RICHARD RIESER and MICHELINE MASON

DISABILITY EQUALITY IN EDUCATION, LONDON 1992
SUPPORTED BY A LOAN FROM CHARITY PROJECTS

DISABILITY EQUALITY IN THE CLASSROOM: A HUMAN RIGHTS ISSUE

FOREWORD TO REVISED EDITION

There is little doubt that Britain's six and a quarter million disabled people have a considerably poorer lifestyle to that of the non-disabled community. Orthodox medical explanations suggesting this is due to the physical and/or intellectual impairments of the individuals concerned are no longer acceptable to disabled people, their organisations, and an increasing number of policy makers throughout the democratic world. It is not impairment which prevents disabled people from achieving a reasonable standard of living, but attitudes and policies which deny them equal rights and opportunities; ie. institutional discrimination.

Sadly, institutional discrimination against disabled people is inherent in the present education system. Children with impairments are marked out for a particular form of 'special' provision which is generally segregated, dominated by medical rather than educational criteria, and given a low priority in the system as a whole. As a result disabled school leavers rarely have the skills and confidence to achieve a full and active adult life comparable to that of their non-disabled counter-parts. Hence, 'special' education helps create the negative stereotypes against which all disabled people are judged. At the same time, the removal of children with impairments from mainstream schools denies non-disabled pupils access to the experience of disability; so perpetuating the ignorance and fear upon which stereotyping and prejudice depend.

Moreover, despite a succession of legislation since the 1944 Education Act endorsing the principle that disabled children should be educated alongside their non-disabled peers, the impetus toward integration has been only slight. The attitudinal and environmental barriers which prevent disabled pupils' successful integration into mainstream schools remain largely in tact, and segregated 'special' education continues to thrive at every level.

While the failure to integrate is often attributable to limited resources it is also due to a lack of knowledge and understanding among all those involved in education – educationalists, school governors, teachers and parents. This book and teaching pack provide the necessary information to resolve this disturbing situation. Written and compiled by two disabled writers together with substantial contributions from several other disabled people – all of whom have first hand experience of the present education system – it provides the most comprehensive and accessible insight into the issues raised by current educational policies that I know of. It is an essential teaching aid for all those who are committed to the abolition of discrimination in education and the creation of a non-disabling society. The authors are to be congratulated for producing it and I cannot recommend it highly enough.

January 1992   Colin Barnes BA Cert ed (FE) Ph.D.
Principal Research Worker for the British Council of Organisations of Disabled People.
Department of Social Policy and Sociology, The University of Leeds.

Acknowledgements

19311

We would like to acknowledge the support of many other disabled people in writing and compiling this book. In particular for the consultation services of Gary Bourlet, Jane Campbell, Liz Child, Liz Crow, Lois Kieth, Paddy Ladd, Elspeth Morrison and Judy Watson; and for the written contributions of Frances Blackwell, Gary Bourlet, Simon Brisenden (died 1989), Jane Campbell, Richard Crawford, Peter Cross, Mary Duffy, Steve Duckworth, Simon Gardiner, Lois Kieth, Barbara Lisiki, Caroline Mackieth, Jenny Morris, Samena Rana, Pamela Roberts, Marsha Saxton, Gioye Steinke, Anna Sullivan, Sharon Sullivan, Helen Todd, Sian Vessey, Judy Watson and Christine Wilson. A special thanks to David Hevey who took many of the photographs. We would also like to thank the following able-bodied allies who contributed: Susie Burrows, David Cropp, Paula Olurin, Pratibha Parmar, Brian Simons, Jenny Simpson, Tim Southgate, June Statham, Carmen Tunde and Christine Yorston.

We would also like to thank the following for allowing us to reproduce articles or illustrations:— Franklin Watts publishers; Beverley School, Cleveland; Sheeba Publishers; Disability Arts in London; Disability Alliance; Exley Publishers; Solicitor Magazine, Charity Supplement; News International; Feminist Arts News; The Voice; National Union of Journalists; Manchester Disability Forum; Manchester Planning Dept.; Parents in Partnership; Spinal Injuries Association; The Centre for Studies on Integrated Education; Community service Volunteers; North South Productions; Rehabilitation International; Camerawork; Campaign for Mental Health; Open University; Community Care Magazine; Same Difference; Office of Population Censuses and Surveys; GRAEAE; Sally & Richard Greenhill for some of the photographs; Brenda Prince.

We also thank the following people for their co-operation without which this book would not have appeared:
Park Barn Comprehensive School, Surrey
Northumberland Park Community School, Haringey
The Children and Teachers of Laburnum School
Haringey Connexions
London Boroughs Disability Resources Team
Typists and Designers and all who helped at Central Reprographic Services ILEA,
Robert Harvey, Mark Lushington, Rae Macey and Susie Burrows, for suggestions and proof reading and to Joe Fisher for obtaining the wherewithall to make possible a more ambitious project than anyone ever imagined.

Finally we would like to thank Lucy for putting up with an absent mother and to Susie, Saffron and Santi for putting up with Richard's grumpiness over the last months due to pressure of work.

Micheline Mason

Richard Rieser

For this partly revised edition we thank CHARITY PROJECTS for providing a loan and PARENTS IN PARTNERSHIP (PIP) for administering it. We also thank Colin Barnes for his forward and Leon and Yvonne Hippolyte RR & MM.

First Published by the Inner London Education Authority
March 1990
ISBN 0 7085 0024 2

Partly Revised and Republished by DISABILITY EQUALITY IN EDUCATION
78 Mildmay Grove, London N1 4PJ
February 1992

Richard Rieser, 78 Mildmay Grove, London N1 4PJ

Micheline Mason, 34a Dafforne Road, London SW17 8TZ

Foreword

In May 1989, the Authority's Consultative Forum for parents of children with special educational needs which meets termly with the Chair of the Special Education Section, Elizabeth Monck, asked the Authority to develop materials for teachers which would provide information on disability issues and would enable them to foster awareness of disability in their pupils.

In September 1989, a disabled teacher, Richard Rieser, and a disabled parent, Micheline Mason, who is a member of the Parents Forum, were asked to prepare materials in response to a brief drawn up by the Forum.

The pack which has been produced has been written by disabled people for teachers in institutions of all kinds and draws on pilot teaching carried out in Laburnum J.M.I. It is a very thought-provoking document and, like any such, is unlikely to be accepted in total by all who read it. It is my judgement, though, that its readers will find their own thinking challenged and that, as a consequence, they will respond more appropriately to disabled people. The authors were working to very tight deadlines in the difficult situation caused by the abolition of the Authority and I should like to congratutlate them on producing such a challenging document in such a short period of time. It is an important contribution to an important debate and deserves the utmost consideration by all working in education.

David Mallen

David Mallen
Education Officer

30 January 1990

Disabled people try to Do things. thay hath to try cos its for ther own life. We must hip them notto mayk it hrd. by Ashton Myrie _ 7

CONTENTS

Section 3
Goods Practices — Page 130

Section 4
Work That Can Be Done In Class — *Pages 217-240*

Resource Cards

1A Statistics OPCS — Disability in Britain

1B (i) Regional Variation in Disability
(ii) Prevalence of Hearing Loss in Great Britain

2A Cartoon

2B Access USA

3A&B Design for everyone

4A&B Design for everyone

5A Hazards in the Home

5B Hazards in the Streets

6A Disability/Race and Class

7A Communication: Braille
7B Communication: Finger Spelling

8A Signed Numbers
8B Language to use/avoid

9A&B Signed Song — 10 in the Bed

10A&B Some Basic Signs

11A&B History: Picture in the mind

12A&B History: Disabled People in Nazi Germany

13A&B Geography: A stitch too late: Polio in India

14A&B Disability in Brazil

15A&B Martina 'Martina'

16A Pre-natal Diagnosis and Abortion

16B English literature

17A&B What we learn from books

18A&B Poems

19A&B NUJ Guidelines

20A&B Press cuttings

21A&B Charity Posters

Introduction

> *"Although special schooling, unit provision and integration within ordinary schools all yield examples of good practice in the education of pupils with a physical disability, such practice is not the norm. The general picture is of hardworking, caring communities which have yet to develop a range and standard of work commensurate with pupils' abilities."*
>
> *HM Inspectors 1989*
> *From a DES report on Educating Physically Disabled Pupils*

Disability is the neglected dimension of equal opportunities. This pack has been written by disabled people for teachers in both mainstream and special schools and nurseries. It aims to open up areas for reflection, discussion and action for both staff and pupils, which will lead to greater understanding of the issues facing disabled people and to changed attitudes and practice.

The discrimination and prejudice directed at people with disabilities in our society has not been challenged in schools generally. In ILEA's equal opportunities policy it receives recognition in the Authority's equal employment policy, but has not been challenged in the school curriculum in the same way as sexism and racism. This major oversight is in urgent need of rectification, particularly in the 'mainstream' or ordinary school curriculum.

Discriminatory attitudes and prejudices must be tackled by all teachers in the curriculum content, teaching methods and materials that they use and in removing barriers to disabled people's full participation in mainstream schools both physical and educational.

Why was disability left out of the race, class, gender formulation of disadvantage adopted by ILEA in 1981? Was it because negative attitudes to, and fears of, people with disabilities are so deeply rooted in our society that most people are not even aware they hold such views?

Was it because regardless of class background, race or gender we *all* can, at any time, become disabled physically or mentally?

So the 'non-disabled' majority classify people with disabilities in such a way as to distance themselves from disabled people. This is extremely damaging; not only to people with disabilities, but more fundamentally, it is damaging to the essential humanity of the whole of society.

As long as stereotyping and prejudice exist towards people with disabilities, scapegoating and violence towards people with disabilities is never far away, whether it be individual, institutional or in society as a whole.

It is worth remembering that forced sterilisation was widespread for certain categories of people with disabilities in many so called civilised countries; that in Germany in 1933 compulsory sterilisation was introduced by Act of Parliament ... "to prevent degeneration in the nation's body by preventing hereditary disease". Only 6 years later a programme for the "*destruction of unworthy life*" was introduced with the tacit support of the churches, which exterminated between 100,000 and 200,000 children and adults with physical and mental disabilities. (see P219)

Our approach is based on the assumption that children are not born with prejudices against disabled people, but acquire them from adults, the media, and the general way society is organised. When children become adults they reinforce and legitimise the misinformation and fear in the form of policies and practices over which they have varying amounts of control depending on how much power and influence they have. Able bodied people always have more power than us with respect to our particular impairment.

As with racism, sexism, heterosexism and class bias we believe that the education system has to make positive attempts to reach the truth when attempting to inform people about history, politics, and life experiences of the different groups within our society. The best way to approach the truth is to enable each group to express and represent themselves, including disabled people. We also believe that each group has a right not only to be consulted, but for their opinions to be *legitimized* in action and policy which will give equality of opportunity to all.

This work was requested by parents of children with disabilities and learning difficulties at a meeting of ILEA's Parents Consultative Forum on Special Educational Needs, in the Spring 1989.

Names were put forward of disabled people who also had experience of Disability Equality Training, teaching, and parenting. Two of us were reasonably free and willing to do the project. We were particularly motivated; Richard Rieser by his experience of life as a disabled person, as a disabled teacher and father of a 1 year old baby; and Micheline Mason by her experience of life and being the mother of a 5 year old disabled child just starting out on her school career.

Although the material has been written or compiled by two of us, we refer to the thoughts and opinions of many other disabled people, who themselves have come to consensus with even larger numbers of disabled people - the Disability Movement. We also put the draft out for consultation with 16 disabled people, whose comments and criticisms have been incorporated in the pack.

If you consider that we were introduced to each other by the ILEA in September given the go ahead to write the pack in October with a December deadline and both of us had many other commitments, Micheline is in a wheelchair, Richard can hardly walk and our collaboration involved darting across London from Hackney to Tooting to work together, you may well be surprised that this book now exists.

We feel there are still areas we wished we could have developed further. We were not able to cover learning difficulties with the depth we would have liked. Similarly we were not able to develop our perspective in relation to race and class in proper consultation with others. We are hoping that phase II will include a development period, followed by a second edition, available nationally. We are also certain that the pack cannot be used effectively by teachers without specific INSET training provided by disabled trainers. A few trainers are currently available, (see resources list), but our task ahead is to train more, and to make sure the courses are available to all teachers.

Disabled people feel that disability awareness, or equality, cannot happen in the absence of disabled people. For this reason we feel that the whole of this pack only makes sense within a much greater move towards integration than the current half-hearted piece-meal approach.

Although the 1981 Education Act, and the consequent Fish Report recommended such a move, the possibility of this happening was anulled, as are all the attempts at legislating for our emancipation, by the refusal to admit that it will require extra resources in order to put right the wrongs our society has inherited and reinforces.

This is particularly obvious in London where most school buildings are old and full of architectural barriers, where teacher shortages are most acute, and where the incidence of pupils needing extra support are highest. In the three countries where planned integration has happened successfully, Italy, Sweden and the USA, there has been substantial additional funding from central resources.

Disabled people believe that our problems as adults will continue to be exacerbated by the able-bodied community, unless the education system accepts its responsibility towards us. We believe it to be our right to be part of the best, most flexible mainstream education system possible in order to prepare us for a useful active adult life within the mainstream. We also believe it is a right for all non-disabled children to grow up informed, unafraid and close to disabled children, teachers, parents, grandparents and to be able to maintain those relationships without enforced segregation at any point. We therefore hope that teachers, parents, governors and all those concerned will join with us to campaign for the resources to be made available without delay.

The book is divided into several parts which are connected to each other. Our history comes first, much of which is still to be recorded, followed by how disabled people define our current situation and issues. Some basic information and guidelines for good practice towards disabled people follow. We have detailed examples of how to include disability in the National Curriculum, and some examples of worksheets, which can be used with different ages in the classroom. The sections form a coherent whole and to benefit from any one piece, the book must be studied in its entirety.

Section 1

by Nicole Moirlie 7

Politics of Disability

Tomorrow I am going to re-write the English language

Tomorrow I am going to re-write the English language
I will discard all those striving ambulist metaphors
Of power and success
And construct new images to describe my strength
My new, different strength.

Then I won't have to feel dependent
Because I can't Stand On My Own Two Feet
And I will refuse to feel a failure
Because I didn't Stay One Step Ahead.
I won't feel inadequate
When I don't Stand Up For Myself
Or illogical because I cannot
Just Take It One Step at a Time

I will make them understand that it is a very male way
To describe the world
All this Walking Tall
And Making Great Strides.

Yes, tomorrow I am going to re-write the English Language,
Creating the world in my own image.
Mine will be a gentler, more womanly way
To describe my progress.
I will wheel, cover and encircle

Somehow I will learn to say it all.

Lois Keith
from Able Lives
©Spinal Injuries
Association

Disabled History or A History of The Disabled
by Richard Rieser

> '**And the Lord said to Moses none of your descendants throughout their generations who has a** blemish **shall draw near, a man** blind *or* lame, *or one who has a mutilated face or a* limb too long, *or a man who has an* injured foot *or an* injured hand, *or a* hunchback *or a* dwarf, *or a man with* defective sight *or an* itching disease *or* scabs *or* crushed testicles.'
>
> *Leviticus 21, 16-20*

"Exceptional - that is different or unusual - individuals have been set aside by other human beings probably since the beginning of the species, certainly for as long as history has been recorded."

"A stone carving in an Egyptian tomb shows an achondroplastic dwarf who was Keeper of the Royal Wardrobe, and wall drawings in another tomb depict blind harpists and singers; in Aztec society the royal zoo included a display of dwarfs, bearded women and deformed humans who lived on scraps tossed in their cages. Throughout European history the careers of court pet, entertainer, jester, circus performer and sideshow exhibition have been assigned to exceptional people. People with physical and behavioural differences have been subject to a whole range of treatment, including being referred to as beloved mascots, found fascinating as freaks, treated with ridicule and marked for extermination."
(Friedberg et al)

Anthropologists in their studies of alternative cultures to our own cultures based on hunting and gathering, pastoralism or farming, have established that all cultures have certain features in common. One such feature is to seek to explain that which they cannot explain 'rationally' or 'scientifically' by the constructions of myths and legends. These often give meaning to that which cannot be explained in other ways. Such explanations often have had practical outcomes for those so identified.

Not all societies treated disabled people in the same way. (Hanks 1948). They range from being outcasts, through to being graded a high social status, the treatment mainly being dependent on the amount of economic surplus.

In Sparta Lycurgus was of the persuasion that children were the property of the state. If "puny and ill shaped" the child was ordered to be taken to Apothetae - a chasm and there disposed of.

This applied to all children not healthy and vigorous" (J. Warkying 1971).

Ancient Spartans also believed that new born infants who were "deformed" showed the displeasure of their gods and so they threw them off Mount Taygeytus. Infanticide was similarly practiced in many cultures. It was often rationalised as in Sparta, but with a practical consequence as well as a divine purpose: unproductive members of society were kept to a minimum where there was only a small surplus of food to share.

In Ancient Rome deformed children were drowned in the Tiber.

These sentiments are very apparent in the Christian version of the Bible. The Jewish faith seems to have a more complex position with some parts of the Talmud advocating disability as a holy state and a means of getting to heaven; similar sentiments are expressed towards those who help disabled people.

'**And the Lord said to Moses**' where there are ancient prohibitions against disabled people being priests:

'**none of your descendants throughout their generations who has a** *blemish* **shall draw near, a man** *blind* **or** *lame*, **or one who has a mutilated face or a** *limb too long*, **or a man who has an** *injured foot* **or an** *injured hand*, **or a** *hunchback* **or a** *dwarf*, **or a man with** *defective sight* **or an** *itching disease* **or** *scabs* **or** *crushed testicles*.

He may eat the bread of his God, both of the most holy and of the holy things, but he shall not come near the veil or approach the altar, because he has a *blemish*, that he has a *blemish*, that he may not profane my sanctuaries'.'

(Leviticus 21. 16-20)

The biblical message is clear that disability is unclean, polluting whilst at the same time, in the Christian New Testament, it counsels charity towards disabled people.

This ambivalence was reflected in beliefs, in the medieval period, when disabled people were viewed as either related to Satan, or as sacred beings - "innocents unstained by normal and sinful human characteristics". Viking and Saxon and feudal law held a person could be judged guilty or innocent by divine intervention based on undergoing physical ordeals. Clearly the message is that the physically exceptional had already undergone divine intervention and been found guilty. Luther was of the view that changelings had *no soul* and advocated that children so afflicted should be taken to the river and drowned. (John Quicke 1985 Page 3). Countless women were identified as witches by the 'Church' if they gave birth to a disabled child. Mother and offspring were then killed.

Much later in the eighteenth century physically disabled babies were often abandoned and deserted as foundlings in the streets of London. The Foundling Hospital was opened in 1745 as a first step in reducing the very high mortality rates among deserted children. Superstition held that a disabled, or deformed child was bad luck, a curse, divine retribution, or that disability indicated possession by the devil, or was the outcome of evil doing.

In medieval times the insane were thought to be possessed by the devil and were mercilessly persecuted and put to death. Asylums were set up to 'rescue' the 'mentally disabled' from this torment. Indeed only very recently have people with learning difficulties been allowed to receive some sacraments in the Roman Catholic Church.

Another historical strand is the association of disability and vagrancy or begging.

The Dissolution of the monastries and the Catholic churches with their 'hospitals' and the Enclosures had turned many disabled people into beggars.

Not surprisingly, many beggars did imitate disabled people to be seen as the 'needy poor'. Finkelstein (Page 8) reports a newspaper report from 1894 on the 'Society for the Suppression of Mendicity (Begging)' which had a museum exhibiting instruments and tools of begging. The Society apprehended at least 1000 beggars a year, many of whom were found to be imposters.

The disabled, or 'crippled', as Victor Finkelstein (1976) would prefer them to be known, prior to the nineteenth century were not separated out or segregated from others in the lower strata; the poorly paid, the unemployed or those 'who had fallen from grace due to vice. (Victor Hugo's 'Les Miserables'). This was Phase 1 according to Finkelstein.

The lack of any real medical knowledge until the middle of the C19th meant that often people were blamed for their disabilities or illness. (Stone '85).

Finkelstein and Stone, from different viewpoints, both identify the C19th as a time when attitudes to disability were reappraised as a result of the increasing importance of labour power and the need to have better ways of distinguishing the disabled who could not work from those who 'did not wish to work'. Certainly disabled people became increasingly institutionalised and seen as being dependent. As Britain and then the United States and other countries industrialised standardised labour become more essential in timed factory production. There was no place for disabled people in the community. The United States forbade the immigration of disabled people from abroad. Increasingly disabled people were segregated into institutions.

It is undoubtedly true that all laboured as best they could in feudal Europe with few exceptions. Only the clergy and aristocracy were exempt. However, once time became money on the assembly line more people were categorised as disabled.

At this time, another strand of thought became influential: the social biology and eugenics movement. Which was to have disastrous consequences for disabled people. Eugenics thinking was based on a wrong interpretation of Darwin's theories of natural selection. Focusing on the hereditary nature of defects, it led to wholesale incarceration and segregation. Later compulsory sterilisation of many mentally disabled, mentally impaired and people with epilepsy was introduced in the United States, Germany, the United Kingdom and other so called civilised countries in the early years of this century. Not much had changed from policies practiced in Rome 2000 years before when mentally defective persons were prohibited from marrying.

The early eugenicists were medical scientists who essentially conducted an experiment in genocide. They sought to improve the quality of the human gene pool by preventing the births of disabled infants. They tried to establish the hereditary nature of such diseases as diabetes, blindness and epilepsy. Misusing Darwin they believed human life was a struggle between the fit and the unfit (feeble-minded, insane, epileptic, diseased, blind, deaf and deformed) who were to be bred out of existence. Techniques of sterilisation were being developed at this time along with wider use of birth control. Since disabled people were of little or no use to the profit makers and so were likely to be a burden on the state, they were to be stopped from producing others like themselves.

By the 1930's 41 states in US had compulsory sterilisation laws for 'the insane and feeble minded', 17 prohibited people with epilepsy from marrying. Today 27 states still have these laws.

In Nazi 'race science' ideology, these ideas had their most horrific application in the final solution for hundreds of thousands of disabled people. (See section on Curriculum for details.)

Suppresion of Deaf Culture

Another off shoot of Social Darwinism was the incorrect view that if deaf people married each other, they would produce deaf children and gradually the human race would become deaf.

For a very long time deaf people without speech were thought to be 'mentally defective'. Then from C17th deaf people had got together and communicated by visual-gestural means that appeared to convey the same information as speech. Deaf schools, clubs and professionals all using sign language developed in C19th.

Then Social Darwininists tried to ban the deaf clubs, marriages of the deaf, get rid of deaf teachers and replace sign language with speech-only communication (oralism). An International

Congress in 1880 did manage to eradicate sign language except in the clubs.

The net result of this oralist takeover led to 90% of deaf people having unintelligible speech, and deaf children leaving school with an average reading age of 8 3/4. (Conrad 1979)

Rights not Charity

All this is very gloomy but disabled people have been making history 'on our own behalf' for some time.

Finkelstein defined phase 2 as the phase of institutionalisation and segregation of disabled people. He saw the present period as phase 3 where we have been overcoming the fragmentation of the *medical* model and developing a *social* movement that unites disabled people locally, nationally and internationally. This movement is based on the understanding that disability is a universal form of oppression, primarily *imposed* on people with physical impairments or learning difficulties; disability as an individual experience is viewed as secondary.

This movement is leading towards a situation where disabled people can live more integrated and effective lives within the community. Entrenched attitudes and practices based on our history are being challenged by disabled people fighting for our rights.

**Cenotaph 1989 —
Richard Rieser laying a wreath for
disabled people murdered by the Nazis**

The Medical Model and The Social Model of Disability

by Micheline Mason and Richard Rieser

> *"We believe that we need to take a holistic approach to educating people about disability issues - that is to say, though we can outline the particular way in which oppression and discrimination affects us as disabled people, it is essential that we link our concerns to those of other disadvantaged groups - to black people, to women, to gays and lesbians, to people discriminated against because of their nationality, religion or class."*
>
> Christine Wilson

A model is a framework by which we make sense of information. A religious model for example would relate things to religious belief and lore. It would give meanings to events otherwise incomprehensible and helps form our behaviour in terms of its own rules- i.e. going to "confession" only makes sense to someone who has accepted the "Catholic" model of belief and not to someone who has accepted a Hindu model of belief. The same event can appear very diffrent to people who have been brought up with different models of understanding.

A model is not necessarily The Truth As Born Out by Scientific Fact, it is just an idea that helps us to make sense of information. "The earth is flat" was a geographical model that served us well until we acquired a piece of information that could not fit into the model - if you kept on travelling in a straight line "across" the earth, you didn't fall off the edge, but instead ended up returning to your starting point, only from the opposite direction. People had to construct a new model that would make sense of this piece of information - i.e. "the earth is round". Hopefully, as we collect more and more information and keep modifying our model to accommodate the information, the model does become an increasingly accurate representation of objective reality and can be tested, e.g. photographs from space reveal that the model was indeed a good guess - the earth is round.

Some things however are not so easily 'tested'. When talking about disability and the possible 'models' that we could employ to understand the issues, the 'test' we have in mind is 'does this accurately reflect life as experienced by disabled people themselves, and does this model allow for progress as defined by disabled people - will it move things on, or not?'

A good deal of our history has used a 'religious' model of disability, usually (but not always) seeing disability as some kind of punishment for evil behaviour, or some kind of embodiment of evil itself. 'casting out the demons', etc. Those who gave birth to disabled children were tainted similarly. This model has in some cultures given way to the medical model of disability. In the West, although vestiges of the religious model still exist, the medical model is the one which has most influenced our thinking and practice towards illness and disability. It assumes that disability is caused by a mental or physical impairment and therefore the impairment becomes the focus of attention. Doctors are people who are trained to cure, or alleviate the effects of such impairments; therefore disability becomes a medical problem. It is understood that if you can cure the patient - i.e. get rid of the impairment - then you have succeeded in curing the disabilty and all is well in the world.

People become individual objects to be 'treated', 'changed', 'improved', made more 'normal'. For the doctor to be successful (s)he must feel herself/himself to be doing their utmost to employ the tools of their trade to this end. **The overall picture is that the human being is flexible and 'alterable' whilst society is fixed and unalterable. We must adapt to a hostile environment.** Many disabled people describe the feelings of 'belonging' to the medical profession who define us in terms of our diagnosis 'she is a spastic', e.g., who assess and define our rights to physical or financial assistance, who plan and manage our health care, whose signatures on bits of paper override our own judgement in even the most personal and fundamental areas of our lives. Because *their* 'success' is dependent on our co-operation in the process of treatment or cure, we

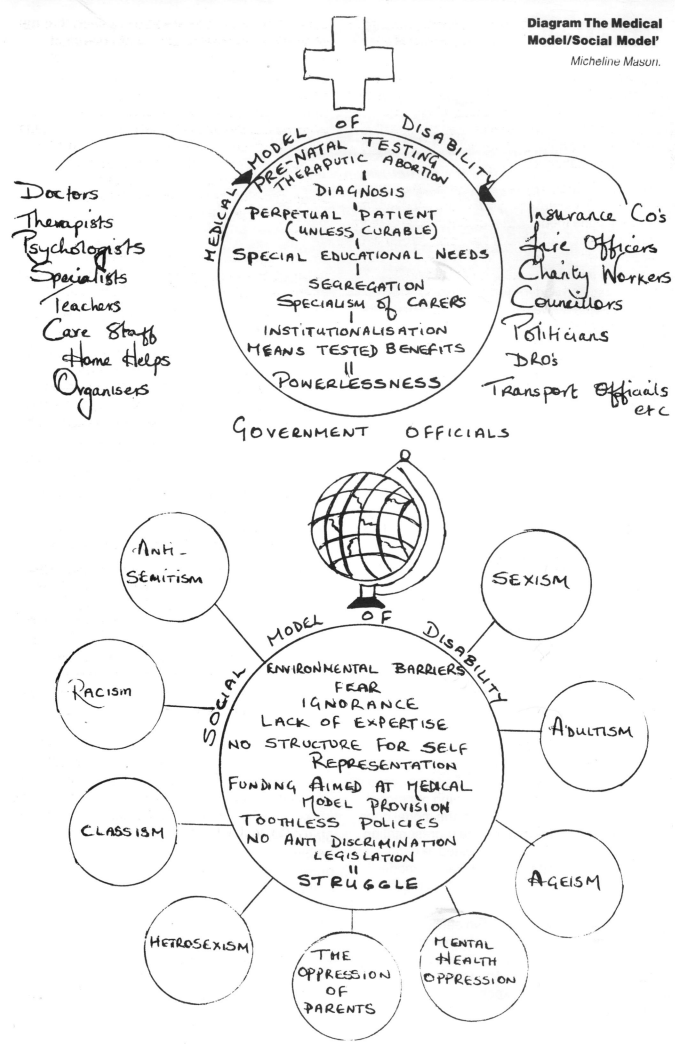

MEDICAL MODEL OF DISABILITY

PRE-NATAL TESTING
THERAPUTIC ABORTION
DIAGNOSIS
PERPETUAL PATIENT
(UNLESS CURABLE)
SPECIAL EDUCATIONAL NEEDS
SEGREGATION
SPECIALISM OF CARERS
INSTITUTIONALISATION
MEANS TESTED BENEFITS
=
POWERLESSNESS

Doctors
Therapists
Psychologists
Specialists
Teachers
Care Staff
Home Helps
Organisers

Insurance Co's
Fire Officers
Charity Workers
Councillors
Politicians
DRO's
Transport Officials
etc

GOVERNMENT OFFICIALS

SOCIAL MODEL OF DISABILITY

ENVIRONMENTAL BARRIERS
FEAR
IGNORANCE
LACK OF EXPERTISE
NO STRUCTURE FOR SELF
REPRESENTATION
FUNDING AIMED AT MEDICAL
MODEL PROVISION
TOOTHLESS POLICIES
NO ANTI DISCRIMINATION
LEGISLATION
=
STRUGGLE

ANTI-SEMITISM

SEXISM

RACISM

A'DULTISM

CLASSISM

AGEISM

HETROSEXISM

THE OPPRESSION OF PARENTS

MENTAL HEALTH OPPRESSION

14

are subjected to all kinds of emotional pressure to conform to the model, to try to get better at all costs. Those who succeed get societies' approval: 'courage', 'independence', 'will-power' are all lauded when a disabled person proves that overcoming disability is a matter of individual effort. Those of us who don't succeed get called 'apathetic' or worse, and are hidden from public view and forgotten about.

The element that is missing in the medical model is disabled peoples' own view of the situation. It is inherent in the medical model that we are objects without power, and without the ability to manage our own lives. It is proving to be a very slow affair to change this because the medical model is institutionalised and therefore does not change as fast as people's awareness. **Disabled peoples' own view of the situation is - that whilst we may have medical conditions which hamper us and which may or may not need medical treatment, human knowledge, technology and**

collective resources are already such that our physical or mental impairments need not prevent us from being able to live perfectly good lives. It is society's unwillingness to employ these means to altering *itself* rather than *us*, which cause our disabilities. This is what we call the Social Model of Disability. It puts the problem outside of ourselves, back into the collective responsibility of society as a whole. The social model includes architectural barriers, inadequate pensions, toothless legislation, a lack of structure for self-representation and much more.

The effects of our actual impairments and the vestiges of society's treatment of us that *we* have internalised will be all *we* will have to deal with.

Why we believe that this model is better than the medical model is that the goals of the medical model are untenable - it doesn't work - whilst the goals of the social model could work on a wide scale because we have already experienced them working on a small scale, in tiny pockets of good practice, all over the world. Furthermore it allows for far greater analysis of society's shortcomings. It makes prevention a priority, and it makes links with the struggle of all other oppressed groups who also suffer because of political injustices. This in turn makes sense for *us* of our experience of disability. It gives us a positive role in the evolution of the human race.

What we call 'Disability Equality Training' is the process by which we all 'unlearn' our habits of thinking learnt from the medical model, and replace them with fresh thinking derived from the social model. It is not necessarily easy. This is why, for example with adults, we do not use 'simulation' exercises such as blindfolding sighted people as a way to understand blindness, but instead use the time to teach 'courtesy' towards blind people. For blind people the problem is not being unable to see although this will effect them their whole lives, it is the lack of skills that sighted people suffer from in relation to assisting a blind person. We cannot give the blind person sight. We can give the sighted person the ability to enable the blind person to do what s/he wants.

PLEASE HELP US
DEVELOP SKILLS
RATHER THAN TRYING TO
TREAT OUR ILLS
Thanks,
Pal
PAINT

The Disability Movement

by Micheline Mason

> "The most common causes of disability - world wide are poverty, economic exploitation, pollution, war and torture. Disabled people are the poorest of the poor. The barriers we face are more than attitudinal or architectural, they are institutionalised in our legislation and in our social practice which ascribes to disabled people the status of receivers and not providers. Our starting point then, is a political one."
>
> Christine Wilson

Segregation is when people are divided up by others against their will. Disabled people have protested against being separated from non-disabled people. 'Why then', we are often asked, 'are you now setting up 'disabled people only' groups and organisations? Aren't you discriminating against the non-disabled?' The answer is simple. We are coming together by *choice*. It is totally different. November 1989 saw the opening of the Berlin Wall. Thousands of East Germans queued for hours, rushed into West Germany, celebrated, bought things, turned round and *went back home* again - FREE. There is a parallel here with disabled people. Once we had a choice in the matter we rushed out into the able-bodied world, said hello, saw the shortcomings of this 'forbidden territory' looked at fellow disabled people and thought 'you seem nice too, now that I have the freedom to notice!' We saw that the able-bodied world has suffered from deprivation of us and our experience, too long. **We saw a common task, to eliminate the disabling aspects of society in order to 'humanise' it for everyone.** But to do that we needed to get each other's support, to learn about each other's experience across the enforced sub-divisions, to forge a common policy, to draw on each other's strengths, to rest from the battle, to practice taking *complete* responsibility, and to develop our own suppressed culture as disabled people. Deaf people probably led the way for us in this with their unshakable pride in their own language and culture.

"At the start of the 1980's there were 200,000,000 children with disabilities around the world.

100 million disabled by malnutrition.

Another 14,000,000 join them every year."

The disability movement is worldwide. It has an umbrella organisation called Disabled People International (DPI) recognised by the United Nations as the representative body of disabled people internationally. It was born in (1981) at a Conference called Rehabilitation International, a professional-led Conference at which the Disabled Delegates made history by withdrawing from the main assembly and setting up their own alternative Conference. It was instrumental in making the UN adopt the World Programme of Action for Disabled persons, which should be read by everybody.

Not everybody who belongs to the movement, knows it. It is not an organisation, although its power comes from disabled people's own organisations, but is rather a political analysis of the problem of disability. Any disabled person who has come to any part of the analysis, and who tries to communicate that through language, policy or practice, is part of the disability movement. What is infinitely preferable to people battling with the world alone, however, is drawing disabled individuals into some kind of a forum to exchange support and ideas. In the first instance this will probably be a locally based disability 'access' group, or an arts group, an 'assertiveness training course' or some such single-issue group. The Youth Service are increasingly providing a forum for young school leavers with disabilities to begin to define their own issues, and run their own services - e.g., youth clubs. There is still a lot of scope for actually bringing that forum into schools and colleges. We make some suggestions in 'Good Practices in the Classroom'.

DAIL.

The British Council of Organisations of Disabled People (BCODP)

In Britain BCODP is the representative voice of disabled people. To join BCODP an organisation must be controlled by disabled people or people with learning difficulties (51% or more voting on the council of management). There are currently (January 1992) 82 membership organisations representing over 200,000 disabled people.

If you would like to know more about BCODP there is a supporters scheme for disabled people and non-disabled allies. For £6 a year you will receive a journal of news, campaigns and activities, and be helping to fund vital work carried out by this body. Donations to the Action Fund will also be gratefully welcomed.

Write to: Richard Wood, Director, The British Council of Organisations of Disabled People, De Bradlelei House, Chapel Street, Belper, Derby DE5 1AR. Telephone: 0773 028182

Self-Representation

by Micheline Mason

"If we accept the premise that one of the major functions of community education on disability is to change and challenge the imbalance of power between disabled and non-disabled people, then I think it follows that the people who should be in control of these initiatives are disabled people. After all, it is our issues that are under discussion -our lives - and we are the ones who have been painfully unwrapping our personal, individual experiences to try to make sense of them and to see how they fit into the whole pattern of human experience. And the purpose of using that experience to develop educational materials and methods is to bring an end to our oppression, and we are wary of it being in any other hands than our own."

Christine Wilson

There are millions of disabled people in the world, 6 1/2 million in the UK alone. We are a complete cross-section of society - all ages, classes, races, abilities. There are as many organisers and leaders amongst us as there are in any other random cross-section of 6 1/2 million citizens, yet we are prevented from leading our own people. The stereotype of disabled people as helpless, inadequate victims unable to manage ourselves, has been so thoroughly institutionalised that the fight for self-representation has become one of the biggest, most time-consuming challenges that we have. There are vast empires which exist to "represent" or "misrepresent" our interest, run by non-disabled people. They often have the word "for" in their titles, and they are well-known - The Spastics Society, Mencap, RNIB, RNID, etc. They have annual budgets of millions of pounds. There is also an umbrella organisation of organisations controlled by disabled people called the British Council of Organisations of Disabled People. They have 52 affiliated groups representing about 10,000 disabled people, and they have almost no money at all. BCODP has not, until 1990, been able to employ one single person, or even produce a decent leaflet because of lack of funding. In 1989 the government gave £35,000 to all those 52 different organisations of disabled people, and £7 million to organisations for disabled people. "Recently disabled people successfully campaigned for GLAD - Greater London Association of Disabled to become an alliance of organisations controlled by disabled people." Recognition of this struggle by potential supporters would be a great leap forward in "disability awareness". In our resource lists we have divided the organisations into "For" and "Of" organisations, and we have divided literature and video lists into "about" and "by" disabled people, but this process we would like you to continue for yourselves.

"Speaking for ourselves": self-advocacy by people called mentally handicapped
June Statham

From Including Pupils with Disabilities, Booth and Swan 1987 Open University Press

In this account of the work of a group of 'self-advocates', June Statham describes how some people who have been categorized as 'mentally handicapped' have challenged that label. The people involved in this group have all attended special schools, and several have lived in mental handicap hospitals. Over a number of years they have worked together in ways that many other groups of 'ordinary' people would envy, to develop their self-confidence and independence. They are collectively challenging the routine oppression they encounter from professionals and public alike.

We want the chance to speak. To speak about different things what we need to talk about, like about the word 'handicapped' and being treated like children and about night classes for people who can't read and write. We want people to listen to us.
(Marion)

> **The most important thing is to be independent. To be your own boss. To be treated like a normal person and a citizen and to have your rights.** (Gary)

Marion and Gary are part of an increasing number of people in Britain who have been labelled 'mentally handicapped' who are now beginning to speak up for themselves and for their rights. Self-advocacy has been a growing movement in this country and others for some time amongst adults with physical and sensory disabilities, but is a fairly recent development amongst those with learning difficulties. Self-advocacy in this context had its beginnings in the mid 1970s in America, and People First groups were established in many states over the following decade. In 1984, the Washington People First group held an international conference which was attended by nine British self-advocates, including Gary and Marion, together with several professionals in the role of supporters. On coming back to England the group decided to set up a London-based People First group, and held their first meeting in October 1984.

Many of those who went to the American conference had already been meeting together for some time to learn the skills and the confidence that would enable them to speak out about their feelings and their rights. Several had been attending classes at the City Lit, which runs speaking and discussion classes as part of their Creative Education courses for people with learning difficulties. Others were members of a group called the Participation Forum set up at the end of 1981, as an off-shoot of a meeting of representatives from Adult Training Centres organized by MENCAP. Most of the group are in their late twenties and thirties. All have in the past been labelled 'mentally handicapped', some have Down's Syndrome, and all have experienced some kind of special schooling. Some members have spent part of their adult lives in hospitals, but they now live in a variety of different situations in hostels, with their parents, in group homes or in a flat. Most spend some of their time at an Adult Training Centre, fitted around their other activities and commitments. The Tuesday morning 'talking session' has become a regular and important part of their lives.

The Participation Forum is a strong, cohesive group. They have been meeting together for four years now and provide each other with a high level of encouragement and support. When two members were waiting for months to move from a hostel to a flat, the others prevented them from becoming discouraged. David and George's training centre announced that it intended to introduce charges for attendance and to lower the already minimal wages, and the group as a whole dictated a letter of protest to the Social Services Department. They help each other and encourage the less articulate or confident members to speak. Tony describes how Lorraine was nervous when she spoke in public for the first time, 'but we all pushed her to make sure she does it and you see her now, she talks like no one's business!' As the newest, Julie, leaves the meeting, Lorraine says 'goodbye love, and thanks for talking'.

David Hevey.

Disabilities photography class — from poster Campaign Liberty, Equality, Disability.

The group has had a big effect on their lives. 'People listen to me more. It's changed me in a lot of ways. I used to have a lot of tempers but I don't get hardly any tempers now. I can say what I want now.' (Tony)

Speaking at meetings, to professionals, parents, students and also to other consumers of services like themselves, is something that the members of the Participation Forum have been doing increasingly over the past couple of years. It is a skill they have developed through coming to the group, through gaining confidence from discussing issues amongst themselves and from the support they provide for each other. For the first two years or so they very rarely had visitors and felt happier talking on their own. More recently they have felt secure enough to allow a wide range of people to sit in on their meetings, including parents, GLC and DHSS staff, student teachers and a Guardian financial page writer, who produced an article on the group's feelings about allowances, benefits and spending their own money. They have organized two conferences call Speaking for Ourselves and Have we a Future?, with the help of John, MENCAP and the City Lit, who videotaped the events. The conferences were aimed at spreading the word about self-advocacy to both professionals and consumers, and the videotapes capture the sense of excitement and emerging control over their lives felt by members of the audience as they come to the front to speak into the microphone for the first time, or join in small discussions to share with others in the same position their feelings about work, education, or the way they have been treated by society.

People call us nasty names or treat us like kids because they're frightened. They don't know what we're like or what we can do ... We're labelled, called mongol, makes me feel not wanted ... Lots of us could live on our own with a bit of teaching and help. Then others could get out of hospitals and live where we are now ... Tell them not reading and writing doesn't mean you're stupid.

A common reaction from the professionals who hear the self-advocates speak is that they are not typical, and that, 'ours aren't like you, they couldn't do what you are doing'. Self-advocacy is a new movement amongst people called mentally handicapped, and those involved are bound to be pioneers who can probably express their views particularly well. But their ability and confidence in speaking up for their rights is something that they have learnt over fairly long periods. The members of the Participation Forum, for instance, spent several years meeting together and exploring ideas in a safe environment before they felt able to speak out in public. They have discovered ways of helping themselves to do this. George is shy and quiet, so the others need to make space for him and he has had to learn to speak louder. Lorraine finds it easier to answer questions directed at her by someone like John, than to speak directly to an audience. Gary described how he sat with a less experienced speaker and held his hand in order to give him the confidence to talk. John feels that the 'ours couldn't do it' attitude of some professionals is a way of avoiding the issues raised by self-advocacy. The fact that the groups of students he works with can communicate so well should be taken not as an

argument that they are atypical but as an example of what people can do given the time and encouragement to learn.

It means that you have to be prepared to spend a long time helping people to build up the confidence and the skills. This group has been meeting for three or four years now. But that's a small amount of time in someone's lifetime, to learn skills that will stand them in good stead for life. *(John)*

The self-advocates themselves know that speaking out is a skill that has to be learnt.

Self-advocacy is about speaking your mind, like I'm doing now. Not to be frightened, just go out and say what's in your mind. There's just one thing that's got me doing it, coming here. This group at MENCAP. *(Tony)*

You wouldn't throw someone in and make them speak to a lot of people. You'd help them to talk. Meet in small groups and get confidence. *(Gary)*

David Hevey.

'A Musical workshop' from poster Campaign Liberty, Equality, Disability.

Eileen, who goes to one of John's speaking classes at the City Lit and is also a People First member, gets annoyed when professionals say 'ours couldn't' about the people with whom they work.

It's always the same when we do talks, they always say that. It makes me angry because I know they can, it might just take a longer time.

Eileen thinks it is important that they go back again to groups they have visited, to provide continuing encouragement and support. 'It's no good just going once and then you don't know how they get on'. She also prefers talking to consumers rather than to professionals. "Because its about their lives, it's more important to them. The professionals can just go home afterwards".

The self-advocates see their movement as being for all those who have been labelled mentally handicapped, and not just the most articulate.

They are concerned that no one be excluded. The People First group uses pictures in their newsletter and shares ideas like drawing shopping lists, to include those who are, in Gary's words, 'hard of reading'; they are campaigning on transport and access issues to include those who have physical disabilities, and members have

It's not just for those that can speak out well. There are other ways, like acting and sign language and music and art. And these are all ways of speaking up for People First. *(Gary)*

visited hospitals to share their ideas with those who have more severe learning difficulties. One member attending his first People First meeting spoke on behalf of his more severely handicapped friend back at the hospital, and was encouraged to bring the friend to the next meeting and help him become involved.

Self Representation 'Gary Bourlet President of People First, London and Thames'.

David Hevey.

Identity

by Micheline Mason

> My disability is a fundamental factor in the being that is "me". I do not want to deny this by calling myself "a person with special needs" or any other such euphemism, nor do I want to deny the collective identity we have achieved for ourselves. Therefore I am a disabled person, and proud of it.

I was born with a condition called Osteogenesis Imperfecta, or "Brittle Bones". I am neither ashamed nor particularly proud of this as it was not of my choosing. What I am very proud of is the kind of person that dealing with this challenge has *enabled* me to become. I think I am a wiser, deeper, richer and more competent person than I would have been had I not had this challenge put before me. I have also had the privilege of close contact with many others who have had similarly enriched experiences of life - my friends at school, my sisters and brothers in the Disability Movement, my own wonderful daughter. I treasure this.

Our aim is to alter the way people feel about the word "disabled" from a negative attitude to a positive attitude, in exactly the same way that "Black" has to be a positive assertion of identity in a racist society. Black people are not "people whose skin tone is slightly different to that of the dominant culture", nor are they people who achieve things, "despite blackness". The term "Black" is a politically motivated identity of a group of people who recognise that (a) they are proud to be the way they are, including their skin colours, cultures, languages, etc, and (b) they belong to a group of people who are systematically oppressed by the dominant culture which is white - i.e. by racism. Disabled people feel the same way.

For young people it is essential that they somehow make a connection with those of us who have - at last - forged a positive sense of identity as disabled people. This is also important for teachers and parents.

The medical model and self image

One paragraph in my copious medical records describes my hips as 'De-mineralized and grossly deformed'. No doubt the same kind of language could have been used to describe every inch of my body. Hardly the stuff that conjures up a sense of personal attractiveness.

Most disabled people, especially those of us who were born with or acquired our disabilities young, have had the most collosal assault on our self-image by the objectivication of the medical profession:

'I was told to walk up and down the ward, naked in my white bikini, as the doctors watched and talked and pointed to the bones on the screen and the bones in my body. One would call me over to him and he'd flex my feet up and down, and command me to stand on one foot, to bend my knees. How hard I'd try to do it right, so maybe they'd leave my body the way it was.' *(Marsha Saxton)*

Hospital

Early hospitalisation can be one of the biggest traumas of a young person's life. Things have been learnt and practices in children's wards have improved over the last few years. In particular rules over visiting times have been relaxed, and in some hospitals it is possible for a parent to stay overnight on the ward and share the nursing care. However, for many families, particularly one-partner families where there are other children, it is not practically possible to accompany a child into hospital, and the vital importance to a young child of having a familiar adult to 'witness' what is happening, is still not really understood, nor are the long-term psychological effects of the experience:

"What affected me most as a disabled child, I think, was being in the hospital so much. For several months every two years or so, I would go in for more surgery on my legs. I remember the feeling of dread when the letter from Shriner's Hospital arrived to announce my scheduled intake ...

... I recall sitting in the rocker, my mother crying. I felt as if a big hand were reaching into my family to pluck me out. My parents seemed powerless, there was nothing they could do to prevent my leaving. I remember, too, how little attention was paid to the surgery happening to help my legs work better. At the time especially when I was young, that just seemed like a ruse to obscure what I knew was really true: my body was defective, so I had to be punished".

Marsha Saxton 'The something that happened before I was born.'

For most of us these experiences have been locked in by the endless chivvying to "Be Brave" and to deny our feelings because we might upset others. However, like all bad experiences, talking about them, playing role-reversal games where the child 'treats' the adult patients, sharing the stories with others, expressing the fear, pain and anger, are all part of the healing. Teachers can help by providing play materials, reading appropriate books, and asking questions that are open-ended - "What was it like for you in the hospital?" rather than "Are you better now?"

Towards a positive self-image

Positive self-image includes the disability. Have you noticed how disabled children often draw themselves as able-bodied? Body image is very important of course, because human beings use our bodies not just to do things, but to feel things, express emotions, give comfort, attract others, defend ourselves, grow children, have sexual relationships and more. Many people, if not everyone, feel themselves to be "wrong" in some ways - blotchy skin, too fat, too short, big nose, ugly hair, etc - and even minor details of someone's appearance can lead to untold self-consciousness and shame. To challenge the negative view people have about more significant physical features such as crooked skeletons, wasted muscles, scars, etc, we are going to have to reconsider our whole attitude towards physical appearance. Acknowledging one's true appearance is a good beginning. Touching all parts of one's body, not just the "normal" looking bits, is very important. Recognising the great deal of beauty and rhythm and grace disabled people often have, even when using our bodies in very unique ways. "Complete Elegance" - we are challenging here a multi-million pound glamour industry that, hand in hand with the health industry, has correlated ill-health with ugliness, health with beauty, and beauty with "goodness". You can look through any library, watch the tele, go to the chemist, etc, and you will have this message drummed into you a thousand times a day. It is very dehumanising for everyone.

Identity 'Striking Poses'

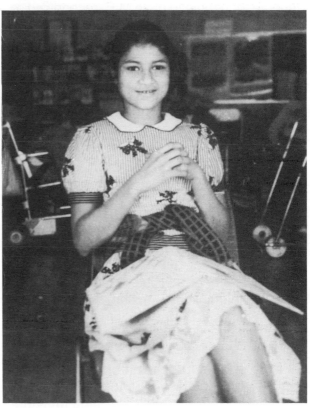

David Hevey.

Mouth drawing by Šaŕka Sýkorová: Exley

People with Hidden Disabilities

by Micheline Mason

Society does not show the same responses towards people with obvious disabilities as towards those people who appear 'normal'. The first group are treated with sympathy, sometimes pity, 'preciousness', over-protectiveness, low-expectations, fear, patronisation, admiration, etc. They are thought of as 'deserving'. Whilst the second group are often treated with disbelief, intolerance, impatience, lack of understanding and the expectation of 'normal' functioning regardless of extra needs. They may get help and kindness in 'acute' stages, but there is generally little awareness of on-going requirements. The struggle for people to have M.E. recognised as a genuine illness and not a form of 'malingering' is an example of this attitude.

(See 'Living with ME' by Anna Sullivan - Teachers Stories.)

Identity as a person with an invisible disability

By the very nature of an 'invisible' disability, there is a choice of identity between 'normal' or 'disabled'. Because of the social stigma still attached to disability, many people will go to great lengths to conceal, deny, minimise or over-compensate for an invisible disability, e.g., by covering hearing aids with hair, hats or scarves; wearing long sleeves or skirts to conceal legs or arms that have some 'difference'; taking medicines in the toilet, etc. **"If I were applying for a job and related my medical history, no employer would be willing to take me on. The advantage of my disabilities being invisible is that I can get away with it. The disadvantage is that in order to get away with it, I collude with my oppressors ... No-one wants to know the truth. Although I can face the facts myself, to reveal the same facts to others seems like courting disaster." Peter Cross**

Because the person may appear to want you 'Not to notice', it is easy to collude with this. It has great parallels with gay oppression and needs to be treated with the same degree of sensitivity.

Individuals do have a right to identify themselves, and just as it is not right to force a gay person to 'Come Out', because she/he may not be willing to confront the negative reactions of others, so it is not right to force anyone to identify as 'Disabled' until they want to. This does not stop others from being aware of their needs and acting appropriately towards that person. When people are able to 'Come Out', it is usually a very liberating experience:

'It had never occurred to me that I might be a person with a disability. Stammering was just something I had to overcome or hide, and as I grew older I did get better at hiding the fact that I can't say certain words.

It is difficult when people feel embarrassed when they see I can't say something. They think they have to know the answer and say it for me or pretend I'm not saying anything. That's not very encouraging to being outspoken or thinking I have important things to say. If people are embarrassed I think it's my job to make the situation more comfortable, so I've pretended that what I was going to say isn't really that important so I won't bother. Once a man a Train Station Ticket Office politely and calmly handed me a piece of paper and a pencil when I couldn't say the name of the station I wanted to go to. I was amazed as it was the first time that someone in that situation had done something really simple and appropriate to make things OK. This man, by his being so completely unembarrassed, showed me that it doesn't have to be an awkward situation, there is always a simple solution, but both the listener and I usually get so caught up into the fear and irritation of feeling stupid that all good thinking seems to stop.

When talking about disability with a friend one day, it dawned on me that I too had been on the receiving end of the oppression of disabled people, and it was a real feeling of elation at being included in a group with this special understanding of the world.'

Caroline Makeith (IFTC 1981)

This group also includes people with mild learning difficulties, Asthma, Eczema, Diabetes, Petit Mal Epilepsy, heart conditions, Dyslexia, stammers, nocturnal incontinence, mild hearing loss, Tinnitus, partial sight, mild co-ordination difficulties, immune deficiency conditions, some

Bradley and Khaleda
by Sevda, Laburnum School.

unlikely that any of these people would have a 'statement' of need even though their lives may be greatly affected by their condition. They are far more likely to be blamed for their condition by both teachers and pupils and labelled in negative ways -'lazy'; 'clumsy'; 'slow'; 'unattentive'; 'weak;' 'a baby;' 'Trying-it-on'; 'cowardly'; 'pathetic'; and so on. They may believe this to be true of themselves, feeling that their difficulties are due to lack of effort or some inherent flaw in their character. This sense of *personal failure* can lead to deep psychological problems later on and, we have noticed it can make this group of people more isolated and 'damaged' than many people with major and visible disabilities.

'For those of us with invisible physical differences the nature of our oppression is summed up in two words - STOP FUSSING. What is much worse, I buy into all the stuff pumped out by the able-bodied - 'Don't make a fuss'; 'Grin and bear it'; 'There are loads of people worse off than you'; 'There is always something the matter with him'; 'He's forever taking pills'; 'All he needs to do is pull himself together'; Yes I have bought into all that. I keep telling myself to stop fussing. I push myself to do things which do not always make medical sense. I kid myself .....'

Peter Cross - IFTC Oct '81

Haemophilia, Sickle Cell Anaemia and Thalassaemia. It may also include the early stages of some progressive conditions like Muscular Dystrophy or Friedrich's Ataxia where there will be a gradual 'slowing-down'. It is

				Our teachers hidden Disabilite
Maureen	No	paula	Eczena	
Shouagh	Eczena	Jean	No	tuesday December 5th
Jane	Diabetes	Gill	No	
			a bit of Eczma	Madeline ✓ Migraine Asthma
Christne	No	Susie		
Roy	No	Carol-Ann	No	by
				William Aimee
Howard	No	Olive	Asthma	Mushiur
Margaret		Elizabeth	No	
Tina	No		No	

Hidden Disabilities — Survey of Hidden Disabilities of our Teachers, Laburnum'
by William, Aimee and Mushiur.

Specific Learning Difficulties

by Richard Crawford

I am dyslexic. It seems a very simple statement to make, a few words to sum up what I am; but to get to this stage has taken a lot of time, caused a lot of pain.

Why? you might well ask. Lots of people come through our educational system without the ability to read or write easily, but I had a 'good' Scottish education and a lot of help from my parents; I worked hard. Yet still, I couldn't read, write or spell easily.

To me, it wasn't fair, I even had to work at my spelling at Christmas. Was I stupid? I did not think so, I knew I wasn't, but yet, neither myself nor my parents could understand why. I always knew there had to be an explanation but could never grasp it, it was always untouchable and meanwhile I struggled with words. In life we are always restricted by language, by semantics, what we want to say is always limited by how we are forced to say it and to me the world had an unfair advantage.

So I went for tests, lots of tests and they told me I was not stupid, in fact kind of smart – that there was an explanation. I was 'word blind' or dyslexic, so they told my parents. At last an explanation, but no great relief, what I wanted was a cure. Then it would be easy, no more copperplate writing, no more spelling exercises, no more striving to please but only getting half way, but nothing is ever as simple as you want it to be.

The more I tried to 'cure' myself, the more I pushed and pushed the worse it became. So there comes a time when the struggling is too draining, too exhausting, then you relax, be yourself and don't have to struggle quite so hard. How you do this is up to you. I was lucky, I found something I was good at, something I enjoyed and can make my living from; that's good, very good.

People ask 'What is it like to be dyslexic?' How do I know? I have nothing to compare it to. I would ask what is it like to be confident enough to write easily without people asking what every second word means and not to always ask 'how do you spell ....' Reading – that's what I find hard, so many people have a snobbery about the books they read. I can count the number of great works of fiction I have read on one hand. So information can only come from the television and radio. I am a TV addict, it's my point of reference but it's limiting and constraining.

Homogenised news, with all the cooked edges and biased views means always having to question why – never taking things at face value - this is no bad thing but sometimes it would be nice to relax!

Today dyslexia is accepted, the education system more tuned into people's needs, though it's very easy to slip through the net; if you are told you are lazy and stupid too often, one day you will believe it yourself! For exams you can have a scribe to write down your thoughts and ideas, there are tape libraries so it's not all bad news, but first you have to work hard. *Don't* give up, I won't say you can overcome it, I will not wake up tomorrow and read fluently the complete works of Tolstoy, but I can control it.

Sometimes my brain runs away, my thoughts cannot go down on paper fast enough or with any order, still I did pass and I got a job with the tax office!

This did not last long, the job included a lot of writing and I was always behind. They sent me to college, where I did get a scribe and I passed my exams easily. That was a start, it got me out of the tax office, I went to a career pyschologist to find out more about my capabilities and what I wanted to do.

I always enjoyed photography, it's something I am happy doing and confident with. I am away from the mundane nine to five routine. Away from the people who can only see the 'handicap'. I am NOT the 'handicap' they are. Never seeing the possibilities, only the problems, they don't see me – the person – the individual, they only see dyslexia. Maybe I should make it easier – walk round with a sign on my back - I AM DYSLEXIC -neatly packaged and synthesised. I bet everyone in similar circumstances feels the same at times!

I do my best for you, can't you come some way for me, that's what I long for - but will it every happen?

Richard J. Crawford

Further reading:

1. *Making Sense of Spelling*
   Millar Robin and Klein Cynttiea, 1986
   ILEA, DCLD. Ebury Teachers Centre 0-7085-9960-5.

2. *Students with Specific Learning Difficulties*
   ILEA 'Learning Difficulties Support Service
   ILEA U&UC Language and Literary Unit

Internalised Oppression

by Micheline Mason

"Internalized oppression is not the cause of our mistreatment, it is the result of our mistreatment. It would not exist without the real external oppression that forms the social climate in which we exist.

Once oppression has been internalised, little force is needed to keep us submissive. We harbour inside ourselves the pain and the memories, the fears and the confusions, the negative self-images and the low expectations, turning them into weapons with which to re-injure ourselves, every day of our lives."

Some people with disabilities suffer from the condition itself, whilst others don't. All of us, however, suffer from internalised oppression.

When the Save the Children Fund did research into the attitudes of black and white children they were shocked to find that by the age of three, black children were already wanting to be white, and that both groups of children valued their white friends more than their black friends. This is the phenomenon of "internalised oppression" - seeing that one group of people are valued more highly than another, and wanting to become like them. This happens every bit as much for disabled children and children with learning difficulties as for black children or working class children.

For disabled children the message that there is something wrong with us can start from birth. Imagine yourself to be a baby. You have just struggled out into the world fully expecting a warm welcome, but instead you get "Oh God! How could this happen to me? Aaargh!" How do you think this would make you feel about yourself? Good? No, of course not. The medical model of disability leads from the point of diagnosis to a lifetime of feeling that we are a disappointment and a worry to everyone. It seems perfectly logical to conclude that having a disability is a bad thing because it upsets everyone, and eliminating or lessening the disability is a worthwhile obsession because without it, you as a person will bring joy to those you love most, instead of misery. Other children play, but you do "therapy". Other children develop, but you are "trained". Almost every activity of daily living can take on the dimension of trying to make you less like yourself and more like the able-bodied. The world is often quite happy to reinforce this rather than being objective.

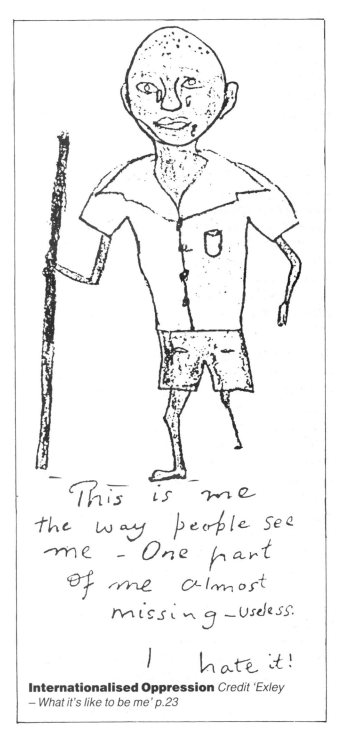

This is me the way people see me - One part of me almost missing - useless.

I hate it!

Internationalised Oppression *Credit 'Exley – What it's like to be me' p.23*

The Joy I Lost For Ever

I really wish I were healthy and had my left hand. Nobody knows how much
I'd like my life to be better, like those who are strong and healthy.
Everybody enjoys living happily, but not me. My life is different. People
sometimes do me harm by laughing at me. It is very painful for me and I'd
like to avoid moments like this at any cost. When it is warm I'd like to put
on a blouse with short sleeves, but I can't. I am simply ashamed.
I hate anybody staring at me and seeing the lack of my left arm. I am very
sorry then, the older I am the more painful it is to me.

Elzbieta Sobiech

When a person feels bad about themselves, and wishes to be like someone else, it is very common to also feel bad about the group one belongs to, and to try to merge into the group which is perceived as superior in the hope that the difference will become invisible. This is the other phenomena of internalised oppression, and especially in the world of disability, has led to us dividing and dividing into smaller and smaller groups, competing with and denying each other, leading many of us to become isolated disabled people living with able-bodied people on able-bodied terms -millions of powerless individuals doing our best to "make it" on our own.

This needs contradiction from outside, not the reinforcement it usually gets. There is a particular danger in attempting to integrate individuals or very small groups of disabled children into a large, established, non-disabled community of children and staff, in that there may be no attempt to foster positive and collective identity as young disabled people within an "integrated" setting, as people see this as a reactionary step. In "Good Practices in the Classroom" we make some suggestions as to how this may be attempted, although there is at present very little "good practice" to follow in this area.

This little boy is in a book Susie got about People with mental disability. by shirley 6

Credit Laburnum School

Internalised Oppression: How it seems to me

by Richard Rieser

I only know what my life was like without a disability from what my mother told me I was like before I was 9 months old, when I got polio. Apparently, I was already walking around, and would have been very 'athletic' if I hadn't caught polio in the hot Summer of 1949.

I can't remember the next six months when I was in hospital alone. Parents were not allowed to stay in those days.

I can feel the scars on the back of my head where I endlessly turned my head while the rest of my body was incarcerated in plaster of paris. It was the theory then to keep the body completely still to prevent 'deformity'.

The Royal National Orthopaedic Hospital at Stanmore did not agree with these 'feudal' methods, and smashed the cast with a hammer when I arrived from Great Ormond Street after my parents had objected to my treatment.

Unfortunately the effect on my mind of enforced separation and incarceration before my first birthday, cannot be got rid of in such a manner.

My memories of my younger childhood were of pain from my treatment and forcing myself to do all sorts of things.

My parents were both of the view that I should learn to walk without a caliper or surgery. I underwent manipulative treatment by the Nurse Kenney method. Mrs Estrid Dane of Notting Hill Gate was to be my mentor. Looking back I shall always be grateful to my parents for this.

Daily we took the 31 bus after nursery, or school had finished. For years my limbs were stretched and twisted until they felt like they were being pulled off. I remember frequently lying in the road, screaming at my mum that I didn't want to go, but she always enticed and encouraged me. This treatment, together with my parents' and my own attitude seems to have been very successful as I grew up to walk without a stick for a number of years. In fact I found a letter from Sir Denis Browne, my Harley Street specialist who saw me when I was 18. He could not believe the progress I had made as he did not think I would walk at all. Physically I could do a great many things, but my personality was less resilient to growing up disabled.

Richard, aged 3. *Credit Boris Ward.*

With my parents 'strong' encouragement I attempted things like walking, swimming, climbing trees, riding my tricycle and later my bike. If I could do all these things with only one arm and one leg working properly, surely I was 'better' than all those around me who seemed to have everything in working order? Of course sometimes there were things I could not do, like running or balancing on a scooter. Reading and spelling seemed to allude me in the same way, and my messy writing and drawings were much ridiculed in my kindergarten (as my dad called it) and at my schools, and indeed still are by my colleagues. Then I felt depressed and sad. Still I was 'tough' and was forever out leading adventures on local bomb-sites and around the streets.

These early pendulum swings of mood have stayed with me most of my life.

I recollect when I was occasionally to glimpse my lopsided gait in shop windows, not believing it was me, but at the same time knowing it was and being shocked and depressed.

I felt these changes of mood most acutely in my teenage years when I thought I was ugly and unattractive. Because I thought I was unattractive I think I made myself so. I was also very unsociable and impolite.

Prior to my fourteenth birthday I had been a semi-illiterate bully, not getting on well at school, and referred to child therapy by Freud's daughter who helped run the school where I ended up for seven years, Town and Country.

The headteacher of our local LCC primary school, George Elliot, had refused to have me at the school. My parents would not send me to the local special school. They kept me out of school in protest until an 'ordinary' school was found which the LCC paid for.

I was also very much against being put with 'those' children. I remember visiting Essendine Special School and feeling sick at seeing all the children with false legs, calipers and wheelchairs. My parents had over-compensated so much that I could not find any connection between 'those' children and myself.

Town and Country could not really be described as an ordinary school. It was a private, co-ed 'progressive school' located in two large Victorian villas in Eton Avenue. It specialised in taking sons and daughters of diplomats and various 'creative' people's children. The teachers were largely

eccentric, traditional and ineffective. I was disruptive, preferring to mess about than learn. There was a big emphasis on foreign languages which I found most difficult, probably because I could not understand the rules of my own language. I was able to act the 'hard' man in the playground and get away with it. This was because I spent most of my leisure time out with my street gang and Town and Country children were a lot softer and more middle-class.

I remember wishing my dad worked in a factory or on the buses like my Scout/street mates and was

Ashton — Moskura *Laburnum JMI.*

Things that richard can do easily

He can swim.
His body dont hurt. then.

by Ashton

things That richard can't do easily

can't
1 carry The. Baby
2 he can't stand
without hes stieck.
3 he can't div The
car easily
4 he carrys heavy
thing with hes
weak arm so it is hard

by moshkura

not an artist and erstwhile teacher. I once told him to get a proper job much to his annoyance. I rejected his artistic side and my own. I think it was also for this reason I blocked foreign languages as my dad could speak at least three fluently.

The need to be tough, to cope, to be what is now called a super-cripple left no space for sensitive feelings and 'soft' creativity.

These feelings of mine were much reinforced by my avid attendance at cubs and boy scout activities. The competitive, physical, cruel, jingoistic attitude that prevailed in the scouts was just what I needed to forget who I was. I threw myself into scouting, gaining all sorts of proficiency badges and eventually becoming the youngest Queen's Scout at 15. I put a brave face on things I found incredibly difficult or impossible. In one way they treated me as if I was just the same as all the others and I suppose that was why I liked it. The problem was I wasn't just the same!

At other times the cruelty of the boys was just too much with their calling me names and jeering at me. On one occasion I was pegged to the ground with wet grass and slops smeared all over me and left in the hot sun for several hours.

This was because I could not peel the potatoes well with a knife, a task I found too difficult due to my polio arm.

This ritual was supposed to make a man of you, but it just made me and the others hard, uncaring and insensitive. This was not good for me as I got rid of my emotions beneath a veneer of bravado. I was unable to feel the strength of character I later found from being open to my feelings and so being conscious of my disability and my limitations, which also led me to try to be more sensitive and empathetic to others.

This contradiction was to make me most unhappy and a fair amount of my time was spent in doing damage to myself, either by excessive drinking or various 'accidents' which led to my damaging various parts of myself. From the age of 15 to 19 I used to arrive home 2 or 3 nights a week in a completely drunken state, quite often being sick all over the place. I broke or damaged my left arm and right leg which I relied upon. I stuck a garden fork through my right foot and messed about with my toe nails which were in-growing so they got septic and required surgery about eight times, and there were many other injuries. This pattern of self-injury continued into my twenties and early thirties and was likely to occur whenever I was

depressed. I didn't like myself and I was pretty sure no-one else did either.

I had a string of psychotherapists at the Tavistock Clinic, but they did not help me as their method was to strip away my defences without putting anything positive in its place. In fact it was not till I was in my thirties that I found a humanistic therapist who used bio-energy. She was really the first person to make me feel good about myself.

But I am jumping ahead. To go back to when I was thirteen. I was becoming aware that Town and Country was not doing me any good. A lot of my mates in scouts were at the local secondary modern, Kynaston, and their stories of events at the school told round the camp fire made me want to go to a 'proper' school with workshops, laboratories, gyms, caning and prefects. I decided with some trepidation to leave the soft cocoon of Town and Country and immerse myself in an all male, streamed secondary modern. The headteacher himself was disabled and that was probably why he accepted me, although I was put a year below my age because of being so 'backward' - I could hardly read and write.

Kynaston was altogether different to anything I had experienced so far. The kids and teachers were tough and there was really no mileage in a crippled bully so I quickly switched into competing with my mind and became more embarrased by my body. I was also made fun of for my German name and for being Jewish.

Anti-semitism was rife as it still is in most schools. I denied my paternal Jewish lineage. Anyway I justified this because my parents had brought me up outside the Jewish culture and as an agnositic. If goaded too far I would still lash out at the perpetrator. But it was the indirect avoidance of me, the whispering, the staring looks that I couldn't hit out at that were far more damaging.

I was not often allowed to forget my body, being the butt of jokes and jostled and pushed in corridors or on the stairs.

Most harmful was being told almost daily that I was an 'ugly cripple' and I would 'never have a girlfriend'.

(One of my therapists told me that if I worked hard everything would be alright at University where I would have girlfriends! I was so worried this would not come to fruition that when I thought I had failed my 'A' levels I seriously contemplated suicide.)

31

In PE and the playground I felt oppressed and belittled by the way I was expected to do things I couldn't do. I skived and joined clubs so I needn't go to games or the playground and eventually I decided to get a note from my mum to exempt me from games and PE. I was not asked by any teacher if I wanted to use the lift in the six storey building for nearly three years. This when I was obviously having problems with the stairs during lesson changes.

Later, although still suffering huge gaps in my formal education I was able to get five 'O' levels, then another three and three 'A' levels. I was now competing intellectually. In this my middle-class background became more of an advantage. My verbal arguing abilities that had really been my main defence against what I viewed as the stupidities of teachers, adults and other children, came to the fore.

I became more concerned with the wider good, equality and justice and by intellectualising these arguments moved into wider political activity.

For the next 20 years I was really concerned with Socialist politics, at University, in geography, in Trade Unions and teaching. I had blocked off those parts of me I found it difficult to deal with. Intellect rather than emotion ruled my life, I did eventually marry and have a child but I could only cope with life by thinking I could do everything.

In the last ten years sexual and personal politics including discrimination of various sorts has become much more important to me. This is also the time I have had a relationship with Susie. When she first met me I projected a strong image of being 'able-bodied'. **I remember going to a pub together in the early days where the seats were all taken. I stood up all evening and was grumpy. On the way home Susie asked me what had been wrong. I had to think hard and then I realised I had been in pain all evening. She said she would have asked someone for their chair if she'd known. I was horrified at the idea of admitting it or letting people know I needed help, and said they would use it against me or think me weak. She was the first person to question my view of myself!**

Over many years I have been indebted to her for supporting me in looking at my own disability afresh which has made it possible for me to join the fight for the rights of disabled people. She has helped me to admit to the things I cannot do, to the physical discomfort and pain I am in most of the time so that I can ask for help with dignity. This is still incredibly difficult for me but is very necessary. I feel I am much more open now. I have also come to terms with many of the spectres of my earlier years.

But also during this period my disability has worsened considerably. I now cannot walk at all without a stick. My old injuries to my left arm and right ankle cause me considerable pain and sometimes prevent me walking at all. I now sometimes use a wheelchair and my fear is that one day this will be a permanent necessity.

When my second child was born I found it much harder than with the first eleven years previously to carry him around and do all the things one has to with a baby. Now he is nearly two, there have been times when I have feared for his life as I have been unable to reach him before he falls. Our local community nursery had never thought that the children of disabled parents should be a priority and despite much argument by us they still don't.

It wasn't until Summer 1987 when, against my wishes, my head teacher identified me for redeployment because by disability restricted my ability to supervise games that I saw the need to fight the discrimination against us as disabled people collectively and move towards the Disability Movement.

Now I know that I need to join with other disabled people who are campaigning and organising against Society's attitudes and discrimination towards us. But I also know that each disabled person has to work through the layers of oppression we have accumulated inside ourselves.

Our personal experiences as disabled people become internalised. Our perceptions of ourself mirror the attitudes and actions towards us. Dealing with this requires more than projecting the blame onto society.

Whatever social changes take place and most certainly these must be worked for, we will still have to deal with the discomfort and pain we may have or the things we want to do and can't. Living with our disabilities will raise questions of valuing ourselves, of self-image of self-criticism and of confidence that disabled people will need to work through.

Even in a society where real equality has been achieved and we seem to be retreating a long way from such a possibility at present, we will still need to gain collective strength from other disabled people as we work through our situation and feelings anew. By sharing this we will continue to have the fortitude for the struggle for life that will always be ours.

Racism and Disability

Shut Down

There was a madman on the train today,
He walked right up and shouted in my face.

I could smell the drink so strong and stale,
His dress was ragged and his skin was
black
His skin was black Two shades darker than
mine.

I knew why he was mad
Inside he was so terribly sad though he
smiled, a terrible smile.

I had to shout back –
Move!
He was invading my space,
who knew what he might do next?

But I knew why he was mad
He was a Black man in this land,
He was a Black man in this land,
Black like me

The tube was packed
and only this could shift
their locked gazes.. yet still
they disguised their interest.

After he'd gone,
My eyes followed,
And watched his every pain.
How could this man have suffered so?
To the point where his mind had to say —
NO
And shut down
And shut down
This Black man had shut down.

I was feeling strong today
Had it been another
I would have just cried broke down and
cried
Broke down
Shut down
Shut down.

From 'Charting the Journey: Writings by
Black Women and Third World Women' 1988
SHEBA

It is not the same thing to be a white disabled person and to be a black disabled person. Disability settles upon anyone, but the effect on any individual is very largely modified, minimised, or exacerbated by who that person is in terms of their age, race and class. Black disabled children and their parents are facing a whole additional set of disadvantages imposed by racism, and this should not be forgotten.

By now we had found out that Sheetal had Sturge Webber Syndrome, i.e., an excess of blood tissue on various parts of her body and had a heamangeoma in her head causing brain damage even before she was born. This caused her to have frequent epileptic fits. Although the hospital staff were courteous and helpful, I found that my questions and insistence on staying with the child was thought to be over-protective and fussy behaviour. On another occasion when Sheetal had a serious increase in fits we took her to hospital where they decided to do a lumbar puncture (a large needle is inserted in the spinal cord to draw a sample of spinal fluid) to check whether she had contracted meningitis again. I almost can't believe it myself when I remember that she was lying there naked for over an hour while the doctor made 17 - yes, 17 - attempts to draw out the fluid in an area of about 1cm sq. Finally I had to ask her either to leave it or let another doctor do it. Then she called the consultant on the 'phone and got instructions after which she managed it. I still wonder how many more times would she have pricked the howling child if I hadn't interrupted her!

The fact that I spoke English helped and the extent of this came home to me only when I found Asians and other non-English speaking people either being given the 'veterinary treatment' or any other parent like myself who was bilingual was called upon to help out. Information on various sicknesses and diseases is almost non-existent in other languages. And of course whereas I could pass the time of day talking to other parents or staff, it must be so lonely and bewildering for those people who differ not only in language but also in culture and custom. Yet even in a multi-racial and multi-cultural city like London, there doesn't appear to be any effort made in order to improve the service in that direction and make it more appropriate to people other than the indigenous British. Even the information on benefits and other services that are available to help people in a predicament such as mine or a different one, often just isn't accessible due to the scarcity of ethnic minority health workers and appropriately written information.

Racism, and prejudice are dirty words, but not dirty enough to be discarded. The only thing that has helped me in achieving what I knew my daughter needed was by being assertive, by persisting until I got, what she needed or at least a satisfactory reason as to why not, but it is not always possible for everybody to do so with inevitably tragic outcome.'
Rameesh Talwar

Extracts from 'Flashes of Pure Joy' GLC Women's Magazine

Not only do Black disabled people and their parents and friends face discrimination in the way they are treated by the medical and hospital system; they also face a whole host of additional problems.

Deaf Black people are often very isolated not having the support of Deaf culture and clubs with additional communication problems, lack of signing and translation.

Discrimination in housing, social service, employment and education which affect the black and ethnics minority populations generally are much exacebated from Black Disabled people.

A recent study of how Black Disabled people fair under Apartheid showed that in South African Townships where the entire black population is forced to live in poverty Disabled Black people were significantly worse off (Disability Handicap and Society 1988).

Nor should we forget that on a global scale the 'white' rich North maintains the 'black' poor South in a state of poverty that leads to vast numbers of easily preventably disabilities. Of the estimated 70 million blind people in the world well over half could have been prevented by cheap dietary changes and programmes of disease prevention. It is the non-white population of the world that contains the vast majority of the 600 million Disabled people.

In the UK the all pervaisive dominant white racist culture has more pernicious effects on the black population.

In what has become a classic study Bernard COARD** (1971) showed how the West Indian child was being made "Educationally Subnormal" in the British School System.

More recently studies in ILEA and Birmingham have demonstrated disproportionately high numbers of Black 'Afro-Caribbean' children as

'Tanya Arif, Northumberland Park, See Northumberland Park

David Hevey.

being referred to Special Schools and Units for the Emotionally and Behaviourly Disturbed.

Many Black people are rightly suspicious of the School Psychological Service and Teachers whose racism has, they believe, led to their children being classified in this way.

Behaviour which is a reaction to the devaluing of black culture and aspirations is often classified as 'the problem' rather than the institutional racism within in the school system.

In "Aliens and Alienists: Ethnic Minorities and Psychiatry"* Littlewood + Lipsedge chart the way the British psychiatric system fails to recognise culture diversity leading to a disproportionately high number of Black people being admitted to 'mental' hospitals.

But Black people on the receiving end of racism can and do break down. Here Carmen Tunde in her poem Shut Down forcibly makes the point (see top of section).

The internalised oppression suffered by people confronting a double oppression is graphically described by Pratibha Parmar in her article 'Fragmentations'.

Extracts from 'Fragmentations'
Pratibha Parmar

In the process of survival and struggle we have to learn to love ourselves as much as we love the causes we fight for. It is important that we don't give time and energy to changing the external forces of our oppression at the expense of our internal needs for self-nurturing and caring.

I came to this insight about two years ago when I had a physical breakdown: a breakdown precipitated by many factors and which manifested itself at the weakest point in my body, my back... One night I woke in the early hours crying out in agony; my shoulders, my neck and my upper back had gone into complete paralysis. Not only was it so excruciatingly painful that I passed out, but I was unable to do anything for myself. I couldn't move or lie down without feeling agonising pain. It was a frightening experience which I would never want to go through again.

Burn out, Burn out, Burn out. My mind kept screaming at me whilst I had been lying on my back unable to move.

I have always found it difficult to discipline myself against doing too much. Since I was twenty I have

constantly been politically involved. The ever increasing spiral of my political life began as I discovered words to explain my perceptions, and met people who gave substance and validation to my experiences of growing up as an Asian woman in a racist and hostile country. Becoming conscious of my 'outsider' status in Britain and taking on the political identity of being Black gave a framework to understand my early experiences of racism. It became quite natural to become involved in the campaigns and groups fighting to challenge racist practices and working to bring about change.

Coming to live in England at age eleven was a tremendous psychological and emotional upheaval. Learning to live with a sense of uprootedness, so common to Black people caught up in the historical processes of fragmentation, has been like piecing together a giant jigsaw.

As I try to recollect the first rude awakening I had of racism, I realise that it was not a gradual process but more like many bolts of lightning striking all at once.

It was 1967 and 'Paki' bashing was a favourite pastime for white kids. The school was still alien to me, we had only been in England a few months and I was in the first year of secondary school. Within a few short weeks I learnt very quickly the strategies of surviving in the playground. There were not many Black kids . . . and we were mostly Asian. I learnt that most of the Asian girls stayed inside in the cloakroom at break times, instead of going into the playground. This strategy avoided getting into fights, and besides most of the time it was warmer.

I remember the first time I was beaten up in the school playground by two skinhead girls. That day is still fresh in my mind. The sun was shining. I wanted to feel the warm rays on my body. I missed the African sun and was miserable with grey English clouds. I went into the playground with my teenage girl's magazine, Jackie, and dreamt about being back in my old school in Nairobi with all the friends I had only left a few months ago. Suddenly, two shadows fell across my eyes and I heard the rasping voice of one of the girls with her crewcut hair demanding me to give her my magazine. Instinctively I knew I should give it to protect myself but I was furious and angry. Who were they to talk to me in this way?

Until my physical breakdown, I had not wanted to see how adversely affected I had been having to resign from my job in a white feminist project because of racism. The fight and struggle prior to this resignation had left me weak and tired. Yet I

---

*Penguin 1982
**COARD Bernard 1971 "How the West Indian Child is Made Educationally Subnormal in the British School System" New Beacon: London.

had not given myself time to heal and there were many scars. I had had many expectations from the job, particularly as it was a feminist project, albeit a white one, and it was an area of work I was committed to. I left with a sense of abandonment and a sense of betrayal, knowing that white feminists were voicing anti-racist sentiments (some of whom were my friends) yet were unable to give any substance of this in their day-to-day interactions with Black women.

I was 'burnt out' from the anger and the work.

It came on top of the loss of a very close, valued and dear woman friend, a friend who I had hoped to grow old with. I had not allowed myself time to grieve over the loss of this friendship and instead turned a lot of my grief into anger and bitterness. Anger that put the lid on the pain of this loss and bitterness. Anger that gave me a crutch to hobble along on.

I had worked hard to numb the emotions, the pain, the frustrations . . . of feeling powerless and hurt. My body's reaction to the stress and strain of these bottled-up emotions was inevitable. It couldn't cope with the pace at which I was moving. The pressure built up so intensely and quickly that my emotional plates were fractured. It was like a volcanic eruption. At first I was numb with shock. How had it come about that my body had to resort to such violence to force me to take notice of my self-destructive pattern?

The numbness took a long time to wear off . . . long after I was physically able and independent. The physical affliction itself only lasted about one month, but it was a turning point. With the support and nurturing my lover so warmly gave me, I was able to 'recover', both physically and emotionally. The warmth and security of my friends offered a safe space to begin the process of picking up fragments of my recently wounded past . . . to make connections with my personal history and unlock dusty corners in my memories.

No amount of sharp, wild words I threw into those two laughing faces could do the damage I wished upon them. Many other fights followed. The humiliation and resentments built up over the years, but the violence of those girls' hatred remains indelibly in my mind to this day. What was it about my Blackness that they feared so much? Why such venomous anger at an Asian girl refusing to cower in front of them?

From 'Striking Poses' A Graeae touring exhibition.

David Hevey.

What is Sickle Cell Anaemia?

Sickle cell anaemia and Thalassaemia are disabilities which may affect some children in any class in London which has black children.

Sickle cell anaemia is an inherited blood disorder which is regarded as a 'Black' disease, and effects approximately one in 400 of the Afro-Caribbean population, and also people originating from Asia, the Middle East, and the Mediterranean. In the last few years more attention has focused on sickle cell, an illness which is more common than haemophilia or cystic fibrosis. This has highlighted inadequate information, services and treatment.

The illness is inherited from both parents who are usually 'silent', healthy, carriers of a 'trait'. 'Haemoglobin' is the component of red blood cells which carries oxygen to all parts of the body. To inherit sickle cell anaemia, the haemoglobin passed on to the child is 'sickle' haemoglobin, so-called because these cells can change from normal shape to a half-moon/sickle shape. If both parents are carriers of sickle cell 'trait' there is a one in four chance that each child could be born with sickle cell anaemia, which is the illness. Sickle cell 'trait' occurs when a child inherits the usual haemoglobin from one parent and sickle haemoglobin from the other. In this case it is not an illness, and never changes to sickle cell anaemia, the illness. In fact it offers some protection against a serious form of malaria. The 'trait' is found in one in ten Black births. Although sickle cell anaemia is present at birth, symptoms do not occur until six months of age, or later. Pain, anaemia and infections are the major problems that may occur in a child with sickle cell anaemia. The main problem is caused by the 'sickling' of the red blood cells. In assuming the 'sickle' shape they also become rigid and can jam up small blood vessels, stopping the flow of blood, causing mild to extreme pain. 'Sickling' occurs when there

'In Brazil Carlos supports his wife and child by selling lottery tickets.'
Ideas: Berkley CA.

is less oxygen in the blood, or if the blood becomes too thick due to less water in the body. Therefore 'crises' can occur with dehydration, under anaesthetics, at high altitudes, following strenuous exercise, with stress, and during and after pregnancy. However, often the reason is unknown.

Although there is no cure, problems and complications can be reduced by access to specialist medical care. Common forms of treatment may include drugs for pain relief, antibiotics to prevent or treat infection, folic acid tablets to help produce healthy red cells, and plenty of fluids. Blood transfusions may also be given.

Sickle cell anaemia is a serious illness and can cause early death. However many individuals survive into middle age.

Interview with J, a Sickle Cell Patient

J: I've known I've had sickle cell anaemia since I was 8. I'm now 25. I've suffered with 'crises' for the last four years. They've steadily been getting worse, and with it the disbelief of the profession of my pain. Because you're Black and you're in pain, you come up against a brick wall; they just think. 'This is trouble'. They're reluctant to do much about it.

D: Do you think that if white people suffered, the profession would know more about it?

J: Yeah! that's true if white people got it as well it'd be taken a lot more seriously. If more care

was taken then people wouldn't suffer, people may not even have died! Sickle cell (anaemia) is something that can kill! The haemotologists (who treat sickle cell disease) know what they're about, know what they want done with their patients. But, they come up against the sister, registrars and housemen, who are in charge of you on the ward. They write up your chart and see you every day. If you've got a complaint or a question they're the ones you see first. Haemotologists? They 'might' see you every day, but they haven't got as much say, they can only give advice. It's only because I stuck up for myself, causing them trouble, worrying my haemotologist, that they all made decisions together.

D: I think the trouble started with you, over your high doses of pethidine (A painkiller used by the medical profession which can be addictive)?

J: My brother has sickle cell (anaemia), he's been on higher doses! There is this stigma about pethidine, they think I'm going to get hooked every time I go in there! Surely after all the times I've been in there, they should know how much dosage I've had, how much I can take, know that when I'm better I don't want it anymore! They thought that a certain amount of pethidine should cure it, but what it 'should' do and what it actually did was two different things. They don't know the extent of 'sickle' pain.

D: So they just assume you're lying?

J: Yeah! I said to a senior staff nurse, 'They're never going to believe me'. After the blood transfusions, injections, and everything else, I was still in a load of pain. They just couldn't understand it! In the end they started giving pethidine to me through the vein, because they realised the injection wasn't getting to me any more! So they contradict themselves.

D: Do you think if you were a black man things would have been different?

J: I met a man in hospital, we were in the same ward for a couple of days. He appears to have had no trouble. My brother goes to a different hospital admittedly, but their attitude is completely different, they take him a lot more seriously. They know that when he's in pain, when he asks for an injection, asks for help, he needs it! More often than not it's, 'Do you need...?', 'Are you in pain...?'. Whereas I had to demand, and maybe two hours later I'd get it. By then I was in double the pain - so that's what they call being 'hysterical'!? Being left in pain!

D: You couldn't win either way, if you kept quiet you weren't in pain anyway!

J: Right! And when I said something I was being 'hysterical'.

D: When you came on my ward, one of the senior nurses said you were 'trouble' when she'd nursed you before. So they all formed this idea of you being a 'problem'.

J: On that ward I reported one staff nurse. After that the sister 'advised' me to ask for a transfer. She knew that if I reported her again, she'd be out. She didn't want that, so she was telling me 'You can get lost'. Her nurses were more important than her patients!

D: Exactly the same thing followed you up to the other ward?

J: Yeah! I thought I was going to get a fresh chance. But no matter how they change the nurses around, your records are always there, so you're gonna have the same problems. I can't go on to either of the two wards I've been on and feel sick and have them believe it. I've never had any trouble on the other ward, but I know it followed me, just because of one nurse. A black student nurse told me a lot of the nurses were scared of me; they didn't want anything to do with me. Anything that had to be done for me they looked to her to do it. One night I had an enema and a staff nurse came in and saw me dripped wet with sweat. I just didn't know what to do! I was on the verge of passing out. I tried to hold her hand, she didn't want to hold my hand. This was so clear to me. She just left me there! Two juniors found me, one of them was the Black nurse. I went through a lot with her, she treated me differently; it shouldn't have made any difference, they were all nurses.

Sometimes I knew my water was coming from an ordinary tap instead of the drinking tap, so we'd spill it behind the curtains so she could refill it. Things like that we had to do for me to survive on the ward. I had to fight. A lot of the time I nearly gave up. After four or five weeks it's no joke any more! I got to the stage where I didn't care what they thought, trouble or no trouble. Being polite was getting me nowhere, so I'd rather drive them mad and get me somewhere!"

*From Spare Rib
Anthology on Health*

So far there is no nationally available information on the incidence of disability among ethnic groups. People with disabilities are not always an easily identifiable group, many have 'invisible' disabilities such as heart disease, diabetes and sickle cell disease (in its mild form). The

Department of Education and Science monitors pupils at special schools by disability, age and sex, and a few local authorities including ILEA have also begun to collect information about school-aged children with disabilities which includes a breakdown of some information according to ethnic backgrounds. There is evidence however that suggests that mothers belonging to certain ethnic groups, etc., suffer disproportionately from ill health.

The support systems, such as they are, for disabled people in Britain are unthinkingly designed around white cultural norms.

Most white people, for example, feel that social services and benefits are a right if you are disabled, whilst a survey undertaken in Islington among the Bengali community revealed that many would regard it as a sign of failure not to be able to support their family financially without turning to the state for help. A Hindu friend of mine has to not only work out the maze of bureaucracy when attempting to acquire an expensive piece of equipment for her disabled daughter, but also has to work out the maze of religious and cultural protocol involved in *not* leaving it all to her brother who is culturally responsible for the material needs of his sister.

Communication of information across language barriers is also an obvious difficulty facing professionals working with families with disabled members. I was amazed when my little friend of four years was given speech therapy by an English-only speaking therapist, although the child only understood and spoke Gujerati. This did not stop the therapist from feeling that she could write a report on the child's language development which, not surprisingly, stated that the child could not communicate!

Images of black disabled people need to be actively sought out, as do black role-models for young people to be proud of. Stevie Wonder is an obvious example, but there are many black writers who describe their own experience of illness and disability, internalised oppression, self-discovery and transcendence with great eloquence and beauty:-

'I am 27, and my baby daughter is almost three. Since her birth I have worried over her discovery that her mother's eyes are different from other people's. Will she be embarrassed? I wonder. What will she say? Every day she watches a television programmed called "Big Blue Marble". It begins with a picture of the earth as it appears from the moon. It is bluish, a little battered-looking but full of light, with whitish clouds swirling around it. Every time I see it I weep with love, as if it is a picture of Grandma's house. One day when I am putting Rebecca down for her nap, she suddenly focuses on my eye. Something inside me cringes, gets ready to try to protect myself. All children are cruel about physical differences, I know from experience, and that they don't always mean to be is another matter. I assume Rebecca will be the same.

But no-o-o-o. She studies my face intently as we stand, her inside and me outside her crib. She even holds my face maternally between her dimpled little hands. Then, looking every bit as serious and lawyerlike as her father, she says, as if it may just possibly have slipped my attention: "Mommy, there's a world in your eye". (As in, "Don't be alarmed, or do anything crazy.") And then, gently, but with great interest: "Mommy, where did you get that world in your eye?"

For the most part, the pain left then. (So what if my brothers grew up to buy even more powerful pellet guns for their sons. And to carry real guns themselves. So what if a young "Morehouse man" once nearly fell off the steps of Trevor Arnett Library because he thought my eyes were blue.) Crying and laughing I ran to the bathroom, while Rebecca mumbled and sang herself off to sleep. Yes indeed, I realised, looking into the mirror. There was a world in my eye. And I saw that it was possible to love it: that in fact, for all it had taught me, of shame and anger and inner version, I did love it. Even to see it drifting out of orbit in boredom, or rolling up out of fatigue, not to mention floating back at attention in excitement (bearing witness, a friend has called it), deeply suitable to my personality, and even characteristic of me.

That night I dream I am dancing to Stevie Wonder's song "Always". As I dance, whirling and joyous, happier than I've ever been in my life, another bright-faced dancer joins me. We dance and kiss each other and hold each other through the night. The other dancer has obviously come through all right, as I have done. She is beautiful, whole and free. And she is also me.

Alice Walker
'In My Mothers Garden'

We have been fortunate enough to get an interview for this revised edition with Yvonne and Leon Hippolyte about their experiences as a black parent and a black disabled person with cerebral palsy and their struggles for an independent life for Leon. *See pages 215-216.*

I'M GOING TO HEAR WITH MY EYES

Above me is a blue sky
filled with clouds so white
I see the trees move slowly
from side to side
but all is silence
and I feel uneasy
sometimes
I just want to run away and hide

Feeling unaware of sounds around me
sounds high, low, fast and slow
I feel these sounds with my hands
the rest I hear with my eyes

I'm not going to let my emotions take control
I'm going to pull through strong
whenever I feel ready to let go
I shall force myself to go on

I shall succeed
through anger, fear
happiness and love
I can and I know it
be something and someone
I thought I could never be

I'm going to come out
and stay right out
of my shell I've lived in for so long
I'm going to take control of my emotions
not let them take control of me

Above me is a blue sky
filled with clouds so white
I see the trees move slowly
from side to side

but now - I feel strong

I can't change the silence
but my hearing is back where it belongs
- back in my eyes

I'm going to hear with my eyes
and move side to side with the trees
and I will continue to succeed
until I reach a point as high
as that clear blue sky.

Helen Todd

Equality for the Deaf Community?

by Richard Rieser

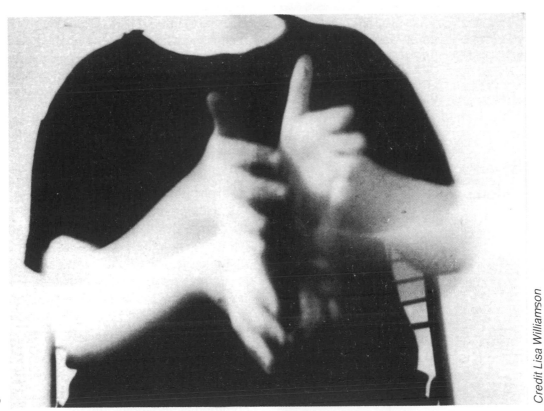

'Signing'

Credit Lisa Williamson

Profoundly deaf people either born deaf or who become deaf in the first five years of their lives have been placed at a *great* disadvantage by educationalists and the medical profession over the last 100 years. (Ladd 1978)

Deaf children born to deaf parents taught British Sign Language as their native language demonstrate a much greater ability to communicate and to understand and to then learn English as their second language.

Only in the last 10 years has it been established by linguists that British Sign Language is a separate visual-gestural language, with full rules of grammar, capable of conveying all the complexities of meaning of any other established language (see Brennan 1987). In the 1970's this had been established for sign language used by deaf people in America, Sweden and Denmark but professionals in Britain had chosen to ignore this.

Like any language, British Sign Language is an expression of a culture, history and values.

The Deaf community are denoted by capital D rather than small case 'd' and are those who consciously choose to use BSL. Not all deaf people see themselves as members of the Deaf community.

Ninety percent of deaf children are born to hearing parents. The main aim of the education of the deaf has been to get them to communicate in English. Where deaf children did use BSL it was seen as a playground language. The use of Deaf adults to teach BSL was not accepted. Medical entry criteria prevented Deaf people becoming teachers. The history, culture and values of the Deaf community were largely denied to deaf children unless they happen to meet adult BSL users in Deaf Clubs or elsewhere.

Nadia Wolley, deaf television presenter, has argued that while there are nearly eight million people in Britain with hearing impairment, only some 55,000 are native BSL users, and that this is a product of the hearing world's prejudice to deaf people and the Deaf community.

The oral method of teaching which has dominated since the Milan Conference of 1880, which banned non-oral means of 'educating' the deaf, has led to the systematic underachievement of deaf children in every country (Conrad 1979). Prior to the Conference deaf children had been educated in their own language by deaf teachers and hearing teachers fluent in sign language, and it had been successful. There were deaf academics, deaf professionals and the great majority of these teachers were deaf themselves (Lane 1984).

The emergence of BSL as a complete language, has allowed Deaf activists to portray themselves not only as disabled, but also as an oppressed linguistic minority. This view has important implications for all teachers as Deaf activists are now arguing against any integration and for separate Deaf schools for all Deaf children so they can learn BSL as their first language (Ladd 1988).

A survey of the British Association of Teachers of the Deaf (1983) showed that although 31,000 children were receiving specialist help from some 2,213 qualified teachers of the deaf, only 3.5% reported using BSL and only another 20% reported using any other signed system like signed English. Even when hearing adults have wanted to learn BSL the lack of understanding of its full linguistic richness has meant until recently they only gained a limited vocabulary that prevented them communicating on anything but a minimal level with deaf children.

However, it is now established that BSL is highly complex but its visual/gestural grammar can be understood in terms of rules.

The gestural 'words' of the language combine in different ways to form signs.
Hand shape, position of the hand in relation to the body, movement of the hand, orientation of the hand and simultaneous use of both hands make up the manual part of the language. The grammar is complex using non-manual features such as movements of the head, eyes, mouth, cheeks, shoulders and trunk; changes in manual inflection denoting different meanings; classifiers and the location of signs in space to express a relationship between signs.

Thanks to the efforts of adult activists in the Deaf community and individual teachers, things are beginning to change. For example the integration of Ben Fletcher who was profoundly deaf but integrated into Birdsedge Primary School, Kirklees. Ben was taught BSL as his first language and has his own sign language assistant. 'Ben' by Sian Downs, Annette Fletcher and Lorraine Fletcher (1987) tells his story and how Ben began to read and write and participate in all aspects of the curriculum through the medium of his own language which in turn gave him access to English. His mother puts forward a forceful argument in 'Deaf Child Deaf Language.... Education' 1987.

Leeds LEA are unusual in that they are now, as a result of Deaf community activity committed to a programme of education which will cater for their needs as the deaf themselves see them. BSL is to become the cornerstone of this policy and hearing children and teachers will also be able to learn BSL. Most LEAs and Government have yet to set these down as an educational policy.

The British Deaf Association has campaigned for a change; to give a central place for BSL in the education of deaf children in deaf schools.

Signing can now be seen accompanying a number of TV programmes. The BBC (1988) put out a programme 'British Sign Language for Beginners' and an accompanying book 'Guide' (Available on Video from BBC or RNID).

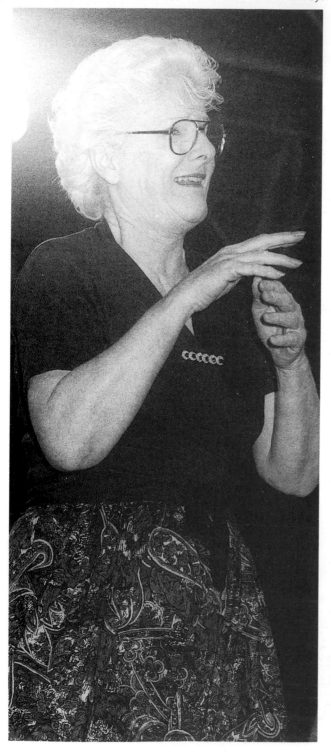

'Dot Miles, signed song'.

David Hevey.

The British Sign Language Training Agency based at Durham University is changing the whole approach to teaching BSL. Attempts are now being made to train more interpreters - urgently needed but there still remains much resistance.

In 1982 the BATOD put out the following policy:

'the use of BSL, recognised as a language in its own right distinct from English, is *not* recommended for use in an educational setting, since the identified goal of education is the development of understanding of the English language'.

This has led in recent years to a number of attempts to simplify BSL so that there is a one to one correspondence between sign and word and a number of made up signs have been added to convey exact English patterns. A number of schools or groups of schools have made up different signs in their attempts to make English accessible to deaf children. This practice is now being questioned by the Deaf community. We would not imagine a situation where each school teaching French or German would make up their own words but effectively that is what these made up languages do.

Certain systems especially the Makaton system are based on BSL but much simplified to teach language to people with learning difficulties.

This is not being questioned, but what is, is the long term validity of teaching deaf children signed English rather than BSL. Firstly, it means that a manual medium is being taught rather than a full language with all its visual-gestural possibilities. The Deaf community see this as a form of cultural imperialism. Secondly, recent research has shown that deaf children taught with these limited signed languages have a strong tendency to re-organise the gestural input in terms of spatial principles even where there are no adults who provide such a model. (Brennan p301)

It makes very little educational sense to teach Signed English in the school or home when there is a far more efficient alternative available BSL

'Deaf Dance Group Southwark' from poster campaign.

David Hevey.

and easily acquireable by the child. This will not stop deaf children learning English rather it will increase their chances of learning it as a second language having learned BSL as their first language.

Some may say this is all very well, but the numbers of profoundly deaf are few and for those with partial hearing 'high tech' hearing aids and dual methods do 'work'. But they still put deaf children at a disadvantage and deny them access to and support from the Deaf community.

As teachers we need to see the deaf and hearing impaired as a linguistic minority and apply the same tenets to them as we would to other children whose first language is not English. The non-discriminatory education of deaf children should include:

(a) Bringing BSL into learning situations for utilitarian and not tokenistic reasons.

(b) Integrate BSL stimulated work in books, work cards, drama with mainstream class activity.

(c) Develop BSL bilingualism in the classroom.

(d) Defend the right for deaf students to choose the balance of BSL/English to meet their individual identity.

The above are based on John Wright's (1982) principles for bilingualism.

In addition the valuation of deaf culture, links with the Deaf community and the possibility of supplementary schools as with other cultural minorities are all necessary developments for equality.

The alternative to this approach will mean increasing pressure from the Deaf community to withdraw the 87% of deaf/hearing impaired pupils 'integrated' without respect for their right to culture or language. Faced with continuing opposition from the oralists, Deaf activists are arguing for separate schools (Ladd 1988).

Only a major shift of practice, and the necessary resources will make it possible for deaf children to remain in mainstream schools and not be condemned to educational failure.

Deaf children have a right to their own language as a first language. All children have a right to benefit from their presence.

Notes

Mary Brennan. 'British Sign Language. The Language of the Deaf Community', p274. Including Pupils with Disabilities OUP. Ed Tony Booth and Will Swann 1987.

Gordon Mitchell. 'The development of educational policy for deaf children', p224, Including Pupils with Disabilities and Ch. 6 and Ch. 14 on Ben -(1988) Sian Davies et al and Lorraine Fletcher.

Paddy Ladd 1988. 'A Hearing Impaired or British Sign Language User? Social Policies and the Deaf Community in Disability, Handicap and Society', Vol. 5 No. 2 p 195-199.

British Association of Teachers of the Deaf 1983 - 'Reports of Survey Concerning Levels of Staffing and Methods of Communication used in Schools in England, Scotland and Wales' BATOD Association News.

Sign and Say 1981, Book 1 and 2. RNID. Useful general introduction.

BBC 1988 – British Sign Language. A Beginners Guide - Video and Book £6.95. Lorna Allsop/Dot Miles.

Lane, H. 1984. When the Mind Hears New York, Random House.

Conrad, R. 1979. The Deaf School Child: Language and Cognitive Function. London, Harper Row

Ladd, P. 1978. 'Communication or Dumification: a consumer viewpoint in Montgomery G (ed) of Sound and Mind: Deafness, Personality and Mental Health. Edinburgh, Scottish Workshop. Publication.

'A Language for Ben' is available on Video from Tyne Tee Enterprises Ltd. a very successful year in nursery, 52mm.

See also 'Everyone Here Spoke Sign Language by N. E. Groce, 1985. Harvard University Press $8.95 paperback.

This is a very interesting book which looks at Martha's Vineyard where deafness was accepted as a normal variation of the human condition. With a genetic deafness trait in the population and social isolation, the community adapted to include them. Everyone spoke sign language.

Two excellent volumes of articles, both reprinted and commissioned, have been produced by the Open University.

Constructing Deafness Edited by Susan Gregory and Gillian Hartley 1991. Pinter Publishers in association with Open University ISBN 0 86187 056 5 £12.50.

Different perspectives on deafness. It examines how deafness and deaf people are viewed within education, linguistics, social policy, psychology, audiology as well as more general presentations in fiction and film.

Being Deaf: The Experience of Deafness Edited by George Taylor and Juliet Bishop. Pinter Publishers in association with the Open University ISBN 0 86187 176 6 £11.95.

Full of valuable personal accounts of what it's like being deaf at school, work, college and in life.

Seeing Voices Oliver Sachs 1990. Picador ISBN 0 330 32090 4 £4.99.

An excellent and readable account of the deaf world.

"I was astonished to learn about the history of deaf people, and the extraordinary linguistic challenge they face, astonished too to learn of a completely visual language, Sign, a language different in mode from my own language, Speech . . . I now had to see the daf in a new "ethnic" light, as people with a distinctive language, sensibility and a culture of their own". Preface

Charities v Rights

by Micheline Mason

'Throughout the history of disabled people's struggle for equal rights we have been undermined time and time again by those who have a vested interest in maintaining disabled people in a dependent position. The legislation that has been placed on the statute book is a pale shadow of the original demands that disabled people put before Parliament. One wheel forward, three wheels back!'

Christine Wilson

In the UK charities, collectively, are now the second biggest employer after the state itself. If the voluntary sector were removed from the scene, we would not have a Welfare State at all. Just try and imagine no Spastics Society, no Cheshire homes, no Red Cross, no Salvation Army no NSPCC, no Samaritans, etc., etc., etc. People are so used to this kind of back-up to the state that many people probably do not realise they are not part of the State, for example the Family Planning Association, the Marriage Guidance Service, the Citizens Advice Bureaux, or even the National Trust. When charities first came into being in the C18th it was unlikely that it was ever envisaged that they would do anything other than channel a little of the excess wealth of the ruling classes to the 'deserving poor'. Charity Law is very different to those laws which govern state spending, laws which are meant to be an expression of democracy with some accountability to the common people through our M.P.s. Charity Law is not democratic at all. In fact Charity Law states that it is illegal for its 'beneficiaries' to be members of its council of management (an attempt to safeguard against vested interests affecting decision). It is also illegal to be 'political' and a charity, and therefore,

Credit LBDRT.

'Human Rights for Human Dignity' — a poster against benefit reductions it is very difficult indeed to be a campaigning organisation unless you are wealthy, or have private access to wealth.

Disabled people know that this is one of the crucial factors in maintaining our powerless position in society.

The thousands and thousands of 'caring' jobs which we are best qualified to do, are taken by non-disabled people whilst many capable disabled people remain unemployed. The images created by the Charity Industry to raise funds reinforce the sad, passive, unfortunate image of disability which we are fighting so hard to eliminate, **but perhaps worst of all they leave us without the fundamental human right to be included in mainstream services as equal**

citizens. We are still beggars, even if that begging has become more sophisticated.

What we would like to see is a society in which charities supporting basic human needs become quite unnecessary. We would like to have it acknowledged that the 'charitable instinct' of kindness and responsibility is a *human* instinct, not confined to the able-bodied, and which should be re-directed into 'social model' provision without the need of recourse of humiliating fund-raising exercises.

A Mori poll taken in 1989 found that most ordinary people still see disabled people as having 'difficulties not from our own making' and would be willing to pay more in the form of taxes to help us help ourselves. *We* would spend the money setting up many local 'Independent Living Centres' managed by disabled people from where we could begin to tackle all the problems society has around disability.

The experience of running our own services and projects will develop our skills and leadership abilities so that far larger numbers of us can take on managerial roles within the mainstream, bringing with us our unique perspective to other life issues such as hunger or poverty. We would not see it as a contradiction that small support groups should form of people with specific conditions, especially rarer conditions, to share information, and to combat isolation, as long as this leads to the development of ever more appropriate general provision, and a wider understanding by everybody of the details of disability, e.g. It *is* alright for the brittle bone society to advise me as to the best make of wheelchair for my four year old daughter, it is *not* alright for them to provide it, when the government refuse to acknowledge that children under five have the right to a decent wheelchair. (Which they do!)

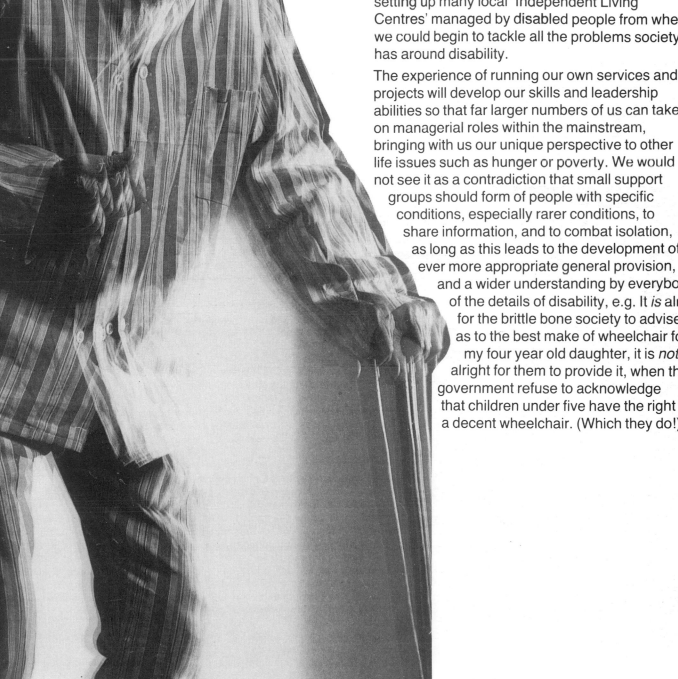

What can teachers do?

Have you thought about your Whole School Policy in relation to charltles? Does your school do fund-raising events, e.g., collecting for a guide dog for the blind? Do you 'Take fruit to the Old People' at Harvest Festival time? What image of blind people or Old people do you think this is giving to your pupils? After one term at her primary school, my daughter informed me that when she grew up she was going to be a doctor, and in her spare time she was going to collect pennies for the poor people in Africa. 'That's being good isn't it mummy?' It must be possible, even with very young children to look at which projects will support people's long-term interest, i.e., self-reliance and human rights, or which will keep people in the role of receivers. We need to look at other ways of expressing our need to give as human beings, especially giving oneself, one's time, one's attention, one's affection, one's talents in order to enable others to achieve equality.

Charities

"Pick the charity of your own choice".
The baked bean label stared at me.
Charity of your own choice; how nice.
Which unfortunate to pick? The
blind, the deaf, the crippled? Shall
I pick...or shall I go for a really
nice one, a crippled child. Pulls
the heart strings to even think about
it. The little crippled child,
unable like his or her peers to enjoy
a 'normal' life. Clink, clink, the
money comes pouring in. Pressed
into the charity boxes or even better
still, handed over with great display. Make an unfortunate's life
better. Bring a smile to those
pitiful lips.

Charities v Rights
'In From the Cold 1984'.

Credit Susan Fairclough.

How About Some Equality of Opportunity for Disabled Teachers?

by Richard Rieser

Conference resolves that the Union as a whole will incorporate equal opportunities for disabled teachers amongst its priorities at national and local level, and calls on all Union members to oppose discrimination against disabled members.'

NUT Conference 1989

My own experience as a disabled teacher (I had polio in my left leg and right arm as a baby) and the casework I have done for others all prove to me a widespread problem. This will only be overcome if those discriminated against, as disabled teachers come together, share their experiences, and exert their combined strength backed by their able-bodied colleagues.

As disabled people we are usually struggling daily to live with out disability and to operate as others do with much difficulty and often in great pain. The union, management and colleagues may be quite unaware of this and therefore do not offer, even in small ways, to make our lives at school easier, or more tolerable. They may not even notice the name calling and abusive attitude coming from pupils and we who spend our lives trying to minimise our disability find it extremely difficult to ask for help. When we may be sacked for being disabled teachers who can blame us?

As a secondary teacher I am aware that the hardness of attitude I have experienced from pupils, replicated in the adult world is not automatically found amongst younger children. I have visited many primary classrooms and talked with children about my disability. 'Why do you walk like that?' 'Why are your feet different sizes' and many other questions come thick and fast. I have found real care and understanding from young children once things are explained. It is *crucial* that we have more disabled people in classrooms to counter prejudice, and ensure the lesson is learned that people with disability are complex and should be valued members of society who cannot be labelled and summated by their physical characteristics.

If people think society's attitudes are not important they should remember it is 50 years since the Nazis set up their first death camps to exterminate the disabled. Over 100,000 were killed, often with their relatives' permission and with the tacit support of the church and others in the German establishment. It is arguable that Hitler would never have introduced the Final Solution for the Jewish population of Europe, if he had not already got away with exterminating thousands of disabled people.

It is hard to believe, that even with this Government's dislike of measures to ensure race and gender equality and their outright hostility to gays and lesbians, that they should also wish to continue to discriminate against disabled people in teaching. However DES Circular 1/88 does just this.

Replacing 11/78 it makes no recognition of a number of criticisms and studies demonstrating discrimination towards disabled people wishing to take up teaching and towards teachers who become disabled during the course of their career.

One would have hoped for a more enlightened view from the Government that introduced Warnock in the 1981 Act. Here handicaps to learning and special needs are viewed as something to be minimised with resourcing once statements are issued. This is alright for pupils, although underfunded, but pupils are to be denied positive role models, as the number of disabled teachers remain severely restricted even though Warnock (1978) strongly recommended in chapter 14 a big change in entry requirements to enable far more disabled teachers into the profession.

For those wishing to be teachers LEA's and colleges must be satisfied ..'*as to the health and physical capacity*' of all teachers and all entering teacher training. Medical Advisers are given the power to assess physical capacity to teach

'Femi' and Richard Rieser on Seaside Trip with Laburnum.

bearing in mind that ...'*teaching makes considerable demands of teachers' mobility and attentiveness*' and to classify as unfit to teach anyone with physical or psychiatric disorders likely to interfere seriously with regular and efficient teaching.

Throughout the circular there is an assumption that anyone who is not able-bodied has to prove they can carry out the same tasks as an able-bodied teacher.

The LEA's and their Medical Adviser's decision is final although they can seek advice from specialists or the DES.

So it is an unidimensional view of physical capacity to teach that prevails, rather than recognising alternative work practices. Team teaching, job-sharing, the providing of ancillary helpers, adaption of buildings and alternative teaching methods would make it possible for many who at present cannot gain entry, or are squeezed out of teaching, to make a worthwhile career.

The threat of physical unfitness to teach hangs over many teachers who therefore keep quiet about their disability. For many who become disabled, during the course of their career, early retirement or the sack are very real threats. This is

a huge waste of training and talent which could be overcome if there was less prejudice from colleagues and a more positive and flexible approach from LEAs and the DES.

Doctor Melvyn Kettle, in his study of 'The Employment of Disabled Teachers', showed how, out of 49 disabled teachers in his study, only 15 were employed full-time and another 11 worked part-time; all but one of the remainder had been retired on medical grounds. And, further, these 'retirements on medical grounds' had come about because of problems of access to work and/or the attitudes of those appointing staff.

Since 1978, the LEA rather than the DES has had responsibility for medical fitness to teach. As one would expect, the attitude of LEAs varies considerably.

In 1985, Dr Jane Lones of Lord Mayor Treloar School noted that fewer of her disabled students - wheelchair users - were getting accepted at teacher training colleges. She wrote to them, 59 - 70% replied. She also surveyed LEAs and 81 replied.

Forty colleges refused applicants on grounds of inaccessibility, which had been worsened by recent amalgamations. Only 10 colleges said they would welcome applications. Only Bulmerche College and Nene College, Northampton said they were completely accessible. This last had also talked to a group of heads and arranged accessible teaching practice.

All LEAs claimed to be equal opportunity employers. 32 LEAs were currently employing chair bound teachers. Three LEAs claimed to have made specific adaptations. Over half LEAs were not employing wheelchair bound teachers. Medical fitness to teach is in the hands of medical advisors and their view of the role of the teacher. Dr Lones reports both employers and college lecturers having a view of what disabled teachers could *not* do rather than what they could *do*.

There is therefore an urgent need for teachers and their unions to take up the question of disabled teachers. The NUT has been pushed into action by disabled teachers. We now have a National Executive Working Party of which I have been elected Vice-Chair. We are planning to draw up guidelines and bring them to our disabled colleagues in a Day Conference of Disabled NUT members.

Drawing from Nothing Special.
Credit Micheline Mason 1989.

The Equal Opportunities meeting at the 1990 Bournemouth Conference will be addressed by four disabled teachers.

The following policy was passed unanimously at the 1989 NUT Conference.

'Disability
Conference recognises that teachers with disabilities face discrimination in obtaining employment and in retaining their jobs. Conference believes that the presence of disabled teachers in schools will enhance the acceptance of children with special needs in mainstream schools, and that they will provide positive role models.

Conference therefore resolves that the Union supports the rights of disabled teachers by providing advice and assistance where employers are over-cautious and reluctant to employ teachers with disabilities.

Conference calls on the Executive to develop firm and progressive policies on the issue of disability, and to ensure that the Department of Education and Science, local education authorities and school governors take steps to accommodate the needs of disabled teachers, and to increase the recruitment and retention of such teachers.

Conference urges divisions to negotiate with LEAs on decision-making with regard to medical fitness to teach, particularly in regard to appointments and continuing employment of disabled teachers who are capable of teaching with flexible work practices, adaptations of buildings, provision of necessary aids and assistance, and support from colleagues.

Conference resolves that the Union as a whole will incorporate equal opportunities for disabled teachers amongst its priorities at national and local level, and calls on all Union members to oppose discrimination against disabled members.'

It is very easy for able-bodied teachers to suffer from feelings of guilt and personal inadequacy about their classroom practice as they attempt to meet pupils' needs with shrinking resources. Think how much more acurately these feelings affect disabled teachers, unless they are equally valued with others in their profession.

We must all campaign for a new approach: from our own unions, from LEAs and from the DES, and the beginning of this campaign and its final success will flow from disabled teachers' determination to refuse to accept discrimination and prejudice in their work places.

This is an amended version of an article that appeared in the Teacher 21 March 1988.

See

(1) Integration at Teacher Level (1985), Jane Lones – Educare Nos 26, p21-24

(2) Backlash – Prejudice Against Disabled Teachers – (1987)
British Jo. Special Education Vol. 14; p58

(3) The Employment of Disabled Teachers (1987) Melvyn Kettle – RADAR

(4) DES Circular 1/88
DES Circular 1/78

(5) Guidelines on Disability – An Equal Opportunities Issue NUT 1991. Examines current position of Disabled Teachers and makes proposals for change in recruitment and employment practices.

(6) Education's Equal Opportunities Policy No Guarantee to Employment. RADAR Contact Winter 1990. Reports a survey of LEA's. Shows that only 0.1% of teachers employed in 140 Local Education Authorities are disabled. Yet 92% of respondents had included disability in their E.Opps Policy.

(7) Don't Disable Teachers with Disabilities – Backlash. Richard Rieser – Sept. 1990. British Jo. Special Education Vol. 17; p94

Further Information from:
Richard Rieser, Vice Chair NUT Working Party on Disability, 78 Mildmay Grove, London N1 4PJ.

POSTSCRIPT. Since the publication of the NUT pamphlet there has been much greater interest in the position of disabled teachers. The draft pamphlet was taken to a working conference of disabled teachers and enriched by their experience. A further conference was held to mark its publication and a summary has been sent to all schools in England and Wales. There have been a number of articles in the Teacher and education and disability press. The NUT working party recently met on a formal delegation Michael Fallon. We were assured that the DES was revising circular 1/88 and that there was now a self completion form for judging medical fitness to initial teacher training. On examining this there is still much need for further change. The Minister also agreed that he would advise LEA's that money could be centrally retained under LMS to pay for the additional costs a school might incur by employing a disabled teaacher. This would be in addition to any funds from the Department of Employment Disability Advisory Service which are available.

Both Hilary Armstrong of Labour front bench and Paddy Ashdown and the Liberal Democrats have committed themselves to increasing the number of disabled teachers. This new found committment from politicians comes none too soon bearing in mind the overall figure of 1 in 1000 teachers that RADAR found in their recent survey.

Teachers' Stories

My Story
by Judy Watson

I was born in London in 1951. When I was four months old, my parents took me to the doctor because my eyes were very red and I had been crying a lot as if I was in pain. The doctor immediately referred me to the Royal Eye hospital where I was found to have glaucoma.

This is an eye condition which can easily be controlled with pills, drops and surgery, but after thirteen operations, it was clear that my sight was deteriorating quickly and I was sent to a school for blind children when I was seven years old. I wore glasses at this time and could see well enough to walk round on my own and was able to read print if I held the book close to my face.

My school was called Linden Lodge and was a mixed boarding school. I was allowed home at weekends which was quite easy because I lived about half-an-hour away by tube. However when I was eleven, I was transferred to Chorleywood College for Girls with Little or No Sight. This was the equivalent to a grammar school to which girls were sent from all over Britain.

Consequently, we were only allowed home four Sundays each term: it was felt that those from Scotland, Ireland and the north would not be able to go home at weekends so no-one should. I hated that and felt that I really lost touch with my family.

I was never very happy at school but gained my O and A levels and left at the age of eighteen to go to Kent University where I did an English degree. By this time my sight was very poor: glasses did not help any more but I could still read newspaper headlines if I had my nose touching the paper. I had a sound academic education and had learnt Braille but was not at all prepared for the 'Sighted' world. We had not mixed very much with sighted people of our own age and we all left school feeling a certain hatred and fear of them. Perhaps I was luckier than most because I have a sister who is two years younger and she had taken me to discos and introduced me to her friends. Many girls at school had never been to a disco or had a boyfriend or even been shopping with someone of their own age. I think this experience has led me

'Judy Watson taking braille register.

Credit David Hevey

to believe passionately that children with disabilities should be taught in mainstream schools.

I enjoyed University life although it seemed to take me a long time to settle. It was very hard work because reading Braille books is much slower than reading print and, in any case, much of the material I had to read wasn't in Braille. This meant I had to ask for volunteers from the other students to read to me. I typed my essays for my tutors and did my exams in Braille. After my exams had finished, I read my answers on to tape and one of the audio-typists transcribed them ready for marking.

While I was at University, I had my fourteenth and final eye operation. This was unsuccessful and I lost my sight completely when I was twenty one and in my third year. It was also at this time that I was married: we were far too young and I was under a lot of pressure and as a result, the marriage was never very successful either. My sight didn't disappear overnight: it went very slowly so that one week I could see a bus-stop in the distance but the next week I couldn't. By the time I got my degree, I was finding mobility a real problem just with a white stick so decided to apply for a guide dog.

I trained in Scotland with my first dog, a golden retriever called Randa, and I was delighted with the amount of freedom this gave me. For the first time in ages, I could go shopping on my own or visit friends. Guide dogs aren't magical, so I have to know where I'm going first in order to give instructions. She follows simple commands like 'Forward', 'Sit', 'Left', 'Right' and 'Find the stairs' or 'Find the door'. When I start work at a new school or move house, I ask someone who can see to teach me my routes and then I can get from A to B with my guide dog. It would be pointless to put me in the middle of London and expect me to find my way round with my dog - we would quickly become lost!

Shortly before I left University, I decided I wanted to be an English teacher and started applying to do a PGCE course. (Post graduate certificate in education.) My friends and acquaintances thought I was crazy: they couldn't understand how I would manage with classroom control, preparing lessons and marking. I knew that I would be able to overcome these obstacles if I thought about it hard enough. Clearly, teacher training colleges shared the view of my friends and I was rejected by nine institutions before being accepted by Christchurch College, Canterbury. September 1973 saw me embarking on my new career with my new guide dog and tons of determination.

While on teaching practice, I quickly realised that I could control pupils with my personality and that I could use my hearing to detect any

'Judy Watson talking with Fifth years.'

Credit David Hevey

misdemeanours. Kids forget that I can smell chewing gum in their mouths and that crisps make a tremendous noise. In my lessons, I always ask that everyone sits in the same place and it is easy to identify who is tapping a pen or talking when they shouldn't be.

I use Braille books in the classroom and plan lessons, mark work and complete various administrative task with the help of readers. Whilst at college and in the early years of my career, my readers were volunteers but now the training agency gives me money to pay someone. It's much better this way. My present reader is called Ruth and she comes to my home in the evenings at seven o'clock so that she can read to me. When we are doing marking, she reads out the work and corrects spelling and punctuation, then she tells me what it was she had to correct and I tell her what mark and comment to write at the bottom.

Having successfully passed my teaching course, I started work in September 1974 at the Sheppey School in Kent, a mixed comprehensive school of 1800 pupils. I was very happy there even though I found it hard work. Teaching requires a great deal of energy and everyone finds it exhausting, particularly when they are new to it. I used to get fed up with working all day and then coming home to readers and having to work every evening as well. I still have to do that and still get fed up with it at times, but most teachers work in the evenings so it isn't that unusual.

I find that everything takes me such a long time: other teachers seem to be able to mark a set of work in an hour or an hour and half; it will take me double that. Some GCSE assignments can be very long and it is not unusual for me to take five hours to mark a set of those! Reading aloud is just such a long process. It is absolutely essential that I am organised. I can't go into school and think, 'What shall I do with my third years today?' I have to plan ahead come what may. I have a filing cabinet at home where I keep my resources and I ask my partner, Matthew, to find a particular worksheet or activity sheet and then I can take it into school ready for photocopying for a class. In fact, Matthew helps me a lot. When I'm getting behind with my marking or I've got a tremendous amount of admin to do for the department, he helps out at weekends. I think he knows more about English teaching than any other non-teacher in the country!

I am now Head of Department in my fourth school and still love teaching. With Matthew's and Ruth's assistance, I think I do a pretty good job of teaching and running the department but it has not always been that easy.

Having worked at the Sheppey School for several years, I was promoted and given a scale two with responsibility for the third year curriculum and administration in the English department. I still wanted more challenges though and applied for so many jobs, I couldn't count but it must have been getting on for a hundred. Headteachers did not even request to see my references; they obviously had many applicants, saw 'blind' written on the form and decided that there was not point in interviewing me. My lucky break came when I applied to do an exchange with an American teacher and was accepted.

In August 1984, Hazel aged eight, Matthew and I flew to Portland, Oregon, and I taught at Beaverton High School for a year. Hazel loved her school and I certainly loved mine. American teachers do not have the same stressful time-table as we do here, the maximum number of classes being five and only two courses being taught. This meant only two lots of preparation, at least one free period guaranteed every day and school finishing at two-thirty. The staff were expected to stay until three-thirty so that they did an eight hour day. (School started at seven-thirty). This meant my readers came to school in the afternoon, I finished marking and preparing by five and then I walked home for a free evening. I really missed that when I returned to England.

Shortly after starting back at Sheppey, I applied for and was given a job as Second in Department at a mixed secondary modern school in Whitstable. I had experienced blatant discrimination at Sheppey where a young teacher in my department was promoted over me to a scale three so I was very pleased to leave. I loved my new job and almost two years later I applied for a Head of Department post at a girls secondary modern in Ashford. I have been doing it for a year now and enjoy it very much. The kids are great! I have always found that though; kids don't have the same prejudices and inhibitions as adults and I always feel very 'Normal' and accepted in a way which doesn't happen with most adults.

My classes are incredibly helpful: someone does the class register, they take it in turns to be 'Hands person' so that they don't all shout at once and I have no end of volunteers to do things when I need them. Two fifth year girls clear my pigeon hole, read me anything urgent and do photocopying, etc. They are brilliant!

I don't want anyone to think that I am 'Super Woman' or anything like that. I am just a very ordinary person who gets cross and is moody and I certainly annoy Hazel a lot of the time now that she is a teenager. I still get angry and depressed about being blind. I don't like it and wouldn't wish it on my worst enemy. I do feel that society should meet my needs more than it does. I don't see why I should always have to compete on equal terms. I know my life would be so much easier if I could see and I particularly regret that I can't read or drive or see my own daughter. I saw a television programme a couple of years ago where a woman had an operation and regained her sight.

It really made me cry and Hazel was very surprised. Just because I usually seem so accepting of my disability doesn't mean to say that I have come to terms with it. I'm not sure that I ever will. I do know though that I am going to try to fight for my rights and the rights of other people with disabilities in the future. It's about time that we said what we wanted and that we were listened to.

Living with ME
by Anna Sullivan

'In March 1988, I woke up one morning, got out of bed intending to go to the bathroom, and found that I could not walk. The pain in my legs was agonising and it seemed that there was no power that would move them. I crawled on my hands and knees to the kitchen and rang work to say I was sick. Six months later I was diagnosed as suffering from ME (Myalgic Encephamyelitus). From that day in March I had never returned to work and now I am medically retired from teaching. There are many fields of research going on at the moment to find the cause for this devasting illness. Is it caused by a virus and/or a breakdown in the immune system, is it caused by stress and trauma or allergy? I cannot say here what is the root cause. The condition is complex in its clinical makeup and the varying degree of disability. Perhaps it is all of these things.

Although my final collapse happended two years ago I know now that I had been ill for much longer. I had been a primary school teacher for fifteen years and like most classroom teachers I never had enough time off when I was ill. Always under pressure from lack of cover staff, teachers feel incredibly guilty if they have sick leave and often drag themselves into school when they should be at home recovering from a bad bout of influenza for instance. Schools are breeding grounds for viruses and the stress of teaching particularly in inner city schools is tremendous. It is not surprising then that teachers are so often sick. In a survey done of ME sufferers by the ME Action Group, it was found that more teachers had the condition than any other professional or social category. The illness has been around a long time but because of wrong diagnosis, dismissive attitudes by the medical profession, it has only recently been recognised as a condition that is real in physical terms. Blood tests usually show no abnormality, you don't look particularly ill and infection is unlikely to be detected. Usually GPs haven't a clue. Many dismiss the condition as neurosis, employers are unsympathetic, and the

'Anna Sullivan'

press have not helped by naming ME as 'yuppie flu'. These attitudes have led to despair and isolation for many sufferers some being driven to suicide. I went through torments of loneliness. I felt I was the only person who knew how ill I was and no one believed me, for ME shows itself only to the sufferer. I also believe that ME is a condition that is of the mind and body. It often strikes at people who live life on the run, people who push themselves to the limit of their energy. I was that kind of person.

As well as being a classroom teacher which is exhausting, I was also an active trade unionist and was involved in community politics especially in anti-racist and anti-fascist work. I had brought up three children most of the time as a single parent. Two years before March 1988 I remember feeling particularly exhausted. I thought it was just because it was the end of term. I was going to meet friends at a restaurant and as I walked along I suddenly felt terrible pain in my legs and they just collapsed under me. The doctor could give no explanation so I just rested for weeks and returned to school. That Autumn I was very ill with a pneumonial infection. I returned to work feeling terrible and now my legs were hurting so much all the time that some days I could barely walk. In 1984 my father had died very suddenly. I loved him very much and his death was very traumatic for me but I gave myself no time to grieve. I was the strong mother the indispensable person in the union branch and anti-racist group. An egocentric assumption but it didn't seem like that at the time.

In 1987 at three in the morning four petrol bombs were hurled through my front room window. My son and I just managed to get out wearing only dressing gowns. I can remember standing in the street watching my house burn and the windows explode and I felt nothing at all. I realise now that I was in a terrible state of shock. The attack on my home and life was a reprisal by fascists for the campaign I had organised against them concerning in particular, attacks on Bengali children many of whom were pupils at my school. This was at the start of the summer holidays and for the whole of that year I had felt very ill and exhausted. By the time I finally collapsed I was getting headaches so terrible that I thought I must have a brain tumour. The pain would wake me in the middle of the night and I would stagger around clutching my head in agony eating pain killers. I had lost the ability to concentrate and found that even reading a newspaper was difficult. The pain in my arms and legs was agonising and walking was now so difficult that I rarely went out. I was so exhausted that I often did not have the strength to comb my hair and a bath took hours to recover from. My digestive system had collapsed and I seemed allergic to everything. The pain affected every part of my body and was relentless, and yet nothing specific could be found wrong with me. I spent three months in hospital and by then was in a wheelchair. My life was turned upside down and I had to completely re-assess myself and how I would cope with this disabling condition. I knew I had to give up my job and I realsed that I would have time to paint to write and rest. I am indebted to my children and friends who looked after me when I was totally helpless and to break my isolation took me to the Theatre, Art galleries even a National Union Conference when I was still in a wheelchair. By now I was officially registered disabled.

It was almost as difficult for them to adjust to the new me as it was for me to. I was visited by a social worker who tried to get me a Home Help.

Even though I could not walk more than a few steps I was denied this facility because I had children. I pointed out that they did not all live with me and they all worked all day and I couldn't even get myself anything to eat. Still they stuck to their decision. Friends were coming in in their lunch hour to feed me. I had not realised until I was affected how difficult just ordinary things were to do, just how many places were inaccessible to people in wheelchairs and how differently people treated me. People who I had not got on with before now were nice to me, and that made me angry. While I was still confined to bed I was visited by a woman representing a group called community link. This group worked from a day centre for disabled people in Islington. They basically set about bringing people like me back into life again. I decided that I would like to go there and attend the creative writing class. I had started to write poetry while in hospital and my doctor, while convincing me that I would get well again, also encouraged me to write. While the day centre caters for people with various disabilities it is true to say that most of the people are in wheelchairs. By the time I went there I was walking, although painfully and slowly. The rest of me looked not particularly ill and I was constantly asked if I was a new worker. Even though I said again and again that I was disabled I felt that many people didn't believe me. When asked to explain what was wrong I found it difficult to do so. How do you explain that some days you can walk and other days you can't. I felt trivial and guilty. I am sure that this happens to a lot of people with hidden disabilities.

I am very slowly recovering with the help of diet and a wonderful herbalist and one doctor who has supported me through the emotional crisis that accompanied my condition. But no one knows of a conclusive prognosis for this illness. Some people recover in three to five years others remain chronic sufferers. We know from research that some people have had the condition for twenty years. Changing your life to deal with disability can be constructive and creative but that is only made relatively possible with lots of support in your personal relationships, because there is little help still outside of that, inspite of various legislation. Physical and mental imagery in a grasping jet aged society does not help the process. I believe that we cannot change things for ourselves unless we address the social issues that shape our society.

Anna Sullivan

Progress with Humanity?
The experience of a disabled lecturer
Jenny Morris *

Being a disabled college lecturer is a paradoxical situation in terms of the status that I am accorded by other people. To be disabled is to be classified as belonging to one of the most 'vulnerable and deprived' groups in society, particularly if your disability is very visible as mine is. It is assumed that such a severely disabled person is unemployed and is dependent on others. Other assumptions are also part of this general image of a disabled person: poverty, lack of ability, lack of mobility, lack of control over one's life. To be a college lecturer, on the other hand, is to be defined as a professional, someone with above average educational qualifications and above average earnings, someone in control, articulate and autonomous.

It is difficult, if not impossible, for people to reconcile the two images. To some extent, they only manage to deal with the fact that I have this contradictory position by ignoring my disability. I thus become an honorary able-bodied person, in the way that many women holding high-status positions become honorary men.

However, I say this now from the position of having been back at work for some time since breaking my back. The initial reaction was to me as a disabled person and my status as such was made very clear when Haringey Council's first response to my disability was to declare my newly acquired contract of employment void, as I had not turned up for work on the first day of term. I was, at that point, just learning to use a wheelchair, having spent nine weeks flat on my back in bed. Haringey is, of course, an equal opportunities employer; its motto is 'Progress with Humanity'. And this was the first lesson that I learnt from my new status. The negative assumptions and views held about disabled people are of such strength that there is many, many a slip between intention and implementation. It's like racism and sexism. The discrimination is deep within people's subsconscious and permeates our social institutions.

I relied on another social institution, my trade union, to fight Haringey's discrimination which they did very effectively and successfully. Yet I have subsequently found out that it was the principle of the matter which primarily motivated the union. After all, if my contract was void then so was that of any teacher who had 'flu on the first day of term in a new job. Most of the individuals involved in putting pressure on Haringey to keep my new job open for me assumed in fact that I would never be able to take it up.

Before I started work at the college, I went in a couple of times to discuss my timetable and to see if there were any problems with accessibility. I was lucky in that the department in which I work is in an accessible building and that various measures had been taken the previous year to enable a bridging course for disabled students to be held there. The alterations that had been done for these students were, however, quite inadequate, and this was another lesson I learnt. Unless you have disabled people involved in making such adaptations then they won't be the right ones. There was an unnecessary lip to the ramp into the buiding which made it almost impossible for those who can't do a 'wheelie' (flipping your wheelchair onto its back wheels) to get up the ramp; the entrance doors were very heavy and there hadn't evenbeen a handle put on at a lower height; rails had been put into the students' wheelchair toilet in every place except the one required; the lift panel was too high and most wheelchair users wouldn't be able to reach the emergency button, or the buttons for the upper floors. All these things are important physical details which increase our dependence on other people and illustrate how the environment can handicap us. The necessary commitment could do so much to minimise our disability.

It took a year since I first got into the college to talk about what alterations were required - nine months since I started work - for a staff wheelchair toilet to be provided. Every time I asked about progress I was made to feel as if I was asking for something which was a great deal of trouble. Indeed, my first reaction on learning that the alterations had finally been done was to be incredibly grateful and to think of writing a 'thank you' letter. However, I didn't as I felt that this would be falling into the trap that had been set to make me feel as if I really had no right to ask for such alterations to be done and that if they were done it was as a very big favour. If education authorities and their employees acted as if disabled people have the right to be students and employees, then the adequate provision of the necessary adaptations would follow automatically and we wouldn't be put in the position of pleading for our exceptional circumstances.

Other changes in attitudes are required when alterations to the physical environment are involved. There are many different types of disability and each individual is affected differently. So it's no good a local authority thinking that just because they have put in a ramped access for a wheelchair user that that is the end of their responsibility for adapting their buildings. What if the next employee or student can walk but has very weak hands? They will then have to make adaptations to the door handles. What if the next person is partially sighted? They may have to paint a white line on the steps or staircases.

Furthermore, an individual's abilities may change over time and thus necessitate further adaptations. If a local education authority is truly committed to equal opportunities for people with disabilities they will need to be continually responsive to new demands.

To get back to people's attitudes to me. Generally, I find there is a combination of total insensitivity to the difficulties which I experience and paradoxically, at the same time, a classification of me as 'unable'. There is a failure to see that being unable to walk means exactly that, and not 'unable' genrally. I am handicapped by various physical obstacles, but these obstacles can be got round given the willingness of people to help. It is just this willingness which is lacking on so many occasions. People offer help when I am doing things which don't require help. I am considered so 'unable' that when I do everyday things like getting out of my car, strangers rush over in a panic of concern. Yet if I am confronted by a couple of steps, their reaction is not to ask me if I would like to be carried up but to assume that yet another place is barred to me. I should mention that I am not a daunting prospect for being lifted up and down stairs; my wheelchair is very light and I weigh under 8 stone.

So many people's attitudes to disabled people are dominated by the assumption that we are alien to 'normal' society, that we don't belong, that we are an embarrassment, an eyesore and shouldn't be allowed out. The problem with being disabled and a college lecturer is that I don't fit into people's expectations of a disabled person.

As I mentioned, I am treated by some work colleagues as an 'honorary able-bodied' person, now that they have got over the strangeness of me being there at all. Yet this being treated as an equal is very much on the surface. Scratch this surface and you find the fear and contempt which underlies much of the discrimination against people who don't measure up to what we consider to be 'normal'. This attitude has come out recently over my having to park my car in a way which blocks other cars because someone else has parked in the disabled driver's space in the college car park. One member of staff threatened to cut my car brakes at the same time as saying to other members of staff how sorry he feels for me. This particular incident has

confirmed my view that the patronising pity expressed for disabled people is conditional on our fulfilling the passive dependent role expected of us.

The second type of reaction I experience at work is from those who I come across as I go through the building who do not realise that I am a lecturer there. Thus I get patronising remarks in the lift, or someone points out that I shouldn't be using the staff toilet, or someone tries to push my wheelchair out of the lift on the third floor under the misapprehension that I am one of the disabled students who are based there.

I do find this reaction very difficult to deal with as I am not normally one to worry about status. Since joining the group of third-class citizens, however, I am more concerned with making as much of my professional status as possible just because it means people do behave a bit more as if I'm a human being if they realise what job I do.

The third type of reaction is from the students that I teach. When I go into a room to teach I am not someone in a wheelchair but a teacher and someone who enjoys teaching at that. You might have thought that when I came back to work after being disabled I would have worried about students' reactions to me. Not a bit of it. When I go into a room to teach, it is the only time apart from with a very few close friends, and with my daughter, that being in a wheelchair is completely irrelevant.

The fourth type of reaction is limited to one member of staff. For months after I went back to work I sensed that there was something very different about this particular woman's reaction to me. I don't always get on well with her so it wasn't so much that there was a sympathy between us, rather that I sensed she had a basic acceptance of me which is lacking in most people. I thought I was imagining it until I discovered that her brother-in-law is a paraplegic and then I realised that she did indeed have a basic acceptance and an assumption that I was a perfectly competent teacher and human being, because her previous experience led her to expect this of me.

This is one of the most important lessons I have learnt. People's expectations of us are formed by their previous experience of disabled people. If disabled people are segregated, are treated as alien, as different in a fundamental way, then we will never be accepted as full members of society. This is the strongest argument against special schools and against separate provision. If everyone, in their childhood and adulthood alike, and at some time during their daily lives, came across people with all sorts of disabilities, then those disabilities would cease to be so frightening and threatening. They would, instead, be recognised for what they are, as handicaps to our functioning, not negations of us as people.

Dr Jenny Morris teaches Housing, Sociology and Social Policy at Tottenham College of Technology. On the day that she signed her contract for this post, in June 1983, she fell off wall onto a railway line while trying to rescue a child. She is now paralysed below the waist. She is a single parent with a two and a half year old daughter. She tells of her encounters with other people's reactions and attitudes towards her and her disability. Reprinted from 'Including Pupils with Disabilities' Booth and Swann 1987 Open University.

JENNY MORRIS UPDATE

What does it feel like to be a member of one of the groups covered by equal opportunities employment policies? Do black employees, women, disabled people, gay men and lesbians feel wanted, appreciated and protected by an employer who professes to welcome us as employees? Or do we feel that, in addition to doing our jobs well, we have to fight for the employment conditions that others take for granted?

In 1983, I was offered a lectureship by an education authority which claims to vigorously pursue an equal opportunities policy. The day I signed the contract I had an accident which meant that I now use a wheelchair. The LEA initially declared my contract void as I had not turned up for work on the first day of term but my trade union pointed out that if this was so, then it also applied to any lecturer who had 'flu on the first day of taking up a new contract. My job was reinstated, but my employer's motto "Progress with Humanity" now sounded rather hollow.

On starting work I experienced problems with both the building and the attitude of staff. I spent two years struggling to get the College management to make it possible for me to use the car park, to use the toilet and canteen facilities, to get into the College without major inconvenience and so on. It was difficult to ask senior management to take up incidents where other members of staff – and occasionally students – acted in an intimidatory and hostile manner. For example, one member of staff threatened to cut my car brakes when I parked in a way which blocked his car; it was a constant source of conflict that I often obstructed other cars because a non-disabled person was using the disabled drivers' parking bay.

After two years of struggling to get my physical access needs met in a satisfactory manner, I gave up. I decided I was at the College to teach, that I enjoyed my job and that forever having to argue and get angry was a waste of energy. I felt I did not want to tackle other people's attitudes to me as a disabled person as I had no support from senior management and I just found it too upsetting.

I therefore worked around the difficulties. I tried to ignore the problems that I had with parking my car although I consistently had to leave classes and move it; I failed to take up the problem of new fire doors which posed a major obstacle; I dealt with the refusal of caretakers to move exhibition boards for me by deciding not to exhibit students' work; I developed wrist injuries through using the too heavy doors throughout the College; I refused to get angry when canteen staff told me I couldn't be served in the staff canteen (they assumed I was a student), and so on, and so on.

I thought I had accommodated myself to the way in which neither the physical environment nor the ethos of the College took account of my needs as a disabled person. The decision not to waste time taking up such issues paid off in that I enjoyed my job and I did well at it. **Like many disabled people, I pretended that my disability was not an issue.**

One day last autumn term I discovered that I had been locked out of the canteen because of new security arrangements. I was devastated. I could not believe that my employer had so forgotten my existence. I instituted a grievance procedure which was finally settled to my satisfaction. Nevertheless, I found it very difficult having to use up my energy getting angry and defending my right to use College facilities.

This summer term I handed in my resignation. During the last seven years, the LEA has continued to assert itself as "an equal opportunities employer". But my experience over these years has been that in order for principles to be translated into reality I would have to fight and campaign to make my voice heard and my needs met. I chose not to do this.

The College Principal asked me to withdraw my resignation, offering to discuss action to address my concerns. But my campaigning energies are already committed to disability issues outside my working life. Surely I have the right to be a beneficiary of my employer's equal opportunities policy, rather than an ever-vigilant guardian of its implementation?

I have opted out but many disabled people continue to face the same battle in their day-to-day employment situation. **Equal opportunity policies may look very good on paper but how much do they rely on the strength, perseverance and tolerance of those of us whose employment rights they are supposed to protect?**

Dr Jenny Morris
June 1990
Published in the Guardian July 1990

Disability Culture

The idea of disability culture begins with the recognition that we are valuable people in ourselves, and that we need not avoid each other or hide behind a cloak of false integration. We no longer need to build our lives on a denial and devaluing of our background and the experiences of pain and triumph, sadness and joy, which form the reality of our upbringing. Disability culture is being built upon a ruthless honesty about people we are and the role we play in society.

Simon Brisenden

This is a concept which has been made possible by the Disability Movement. It consists of two things - firstly the skills which we have developed in order to live well with our particular conditions, and to communicate with fellow humans. Wheelchair skills, sign language, long-cane skills, our humour, our 'secret' knowledge that we share only with each other, all this is part of our culture. Secondly it is the development of our artists, poets, dancers, actors, singers, comedians, writers, film-makers, photographers and musicians who are using our talents to express the experience of disability from our own perspective.

'Ultimately Disability culture should be recognised as one of the many strands running through contemporary multi-cultural society. A lot of Disabled People believe there is a great value in making links between ourselves and other oppressed groups and artistic expression should facilitate this in all sorts of ways. In time we will have our own body of artistic work about, or informed by, the experience of being disabled in the same way as there is already much work created from the point of view of women, people from ethnic cultures, and from lesbians and gay men.'
Sian Vasey

What is Disability Culture?
Simon Brisenden

Some disabled people avoid the issue of disability culture simply because it touches areas of their lives that they would rather not think about. If you have carved out a life against all the odds as an alien in a non-disabled world, you do not want to think too hard about the price you have had to pay.

'Heart and Soul at Covent Garden'.
Credit Chris Killick (Disab Artic)

You may not want to think, for instance, about the world of disabled people, for you now belong to a different world. The idea of a culture of people with disabilities, a set of common experiences and aspirations belonging to us all, seems to undermine everything you have achieved. It seems to threaten the basis upon which you live. If you have struggled and fought to become assimilated, to merge with the majority, you do not want this achievement to be knocked, you do not to be reminded of what you have left behind.

The overwhelming urge to become part of 'normality ' leads one to devalue the world of disabled people and to avoid contact with that world. It leads one to avoid like the plague any association with other people with disabilities and their organisations.

The concept of disability culture is deeply threatening to this point of view because it values the lives and experiences of disabled people as important in themselves. More than this, it says that the world of disabled people should be valued on a par with the world of 'disability'.

'Three resource — users Jackson's Lane Community Centre'

David Hevey

The idea of disability culture begins with the recognition that we are valuable people in ourselves, and that we need not avoid each other or hide behind a cloak of false integration. We no longer need to build our lives on a denial and devaluing of our background and the experiences of pain and triumph, sadness and joy, which form the reality of our upbringing. Disability culture is being built upon a ruthless honesty about the people we are and the role we play in society.

Out of the recognition of our value comes the ability to organise ourselves, to put on events, to mobilize our forces, to produce works of art, to run workshops and newsletters and generally to get together and share the common language of our experiences. Only people who value themselves, and listen carefully to their own voices have a culture of their own rather than a secondhand culture gifted to them as the price of a silent acquiescence to unthinking 'normality'.

So what is disability culture? It is, in general terms, that which is common to our lives and which informs our thoughts and activities. It is our aspirations and our dreams as well as our struggles and our nightmares. It is the things we cannot forget as well as the things we want to remember. It is the schools we went to, the day centres we inhabit, but it is also the art we produce and the organisation we have built. It is so many things but it is no one particular thing.

Many of us have found the idea of disability culture extremely valuable because it has given us the opportunity to share experiences, to come out of the shell of private confusion and into the public world of politics and performance art. Speaking as a poet it has given me the one thing I wanted above all else - an audience I could

'Downs Syndrome Dance Group from poster campaign, Southwark'

David Hevey

'Hamish, performer with Graeae Theatre Company'

Credit David Hevey.

'Hamish, performer with Graeae Theatre Company'

identify with. This is true for other artists too, who have been given strength and encouragement by the realisation that the subjects they struggle with are not isolated incidents but have a deeper cultural significance.

We now live a multicultural society and we must proudly take our place alongside the other cultures and lifestyles that are demanding a space to communicate and be themselves. We must learn to relish our differences and not disguise them. We must take control of our lives and our organisations so that we can create a form of politics that is born out of our uniqueness, and which is not led by professionals or other non-disabled people.

The culture of disability comes out of our ghettoes as a form of defiance just as it comes out of the ghettoes of women, black people and ethnic minority people, gay men and lesbian women. A ghetto is not only a place of physical degradation, a slum, but can also be a spiritual dungeon, a psychological prison in which the mind is chained and tortured. So it is not just a question of closing down the special schools and the day centres but of opening up our minds to the value of our existence. We can only work against these mental ghettoes by getting together and sharing the common themes of our lives. It can be a thrilling and liberating experience.

The culture of disability is the web that binds us together on the basis of what is common but leaves us room to move and grow. It is built upon appreciating and valuing many things, including things that may have been patronised or ignored in the past. For instance, an important element of our culture is our history. We should not wait for the academics to decide this is important, but we must begin charting it ourselves by listening to and recording the reminiscences of older people with disabilities. Their stories are our lost history, a central element of the culture we belong to.

But a disability culture is not only rooted in the proper appreciation of the past, it must also celebrate the present and the future. This sense of celebration and freedom has been strongly in evidence at some of the artistic events that have taken place up and down the country, where audiences and artists have merged together and aparticipated in a collective event arising out of desire to express themselves. Disability culture is about expressing ourselves in whatever way comes naturally, and about realising that these expressions are valuable.

It is not a question of shutting ourselves off from society, as some people seem to think. On the contrary, we must take our place in society fortified and empowered by the knowledge that we do not need to discard our cultural identity as the price of integration.

Disability Arts in London

There has been a real bursting forth of creativity by disabled people in London in the last few years. It is one of the major ways of developing pride and identity as individuals who belong to a group of people who are moving out of repression, literally into the limelight. We think that it is vital that young people are:

(a) Encouraged to develop their arts at school.

(b) Exposed to the Arts Movement through attending performances or workshops, or inviting artists into the school to perform or lead workshops or to do Arts Projects.

(c) Challenging the discrimination which exists in the professional arts world against disabled people (e.g., entry requirements for RADA).

For more information contact:

London Disability Arts Forum, The Diorama, Peto Place, London NW1

Telephone and Minicom 01-935 5588/ 01-935 8999

LDAF exists to clarify, explore and define Disability Arts, as well as promoting Arts by Disabled People. The organisation also provides a forum of Disabled People to further the participation and representation of Disabled People in the Arts.
Publishes DAIL magazine

Shape London, 1 Thorpe Close, London W10 5XL
Telephone and Minicom 01-960 9245
'An Arts development organisation established in 1976. It works throughout London to create greater equality of access to and opportunity in the arts for people with disabilities and other under represented groups.'

Artsline - 01-388 2227. London's information and advice service on arts and entertainment for disabled people. (Detailed information on access to arts venues, etc.) for older students and teachers, etc., LDAF have a cabaret club called 'The Workhouse' - 'Disability Arts in Action' ... featuring Theatre, Music, Comedy, Mime, Signed Song, Poetry' for more information contact LDAF.

Nice Face, Shame About The Legs...!
Confessions of a Disabled Female Stand-Up Comic

At a Cabaret evening a few months ago I made a decision. When I told people about it they all laughed (nervously) or gaped, or said 'you're so brave'. As a woman with a disability these reactions are familiar. Boring even. But I hadn't told them that I feel fine with who I am, that my disability is part of me and shaped my life experience and world view, or that I was travelling alone around the globe checking out accessible venues. I had merely said that I was entering the world of stand-up comedy.

It is difficult to know exactly when the seed of an idea gets sown, extroverts act, creative types write novels or poetry. What possesses the person who will get up and put themselves in front of a bunch of total strangers and undertake to make them laugh - and keep laughing?

Sitting in this 'alternative' cabaret venue, listening to a double act of boys- they were big boys in long trousers, probably graduates - being silly and quite tedious, my attention was drifting. Then I heard the line:

'What's the difference between the Labour Party and a real spastic? Answer: There are no Socialists in the Labour Party.'

The audience giggled and I found myself heckling vigorously. That night I thought - Disability Arts is flourishing - theatre, poetry, music but only a couple of 'Stand-ups' (as they're known in the trade ....) - both men. Thus was born Wanda Barbara.

There are female comics - some very good. I was impressed with the range a couple of years ago at the Edinburgh Fringe Festival. Yet even they think disability and disabled people are legitimate 'targets' for humour. I went right off Hattie Heyridge, who I do think is funny, when she stuck in a gratuitous and offensive quip about blind people and guide dogs.

I think the reasons are deep rooted. These 'alternative' artists who would shudder at the very notion of being sexist, racist or heterosexist, suddenly lose all their politics on the subject of disability. And the reason they can't be humorous about disability is because they usually fear it. As many of you reading this article fear it. This fear then manifests itself in, at best, stupidity (as with Hattie Heyridge) or the thinly disguised hostility and hatred displayed by the aforementioned boys.

Much alternative comedy was based on people's previously taboo experiences. So we got a lot of stuff about willies, wanking, sexual inadequacy, drink and vomiting and how generally uncouth men can be. On the other side of that coin was periods, spots, hairdos, clothes, boring sex, school and repression and how generally uncouth men can be .....Some of that still persists and is not funny any more-at least the content could be, but the form definitely isn't.

I knew what sort of scenario awaited me on the alternative comedy circuit, and I've been hesitating about it ever since. My debut, at the big, broad and massive Workhouse, a venue organised and run by London Disability Arts Forum, was sort of 'safe'. The audience was predominantly people with disabilities and a lot of friends, (some non-disabled).

This was just as well because most of my act focused around disability and the essential humour inherent in our lives. Contrary to popular opinion, we are not tragic victims, or brave, stiff upper-lipped individuals. We live complex, even interesting, lives.

What I tried to do was pick up the theme from the point of view of the oppressed person, thus overturning the oppressor's viewpoint and showing its absurdity at the same time. But the act is not vicious. I think this is part of the 'femaleness' of the material - which I devise myself - it confronts without being confrontational and it satirises without rubbishing individuals. A friend was mortified because I made a small comment about her in the show.

'A real raver, stays up 'til half past nine, every night'!'

But we knew the joke - many of the audience laughed (including her). People with disabilities who have to be helped to bed by a district nurse, giving no choice about what time to the individual. People whose levels of pain mean that they have to go to bed early because of sheer fatigue. It's the kind of joke that could only be made by one disabled person about others because in the delivery there is no malice or mockery. A common understanding exists. There is a whole area of humour that belongs to oppressed groups only. Those groups have made sense of the world in their way - by showing how insensible, how irrational, how contradictory much of what goes on around us actually is.

'Wanda Barbara' *Credit DAIL.*

What is funny to a disabled audience, however, may leave a non-disabled audience cold. I have had to think about this a lot. Originally, I devised material that was accessible and humorous for the cognoscenti, the audience of people with disabilities. I did not think about taking it beyond the audience - it was enough that a woman had had the bottle to stand up and be counted in this field and had done it successfully within the Disability Arts circuit. New acts create interest, though, and soon I was getting bookings outside my safe and chosen environment. I accepted them knowing the risks, but also knowing what dross there is on the cabaret circuit - I could, and I would do better than many of the current acts. I have had to rethink my material, mainly in order to make it comprehensible to an able-bodied audience. More explanation is needed. But people are often scared to laugh.

This frustrates me, not because I think they should laugh - if they don't find it funny - but because what enables them to laugh at schoolboy 'spastic' nonsense, is also the mechanism that prevents them from finding disability funny from a disabled person's perspective. So what I do is get up there and say 'I'm a disabled woman'. My existence has been mocked, scorned and misrepresented and by being up here I'm not allowing that to continue. No longer can audiences ignore the experience of people with disabilities, but they have it presented to them in a strong and humorous and most of all political way.

So disability is the central theme which informs what I do - but it isn't only all about that; my presence reminds people that disability can't be ignored. So the stand ups who tell silly, offensive, pointless stories on disability can no longer assume that they have an audience who will collude with them, and that because a venue is upstairs there won't be any 'cripples' there. And only I can use the word cripples - in my way, because while we continue to be used and abused, that language on able-bodied lips is part of the problem. From mine, coming from the disability movement, it's part of the solution.

Think about that next time you run for the bus...

Wanda Barbara a.k.a. Lisicki

Pamela Roberts' Videomaker

I have sickle cell anaemia, a hereditary blood disorder. At the time of growing up, sickle cell was not classified as a disability, but as social leprosy, due to the ignorance and lack of information that surrounded the disorder.

Having left school, I worked on various community projects and was involved in women's issues. In 1983 I co-founded an educational and resource project for girls and young women in the borough of Waltham Forest. The building we acquired for the project was the pits. It was whilst renovating the premises that I picked up an infection which developed into pneumonia leading to both my lungs collapsing.

I was hospitalized for three months and came out barely more than a skeleton. The months that followed I was constantly in and out of hospital with repeated crisis: blood clotting in the joints. It got to the stage where a friend commented, you only come out to get your hair done just in time to go back in again! The constant 'sickling', the clumping together of blood cells, led to the deterioration of my hips, now leaving me walking with the aid of crutches for short distances and using a wheelchair for long distances.

To take my mind off my now visible disability, I was introduced to video as a form of therapy. However, my interest developed beyond shooting friends' party videos and I shot my first professional video 'Is it a bed of roses?': a 30 minute documentary looking at the social prejudices faced by a young unmarried mother.

January 1988, the Girls' Project folded and I decided to focus my energies on developing a career in the media aiming to become a director. I realised with just one video to my name, I wasn't going to get far and needed specialised training. By chance I came across an advertisement from the British Film Institute offering production awards for 'New Directors' to make a 20 minute film. This seemed ideal.

After managing to book an appointment to see the contact person I was told in a sickly sweet way, that 'It's not meant for the likes of you.' Unperturbed, I set off for the heart of the British film industry: Wardour Street, Soho. As I didn't know where to go and what to ask for, I just walked into Warner Bros and told them what I wanted to do. When the doorman told me to go to Walt Disney I thought he was taking the piss, until he pointed me in the direction of Golden Square.

It soon became apparent that what I was doing was totally unheard of. The industry was being confronted by a Black, disabled woman. Producers would gasp in astonishment, mop their foreheads fervently and adjust their glasses to make sure they saw right.

After constant knock-backs and insults I set out on a one woman crusade to train myself. Hurdle number two, training courses were expensive and definitely not designed for people with disabilities, but a certain amount of letter writing and grovelling to sponsors resulted in obtaining a couple of courses.

In the last year I have gained training into every aspect of production from script development to computer graphics. I was awarded 'Newcomers' for first time film makers to attend the Edinburgh Television Festival.

'Is it a bed of Roses?' has become a success, distributed by the British Film Institute. Offers of purchase have come from the Health Education Council with international recognition from the New Zealand Health Authority who've also requested a copy, but the cherry on top of my cake is a trainee directorship with a production company.

My observations and experiences that I have met with over the past two years have not been put to one side as a bitter memory. In my capacity as a freelance course organiser, I have initiated and am now co-ordinating a video production training course for Black disabled women. I hope that the course will provide a vehicle for Black women who want to develop a career within the media and address a serious issue with the industry.

Pamela Roberts

" 'Pamela Roberts' Independent Film and Video Maker."

Credit Patrick Friday) Disability Now.

A Venture into Art with a Magnifying Glass and a White Cane

by Gioya Steinke

The usual question I'm asked when visiting some Gallery or Museum is 'how do you see?' The answer being the old corny musical hall joke, 'with great difficulty'. As for the other query 'why do you go?', I just don't know. Certainly not because I had any early art training or knowledge, and not because I wish to get anywhere with my present drawing and 'viewing'. It is a 'thing of the moment', something that gives an inner glow and identity with the colours I can still see, the curve I can still follow, and the pattern and shape that are revealed to the poor hard-worked hazy eye.

I was recently at the Royal Academy, renewing my passion for Henry Moore, and visited their restaurant for a cup of tea. The person sitting opposite asked if I would keep an eye on her bag while she collected a second cup. It was best to inform her that I was willing but could not actually see her bag from across the table. She stared with quite an amount of hostility and said 'Why on earth do people like you come to these places if you can't see?' (Yes, I did count up to more than ten before I answered). So I explained HOW much any disabled person, visual and otherwise, can get out of any venture that really holds an interest and a challenge for them: I told of the many 'Touch' exhibitions and workshops that have been held in the last four years, the expertise and stimulation one experiences from the touching and handling of sculpture and just how many disabled artists, past and present day, are making a name for themselves in the work of Art. Did I convince her? I don't know, but she did admit that I seemed to have enjoyed my Gallery visits more than she had! Actually, she added that she had noticed that the disabled person often appeared to have an increased capacity to 'get more out of life'. Maybe that's it - we who struggle with whatever our limitations, Do 'get more' out of our ventures. WE put more in....

So, how did my adventure start? I think it was with the Exhibition for the Blind and visually disabled, held at the Tate Gallery in 1981. It served to make me aware that there was a further interest in art to be had other than my compulsive collecting of art postcards. A new dimension was opened up for this 'blind old bat' (a fond family quip, no insult intended). One saw there was an immense field ahead in the magic world of art that could be explored and appreciated in whatever way it 'appeared' to the impaired vision, and it could be completely of one's own. I started taking small groups of my visually disabled colleagues from

'A Venture Into Art with a Magnifying Glass' 'Gioya Sleinke in action'
Credit: FAN..

our local Adult College to various Galleries and Museums. Most of them have something to offer that can be handled, and if one contacts their Education Department first, one gets much help and even a guided tour. Incidentally I now have a most comprehensive list of Museum and Galleries and their various facilities that are offered or available. The R.N.I.B. have sent me so much information that I am to be given a small notice board at the Adult College to pin up any relevant information, etc.

I joined an Art class last year after much thought as to exactly what I could manage. A few sessions with watercolour reduced me to tears, literally, probably because I looked at the lovely work the other sighted students (with talent) were producing. The teacher kindly suggested that I might try pottery or sculpture instead. Now I knew I loved touching these things, but I have no wish to produce them. Realising that it's the contact of the pencil or crayon on paper that gives me the urge to 'follow through' what I can see led me to the Life Class.

It is quite amusing, I'm told by other students and the models, to see me peer and then check some unseen point on my own limbs. (Got a bit stuck with my first male model though). Now it's no longer a trauma. I depict only what I see and can feel on myself. The other students are most interested in another 'view' and gradually accept that the way a visually disabled person 'sees' is merely another part of the spectrum of how we all see. I got this quote from a recent Conference I was invited to attend in Cardiff. This was indeed an ADVENTURE, and served to show just how much there is in 'Creative Seeing' (The name of the conference). This was organised by the Welsh Arts Council and the many speakers were all a great joy to hear and meet. The emphasis was made that the 'sighted' public do not realise that 80% of those registered as Blind have some small amount of useful vision. And HOW this small amount is used and valued is what counts and provides a fulfilling way of life. It was also mentioned how an interest in art can lead to an increased confidence and a sense of identity and

dignity. I can well agree with all of this. All my gadding about has restored my respect for my own needs after the years of bringing up a family while coping with severe visual and other problems. A few lessons in the technique of using the long white cane have been tackled, just in order to get about on my own to any venue that offers a further ' moment of being and seeing'.

The meeting and sharing views and experiences with other people is all part of this, there is always something fresh to ponder over and follow up. A chance letter to that excellent magazine, Disability Arts in London, (to thank them and mention my visit to the garden for the blind at the Chelsea Flower Show) was kindly published. This filled me with zeal and an excuse to finally give up trying to keep the house clean (the operative word is 'trying') and my need for contact of pen and paper is being filled by the writing up of my past 'journals'. I shall be called more than a blind old bat if they ever get into print.

Heart 'n' Soul Dancing

Credit David Hevey

Disability and Photography

An article which first appeared in 'Polareyes' - a one-off publication of black women photographers work

Disability is about values, and as we live in a society where the emphasis is on being visually 'perfect' a person with any kind of handicap is therefore a person who is not 'perfect'. Whether it's in looks, colour, ability which may be physical or mental, a hidden one, or an apparent one, one is heavily discriminated against.

I am an Asian disabled woman, photographer and a teacher. Some people would say I'm in a position to be able to relate to all of these minority groups. Yes, I think I can, but what has had the most effect on my life is the disability aspect.

I wanted to write this article to try to illustrate some of the problems I have come across; especially whenever I have tried to do anything which has challenged existing attitudes. I hope that some people will benefit from my experiences, and that their awareness, it does not matter how small and practical, can make a big difference to someone's independence.

I started doing photography about five years ago when I enrolled at Sir John Cass School of Arts to do a part-time photography course. I was told that I would be a fire hazard, because the class appropriate to my level was on the second floor and I had to use the lift to get there and in the event of fire I would not be able to use the lift. There was no other way of getting down. After a lot of persuasion and heated arguments I managed to convince the Principal that I did not mind being carried down the stairs if there was a fire. The darkroom there was totally inaccessible; the lectures however were very supportive, but I found it very frustrating to sit and watch other people doing their developing and printing, so I left and approached 'Camera work' to modify a darkroom. That was the beginning of a very big and drawn out process of finding an accessible darkroom and someone who could modify cameras.

Photography has always meant a lot to me as I like to capture certain moments which possibly will never occur again, because a certain combination of factors may not gather again in the same manner. I love people and colours, and photos are a way of sharing and saying so much, which words would not be able to express.

A year and a half ago I actually started to do my own developing and printing of black and white photos. This was at the Battersea Arts Centre where S.H.A.P.E. had started a darkroom which was accessible. What bliss! Even though finding the transport to get there was extremely difficult.

'Camera work' finished their darkroom as well. That is brilliant; so now I don't have to make the long journey to Battersea anymore. I can actually spend my time and energy on doing the work instead of finding access and persuading people that it's a good idea to invest in darkrooms which can be used by People with disabilities.

Being a little bit more positive I can see that attitudes are changing and that things, the Dial-a-Ride service in my area is an example, are getting better. There are people who argue whether it should be 'Disabled People' or 'People with Disabilities' or whether 'helpers' should be 'facilitators' or 'arms and legs' or whatever. I personally don't care, because to me, disability is not a game of words but a way of life, which is full of physical limitations, and mental and emotional barriers which create the loss of opportunities to participate in the community on an equal level. These frustrations are created by society's ignorance and the absurd attitudes which exist towards disabled people, whether they be partly or totally blind, or deaf, or in some way physically impaired. Also those who are mentally ill or who have learning difficulties or whose speech is impaired, and who have hidden or apparent disabilities resulting from epilepsy or ageing.

It would be encouraging to see more practical constructive improvements made in the field of the Arts, especially in Visual Arts. This would enable more disabled people to make their own initiatives, instead of endless meetings and conferences held on their behalf by able-bodied people, when disabled people can't get there because of the lack of adequate transport.

Samena Rana

Disability and Photography 'Somena Rana at Work'

Credit Claire Wheeler/FAN.

Credit Somena Rana.

'Pakistan 1988'

73

Disability Culture: It's a Way of Life

Meanwhile cast your mind back for a moment or two and try to remember whether you have ever, for want of anything better to do, glued yourself to a toilet seat. Now, of course it's none of my business whether you have going in for that sort of activity, or not. I only bring the matter up, because I am sure that if you did try a little of this non-addictive experimentation with solvents, you would find the effect pretty similar to one of the humdrum but nevertheless, important experiences of my daily life and the daily life of a lot of Disabled people - you would find yourself unable to get up off the loo. Come to think of it I cannot get myself onto the loo either, but sticking, pardon the pun, to the initial problem, I am sure you can imagine the difficulties this raises. Incidentally, I hope you are finding my attempt to find a way of making the experience real for you as well, useful. Not everybody favours the school of 'disability-awareness training', which requires able-bodied people to smear vaseline on their glasses and stuff cotton wool in their ears so they can know what it's like to be Disabled. As far as I'm concerned, if you really want to get into the subject of Disability I strongly suggest that you go and dig out the Araldite and get into the bathroom just as soon as you've finished reading this article.

So what has this got to do with Disability Culture? Well, not unsurprisingly, being unable to get on and off the loo without help does have quite a significant effect on the lifestyle of the individual and what is culture if not almost another word for lifestyle? This loo business is a very specific and unequivocal example of the Disability experience and I don't want to mislead you into thinking that I am talking about something uncomplicated here. Being Disabled weaves itself into the fabric of life in all its aspects and very importantly it is not an entirely negative experience. For example, in the course of being helped in the loo I have made any number of friends, in fact I often find the bathroom is an ideal place to get to know people, or cement a relationship.

The experience of being a Disabled woman is an interesting one. A lot of us would agree that in many ways we are treated as the ultimate in non-persons.

We are not generally seen as having any sexuality and as it sometimes seems that the majority of men can only relate to women through sexuality this can mean a certain amount of isolation. However, once you've come to terms with the fact that you're not going to win Miss World, disability for a woman can be quite a liberating experience. We are not usually snapped up in the flower of youth for our domestic and child rearing skills, or for our decorative value, so we do not have to spend years disentangling ourselves from wearisome relationships as is the way with so many non-disabled women. This means that we are free to get on an live our lives without the daily burden of being treated as sex objects. This is obviously a wild generalisation, but it is certainly a fact that the disability arts scene, for instance, includes a lot more women in key roles than other scenes I can think of.

In the rare moments that I am not organising my social life in the lavatory I am a worker for the London Disability Arts Forum, (LDAF) which is the London wide organisation of Disabled people interested in the arts. One of the reasons for forming LDAF was to provide an opportunity and a focus for Disabled people to start exploring this notion of our culture and to create environments that encourage its expression through the various art forms. Now of course it has to be said that obviously someone deaf, or blind, or learning Disabled would not find the toilet example an even remotely useful illustration of their lifestyle in the practical sense, but it is probably true to say that we all have similar emotional and social experiences because of our impairments and the Disabilities, which ensue from them. Through the arts we can make discoveries about what we have in common and place the emphasis on those things rather than on our differences, thus countering the traditional charitable model of Disability that has historically kept us separate from each other. If you are not sure what I mean just think of organisations such as The Royal National Institute for the Blind, The Royal National Institute for the Deaf, the Spastics Society and a host of others all dedicated to the welfare of one type of Disabled person or another.

I do not believe there is any doubt that Disabled people have our own culture in that our lifestyles, in the main, are distinctly different from those of non-Disabled people. Whether Disabled people en masse want to term this difference a culture remains to be seen. Certainly a lot of Disabled people shy away from acknowledging that they have anything to do with disability as a movement and there are indeed strong pressures on us to be 'normal' and to fight on an individual level against the injustices we face, which work against our collective strength. However, LDAF has about one hundred members, other Disability Arts

Forums are springing up all over the country and the indication is that there are an awful lot of Disabled people around who want something other than integration into mainstream culture - whatever that is - and who do want the time to explore our identity as Disabled people.

Sian Vasey

'Asking for it'
**Beyond the Barriers: Camera work
Touring Exhibition (Disability, Sexuality
and Personal Relationships.)**

Credit Mary Duffy.

Asking For It

Mary Duffy

I like to make real work about real life. My disability is central to my perception of reality, and my disability is often central to my work. But my work goes beyond disability issues. I have learned slowly that how I feel about my body, my life is not really very different from how non-disabled people feel about themselves. It's simply that they wear the cloak of normality, a concept which renders me naked.

We both live in the shadow of stereotype. I'm simply lucky enough to be on the fringe, rejected by the stereotype, forced to forge my own identity, my own reality, and to create it anew,.....beautiful, proud and disabled.

I remember the feeling of being embraced and not liking it.

I remember the feeling of wanting to embrace, and not being able to.
I remember the feeling of being tied because both my feet were on the ground.
and I remember feeling like this about sex.

I wonder what you feel when you embrace me, when you wrap your arms
around me, tight.
You tell me you can feel me standing on my tippy toes and burrowing my face in your shoulder.
That you can feel me wanting to hug you.
And I tell you that for me wanting is not always enough.
You tell me you like to hug trees; you feel they appreciate it.

Sometimes I feel like a tree when you hug me, warm, radiating and

rooted. Other times I feel like a telegraph pole, straight,
unbending and wired. You find it hard to understand this, and say that
It must feel more like being in a straight jacket. I tell you that being in a straight jacket wouldn't make a lot of difference to me, and we laugh a little.

I know you miss me not hugging you back. I know that you miss those warm, woolley, soft, wrapping hugs.
What I want to say to you is that only by doing things differently can I
be true to myself.

As a child, I learned quickly that if I worked hard enough to be
'normal' meaning not disabled, I'd be accepted as ablebodied. Being
accepted meant never asking for help, never saying I'cant
never admitting to failure, never feeling hurt or vulnerable, and never, ever feeling helpless.

It meant being fearless, invulnerable and independent. And it meant always being very, very controlled.

I've had lots of success at what people call 'overcoming my disability',
but my real major triumph is being able to ask, to ask for simple,

Credit David Hevey.

real, and important things like touching and being touched, embracing
and being embraced. I remember asking for hugs, specifically and
physically on my terms.

I have great freedom and sensation in this simple expression. It is
difficult to ask. I am afraid of my own fear and of your fear. Fear
that I am inadequate. Fear that feet and legs are not hugging.
A fear that I fiercely defend and justify. I can wrap my
legs around you. Envelope you. Squeeze you gently or tenderly. I can
hug you fiercely and fervently. I can embrace you in fun,
and when you are frightened.

I can embrace you spontaneously, sumptuously and passionately.
Fear of difference encourages invisibility and keeps everyone apart.

I have choice.

Mary Duffy

Sian Vesey from Link, Jane Campbell LB DRT and Geoff Armstrong from London Disability Arts Forum, at the Moving on Festival Summer 1989

Section 2

Things You Need To Know

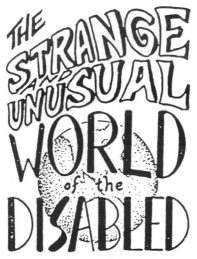

How to be an ally — The Role of Non-disabled People

by Micheline Mason

The truth is this: we do need you, not to be 'experts' or managers of our lives, but to be friends, enablers and receivers of our 'gifts' to you.

The history of disabled people and the development of the medical model of disability means that *all* people are victims of "health system oppression". It affects the non-disabled - or temporarily able bodied -in several important ways. Firstly our health is seen to be "owned" by the medical profession whom we go to to be "made better". In order to maintain the power of the medical profession, lay people are kept systematically ignorant about basic physiology and biology, and even more so about "pathology" - what happens when things go wrong - and about basic treatments, the body's self-healing powers, drugs, therapies, etc. Consequently the experience of illness or disease is often a frightening sense of loss of control, dependence and powerlessness. We see it as a negative thing which happens *to* us and which needs to be taken from us by someone else. People who have never experienced a serious illness or disease are often more frightened of the *idea* of it than are people who have actually had the experience, because it is only the experience which allows one to become aware of our own resources for healing, and adaption, which are HUGE.

How the body works, its powers for self-healing - how doctors and nurses can help if necessary - the limits of medicine and the existence of physical and mental disabilities needs to be taught, *and can be understood*, from the earliest age. Talking about disability has become taboo but this embarrassment needs to be overcome. Another way non-disabled people are affected is by being segregated from disabled people and told that only "special" people can look after us. This, coupled with the ignorance previously described, leaves non-disabled people feeling a deep lack of confidence in their ability to "cope" with disabled people.

This lack of confidence makes a terrible partnership with the main role non-disabled people are supposed to fulfil in relation to disabled people - that of "carer", "helper", "expert". You are *prevented* from knowing and yet you are *supposed* to know what is best for us, and how to

help us. No wonder you find this difficult. No wonder it feels easier to back away and leave things up to the parents, or the professionals. However, disabled people are no longer willing to be "backed away from", especially when the fear becomes justified and acted upon by policy makers and planners who consequently limit severely our choices in life.

The truth is this: we *do* need you, not to be "experts" or managers of our lives, but to be friends, enablers and receivers of our "gifts" to you. We need you to admit cheerfully what you don't know, without shame; to ask us what we need *before* providing it, to lend us your physical strength when appropriate, to allow us to teach you necessary skills; to champion our rights, to remove barriers previously set in place, to return to us any power you may have had over our lives. We may also need you to remind us of our importance to the world, and to each other, at times of tiredness and discouragement. We can live without patronage, pity and sentimentality, but we cannot live without closeness, respect and co-operation from other people. Above all we need you to refuse to accept any "segregation" of one group of humans from another as anything else but an unacceptable loss for all concerned.

The Human Condition

by Micheline Mason

The human body is very complex and is still not very well understood.

Every function of the body may go "wrong" and does go wrong in some people. Medical science has recognised a few of these things and given them labels in order to help decide on any possible treatment. There are still many "dysfunctions" of the body that are not understood and which do not have clear labels. Although each one of these can be called a "rare medical condition", there are a lot of them, so the instance of undiagnosed and little understood conditions is surprisingly common. Also there are headings which cover a group of different conditions that may affect people in very different ways, e.g. "Developmental Delay", "Chromosomal Disorders", "Brittle Bones", "The Dystrophys", "Cerebral Palsy", "Phocomelia" (limb deficiencies). Most recognised conditions have organisations of people who have the condition (or parents of young people who have the condition) who publish information about each particular one. These are usually the most accurate and up-to-date sources of information, and we would recommend that every school builds up a resource pack of its own by writing to these organisations. Some, e.g. The Brittle Bone Society, have special literature for teachers on assistance they can give to pupils in schools. They may also be able to send a specialist advisor to a school who has a child with a particular condition. (See resource list.)

There are broad categories of conditions which have certain characteristics which it may be useful to be aware of.

Central Nervous System Disorders

Nerves send messages to the body from the brain, and take information from the sense organs to the brain. They control both voluntary muscles such as biceps, and involuntary muscles such as the heart.

Conditions which affect the central nervous system include cerebral palsy, spina bifida, poliomyelitis, spinal injury, multiple sclerosis, Parkinson's disease, Friedrick's ataxia, stroke.

Damage or dysfunction of nerves can lead to a loss of movement, sensation, control or information. It does not usually make the person feel ill or in pain, athough some people may feel either or both of these things. Some people may lose "feeling" in parts of their bodies and some people might lose their sight or hearing or sense of smell due to nerve damage.

Brain cells once damaged never "regrow", and most damage to nerves is irreversible. However we can learn to transfer functions from damaged brain cells to undamaged brain cells, and we can also learn to use undamaged nerves to compensate for damaged nerves, to some degree. We can also learn to "control" involuntary muscles - swallowing for example - if we have to.

Some conditions are static, i.e. they stay the same, some "improve" with time, and some are progressive - they get worse. Because there are so many different specific conditions that have different "prognoses" or future likelihoods, it is not useful to try to make simple generalisations. For example there are many conditions which lead to progressive weakening of the muscles, Duchenne muscular dystrophy being just one of them. However they do not all lead to death in adolescence and for many people the exact diagnosis has only been made after adolescence when the original diagnosis was proved inaccurate - i.e. the person stayed alive. As you can imagine these sort of mistakes have enormous effects on the people concerned and their loved ones.

Skeletal Disorders

Osteo - means "bone"
itis - means "inflammation of"

These include phocomelia (absence or unusual formation of limbs), spinal curvatures, the brittle bone syndromes, osteo arthritis, rickets, congenital dislocation of the hip, club feet and many other unusual conditions. Because the skeleton shapes the body, conditions which affct bones often are very "visible". They may well affect growth as well as proportion and fine features of the face and body. Teeth are part of the skeletal system. Ears have bones in them and some skeletal disorders can affect hearing. This kind of hearing loss is called "conductive deafness".

Apart from the physical affects of these conditions, young people often have to deal with people's reactions to their appearance, and words used to describe them such as "deformed" or "stunted".

Bones hurt when they are injured or broken or inflamed or operated upon, as do the surrounding muscles which often go into "spasm" in order to try to support the injured bone. However this is usually "useful" pain, designed by the body to make people keep still so that the bone can mend. Bones are living tissue which can regenerate itself and which can heal itself from enormous damage.

Disorders of the Organs

This is a very large group of disorders including diabetes, haemophilia, cystic fibrosis, sickle cell anaemia, and many other conditions. They are usually unstable in that people with them often have "good times" and "bad times". They usually require on-going medical management or intervention. They may make the person concerned feel ill at times. The person may have to use drugs intermittently or permanently and the drugs themselves may have undesirable side-effects. Many of those conditions in children are of genetic origin and are treatable but not curable. Other members of the family may be affected, i.e. it is a hereditary condition. Some conditions such as cystic fibrosis do shorten the person's life expectancy although "naming dates" is not a useful exercise.

Allergy based Disorders

These include asthma, eczema, food allergies, hay fever, chemical allergies, migraine and other environmentally caused disorders. They are often made worse by stress. The body over-reacts to contact with particular substances - e.g. dust, pollen, milk, food additives, bee stings, resulting in an enormous range of symptoms - difficulty in breathing, rashes, sores, changes in mood or behaviour, bed wetting, pains, etc. Allergic reactions to medicines can be fatal. Asthma is one of the most common childhood disorders and is the most common reason to hospitalise a child. About 400 children die of asthma every year (death is actually from heart failure caused by exhaustion).

Obviously the allergic substance needs to be identified and avoided if at all possible. Extractor fans can help lessen airborne allergenics at school, but many allergenics will be primarily found in the home of the person concerned, living in the dust in carpets and soft furnishings for example, and are very difficult to eliminate. Allergies can appear overnight, and they can also disappear without apparent reason. Many allergic

reactions do lessen or vanish as a young person grows up. Why this should be is not really understood.

The Epilepsies

Epilepsy is not yet understood. It is a dysfunction rather than an organic disease, in that the electrical connections between nerves in the brain suddenly start to become disordered, erratic, exaggerated - like a storm of electrical impulses - and can return to normal, for unknown reasons. The result for the owner of the brain is a temporary loss of consciousness possibly accompanied by muscular spasms called "fits".

There are two main types of epilepsy. Firstly petit mal epilepsy where "fits" are mild, not necessarily involving full loss of consciousness. These fits may only last a few seconds and may appear to be "daydreaming". They are sometimes accompanied by compulsive "movement" such as "picking" at one's own clothing. The person will experience the fit as a gap in memory. The teacher will need to be aware that this may happen at any time and could mean the person not absorbing instructions properly, and not necessarily being aware themselves that this has happened. It could be quite easy to accuse the person of "not paying attention" for example, instead of understanding the profound effects an almost invisible disability could have on someone's life.

The second type of epilepsy is called "grand mal" where fits involve loss of consciousness with varied physical movements. Every person with epilepsy has a type of fit unique to them, although there may be similarities. The individual must always be consulted as to their particular needs. Some people have several fits a day, some have "nocturnal" fits only when asleep, and some people may have one fit a year or less. Some people have "warnings" and can get themselves to a safe place, others don't have any warning at all. Some people's fits last a few seconds, or a few minutes, whilst some people stay unconscious for an hour or more. Some people take a few minutes to recover, and others may take a day or two. Most people are a bit "disorientated" after a fit and may need to be reassured and told what the time is, where they are, and offered some assistance to get to a place to rest and recover.

Some people have "controlled epilepsy" which means that as long as they "keep taking the pills", they don't have fits. These people may drive a car if they have been without a fit for more than 3 years. The "pills" however may have side-

80

'The Human Condition!'

Credit Sally and Richard Greenhill.

effects which everyone should be aware of, such as drowsiness, and some people with epilepsy have have found these side-effects more of a problem than the "fits" which may worry the onlooker more than the person having the fit. They may opt to come off drugs and "live with it", which of course means that we all have to learn to "live with it" too.

Auto-Immune System Conditions

These conditions are caused by the body's defence system turning on itself and destroying its own tissue. They are not that well understood. They include multiple sclerosis, ME, cancer and rheumatoid arthritis. Some diseases and viruses can also weaken the immune system and make the body less able to fight off infection. Glandular fever is an example of this. AIDS, which stands for Acquired-Immune-Deficiency Syndrome, is a condition in which a virus attacks the body's defence system making it unable to work. As most people are now aware, once the virus becomes active the person with it will become more and more ill. Some children are born with this virus with which they have been infected in utero. Quite a large number of haemophiliacs have also got the virus from using infected blood in the production of their "factor 8" injections which help control clotting of the blood. (Blood and blood products are now screened for the AIDS virus.)

Sensory Conditions

Impairments to the five senses of sight, hearing, taste, touch and smell can happen from genetic factors, injury or disease. They are all connected to the central nervous system and damage to that system will probably effect one, some or all of these senses. Once damaged, little can be done to repair it. Impairments that are not caused by damage to the nerves may be "treatable" by surgery, e.g. cataracts, or by "aids", e.g. hearing aids, glasses, etc.

The Limits of 'Medicine'

by Micheline Mason and Richard Rieser

Many of us have had our lives saved by surgeons. Micheline for one would not be alive, and nor would my daughter, if someone had not been able to perform a Caesarian Section when my baby needed to be born. Doctors, hospitals and drugs do have a place in our lives, there is no doubt. However, when you have a disability, and when you have met hundreds of other people with disabilities, you get to put the medical role in proportion. As well as saving our lives, and lessening our pain, cutting things out of us that might poison us, straightening injured limbs and

Limits of Medicine
Credit stolen childhood Mark Edward/Paros Pictures.

such like services, the medical profession also make mistakes, don't know, and are using tools of their trade in the form of medicines that are often a mixed blessing. Allopathic medicine also tends to objectify a person's disease or impairment, whilst holistic medicine uses approaches which treat the whole person. Many people who have been patients have stories to be told which graphically describe the shortcomings of the health system, yet we still tend to ascribe to it authority and power in the vain hope that illness and disease will become a thing of the past. It won't. In fact the development of society not only eliminates diseases such as smallpox, it creates disease and disability such as heart disease or lung cancer. It also injures people in traffic accidents, at work and in wars. **Poverty, unsafe working conditions, malnutrition, pollution, unsuitable living conditions, lack of clean water are the main causes of disease, disability and premature death in the world, not the lack of a bottle of aspirin.**

For young people the disadvantages of medical treatments need to be weighed against the possible advantages. Children are not usually asked if they want speech therapy, physiotherapy, orthopaedic surgery, hospitalisations, drugs or cumbersome and ugly 'aids and appliances'. We are not asked if we want to be put on daily regimes or programmes that use up hours of precious play-time. All these things are just imposed on us with the assumption that we share our parents' or therapists' desire for us to be more 'normal' at all costs. We are not even consulted as adults as to whether we think those things had been necessary or useful.

It seems that the most insidious argument comes from international proclamations that medical intervention, far from lessening the incidence of disability world-wide is increasing it, because they save the lives of people who would otherwise die 'As we avert death we often do so at the price of a life-long chronic health or disabling condition' (Gerben de Jong International Rehabilitation Review September 1989) -connecting medical power with the control of disability. It has yet to be proved statistically that there is any truth in this hypothesis. Whilst there is an alarming increase in the numbers of children and young adults who have or acquire disabilities - analysis of the data from the annual National Health survey indicates that in the 25 year period from 1959 - 1984 the prevalence of people of working age being unable

500,000 workers a year are permanently disabled in industry.

Credit Ideas: Bentley CA

to carry on their major activity because of a health condition rose by 178% and the prevalence of children who are restricted in their school or play activities because of a chronic health restriction rose from 1.7% to 5.0% - what is causing this has yet to be objectively studied. Our own view is that medicine does not appear to save the lives of many people whose conditions are of the kind that lead to death and that the increase is in chronic illness such as MS or ME, diabetes and asthma all of which are more likely to being caused by social factors such as pollution or stress, or medicine itself which no-one wants to look at seriously because the implications are so much more profound.

Vast amounts of resources are used up by the medical profession, particularly in the area of 'research' which may be more usefully applied to eliminating the sociably caused dis-ability. Millions have been spent, not one single cure found for any major disabilty other than those caused by bacteria which can be treated with antibiotics. Some viral diseases have been eliminated or greatly reduced by immunisation programmes, and some surgical techniques have saved lives such as implantation of shunts for people with hydrocephalus, but one has to ask oneself who has really benefited most from the allocation of such vast amounts of money -

researchers, drug companies, fund raisers, or disabled people?

No where is this more clearly demonstrated than in the Third World.

At the start of the 1980's there were 200 million children around the world with disabilities - 100 million disabled by malnutrition. Another 14 million children join them every year.

At present most of the Third Worlds health budget is spent on western-style curative care. What isn't spent on training doctors and maintaining large hospitals is spent on importing expensive drugs: up to 50% of Third World health budgets are spent on imported drugs (A. Vittachi p132).

Such expensive health care is only available to a tiny minority who can afford to pay for it.

Primary Health Care needs to be given priority over the high tech western system. 'Barefoot doctors' can be trained for as little as one thousandth of what it costs to train a doctor and they can be more effective in preventing disability and promoting good health. **For example, showing families why they should eat vitamin A rich green leaves. Five cents worth eaten each week could save the eyesight of 250,000 children every year.**

PHC workers can also encourage breastfeeding, help build safe latrines, keep the local water supply clean, report family planning methods, advise on immunization programmes, the use of oral rehydration salts for diarrhoea - a huge killer.

Such efforts could dramatically reduce the number in poor countries who die or are disabled.

The vast majority of the disablement is not caused by acts or God or nature: it is allowed by political neglect.

The spread of most disabling diseases in the Third World is related to economic inequality via malnutrition, unsafe water and poor sanitation - and this could be altered. It has been estimated that three quarters of the world's disease could be prevented by cheap, widespread primary health care at a cost of an extra 50 billion dollars per year for the next 20. Thats 2/3's of what the world spends on cigarettes, half what is spent on alcohol and 1/20th of military spending (A. Vittachi P136).

SIMON BRISENDEN'S POEMS

– for further info write to:
Hazel Peaseley
19 Blighmont Road
Southampton SO1 3RH
Phone: 0703 776451
Proceeds will go to
Simon Brisenden
Independent Living Trust
There are two volumes
costing £4 each

Vegetablism

I am a child of the earth
I've been a vegetable since birth

I went to a school for vegetables
and learnt how to go with meat
I grew up and wore the stigma
of being something people eat

And in my very early vegetable days
I went through a religious phase
And asked God why he had made me
just to drown in a pool of gravy
But his answer was not detectable
so I became a Marxist vegetable
and bringing in elements
of a feminist critique
I formed a vegetable
liberation clique

The vegetable is political I said
and tried to undermine the state
We advocated passive resistance
to the knife the fork and the plate

And now I am writing a history in three
    volumes
(from a post-structuralist point of view)
of all the anonymous vegetable victims
who have perished in hot-pot stew.

Simon Brisenden

The Language We Use

by Richard Rieser

'I am not a disability, I'm me. I have dyslexia and I've had polio but I'm not 'a dyslexic' or 'a cripple', I'm me'

John Swan, 14 in 'What it's like to be me' Exley 1981

'The sloppiness of our language makes it easier for us to have foolish thoughts'

George Orwell

Language carries many messages. It categorises, labels and reinforces stereotypes. It is therefore important to define our terms.

The terms and parts of speech many people still use cause harm and hurt to people with disabilities, but also cut-off the users of that language from a greater understanding and empathy with people with disabilities. Ultimately the use of such language cuts off the user from a deeper understanding of themselves and others.

Much official literature on disability makes the distinction between *impairment, disability* and *handicap* and a useful starting point will be to examine these terms. The United Nations and World Health Organisation define these in the following way:

Impairment is a physical deviation from what could be considered *usual* in terms of structure, functional, physical organisation or development. It is objective and measurable, e.g., sickle cell anaemia, spina bifida, cystic fibrosis, epilepsy, scoliosis or a certain amount of loss of tissue or sensation of a part of the body.

Disability is the functional limitation experienced by the individual because of an impairment. It refers to what the individual cannot do in the usual or expected way because of an impairment. Although to some extent measurable, the severity of a disability is related to a number of variable factors such as the age, occupation, wealth, culture of the person effected, as well as, how they themselves view their disability. The functional limitation is often more important than the cause. So having a sight or hearing loss is more important than the reason for the impairment.

Handicap is the disadvantage imposed by an impairment or disability. It is the social and environmental consequences to the individual. It is not measurable, but experienced. The actions and reactions of others and of the person with the disability to the impairment all interact to give a degree of disadvantage.

I can illustrate these different terms by looking briefly at myself.

When I was nine months old I had polio. It left me with an impairment to the muscles of my left leg, chest, back and right arm. As I grew the bones and muscle development were affected so my legs and arms are of different sizes with a restriction of motor ability.

In the affected limbs, my disability has progressively worsened since my youth and I now need a walking stick at all times, whereas previously I had only needed this for long walks. The fact that my impairment was caused by polio is less important to me than the restriction of my mobility. However, the doctors' reaction to my impairment was that I would not be able to walk or use my right arm, but my parents brought me up to use them very effectively. Mentally I over compensated and this undoubtedly was a formative influence on my personality, which at the age of 40 I am only now coming to terms with. It is important for me to know my limitations in order for me to challenge the handicaps that society places upon me. Why should I exhaust myself and become irritable by using the stairs when my employer should be forced to install lifts where I need them in my school and at the Hackney Teachers' Centre. Why should I suffer pain filling my car with petrol or queuing in a restaurant when people should be employed to serve me. Why should I stand in a shop that has no seats.

My experiences as a teenager in a mainstream secondary modern of continual name calling, bullying and the uncaring attitude from the majority of teachers led me to adopt a supercripple stance and attitude to myself which meant a tendency to over reach my capabilities with the subsequent impact on personality. When 12 years later I returned as a teacher to a boys comprehensive I still experienced name called from the kids and other teachers' ignoring my needs. This must be happening to most disabled people in schools.

As handicap is largely imposed upon me by society, and was tacitly accepted by me, I have had to develop my awareness of myself in order to reject the view of myself I have internalised from society. Therefore, for me and thousands of others to be described as the handicapped is quite wrong.

Handicap is viewed as a negative term by many people with disabilities. The word *handicap* derives from C14th horse racing when a rider of a good horse had to race holding his cap in one hand. The word, therefore, signifies imposed disadvantage. It has come to reflect the dependent position in which disabled people are placed by society. Handicap and begging for charity became at certain times and places synonymous. In John Gay's 'Beggars Opera' set in C18th London, or Thailand in 1988, where children are sold and then mutilated by unscrupulous businesses, to increase the amount of money they can earn by begging, the message is the same. The recent extravaganza on London Weekend Television - the Telethon -was a good example of how the charity approach to disability is still very much with us. Charity puts people with disabilities in a dependent position, rather than independent with equal rights.

*Handicapism**: The term handicapism was adopted by disability rights campaigners in the USA some 18 years ago. *Handicapism* refers to the stereotyping, prejudice and discrimination practised by society against disabled people. *Handicapism* is an acceptable use of 'handicap' as it reflects the negative connotations which reflect society's oppression of disabled people.

The Disabled Rights Movement was described by Frieda Zames*, a New York activist, in the following terms:

---

*See Inter-racial Books for Children Bulletin Vol.8 No.6 and 7 1977 -special issue on Handicapism in Children's Books. Chapter 2 and 3 of 'Accept Me as I am' by Friedberg, Mullins and Sukiennik provides a useful summary of mainly American work that is difficult to get hold of.

'We who are disabled are tired of adjusting our lives to fit a society that ignores or insults our existence. We demand, and are struggling to achieve, a restructuring of society to accommodate our needs and to affirm our equality with other human beings.'

This is particularly true in the teaching profession where medical fitness to teach is still assessed on a unidimensional scale and at any time teachers can be PU'd - declared physically unfit to teach. See 'How about some Equality for Disabled Teachers'. Clearly such rigid thinking from the DES and LEA's will and does hamper attempts to develop a disability curriculum, engendering as it does, an inflexibility and intolerance of their colleagues amongst many teachers.

We can certainly benefit by adopting Alan Sutherland's (1983) radical approach and demolishing the false dividing line between 'normal' and 'disabled'. We must recognise that disablement is not merely the physical or mental state of a small minority of people; it is the normal condition of humanity. Certainly if such a view is adopted in the classroom it would lead to far greater tolerance and acceptance of each other's physical differences, which can then be built upon to incorporate understanding and acceptance of more obviously or severely disabled people. This could be termed the continuum approach.

However, Sutherland is not utopian. He recognises that we live in a society where a minority of the population are particularly strongly discriminated against because of their disabilities.

He, therefore, proposes a definition of disabled people as all those who are stigmatised against on the basis of their physical (mental) condition.

Therefore, he argues people with disabilities include the chronically sick and disfigured, indeed all those who can recognise what we have in common and counteract our shared oppression by developing a group identity and a common awareness of our situation.

The Disabled Persons International DPI founded in 1981 to represent organisations internationally that have at least 51% disabled people on their controlling committee took issue with the World Health Organisation definition.

They put forward and adopted the following:

'*Disability* is the functional limitation within the individual caused by physical, mental or sensory *impairment*.'

'*Handicap* is the loss or limitation of opportunities to take part in the normal life of the community on an equal level with others due to physical or social barriers' (Dione Driedger -1989 p92).'

With this definition the DPI wanted society to cease to point to the disabled individual for her/his lack of participation, and instead break down the barriers it had erected. These barriers were on the one hand paternalistic attitudes and on the other the physical inaccessibility and communication barriers to the goods and services enjoyed by the rest of the population.

I prefer the DPI definitions as it provides for a collective strength as disabled people. I also believe that the internalized oppression we face as disabled people is a factor we have to recognise in building a mass movement of disabled people. In my view to reduce us to our impairments denies us an identity as different but equal. We are still handicapped by society. Just because society misuses this word does not deny this truth.

The disabled united are strong we come together around the oppression we face as 'the same difference'.

The British Council of Organisations of Disabled People have followed a different definition originating from UPIAS -Union of Physically Impaired Against Segregation (one of the first disability rights organisations in the UK).

Impairment - lacking part or all of a limb, or having a defective limb, organ or mechanism of the body.

Disability - the disadvantage or restriction of activity caused by a contemporary social organisation which takes little or no account of people who have physical impairments and thus excludes them from participation in the mainstream of social activities - physical disability is therefore a particular form of social oppression.

Language to avoid

As can be seen from the previous section language has a social meaning and this changes all the time.

What is acceptable in one period is not in another. What largely determines this is the self-activity of the group described.

The last 20 years of the Disability Movement have lead to the re-examining of the language. This process is continuing.

However, certain language which is offensive to disabled people or dehumanizes or objectifies us should be avoided.

Disabled is acceptable as our word for ourselves. It does not have the paternalistic and patronising association of *handicapped*. A parallel can be drawn here with racism. Black people feel proud

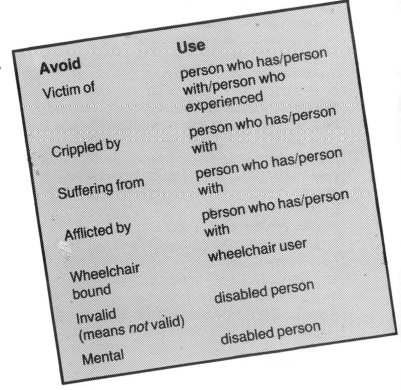

Avoid	Use
Victim of	person who has/person with/person who experienced
Crippled by	person who has/person with
Suffering from	person who has/person with
Afflicted by	person who has/person with
Wheelchair bound	wheelchair user
Invalid (means *not* valid)	disabled person
Mental	disabled person

Recently the DPI have adopted the BCODP definition and advocate the dropping of the use of 'handicap' altogether, as it is misused so widely. Most organisations controlled by disabled people are now advocating this two fold definition. The debate will continue, but non-disabled people should be guided by disabled people in the langauge they use.

to call themselves Black. They reject coloured/Negro/nigger as the word their oppressor used for them. Similarly we reject handicapped/crippled. Despite this the Warnock report, Fish report and US legislation for disability rights use handicapped as interchangeable with disabled. This is both unacceptable and a wrong usage.

Don't use the word 'disabled' as a noun on its own, i.e. 'The Disabled'. We are people with disabilities or 'Disabled People'. Disabled should be spelt with a capital D in this context.

Also avoid reducing a Disabled person to their impairing condition. For example, 'A paraplegic' or 'Arthritic'. We are disabled people *with* these impairments in different degrees. In any case the label does not tell you much about the person.

A number of words associated with disability should be avoided because they create a negative image.

In general language usage we should stop using words like deaf, blind, paralysed as adjectives or adverbs with a negative connotation e.g.

> blind drunk
>
> blind rage
>
> blind to
>
> blind side
>
> blindness

How far one goes with this is difficult. See and hear are part of the language but where there are other words which have the same meaning we should start to use them. Do you *see* what I mean could be easily changed to do you *know* what I mean.

Insensitive use of language can be damaging and embarrassing.

Special Educational Needs: Just another label
by Micheline Mason

This phrase came about as an attempt to de-medicalise the labelling of children with disabilities, e.g. retarded, sub-normal, crippled, maladjusted, to what was hoped to be less negative labelling based on educational need. Disabled people welcome the spirit in whch this was done. "My special child" is certainly better than "My little invalid" (my mother's phrase!). However it again overlooks the political

dimension. We do *not* consider ourselves to be special. We consider disability to be a norm within every society, borne out by statistics, and we want our needs to be taken into account as normal human needs. It seems questionable that even 20% of young people can have "special needs". It seems ridiculous that 45% of young people within inner city areas can have "special needs". Surely the question is how does the education system fail to answer the needs of 45% of its users?

However, for the present the official terminology will be used. SEN includes disabled children, children with learning difficulties and children with emotional and behavioural problems. For the

Preferred	Offensive
Disability, Disabled Person	Handicap, Handicapped Person
Cerebal Palsey	Spastic
Deaf or Partial Hearing	Deaf and Dumb, Deaf/Mute
Downs Syndrome	Mongoloid
Disabled Person or Mobility Impaired ambulatory disabled	Cripple/Crippled
Blind Person, Partially sighted	The Blind
Deaf People	The Deaf
Learning Difficulty,	Mentally Handicapped, Backward/Dull
Developmental Disability	Retarded, Idiot, Imbecile, Feeble Minded
Speech Difficulty	Mute, Dummy
Emotional Disability,	Crazy, Maniac, Insane,
Mental Disturbance	Mentally ill
Exceptional/ Different	Abnormal

by Vid

Word-Power

The issue of language with regard to disability is an important one.

Look at the following words and ask yourself whether they imply a positive or negative image.

wheelchair-bound ......positive/negative/neither

the disabled ....positive/negative/neither

people with
disabilities ....positive/negative/neither

disabled person ....positive/negative/neither

cripple ....positive/negative/neither

invalid......................positive/negative/neither

integrated ....positive/negative/neither

spastic......................positive/negative/neither

handicapped.............positive/negative/neither

people with learning
difficulties ....positive/negative/neither

spina bifida ....positive/negative/neither

independent ....positive/negative/neither

sufferer....................positive/negative/neither

special.....................positive/negative/neither

mental patient...........positive/negative/neither

purposes of this pack we are including young people with any physical and mental condition, be it permanent or temporary who are affected in some way by society's attitudes towards disability.

Lois Keith poem (p 9) is a good example of how much we describe things in terms of physical attributes.

caroll pinkham and the students of poplar college

when I am going out with my mum or my sister, people start to stare at me. I feel like swearing at them – especially little children playing in the street – they always stare.

When I go out to a crowded place with my sister people always tend to walk in front of my wheelchair. They can see me behind them but they just ignore me until I accidentally bump into their ankles, then they quickly move out of the way. We say 'excuse me', but they still ignore us.

At home if someone comes round to visit, whom I don't know, but my mum does, then that person will ask my mother what's wrong with me, and why I am in a wheelchair. I'm sitting in the room with them and they still ask my mum. I hate it when they don't ask me. It makes me angry. Sometimes they pat me on the head and say 'poor thing'. I hate people feeling sorry for me because I'm in a wheelchair.

It also makes me angry that I can't go out by myself because I can't cross the road because there isn't a dropped kerb. I hate to sit indoors all the time. For example, at weekends I stay indoors because I don't have anybody to go out with. I go to a club in the weekdays – which is good because I get to meet friends who are disabled and able-bodied. The people there treat me like they would treat anybody else.

Faeza Patel

Technology and aids in relation to Disabled People

by Micheline Mason

Everyone uses aids - a fork, a toothbrush, a spade, all these are aids. Some of them are very cheap like knitting needles and some are expensive like cars or computers. Some are for very specialised work like an electron microscope. There are a wide range of aids specifically designed to overcome the physical limitations of some people, such as wheelchairs. The difference is not in the myth that some people need aids and other don't, but in the fact that disabled people often cannot afford the aids we need in order to function as well as we can. This leads to assessments by professionals, long waits, lack of choice, unequal provision, and many other disadvantages known only too well to those of us who have to go through the humiliating procedures repeatedly.

Imagine that all babies were born without legs, and that legs were something for which you had to apply to the Government. You would have to prove that you couldn't manage without them, that you would be able to make adequate use of them, that you cannot think of a cheaper alternative. You would have to persuade a social worker and a doctor that you were a genuine case, and then you would have to wait weeks or months for your first fitting. You would have to go to the 'limb centre' to be measured, etc. You would have to wait for your second fitting where your 'legs' would be tried out and any alterations or problems sorted out. You would then have to wait weeks or months for your standard model, functional if unattractive legs to arrive - by which time you may well have grown out of them.

'Wheel Power'

Credit Everaids.

The right piece of equipment can make a tremendous difference to a persons life:

Daniel came running through the door, yelling things like, WOW' ...., WHOOP-PEE' AND YEH'.

'It must be something pretty good to get him that excited,' said his Gran, who was visiting us as the time.

I looked at his face all hot and red, which showed the speed of his journey home. I knew what his news would be, but waited with Gran for him to tell all.

'Calm down Dan, go and wash your face, it's so hot love,' I could hear Gran saying.

He ran to the bathroom, more 'WHOOP-PEES' sounding throughout the house. I thought back, could it really be four and half years since I first stood in front of his teacher, telling her I thought there was something wrong.

'No,' she said, reassuring me, 'some children do stop learning for a while, but Dan will be fine next year, you wait and see.'

Next year came and went. My concern increased with his lack of progress.

'Please can't you do something,' I pleaded with a stern faced teacher. 'What makes you think your son should be intelligent?' she said to my amazement.

I went to see the Head, who gave me a cup of tea to calm me down. 'I really am worried,' I shook with rage with what I thought was lack of concern. It was arranged I should call in each week and see his work and how he was getting on. Each week as Dan struggled to cope brought more concern on my part and a more defensive attitude from the Head and the Teacher. I begged that he be statemented. It took months before I saw an Educational Psychologist, but she couldn't do much because it was the end of the school year and anyway she was leaving, but would pass her findings on. I had Dan independently assessed at the Hornsby Dsylexia Association who confirmed that Daniel has an IQ of 120, but is dsylexic.

Dan's next teacher was straight from Teacher Training College.

'Hello,' she said, 'I'm glad you've come in. I was going to write and ask you to come and see me.'

'What's wrong,' says I.

'I don't want to upset you, but did you know that your Daniel has a problem with his reading and writing?'

I sat down and told her of my past efforts to get him some help. 'Leave it to me, I'll see what I can do.'

My shoulders felt a little lighter as Dan and I walked home. The new Educational Psychologist came, we saw the school's Doctor, we saw the Educational Welfare Officer, and a speech therapist. The statement provided a point 2 teacher for Dan, this gave him two individualised teaching sessions per week. The sessions started last September (1988).

The relief on Daniel was enormous, and it showed. His confidence began to grow and slowly and with much effort he began to read. Each Tuesday and Thursday he goes into school with a spring in his step, but the other eight sessions with his class teacher are a trial. Whilst pleased with this help I still worry that it's not enough. I know how desperate he gets on those other days. I know I have to find other ways of helping him.

I received a postcard from Daniel who was on holiday with the school. DEAR MUM AND DAD, ... It started, the rest was so short I knew he had struggled to find words that he could spell. I cried clutching the postcard. I love this child so much, why can't I help him. There are doors that can open up to him the education that he needs, but where do I find the key.

Well, I think I may have found our key - or at least part of it, thanks to another parent in PIP* who suggested I telephone the ILEA centre for Motor and Associated Communication Handicaps. They may be able to help, or at least advise. I did phone and was shocked that I did not have to beg or plead with them to help me. I told them Daniel's next statement review was on the following Wednesday. They said they would phone the school and see if they could assess him before Wednesday. They saw Daniel on the

---

*Parents in Partnership (PIP) 37 Woodnook Rd, London SW16.

following Monday. He came home full of excitement and whilst making a jam sandwich (because he was starving) he told me all about this wonderful lady who had come to see his work and talk to him. He'd done some more for her while she looked on. (He did not even realise he'd been tested.) He'd also worked on this machine, but he wasn't going to tell me about that, because she had said he might get one after next Wednesday's review, but he would have to wait until then to know.

'It's so terrific, Mum, I know if I say anything it won't come true, so I'm going to wait until Wednesday when I'll be told.'

The report was written and delivered in time for this morning's meeting which I attended. Everyone admitted that whilst Daniel was making progress it was very slow. His problems are considerable, but should he have one of these machines? Would his written work suffer? The Educational Psychologist pointed out the CENMACH report - it read:

'It is unlikely that Daniel's written work will ever provide him with positive feedback with his spelling or allow him to have a sense of pride in his work.'

He will be issued with the Canon 90 electronic typewriter to use in the classroom. He will be able to type out his work, check his spelling, save his work and print it out when correct. It will stay with him for as long as he needs it, and he can use it at home to do his homework. The statement was amended for its allowance and Daniel would be told today that he would be getting it.

'WHOOP-PEE,' Daniel came back into the kitchen, 'Can I have a jam sandwich Mum, while I tell you and Gran my great news.'

As he ate the sandwich his face shone with excitement. He was so pleased and as I cleaned the mess he'd made making the jam sandwich, I too smiled to myself, had I as last found one of those keys?

Daniel's Canon typewriter with word processing facilities should arrive by September 1989, when he starts his last year of junior school. For the first time in five years Daniel is looking forward to going to school all week.

Jenny Simpson
Reprinted from PIP Newsletter
Nov. 1989

'Smestow Comprehensive Wolverhampton' *Credit CSIE.*

When a pupil comes to a school they may well bring some personal equipment with them, such as a wheelchair. If the need for further equipment arises during their school career, it would be requested by a member of staff in a 'special needs dept', or a local Authority O.T., or a specialist aids advisor from an appropriate voluntary organisation. The equipment usually, but not always, is attached to a person, not a school. Therefore if a partially-sighted pupil leaves your school, he/she will probably take their closed circuit television with them.

The range of technology available is developing rapidly and is leading to very exciting possibilities. There is a large exhibition held annually in Britain, called 'Naidex' where the latest equipment can be seen and tried.

We would like to see many more local centres where we, the clients, could examine the full range of equipment available, borrow them, rent them or buy them as makes sense. This is especially true for disabled children as their need for aids can change as fast as their need for new shoes, or toys.

Wong Sai Ming

I don't want your pity
And I don't want your help
I just want a fair chance
And acceptance as myself
I know I'm not the same as you
      Chrissie Chadwick

Exley

94

Mainstreaming with Micros*
Microtechnology and special needs
in the ordinary school

Changing Trends

More disabled children are now educated in ordinary primary and secondary schools than would have seemed possible only a few years ago. The trend towards integration is increasing and is encouraged by two quite recent developments. First, there has been a marked change of attitude among both the parents of disabled children and the professionals who work with them. In the past, many parents welcomed the idea that their child should be educated in a special school with its sheltered atmosphere and specialist staff and equipment. This segregated setting seemed an attractive alternative to the large and apparently impersonal neighbourhood school. Today, however, many more parents are becoming increasingly aware of the advantages for their child of at least some experience of the curriculum and social contact offered by the ordinary school. Professionals, too, have increasingly come to recognise how difficult it is for small special schools to provide adequately for all needs of developing children while staff in many ordinary schools now accept that they have a responsibility for the education of children with a much wider range of needs.

The second development is the rapidly increasing range of aids available to enable disabled children to be integrated and gain access to the ordinary curriculum. Only a few years ago, aids for disabled students in education were either non-existent or were bulky, inflexible and expensive; they were certainly not suited for use in the ordinary classroom. Many of the new aids, on the other hand, are small, light, reliable and relatively inexpensive. Moreover, they provide disabled users with access to activities that previously have seemed impossible. This flexibility and power is the result of the application of microcomputer technology to the problems of the disabled.

Liberation

The interchange of information is the basis of human communication but any children with physical and sensory impairments have severe communication problems because they are not able to enjoy a full exchange of information with those around them. The degree to which a person's disability is a handicap depends upon the circumstances in which he or she is required to operate. The inability to handle information sufficiently fast enough has frequently led to children being segregated because they 'cannot' keep up' in an ordinary classroom.

With the use of computer becoming more widespread in ordinary schools, the inability to handle ordinary computer programs may prevent access to certain areas of the curriculum. As an example the Keymaster is a new device which can be operated using one or two switches but which enables the user to access a BBC microcomputer. This in turn, can be used for word processing or to run one of the many other educational programs now available.

Janet, who is fourteen, and thirteen year old Nicky do not need all the facilities offered by a microcomputer. However, as Nicky has muscular dystrophy he finds writing very tiring. When provided with a Brother EP-20 portable electronic printer he was able to use this for his written work and maintain sufficient written output to remain in a comprehensive school. The Brother printers are battery powered and can be easily taken around the school and home in the evening. They also have an additional feature which is very useful for Janet who is cerebral palsied and whose poor hand control makes writing, and typing, difficult. When keys are pressed the letter appears in a seventeen character display just above the keyboard. Not until this display is full is the first letter printed so that Janet, whose Brother EP-44 has a very high quality print, is able to correct her mistakes before they reach the paper. A recent addition to the Brother range, the BP-30, can write in three sizes and four colours and therefore has considerable potential as a writing aid for younger children who are integrated into primary schools. The Canon Typestar 6 also has a large print and is available at discount to disabled users.

Children with Visual Impairments

The problems of handling ordinary text have frequently result in the segregation of blind and partially sighted children from an early age.

---

*From a Fact Sheet by The Centre for Studies on Integrated Education. See address list

Television magnifiers to enable partially sighted people to read ordinary printed material have been available for some years and have made it possible for some children to be educated in ordinary schools. However, they remain bulky and are not easily transported.

A recent device, the Viewscan, overcomes this problem by employing a tiny, hand-held camera which is scanned across a written or printed page. The image of the text is displayed on a large illuminated display which is completely portable. A similar concept is used in the Optacon which is designed for use by blind people. A camera is used to scan the text but, instead of the image being displayed on a screen, it is converted into a tactile form and detected through the fingertips.

The very small market often makes aids for the visually handicapped expensive and this could inhibit their use as aids to integration. However, the trend is now to move away from costly, purpose-built aids towards the use of devices which enable blind and partially-sighted children to use a standard microcomputer. In the Workstation for the Blind, devised by Tom Vincent

'The Magic Micro: Quintin Kynaston'.
Credit Sally and Richard Greenhill.

of the Open University, a braille overlay on a Concept Keyboard enables the user to operate a word processor program on a BBC computer.

Work is printed out on paper while a speech synthesiser also 'reads' the output aloud. An alternative to spoken output is provided by the Soft Copy Brailler in which the text is read on a transient braille 'display' as it is printed out.

Children with Hearing Impairments

The normal hearing aid, issued by the Department of Health and Social Security, has a very short range and is particularly sensitive to background noise, echo and reverberation. It is therefore quite unsuited for use in the ordinary classroom. A radio hearing aid, on the other hand, enables the teacher to speak directly to the child over a considerable distance withot loss of quality. Such devices have been practicable for some years but microelectronics has enabled the size and weight to be reduced and so made it possible for many profoundly hearing impaired children to benefit from integration.

Unfortunately, the DHSS regards radio hearing aids as educational aids and does not supply them. Instead, the money has to be found by local education authorities or through fund-raising.

Children with Learning Difficulties

Much of the power of microtechnology results from its flexibility. Good special needs software provides the teacher with a powerful tool which can be used to individualise the curriculum to suit a particular child.

All of these aids are, as yet, only just beginning to reach those children who can benefit from them. In part, this is due to a lack of experience, information or advice. Recognising this problem, the Microelectronics Education Programme (MEP) provided funds to open a communication aids in education centre in Oxford. At a national level, the ACE Centre (ACE stands for Aids to Communicate in Education) gathers and disseminates information about aids. At an individual level, the Centre has facilities for those who wish to see and try aids for themselves; it can provide technical advice and, where appropriate, provide assessments of particular children's needs.

Whether or not an aid recommended is then provided by a local authority is, of course, another matter and, in the past, schools and parents have often had to raise funds themselves. Local education authorities, under financial pressure already, are not rushing foward with open arms to embrace the costs of providing individual chidren with the aids they require.

Useful Ally

The 1981 Education Act ought to be a useful ally in this situation. If, attached to a child's statement of needs, is the professional view that a particular item of equipment is essential in order for child's educational needs to be met, it would be difficult for the authority to ignore it. However the authority may respond that it does not have the money and that it may be a more efficient use of resources to place the child in a special school where the staffing ratio and limited curriculum makes an aid unnecessary.

Part of the Education Support Grant scheme operated in 1984 by the Department of Education and Science (DES), was intended to encourage education authorities to use some of their resources to provide microelectronic aids designed or adapted for use by children with special educational needs. The DES provides 70 per cent of the cost of such aids but, unfortunately, the local authority has to find the other 30 per cent and many may be reluctant to do so.

In the next few years we shall see further progress in the use of microtechnology-based aids for disabled people. We can expect that it will soon be possible to carry around enormously powerful communication systems on a wheelchair or even in the pocket. A person whose mobility is limited will be able to retrieve information without having to go to a library but mobility problems will also be diminished with the application of microtechnology to wheelchair control. It may not be long before a severely disabled person has only to select the room they want to go to and their wheelchair will take them there by the best route and without bumping into anything on the way!

The use of speech synthesis for those with severe speech difficulties has been the subject of much investigation. Within a few years we shall see high quality speech synthesis of unlimited vocabulary becoming widely available and portable communications incorporating this technology will enable non-verbal people to communicate much more naturally with those who cannot understand signs. Synthesised speech will be increasingly used to give the visually impaired access to ordinary written material.

A Right to Communicate

Communication should be seen as a right, and an essential component of education and children with communication difficulties should not have to wait while central Government and local authorities are persuaded to provide for their needs.

Tim Southgate
Head of Ormerod Special School, Oxford

Stereotypes of Disabled People
by Richard Rieser

The pre-conceived attitudes towards, assumptions about and expectations of disabled people are one of the biggest barriers to our equal opportunities.

These stereotypes are portrayed on television and the radio, in local and national newspapers and magazines, in comics, in childrens books, in adult literature, in films and in advertising.

In part these stereotypes are based on superstitions, myths and beliefs from earlier times, but they show remarkable persistence and are rooted in deep seated and childish fears we all have about disability.

We can all, at any time, become physically or mentally disabled as well as die. Perhaps the need to distance ourselves from this reality makes it convenient to rely on stereotypes of disability. They are less troubling than accepting the individuality, the joy, the pain, the appearance and behaviour and the rights of disabled people. The refusal to acknowledge this rich variety of human experience diminishes the humanity of the able-bodied.

Disabled people have been and are challenging these negative attitudes and images of ourselves.

Teachers, parents, librarians, publishers, writers and illustrators, photographers, designers, advertisers, journalists and all who collaborate in maintaining these images have to be made to see the damage they perpetrate.

What are the Stereotypes of Disabled People?

Biklen and Bogdana (1977) in their study of 'Media Portrayals of Disabled People' identified 10 commonly occurring handicapped stereotypes. We shall use this as a basic framework.

'Crippled Clara'
Credit Bunty Magazine.

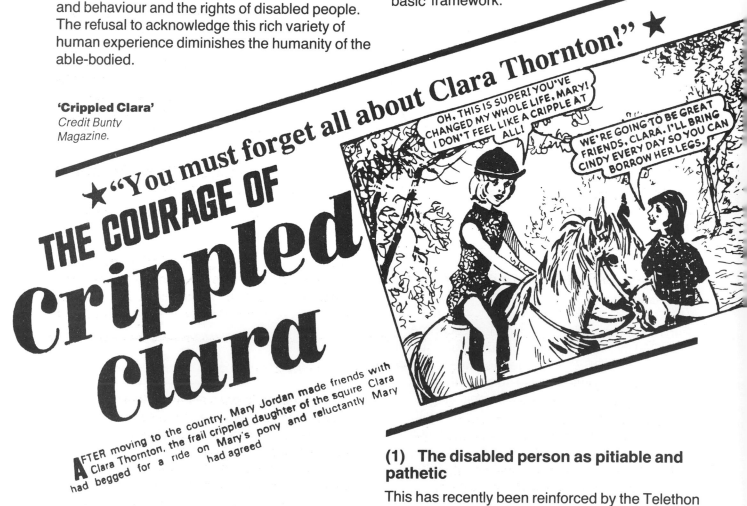

★ "You must forget all about Clara Thornton!" ★

★ "You must forget THE COURAGE OF Crippled Clara

AFTER moving to the country, Mary Jordan made friends with Clara Thornton, the frail crippled daughter of the squire Clara had begged for a ride on Mary's pony and reluctantly Mary had agreed

OH, THIS IS SUPER! YOU'VE CHANGED MY WHOLE LIFE, MARY! I DON'T FEEL LIKE A CRIPPLE AT ALL!

WE'RE GOING TO BE GREAT FRIENDS, CLARA. I'LL BRING CINDY EVERY DAY SO YOU CAN BORROW HER LEGS.

(1) The disabled person as pitiable and pathetic

This has recently been reinforced by the Telethon to raise money for the disabled. In adult literature Laura in 'The Glass Menagerie' or Philip Carey in

'Of Human Bondage'. The inclusion of the disabled character is often used as a literary device to show another character's goodness and sensitivity. Tiny Tim in Dickens's: 'Christmas Carol' 'Alas for Tiny Tim, he bore a little crutch and had his limbs supported by an iron frame'; Porgy in 'Porgy and Bess', Gershwin's opera is another example. This patronising stereotype springs in part from feelings of superiority of the non-disabled to the disabled and is patronising.

The disability charities operate on this stereotype reinforcing the passive, pitiable dependency of disabled people. Much public information comes from, and government funding, goes to these charities, which are *not* controlled by disabled people.

For many years one of these charities allowed the absurd sight of little girls wearing callipers to sit outside shops begging for money!

As the charities compete for money, they outdo each other in projecting pitiable images of disability.

(2) The disabled person as an object of violence

In reality, disabled people are often victims of violence. But the absence of other roles in media and literature reinforces society's view of people with disabilities as totally helpless and dependent.

Films like 'What Ever Happened to Baby Jane' in which Joan Crawford confined to her wheelchair is wholly at the mercy of her murderous sister Bette Davis or, Audrey Hepburn's blind character in 'Wait Until Dark'.

In television too the disabled are apt to be victims.

The tabloid press will use this stereotype, but they seem less horrified when reporting the mistreatment of the mentally disabled in institutions.

(3) (a) The disabled person as sinister or evil

This is one of the most persistent stereotypes.

William Shakespeare's Richard III is a classic example. For dramatic effect the character is given a disability to accentuate the evil dimension of his personality.

In fairy tales 'the dwarf' Rumpelstilsken, and the mean witch (leaning on her crutch) in Hansel and Gretel, or Captain Hook, in J.M. Barrie's 'Peter Pan'.

In Collodis' story Pinocchio, where a fox and a cat, in order to steal from the hero, pretended to be paralysed and blind. At the end of the book their feigned afflictions became real: is this not meant to be their just punishment for their deceit?

Stevenson's Treasure Island begins by using disabled characters Blind Pew and Black Dog to evoke terror and suspense.

Many of the villains in films are given a disability. Dr Strangelove, Dr No and a whole host of characters in horror and science fiction movies; where the evilness of characters is matched to their grotesque appearance.

Wahl and Roth (16) 1982 in conducting a media watch in Washington found that 'the image of psychiatric patients as frightening and dangerous came across clearly in television portrayals'. Mentally ill persons were shown to be active confused, aggressive, dangerous, unpredictable and male. Such an image is inaccurate; mentally ill persons, in general are much more likely to be withdrawn and frightened; than violent and aggressive; they are more likely to avoid than to attach others; they are as often female as male.

(b) The disabled child as the reward for the evils of the parents.

Nowadays confined to fantasy as in the film 'Rosemary's Baby'.

Throughout Europe from the Middle Ages up to 1800's it was widely believed that deformed or disabled babies were changelings. The devil or fairies had changed the baby. This was because

---

In real life Richard III was not disabled at all

'I, that am curtail'd of this fair proposition
Cheated of feature by dissembling nature
Deform'd, unfinish'd, sent before my time
Into the breathing world, scarce half made up
And that so lamely and unfashionable
That dogs bark at me as I halt by them

Why, I, in this weak piping time of peace

Have no delight to pass away the time
Unless to spy my shadow in the sun
And Descant on mine own deformity
And therefore, since I cannot prove a lover,
To entertain these fair well spoken days
I am determined to prove a villain
And hate the idle pleasures of those days (Act 1 Sc. 1)

'Bunty'

of the sins of the parents. Infanticide of such children was common.

Many thousands of women who gave birth to such babies were burnt at the stake as witches. To give birth to a disabled baby was proof positive of intercourse with the devil.

(4)   The disabled person as atmosphere

Blind musicians, news dealers and the blind man with the cup are frequently thrown in for seasoning in films and TV stories, a practice which dilutes the humanity of disabled people by reducing them to the status of colourful or curious objects. Related to this stereotype is the depiction of people with disabilities as exotica. People displayed in this way at 'freak shows' are the victims of this stereotype. In the USA despite higher profile campaigns against handicapism than in the UK, the 'freak' remains a feature of state fairs. The headline in Newsday 5 September 1983 read:

'Farmers, freaks, fun: 142nd State fair'. At the entrance of the Great Sutton's circus sideshow there's and old thin man, about 3 feet tall. Then there's Otis, the Frog Boy, a middle aged man with deformed non-functioning legs and hands.'

British circuses still feature dwarfs and bearded ladies amongst their attractions.

These exotica and interest in the physical condition of people is forever focussed upon in comics and horror and science fiction movies, and it would be true to say that these continually reinforce the idea that physical appearance is linked to the moral character of the person so portrayed.

(5)   The disabled person as 'Super Cripple'.

Disabled people are often portrayed as having super human attributes. 'Ironside' the wheelchair bound detective has extraordinary mental powers as well as an unusual calm in the presence of adversity. Longstreet, another TV private eye, who is blind, is given superhuman hearing.

Readers Digest and other magazines often feature the extraordinary achievements of disabled persons who 'overcome' so becoming 'acceptable'. TV news also regularly feature people with disabilities who have taken part in sports events such as the London Marathon, the Wheelchair Olympics or water skiers with one leg.

It is not that people with disabilities do not participate and enjoy these events, rather it is that the media in showing mainly this perspective of disabled people's achievement encourages the stereotype that disabled people have to over-compensate to win acceptance in the wider community. By always making examples of people like Helen Keller and other disabled superachievers our society implies that the experiences of ordinary people who are just struggling to cope are unheroic or irrelevant.

Another side of the same coin is heaping excessive praise on the disabled person for carrying out some perfectably reasonable act. We are not being seen as people.

(6)   The disabled person as laughable

Mr Magoo is the fool in showing society's view that certain conditions of being - in this case physical disability - are humorous. People with hearing loss are frequently made the butt of jokes in comedy routines and 'jokes' when they misinterpret what is said to them. Harpo Marx built his career of humour on not speaking. The 'Thalidomide' joke or more recently the jokes about the victims of the Kings Cross fire which pass around schools and playgrounds and can be heard to be repeated in staffrooms, show that this stereotype is very much with us. Laugher may often be used to deal with difficult or embarrassing situations. All the more reason for

When you buy a copy of Anti-Social for the Disabled, you help the handicapped 5 ways:

Give so others may live!

all teachers to take up and discuss with a class the whole area of disability.

Recently the film 'Hear No Evil, See No Evil' featured a blind man and a deaf man thrown together having to solve a crime with 'hilarious' consequences. Here both blind and deaf are the butt of the joke.

(7) The disabled person as her/his own worst enemy - blaming the victim. This is also common in racist and sexist attitudes and behaviour.

Disabled people are often portrayed as self-pitiers who could 'make it' if only they would stop being 'bitter' about their 'fate', think positively and rise to 'the challenge'. The legitimate anger which disabled people feel about society's abuse is misrepresented as unfounded bitterness that has its roots in the person's character. The parallel with the 'male' view of women complaining of sexual harassment or rape victims 'as asking for it' is obvious. Similarly in racist attitudes and behaviour, which classifies those in the black community who react to racism as the problem, we see the blaming of the victim. TV medical shows such as 'Marcus Welby MD' are particularly prone to this approach. This may well have its roots in the clinical approach to disability that does not put it in a social context. Certainly my experiences at the Royal National Orthopaedic Hospital lead me to believe this is a fairly general attitude in hospitals dealing with people with disabilities.

Children's authors seem especially fond of this stereotype. An example is 'The Door in the Wall' by Marguerite de Angeli (Doubleday 1949). Here Robin reacts angrily when a child calls him 'crook shanks' because his legs are disabled. Robin's guardian, Brother Luke, both criticises and laughs at his anger. Later Robin 'overcomes' and so Robin changes from a person who naturally defends his rights into one who submits to society's narrow minded expectations. The reader is left with the impression that this change is desirable.

Another variant of this is the *Disabled person as using their Disability*. This is especially common amongst professionals dealing with disabled children.

Disabled children are not believed in their own assessment of how much, or how little they can do. 'They exaggerate their disability to manipulate.' This draws on another common assumption *that disabled people are all stupid or not intelligent*, the 'Does He Take Sugar' syndrome.

Both views derive from the Medical model of disability, that the doctors, psychotherapists, etc., know what is best and assess our capabilities. Yet they get it wrong so often. IT MUST BE REALISED THAT THE DISABLED PERSONS ARE THE BEST EXPERT ON WHAT THEY THEMSELVES ARE CAPABLE OF.

(8) The disabled person as a burden

This stereotype is linked to the concepts that all people with disabilities are helpless and need to be taken care of by 'normal' people. Many

Avoiding Handicapist Stereotypes: Guidelines for writers, editors and book reviewer

- **Shun one-dimensional characterisations of disabled persons. Portray people with disabilities as having individual and complex personalities and capable of a full range of emotions.**

- **Avoid depicting disabled persons only in the role of receiving: show disabled people interacting as equals giving as well as receiving. Too often the person with a disability is presented solely as the recipient of pity.**

- **Avoid presenting physical**

- **characteristics of any kind as determining factors of personality. Be especially cautious about implying a correlation between disability and evil.**

- **Refrain from depicting persons with disabilities as objects of curiosity. It is entirely appropriate to show disabled people as members of an average population or cast of characters. Most disabled people are able to participate in all facets of life and should be depicted in a wide variety of situations.**

- **A person's disability should not be**

disabled people have fought hard to assert their right to independent living in the last 20 years; their right to be supported by society in overcoming the barriers society imposes. The idea their special needs are a burden comes from the difficulties society imposes on meeting their needs. The burden image objectifies and dehumanises. It is important to recognise that people with disabilities are human beings who are capable of much independence and of interacting with others in mutually rewarding ways.

The popular TV series 'Beauty and the Beast' set in New York portrays the disabled, disfigured outcasts as having to live a subterranean existence. It also underlines the unacceptability of the different and that they are dangerous and must be segregated.

(9)   The disabled person as non-sexual

Disabled people are almost always portrayed as totally incapable of sexual activity. In 'Lady Chatterley's Lover' by D.H. Lawrence, her husband is disabled and non-sexual leading to her affair with the socially inferior but sexually potent gamekeeper, Meadows.

(Battye - The Chatterley Syndrome in 'Stigma' 1966)

Although some disabilities may limit an individual's sexual activity, the assumption that disabled people are non-sexual beings is false and unreal.

The film 'Coming Home' with Jane Fonda and Jon Voigt was particularly good in portraying how a love affair develops between a paraplegic Vietnam war veteran and the attractive able-bodied wife of an army officer, Jane Fonda. Faced with the reality of this her husband can't take the 'insult to his virility' and tries to kill them, and then having been dissuaded by argument, kills himself.

Sexuality always arouses powerful emotions and nowhere more than put alongside disabled people. This probably explains why most portrayals ignore sexuality.

The opposite view of disabled persons as sex starved and degenerate, as featured in comics, TV crime and horror films is a strange reversal. Perhaps this links back to the thesis about those who are different challenging our primal insecurities including sexuality.

Certainly this ambivalence is suggested by the way men with certain mild disabilities - especially sustained in war -are viewed as brave and/or sexy, i.e., Nelson or Mosha Dayan. Of course this does not apply to women in a similar position. Women with disabilities have had to fight particularly hard to reclaim their sexuality. (See section on Women and Disability.)

I wonder if 'Coming Home' would have got released at all if Jane Fonda had been the paraplegic rather than Jon Voigt.

(10) The disabled person as incapable of fully participating in everyday life

This stereotype is mainly perpetrated by disabled people being absent and not being shown as integral and productive members of society - as ridiculed or made the butt of a joke. (Blind people do not mistake fire hydrants for people or bump into every object in their path, despite the myth-making of Mr Magoo.)

- **Avoid the sensational in depicting disabled people. Be wary of the stereotype of disabled person as either the victims or perpetrators of violence.**

- **Refrain from endowing disabled characters with superhuman attributes. To do so is to imply that a disabled person must overcompensate and become super-human to win accceptance.**

- **Avoid a Pollyana-ish plot that implies a disabled person need only have 'the will' and the 'right attitude' to succeed. Young readers need insights into the societal barriers that keep disabled people from living full lives -systematic discrimination in employment, education and housing, inaccessible transportation and building, and exorbitant expense for necessities.**

- **Avoid showing disabled people as non-sexual. Show disabled people in loving relationships and expressing the same sexual needs and desires as non-disabled people.**

part of the work force, families, schools and colleges. The absence of such portrayals feeds the concept that disabled people are inferior human beings who should be shut away and segregated. This is one of the biggest problems with nearly all literature, textbooks and curriculum materials, and with very few exceptions people with disabilities do not appear. **Over the last 10-15 years black people and girls have appeared as almost obligatory token figures in much children literature. Do images of the disabled, largely absent apart from specialist books have to go through the same tokenistic phase?** Regular inclusion of disabled people as participants in all facets of society would lend emphasis to the wide range of things we can do rather than to what we cannot.

The Way Forward. The portrayal of the disabled should ignore the 10 stereotypes outlined above. A number of guidelines have appeared which would be useful to reproduce here to help us with the above task.

The guidelines on pages 102-3 were prepared by the Center on Human Policy, the Center for Independent Living in Berkeley, Disabled in Action of Metropolitan New York and the Council on Inter-racial racial Books for children. They are offered as suggestions to assist authors, editors, reviewers and readers in counteracting the common stereotypes about disabled people.

Update – The stereotypes are still very much with us. The Campaign Against Patronage has been established by Disabled People and has taken direct action against the images of disabled people that are used by the big charities and against the way disability is portrayed on Telethon, Children in Need and Comic Relief. The latter allowed a film putting the Campaigns case, to be screened, but late at night. The press still continues to reinforce the image that disability is something to be frightened of or is a tragedy or outside society. 'What the Papers Say and Don't Say about Disability' (Spastic Society 1991 £2.95), looks at 335 stories in the national press and analyses their treatment of disability.

Films continue to reinforce stereotypes. 'Dick Tracey', directed by Warren Beatty portrayed all the baddies as disabled or disfigured. This was seen worldwide by more than 500 million children. Spielberg's latest film released in the UK 'Hook' reinforces the old stereotype of vengeful evilness caused by disability. The horror movie has always used appearance as a metaphor for character. However, with the increasing use of cartoons, such as the Turtles and others, children are now getting a daily diet of animated horror "comic morality" in which all that is evil is disabled, different or disfigured. This issue must be addressed by educationalists and parents. The producers of images must be made accountable to the public. Advertisers also feel free to use images of disability (see below) or the recent Guardian Advert featuring Britannia in a broken wheelchair (page 129).

Dick Tracey

Packaging of Lebkuchen biscuits featuring the witch from Hansel and Gretal as disabled/evil

Footnote
BCODP are producing a guide ''Disability Stereotypes in the Media'' in the spring 1992, which will include Charity Advertising and a proposed Code of Ethics. This should be very useful.

See also **The Creatures Time Forgot: Photography and Disability Imagery** by David Hevey, Routledge April 1992.

Children's Literature

by Richard Rieser

Children's literature can provide a powerful influence on beliefs, and if books are chosen with care they can refute stereotypes and construct positive images about people with disabilities in the mind of the reader.

Proponents of this view claim that:

'In depicting the human dilemma, a literary account is often more vivid than even our everyday experiences because essentials are winnowed from the ephemeral and highlighted.

Novels - can translate objectively defined societal problems into subjectively realised experiences.

Fiction provides distance and intimacy. Being both fantasy and reality it permits the reader to be both a spectator and participant.

Through books some parts of the reader's conception of the world is either confirmed, modified or refuted and that changes the reader'.

It is difficult to assess the changes effected by private reading, but there is growing evidence that deliberate use of books, followed by discussions or other exploratory activities, has a measurable impact on attitudes. (Baskin and Harris p.30)

Baskin and Harris 1984 p.31-32 quote a number of studies that show a substantial and lasting shift in children's attitudes toward people with disabilities after group reading of selected fictional works, featuring characters with disabilities.

They go on to suggest that the best books do not have a 'message' that overwhelms the narrative. The central characters must be created in the illusion of fullness, roundness - must be shown as complete human beings. Good childrens' literature should help the readers discover the truth for themselves, rather than seek to convert the readers to a cause.

Baskin and Harris in 'Notes from a Distant Drummer' (1977) state that some critics (of childrens' literature) appear to feel that any book about a person with special needs serves an important social goal and therefore critical analysis is bypassed (p.63)

This fault is serious when particularised knowledge is urgently needed. If critical or analytical comments are not made about works that evoke pity, purvey misinformation, present faulty models, or otherwise include basically inadequate material, critics are abdicating their professional responsibility (p.62). This comment needs to be extended to those reviewing children's literature featuring people with disabilities, many of whom have been far too uncritical and have recommended the use of books that re-inforce many of the 10 stereotypes (see stereotypes section) derived by Biklen and Bogdana.

Albert Schwartz 1977 in an article entitled 'Disability in Children's Books: Is Visibility Enough' applies Biklen and Bogdana's criteria to modern children's literature, and found most of it re-inforced one or more of the stereotypes. Schwartz is only able to recommend six books out of all the hundreds available, and most of these had some drawback.

In the same year Baskin and Harris produced their much weightier 'Notes from a Different Drummer'. This book for the first time brought together most modern childrens' books that had a character with disability, produced in the English Language, from 1945 to 1976. Apart from some very useful introductory chapters on 'Society and Handicaps: the Literary Treatment of Disability' they then go on to map out the changing treatment of disability in childrens' literature.

Historically childrens' stories were not judged as literature, rather they were vehicles for re-inforcing moral instruction, or providing academic information in a palatable form. The popular Victorian writer, Charles Kingsley, in 'The Water Babies' said ... 'for you must know and believe that people's souls make their bodies' and here he echoes medieval ideas on disability. (See Curriculum sheet on Classic Children's Literature).

When stories did feature people with disabilities, they were portrayed as paragons of virtue, wonderfully patient, good natured and brave under all circumstances or alternatively as evil. In 'Heidi', Clara the wealthy 'crippled girl' was taught to walk by Heidi - buoyed by Heidi's cheerfulness and determination she made an almost instant recovery. Often the disabled character is only known by his disability - 'The Blind Man and the Talking Dog'.

As the Twentieth Century progressed, descriptions of real problems associated with disability are intermixed with totally unrealistic resolutions. Although a carefully laundered view of life continued to dominate, coinciding with World War II, a new trend was emerging. Some writers began to realise that efforts to protect children from capricious knowledge of a threatening, unhappy or capricious world, rather than providing security, left them unprepared and vulnerable. Gradually more honest and realistic presentations occurred.

However, the vast majority of the 311 titles reviewed by Baskin and Harris reinforced prejudices against the disabled that predominate in society. They provide a plot synopsis focusing on the aspects to do with disability and then an analysis of its treatment in the book. While critical, they are far more easy going than Schwartz.

Bonnie Lass and Monica Broomfield (1981) using Wolfensberger's (1972) stereotyped roles of the disabled construct criteria for choosing books that give 'a fair shake' to disabled people, and which will foster a positive attitude in the classroom.

**Children's Literature
'Peter Pan', Hodder & Stoughton**

Wolfensberger identified disabled persons as being seen as:

(a) perpetual children;

(b) menaces to society;

(c) subhuman or superhuman;

(d) objects of pity, charity or ridicule.

Using their criteria which also rejected books where people with disabilities were segregated, they could only recommend 12 books.

Their laudable attempt at selection, however, highlights a problem. In a more detailed review of childrens' literature, as it deals with hearing impairment, Albert Schwartz (1980) goes on to list additional flaws in books dealing with deafness. As a result he excludes two of the three books recommended by Lass and Broomfield.

He reviews 70 titles and finds 3 acceptable. Schwartz includes the following useful flaws:

(a) Deaf people are frequently presented as isolated both from the hearing world and deaf community.

(b) Many books give an inaccurate picture of deafness presenting it as a completely silent world or cureable by a hearing aid.

(c) The oral method is presented as the best or only way for deaf people to communicate. Four books mention sign language. Yet sign language is the first language of the deaf community.

(d) No books mention American sign language or its important role to the deaf community.

Clearly then we have to get our criteria of what constitutes an acceptable portrayal of various people with disabilities from those people themselves. This will not be a fixed level of acceptability, but will change as disabled people gain confidence and independence in their struggle to eradicate the handicaps society imposes upon them.

In 1925, Jessica Langworthy analysed 311 works of fiction containing blind characters and found four sorts of blind persons:

1. The idealised and abnormally good.

2. The repugnant and abnormally bad.

3. The extremely clever.

4. The normal and well described.

Of all types Idealised Blind Persons occurred most often, reflecting what Langworthy maintained was sighted author's uninformed perceptions about what non-sighted people should be and do.

All the reviews mentioned so far are American. There has been much more work done in this area there, prompted by the mainstreaming of children with disabilities. There are some reviews in the UK, but they are on the whole much less critical. Quite often they use language disabled people find insulting and they perpetuate negative stereotypes.

'Count Me In. Books for and about Disabled Children' (1981) provides short summaries of 52 works of fiction and 24 biographies that are recent and accessible. The author excludes indulgent books that bestow special powers on people with disabilities. She also excludes historical novels as these reflect the values, superstitions and prejudices of their time.

Grace Hallworth (1982) produced for Hertfordshire Library Service 'My Mind is not in a Wheelchair'. Here, 125 childrens' books with characters with disability are listed and classified by type of disability. The use of the terms 'mongol', 'mute' and 'handicap' in unfortunate.

While the selection steers away from the mawkish it does not examine other commonly occurring stereotypes. At one point the author uncritically states '*Two handicaps* - racial prejudice and blindness - are linked in these stories'.

ILEA Centre for Learning Resources 1981 also produced an annotated bibliography of childrens' books featuring special needs for the International Year of the Disabled. This unlike some of the other reviews contains a short summary and the relevant reading age. However, it is not critical of the negative stereotypes of disability contained in some of the books listed.

Perhaps one of the main reasons that English reviewers are less critical than those writing in the USA is that there are less books published in the UK and many of the best American books are not readily available in the UK.

But if reviewers, parents and teachers are not critical then publishers and authors will continue to reproduce negative stereotypes.

Margaret Marshall (1985), still sticking to the wrong use of 'handicapped' lists 30 titles and states:

'The handicapped child is an ordinary child who may need special help in some things, including reading books and library use. But the 'ordinary' child who is not *handicapped* in the usual sense is handicapped by society's view of disability. They provide an all too rare opportunity for handicapped children to find themselves in books and for the 'ordinary' children to develop empathy and understanding'.

If this is Margaret Marshall's aim why is she so accepting of books rejected for their damaging re-inforcement of stereotypes by other reviewers?

John Quicke (1985) in a much more deeply thought out approach presents childrens' fiction as a means of changing attitudes. An advocate of integration, he sees acceptance by normal peers as central to the success of integration.

Quicke argues - 'there is enough evidence ... to justify a teaching intervention which tackles the problem directly, by including a planned element in the curriculum specifically designed to encourage positive attitudes and actions towards peers with special needs, just as there is a case for curricula to foster racial tolerance and awareness of gender issues.'

He argues that fiction is less traumatic than a visit; that matters not easily dealt with in any other way, such as sexuality and the physically disabled (except it is still ignored) can be explored; that it provides a total picture of the experience of

'Heidi'

disability, and that separateness is not over-emphasised as disability is dealt with in lessons exploring all forms of human relationship.

Quicke, unlike other English authors writing in this area is familiar with American work in this field. He is critical of Baskin and Harris for not providing serious evaluation, and then goes on to examine books from the point of view of his integrationist view, and from a socio-psychological perspective.

'Most of the problems around which the plots (of the books selected) are constructed are those faced by many children disabled or not.'

The idea of grouping books by disability labels is rejected. Instead books are grouped by 'the struggle to be myself', or 'friendship across the divide', or 'the special relationship' of siblings one of whom has a mental disability.

Although Quicke provides many insights and detailed analysis of plots, he appears to find it acceptable to include books that provide negative ideas on disability. For example in 'Unleaving' by Paton Walsh, in which Paul pushes his Down's Syndrome sister, Molly, off a cliff, Molly has no real character in the book and this Quicke rightly criticises. But the real question is whether such a book should be recommended as a means of 'encouraging positive attitudes and actions towards peers with special needs'.

Perhaps it is for this reason that Emily Strauss Watson (1982) looking at 'Handicapism in Childrens' Books: A Five Year Update' (of the Albert Schwartz (1977)) article reviews 74 books, but rejects all but 21 because they re-inforce the negative stereotypes outlined earlier.

While the disabled person is not portrayed as evil or sinister they are still portrayed as:

1. **Pitiable or pathetic**
2. **An object of violence**
3. **A 'super crip'**
4. **Laughable**
5. **Her own worst enemy**
6. **A burden**
7. **Non-sexual**
8. **Incapable of full participation and/or isolated.**

A number of the titles Strauss Watson rejects on these criteria, John Quicke recommends. Perhaps this is because Quicke believes in the interaction of the reader with the plot and

This is christopher with his beaker. He goes to a special Playgroup where disabled and able-bodied children Play together. by olu

characters. 'The child reads him or herself into the world created by the author, and by so doing begins to see almost without realising it, *how disability functions in a particular social, emotional or even historical context*.'

This view is just a little idealistic from a teaching point of view. We do not encourage children to read racist books to understand racism except in a very structured situation. No more, given the choice of the large variety of books featuring disability, should we select handicapist texts.

The selection by Emily Strauss Watson is reproduced below, as a set of books that disabled reviewers believe present disability in a non-stereotyped way in good literature.

Slapin, Lessing and Belkind (1987) present a more up to date list of good American children's literature and reviews some examples of good, bad and indifferent with regard to non use of handicapist stereotypes.

I have added titles that I consider meet the same criteria that have been published since.

This man cannot use his hands but he can still write by using his head to type. by uche Anichebe

**'Drawings from Books,
Children in Reception Class.**
Susie Burrows, Laburnum'.

Unfortunately a number of these books are only published in the USA and have proved very difficult to get in the UK.

Baskin and Harris in their second volume review 348 volumes produced in 6 years. Their more far reaching analysis points to an increase in violence towards and by disabled characters, including rape. But on a more positive note they point to more new books which feature severely impaired protagonists for whom impairment is only one of a host of attributes that affect their lives. They also note the growing casual treatment of minor disabled characters as though they were simply a natural part of the passing scene.

This point has been addressed by publishers recently with regard to gender and ethnicity in their illustrations of fiction and non-fiction. This is an important part of the curriculum. The time must now surely be right for teachers to examine all teaching materials for their portrayal or much more commonly their non-portrayal of people with disabilities.

The publishers Franklin Watts have recently produced a number of books such as 'My Class Visits a Nature Reserve' which features children with disabilities but not as the main theme. The New A-Z series by Matthias and Thomson is well illustrated with colour photos and the simple sentences accompanying each photo is also given in signed English and the letters are also given in finger spelling. There are so far four on food, my body, animals and transport. It is not easy to get the right balance and 'Our Riding Stable' by Sue Corbet produced by Hamish Hamilton concentrates on riders with different disabilities in a book with good colour photos, but with a text for junior children. It might have been better not to have chosen the disability of the riders as the unifying factor since, as a result, it is rather self-conscious as a book.

Wayland have published some excellent books in their Children Need series. In Children Need Education, Deborah Parsons weaves into an excellent book for junior children positive images of disability.

The Community Services Volunteers have produced some very useful packs e.g., ''In Our Own Right'' on disability - physical and mental - which can be used as a resource for teachers with secondary pupils. They have also produced a booklet on how to and how not to develop projects with schools. Also many of the National Organisations have materials that can be of use.

There are not enough books and materials available and teachers will have to make use of what there is to construct their own books and wall displays and images to include people with disabilities in every aspect of life presented to children as part of the curriculum.

Recommended Books

Code Disability
DV - Visual
DH - Hearing
DP - PhysicaL
DM - Mental
DG - General

For Young Readers

The balancing girl by Berniece Rabe, Dutton 1981 - DP
Darlene by Eloise Greenfield, Methuen, 1980 - DP
Giant Steps for Steven by Carol J Bennett, After School Exchange, 1980 - DP

Grandma's Wheelchair by Lorraine Henroid, Whitman, 1982 - DP

My Friend Jacob by Lucille Clifton, Harper and Row, 1980 - DM

My Sister is Different by Betty Ren Wright, Raintree, 1981 - DM

Rolly Goes Exploring by Philip Newth, Philomel, 1981 - DV - 3 others in series also good.

Through Granpa's Eyes by Patricia MacLachlan, Harper and Row, 1979 - DV

What's That? by Virginia Allen Jensen and Dorcas Woodburry Haller - DV William Collins and World, 1980

Nick Joins In by J Lasker, Albert Whitman, 1981 - DH + DP

***Don't Forget Tom** by Hanne Larsen, A & C Black, 1974 - strong, positive image of mental disability -lacks multi-racial characters - DM

***Janet At School** by Paul White A & C Black, 1978 - positive image of Janet with spina bifida at ordinary school but no multi-racial characters - DP

***Good Morning Franny** by Emily Hearn, Womens' Press of Canada, 1984 - good illustrations and story of Franny's friendship with Ting. Activities and play are the focus and Franny's wheelchair becomes unimportant. - DP

***Race You Franny** by Emily Hearn, Womens' Press of Canada, 1986 - Franny's adventures with Donny while she jokily prepares for wheelchair olympics. - DP

***Cromwell's Glasses** by Hally Keller, Hippo Scholastic, 1987 - Visually impaired rabbit's trials and tribulations. - DV

Also for incidental featuring of disability which is still rare:

***A Bag Full of Pups** by Dick Gackenhach, Picture Puffin, 1981 - 2 of 11 adults want pup as aid to blindness and hearing impairment. - DH + DP Illustrations of all adults a bit caricatured and few multi-racial characters - Infant

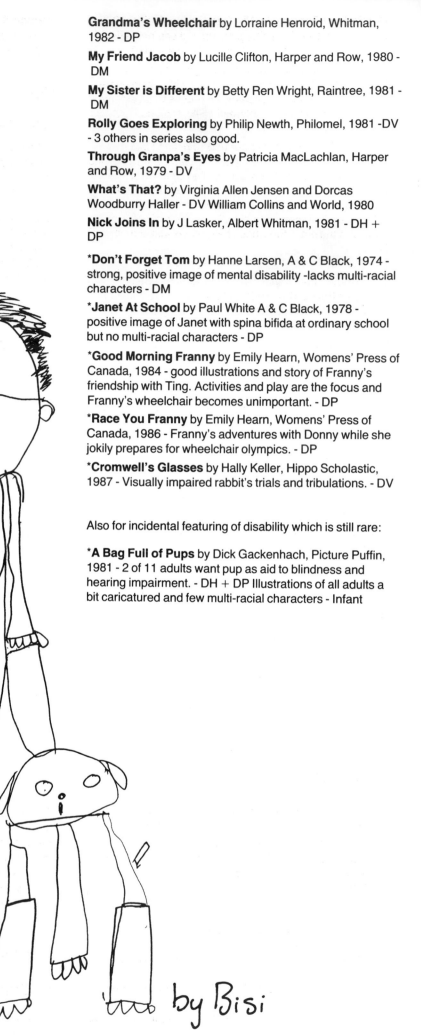

by Bisi

*Not So Fast Songolo by Niki Daly, Picture Puffin, 1985 - Sheplands granny long shopping trip, but she has difficulty walking - a good story, well illustrated - Junior - DP

*Wilfred Gordon McDonald Partridge by Man Fax, Picture Puffin, 1984 - How a young boy with a long name finds out about memory and how he relates to an elderly women who forgets a lot. Interesting illustrations - Old Infant/Young Junior. - DM

*How We Play by Anita Harper and Christine Roche Kestral Books 1979. This book shows black and white girls, boys and disabled all as part of life. The pictures are funny and interesting. It contains very strong messages (but without being boring) just by the way the writing and pictures are juxtaposed. Infants. Shows argument over game and the girl in the wheelchair, reacts just like others. - DG

'**How we feel**' and '**How we live**'are good also.

*A Garden in the City by Gerda Muller. MacDonald Children's Books, 0-356.16825.5. A beautiful book about plants and gardening. The story features a group of children one of whom is disabled.

*Library Day by John Cowley. Heinemann Educational Books 04-35-00226-0. A disabled child as one of a number attending story time in the library.

*Different and Alike, Nancy P. McConnell 1988. Current Inc. Colarado Springs C080941 - ($2.95. Soft) Sensitive and humourous guide to what it's like to be disabled.

Sign Language Books.

These are particularly useful in developing an understanding of how the deaf people communicate. Most primary age children find them fascinating.

*Where's Spot by Eric Hill ISBN 0-904-691-30-6, £6.95, 1986 - DH

*Spot Goes to School by Eric Hill ISBN 0-904-681-306, £6.95, 1988 - DH
Both published by National Deaf Children's Society, Distributed by Baker Book Services Unit, 10/11 Manfield Park, Guildford Road, Cranley, Surrey, GU6 8NO (0483-275444). School Discount. Both the above are English/Sign Language - DH

*Beverly School for the Deaf sell a number of sign language books they have produced. **First signs-animals, colours, clothes, food, toys, Signs for Beginners and Song in Sign**. They also sell a **Dictionary of Sign**, £5.50 plus 1.50 postage - DH
Beverley School for the Deaf, Beverley Road, Saltersgill, Middlesbrough, Cleveland, TS4 3LQ. These are signed English not BSC. Signed English.

*Heathlands Primary School produce **The Beginners Book of Signs, Easter, Summer, Christmas and Countries book of signs**. Heathlands Drive, St Albans, Herts, AL3 5AY - DH. Signed English.

*Beverly Mathias and Ruth Thomson 1988 have produced four ABC books with finger spelled letters and English/Signed translation on the topics of:

Animals: ISBN 0-86313-784-9, Franklin Watts, London, £5.95
My Body: ISBN 0-86313-695-8, Franklin Watts, London, £5.95
Transport: ISBN 0-86313-782-2, Franklin Watts, London, £5.95
Food: ISBN 0-86313-783-0, Frnaklin Watts, London, £5.95
These books generate a lot of interest in signing and finger spelling.

*British Sign Language: A Beginners Guide. BBC Publications Video £9.99, Book, Lorna Allsop 1988 - £6.95 - Highly recommended.

Non Fiction

Talk it Over Series

*The Dinosaur Series by Althea Braithwaite. These books are widely available, but the story line is weak but they do give some understanding of the problems encountered by children with various disabilities. They have colour illustrations by various illustrators and they do tend to reinforce a number of a stereotypes of people with disabilities, £2.95 hard back and £1.75 paper back.
I Use a Wheelchair ISBN 0-85122-381-8 (382-6 hard) 1983 - DP
I Can't Hear Like You, ISBN 0-85122-500-4 paper, 1985 - DH
I Can't Talk Like You, ISBN 0-85122-344-3 (345-1 hard) 1982 - DG + DH
I have Diabetes, ISBN 0-85122-384-2 hard - DP
I have a Mental Handicap, ISBN 0-85122-685-X paper 1987 - DM
I have Epilepsy, ISBN 0-86122-672-8 (439-3 hard) 1987 - DM + DP
I have Eczema, ISBN 0-85122-712-0 paper - DP

*Kevin and Lee Play Together, ILEA Learning Resources Branch, Phototalk Books, 1984 ISBN 0-7085-9995-8. Kevin is shown playing in an unselfconscious way with Lee and using his specially adapted scissors, electric bike and standing frame - DP

*I'm Louise by Anne Rooke 1986, Living and Learning, Cambridge ISBN 0-905-114-22-1. Shows Louisewith Down's Syndrome in various aspects of her active life. Simple text and colour photos £1.95 -DM

*Jessy Runs Away by Rachel Anderson and Shelagh McNichols, A&C Black London 1988. ISBN 0-7136-3059-0 hard £3.95. Story of the adventures of Jessy with Down's Syndrome illustrated with black and white drawings. This is a good story but a bit contrived, but it does raise many questions about mental disability. - DM. Still uses 'handicapped'.

*Children Need Education, Deborah Parsons, Wayland, 1987, £6.95. ISBN 1-85210-107-5 hard. Includes positive images of children with disability in different parts of the book. Also includes charter of childrens rights and forward from Princess Anne including disability.

*Nothing Special Micheline Mason 1989 Published Working Press. Available Central Books - 14 The Leathermarket, SE1 3ER ISBN 1-870736-028 0 £2.50. Large orders at discount (30 or over) from author at 34A Dafforne Road, SW17. Is an account of a totally integrated primary school. A tale of the future. What things could be like although all the practices shown already occur but in different places. Good line drawing illustrations.

*I can do it Myself W. Van Leuwen + H. Elzenga 1986 - Spindleweed ISBNO-907349315. A very readable little book of text and drawings showing adaptions that give independence.

For Older Junior/Young Secondary

Fiction

Alesia by Eloise Greenfield and Alesia Revis, Philomel, 1981 - DP

A blind girl reading braille
by Bereni

Home Town Hero featuring Scott Whittaker with asthma, 0-091477-04-5 - DP.

A Portrait of Me featuring Christine Notts with Diabetes, 0-0941477-0503.

Trick or Treat or Trouble featuring Brian McDaniel with Epilepsy, 0-941477-07-X

These 6 books are excellent junior stories with informative appendices. The individuality comes before disability.

Non-Fiction

Like It Is: Facts and Feelings about Handicaps from Kids Who Know by Barbara Adams, Walker, 1979 - DG

What If you Couldn't ....? by Janet Kamien, Scribner's, 1979 - DG

Wheelchair Champions by Harriet May Savitz, TY Crowell, 1978 - DP

Mark's Wheelchair Adventure by Camilla Jessel, Methuen, 1975 - Weak characterisation but Mark shown making friends and active with spina bifida also features Tessa with cerebal palsy. Realistic photos - Old Junior/Young Secondary. ISBN 0-416-63740-X. £4.95 paper - DP

Disabled People Peter White 1988 Franklin Walls - A 863137962. Good informative account with colour photos. Lacks politics of disability £5.95.

Apple is my Sign by Mary Risking, Houghton Mifflin, 1981 - DH

Belonging by Deborah Kent, Dial, 1978, New York - DV

God, Why Is She the Way She Is? by Linda Jacobs Ware, Concordia, 1979 - DM

Just Like Always by Elizabeth-Ann Sachs, Atheneum, 1981 - DP Scoliosis

A Little Time by Anne Norris Baldwin, Viking, 1978 - DM - Down's

Silent Dancer by Bruce Hibok, Messner, 1981 - DH

I Can't Always Hear You Joe Zelonky 1982 Basil Blackwell 0-86256 009-8
Partial hearing non-stereotyped portrayal well illustrated.

My Sister is Different Betty Wright 1982 Basil Blackwell - 0-862560071
Shows change of attitude of brother.

Kids on the Block Book Series published by Twenty First Centuary Books
38 South Market Street, Maryland 21701, USA.
$12.95 plus postage. 48 pages well illustrated. Each book has a strong story line and good ethnic and gender balance. Written by Barbara Aiello and Jeffrey Shulman 1988.

Business is Looking up featuring Renaldo Rodriguez with visual impairment - DV 0-941477-00-2

It's Your Turn to Bat featuring Mark Riley with cerebal palsy, DPO 941477-02-9

Secret's Aren't (Always) For Keep featuring Jennifer Hauser with learning difficulties 0941477-03-7, 1989 - DM

*Our Riding Centre Sue Corbett Hamish Hamilton London 1988 0-241-12442-5 hard, £4.95. A good book for all primary aged children showing, with good photos and limited text people with various disabilities learning to ride a Polehill Riding Centre. It would have been better if the disabled riders were part of a larger group - DG

My Class Visits a Nature Centre. Vivien Griffiths, Franklin Watts London 1987. ISBN 0-86313-503X hard £5.25. Features physically disabled children on an active visit to a Nature Centre. Well presented. -DG + DP

*What It's Like to be Me Exley 1981. Contains many excellent pictures and poems by children with disabilities of all ages from all over the world. Edited by Helen Exley. Available through letter box library, 8 Bradbury Street, N16 - DG

One World Series by Franklin Watts London 1988 have produced a semi-autobiographical Series. They show children with text and photos with different disabilities. There is more detail about each disability at the back of the book, whilst the text is in large Handired type. These books are better than Dinosaur as they feature real children with photos of their lives. Author is Brenda Pettenuzzo.
I have Asthma, 0-86313-745-8 - DP
I am Blind - DV
I have Cerebral Palsy - DP
I have Cystic Fibrosis - DP
I am Deaf featuring Amina Munir and her family, 0-06313-571-4 (Oralist)
I have Diabetes, 0-86313-561-7 - DP
I have Down's Syndrome, 0-86313-572-2
I have Spina Bifida, 0-86313-562-5

This girl is blind but she can still ride a horse.

by Aysha

In the book "Darlene" she plays with her cousin.

by Alvan S.

Overcoming Disability - Brian Wood 1989 Franklin Watts. Mainly medically based. Despite the terrible title quite informative. No politics of disability.

For Older Readers

Fiction

Little, Little by ME Kerr, Harper and Row, 1981
Passing Through by Corinne Gerson, Dial, 1978
Run, Don't Walk by Harriet May Savitz, Watts, 1979
Signs Unseen, Sounds Unheard by Carolyn Brimley Norris, Alinda Press, 1981
The Swing by Emily Hanlon, Bradbury, 1979
*Down All the Days 1971, Christy Brown, C.P. Pan

I Looked in a book and I Saw a dissaybold man and he dident have a no leg's becos of The worr And he had To be in a weeyolchef. BY Bereni. Aged 5.

*Shadow of Summer, Pan. Christy Brown

*My Left Foot, Autobiography 1954, C. Brown, Mandarin, 1989

*Dam Burst of Dreams, Christy Nolan – Written with a Unicorn attachment when 12

*Under the Eye of the Clock, Christy Nolan.
Both are very dense language but could be read to a whole class

Non-Fiction

See Me More Clearly: Career and Life Planning by Joyce Slayton Mitchell, Harecourt Brace Jovanovich, 1980,

*Images of Ourselves, 1981 - Ed Jo Campling: Disabled Women Talking, 0-7100-0822, Routledge and Kegan

*A Change of Rhythm: The Consequence of Head Injury, Jackie Kiers, 1986, 0-9511398-0, Headway, £2.25.

*Voices from the Shadows: Women with Disabilities speak out. Gwyneth Ferguson Matthews, 1983, Women Press of Canada.

*A Celebration of Differences: Bristol Broadside 1985. Tells life story of different physically disabled people.

*Coping with Disability 1986, Millicent Isherwood - Chambers

*With Wings: An anthology of literature by Women with Disabilities. Ed by Marsha Saxton & Florence Howe, Virago 1989.

*Sex for Young People with Spina bifida, Cerebral Palsy by Barbara Newman, Published 1983 by Ass of Spina Bifida and Hydrocephalus -0906687-03-9. 1983

*Everyone Here Speaks Sign Language N.E. Groce 1985. Harvard University Press $8.95

*Able Lives. Ed by Jenny Morris, 1989 Spinal Injuries Ass Women's Press

*Ups and Downs - Poems by David Sheppard (Downs Syndrome) 1988. Margaret Sheppard, 76 Woodlands, North Harrow, Middlesex.

*Art Ability: 50 Creative People Talk About Ability and Disability: 1989 Simon Goodenough. Pub. Michael Russell 0-85966-159-8 £6.95

*Keep Fit Exercises for Disabled People by John MacGrath, ILEA Adult Ed.

*A Sense of Self 1988. Positive images of disabled people. Camerawork, 121 Roman Road, London, E1 ISBN 1 871103010 £4.50.

Update

Young Children Fiction

*Something Else, Wendy Lohse 1990, Hodder and Stoughton. ISBN 0 340 50927 9. An excellent picture story book of a girl with no legs and what happens when she goes to a new mainstream school.

*Franny and the Music Girl, Emily Hearn 1990, Magi Publications, London. ISBN 1 85430 183 7 £2.95. Continuing this excellent series of the adventures of the girl in the wheelchair. A good story well illustrated.

*Jonathan of Gull Mountain, Jens Ahlbom, R&S Books. ISBN 91 29 575907 £6.95. An excellent and sensitively told story raising many points about disability. Jonathan is the only person who does not have wings, and the book charts the problems he encounters growing up and going to school.

Young Childrens Non-Fiction

*Talk to Me, Sue Brearley, Photos Jenny Mathews, A & C Black, London, 1989. ISBN 0 7136 31929 £4.95. This well illustrated book shows in a how we can talk to each other in different ways.

*How Babies and Families are made, Patricia Schaffer, 1988, Tabor Sarah Books Berkley, California. A sex education book showing the different ways children are conceived. It is notable for its straight-forward treatment of this subject but also for the illustrations which include disabled adults, parents and children.

Older children Non-Fiction

*Let's discuss Disability, Ruth Bailey, Wayland 1989. ISBN 1 85210 497 X £6.95. Focusing on Access, Employment, Education, Independent Living with useful case studies for Secondary or top Juniors. This is a welcome addition putting a social rather than a medical view of disability. The black and white photos make it a bit drab.

*Johnny Creschendo Revealed: Autobiographical songs, poems and photos from one of the Disability Movements best performers. £1. Available from: 1 Royal Oak Court, Pitfield Street, London N1 6EL.

*These books are not included on Emily Strauss Watson's list, but because of the difficulty of obtaining a number of the titles she recommends and because other books have been published I have included the best of these.

OPCS Surveys on Disability in Britain

The OPCS Report - Their Significance

The new national surveys on disablement - by the Office of Population, Censuses, and Surveys (OPCS) - are the first such surveys to be carried out in Britain since 1969. The surveys were commissioned by the Department of Health and Social Security in 1984 following the 'Fowler Reviews' of social security which had been set up to look at supplementary benefit; housing benefit; retirement pensions; and benefits for children and young people. At that time, the Government argued that it did not have enough information about disabled people, their incomes and needs to carry out such a review of benefits for people with disabilities.

The Government committed itself to review disability benefits following the results of the OPCS surveys. In a Parliamentary Answer in March 1987, John Major, then Minister for the Disabled, stated:

"The results of the survey are expected to be published in 1988 and will provide the evidence for a comprehensive review of benefits for sick and disabled people."
(Hansard, Written Answers, 4 March 1987, col.623)

The first two reports were published in 1988 with the sixth, and final, report being published in July 1989. At the time of writing the Government had made no announcement as to any aspect of the disability benefits review which it had committed itself to carrying out once all the OPCS reports were available.

Disabled demonstrators hold up traffic in Oxford Street in September, causing chaos on the roads in central London. They were protesting about inaccessible buses and trains. Thousands more turned up to the Disability Benefits Consortium rallies in London, Glasgow and Manchester to demand "proper incomes" rather than disability benefits.
Credit Disability Now 1990 Rebecca Reynolds

Summary of Main Findings

The following are the main findings from the 6 OPCS reports on disability:

Prevalence of disability

- There are at least 6.5 million people with disabilities in Britain - the first report showed there are 6.2 million disabled adults, more than double the previous official estimate. The third report estimated there are some 360,000 disabled children.

- Over 14 per cent of the population of Britain have a disability such as to be classified as disabled for the purposes of the OPCS survey.

- 5.8 million disabled adults live in private households with an additional 422,000 in communal establishments, i.e. in some form of residential institution. OF the 360,000 children under 16 with a disability, less han 2 per cent - or 5,500 - live in communal establishments.

- Most disabled adults - especially those most severely disabled and those in communal establishments - had more than one type of disability. The majority of disabled children also had more than one type of disability.

- Of the 5.8 million disabled adults in private households, 58 per cent (3.4 million) are women. The survey also shows that there is a higher rate of disability amongst elderly women than amongst elderly men.

- The rates of disability for "Asians" and "West Indians" (OPCS classifications) are 12.6% and 15.1% respectively. The equivalent figure for "Whites" is 13.7%.

Aged and disability

- 4.2 million disabled adults (or 69%) in Britain are aged 60 or over.

- The prevalence rate of disability for people over 60 is just 355 per thousand of the population, showing that the majority of pensioners are not disabled. Only amongst those who are aged 85 or more are the majority disabled.

Types of disability

- Amongst disabled adults, locomotor problems are the most common types of disability, affecting over 4 million adults. Around two and a half million respectively have hearing difficulties and personal care difficulties. Disabilities related to intellectua functioning were more common amongst people in communal establishments than in private households.

- Amongst disabled children, the most common types of disability had to do with behaviour followed by communication, continence, locomotion and intellectual functioning.

Employment status

- Only 31% of disabled adults below pension age were in paid employment compared with 68% of the general population.

- The overall unemployment rates for economically active disabled men and disabled women were 27% and 20% respectively. At the time the OPCS survey was carried out, about 11% of economically active men and 9% of economically active women were unemployed in the general population. Thus, disabled people were more than twice as likely to be unemployed as people in general.

- 48% of people in the least severe disability category 1 were working, compared with only 2% of those in the highest severity category 10.

- The unemployment rate is higher amongst parents with disabled children than in the general population.

Financial circumstances

- The incomes of people with disabilities are substantially below the income levels of the rest of the population.

- Three-quarters of disabled adults in private households - 4.3 million people - rely on State benefits as their main source of income - with an average total income of only £65.20 per week.

4.5 million disabled people live in households where there are no earners. The highest proportions of households with earners were found amongst married people under pension age.

The earnings of disabled people who do have jobs are substantially lower than those of non-disabled employees, and drop further with increased severity of disability. When parents of disabled children are in paid work, their earnings tend to be lower than other parents.

The gap between the average income of disabled people and non-disabled people was over £39 per week at 1988 prices, once the extra costs of disability are taken into account. Based on the OPCS findings, the total average gap between the incomes of disabled people and non-disabled people is estimated at nearly £8 billion per year.

The gap between the weekly income of families with disabled children and other families was over £24 per week, once the estimated extra costs of disability are taken into account.

- Over 5 million disabled people get no non-means-tested help with the extra costs of disability - disabled people have to depend heavily on means-tested benefits.

- Over 70% of disabled adults were on incomes which were three-quarters or less of average income, and 35% were on incomes below half of averages income (once estimated extra spending related to disability was taken into account).

- Over 2 million disabled people with disabilities estimated that they spend over £5.20 per week on costs arising from their disability; over 1 million spent more than £10 per week; over half a million spent over £15 per week; and 1.4 million felt they needed to spend more than they were able to afford.

- For mobility allowance and attendance allowance respectively, 45% of those not receiving the benefit had not heard of it. Only 5% of those getting attendance allowance had a carer who received invalid care allowance (the specific carer's benefit - entitlement of ICA is linked to the disabled person being in receipt of attendance allowance).

- Only 46% of disabled householders were owner-occupiers compared with 59% of the general population. The rate of owner-occupation amongst families with disabled children was 52%.

Informal Care and Help

- 22% of disabled adults living at home needed help with self-care activities such as getting in and out of bed or a chair, washing, dressing. The proportion of those needing this type of help rose to 94% in the highest severity categories 9-10.

- OPCS estimate that there are 1.2 million people in Britain who are providing varying amounts of help with self-care needs of people with disabilities. 40% of them are aged 65 or over; and 65% are women.

Services

- 30% of disabled adults in private households lived alone. Those who were living alone were more likely to have received local authority social services, such as meals on wheels and home help.

- When disabled adults were asked about services they would like more of, chiropody, local authority home helps, and community nursing were amongst those most frequently mentioned.

Social activities

- 15% of disabled people in communal establishments said they never had visitors, compared with 4% of people in private households. Visitors were also more frequent for people in private households: 80% had a visitor at least once a week whilst this was the case for only 25% of people in residential establishments.

- Half of the total of adults in private households had been on holiday or respite care in the past year, compared to 20% in communal establishments.

How OPCS Measured Disability

OPCS defined disability as "... a restriction or lack of ability to perform normal activities, which has resulted from the impairment of a structure or function of the body or mind." (OPCS 1; p.xi).

This is based on the concept of disability proposed by the World Health Organisation's International Classification of Impairments, Disabilities and Handicaps. Thus, rather than focusing on the precise nature of a person's impairment - whether physical or mental - OPCS used a definition of disability which looks at the results of an impairment i.e. the things that people cannot do in terms of every day activities.

OPCS also took the view that disability should be thought of as a "continuum" ranging from slight to severe disability. So the precise definition of disability for any particular survey depends on setting a threshold level along this continuum. Estimates of the prevalence of disability are, therefore, based on how many people are found to have disabilities above this threshold level.

People interviewed for the survey were asked questions about what they can do rather than what they do do. OPCS

Day Centre Cardiff from CSV annual Report.
Credit David Hevey.

stated that this was because benefit assessment is made on this basis.

A panel of judges was used to construct the overall measure of severity of disability (for detail as to how this was carried out, see OPCS Report 1 and Disability Alliance briefing on OPCS Report 1).

The overall severity scores were then grouped into ten categories of severity of disability from 1 - the least severe -to 10 - the most severe.

OPCS - Still an Underestimate

The OPCS findings are an indictment of successive government policies concerning the incomes of people with disabilities, and highlight the need for an adequate system of disability benefits together with positive action on employment opportunities. However, even these figures under-estimate the true situation:

- the definition of disability and the disability 'threshold', used for the OPCS survey, excluded a number of disabled people who nevertheless have extra costs because of their disability.

- The extra costs of disability were seriously under-estimated, partly as a result of the OPCS interviewing techniques where there was insufficient time or opportunity to get full details of people's expenditure. As OPCS states: "...people found it very difficult to estimate what proportion of the total cost of, say heating was incurred because of their disability. In effect we were asking questions about a hypothetical situation in which they were not disabled." (OPCS 1; p.35).

There is also the inescapable fact that many people do not incur extra costs because of their disability as their income is too low; to put it crudely: "If you haven't got it, you can't spend it."

OPCS itself states that "Because of the problems ... in obtaining reliable estimates of extra expenditure, all the results presented in this chapter should be treated with some caution." (OPCS 1; p.36).

- Northern Ireland was excluded from the survey. Belatedly, similar surveys have been set up in Northern Ireland but will not be completed for at least another two years.

- The findings on financial circumstances of disable people were based on information collected by OPCS in 1985 and take no account of the massive cuts in social security benefits which have taken place since then. In particular, the Disability Alliance estimates that over 1 million people with disabilities lost out because of the April 1988 benefit changes (implemented as a result of the 1986 Social Security Act).

- Any examination of the OPCS findings on the financial circumstance of people with disabilities leads to the clear conclusion that poverty is the reality of everyday life for the majority of disabled people and their families. But the most notable omission in the reports is any reference to poverty.

With thanks to Disability Alliance for permission to reproduce.

Disability Alliance
25 Denmark Street
LONDON WC2H 8NJ
October 1989

Notes

1 OPCS surveys of Disability in Great Britain: Report 1 -'The Prevalence of disability among adults, HMSO, ISBN 0-11-691229-4, price £10.70

OPCS surveys of Disability in Great Britain: Report 2 - 'The financial circumstances of disabled adults living in private households, HMSO, ISBN 0-11-691235-0, ptivr £11.50.

OPCS surveys of Disability in Great Britain: Report 3 - 'The prevalence of disability among children', HMSO, ISBN 0-11691250-2. price £10.60.

OPCS surveys of Disability in Great Britain: Report 4 - 'Disabled adults: services, transport and employment', HMSO, ISBN 0-11-691257-X, price £15.60.

OPCS surveys of Disability in Great Britain: Report 5 - 'The financial circumstances of families with disabled children living in private households', HMSO, ISBN 0-11-691264-2, price £9.00

OPCS surveys of Disability in Great Britain: Report 6 - 'Disabled children: services, transport and education', HMSO, ISBN 0-11-691266-9, price £14.30.

2 Social Security Advisory Committee, Benefits for Disabled People: a Strategy for Change, HMSO, ISBN 0-11-3211-84-8, price £5.90.

The Disability Alliance also has various materials available relating to the case for a comprehensive disability income scheme:

- "Poverty and Disability: Breaking the Link - the policy statement of theDisability Alliance - is available price £3.00 post-free. A 16 pager summary is also available free of charge. We can let you have as many copies of the summary as you need, so please distribute it as widely as possible.

- Briefings on the first two OPCS reports are available from the Disability Alliance priced £2.50 each post-free.

- A brief summary of the findings of the two OPCS reports and the SSAC report are contained in an article in the 14th edition of the Disability Rights Handbook, currently available priced £3.75. The Handbook also contains an article on the effects of the April 1988 social security changes on people with disabilities.

Disabled Parents

Micheline Mason

Because the stereotype of disabled people has, for so long, been that of a dependant, cared for by others, it has been very difficult for society to even acknowledge that disabled parents exist. If we exist, then not only are disabled people 'carers' ourselves, it must also mean we have had sex, another thing disabled people 'don't do'. We could not find *any* examples of films, books, plays, TV programmes or anything else generally available to the public which portrays the experiences of disabled parents. Yet, of course, there are many, many of us. Some of us have children who also have disabilities, such as myself. Being a parent is the best and most important thing in my life, at present. My love and commitment to my daughter is the motivating force which spurred me to doing this pack. Richard Rieser is also a parent as are many of the other disabled contributors.

Judy Watson

In my second year of teaching at the Sheppey School, I became pregnant and my daughter, Hazel, was born in March 1976.

I went back to work when Hazel was eight weeks old and her father and I separated when she was

'Lucy and Micheline' *David Hevey.*

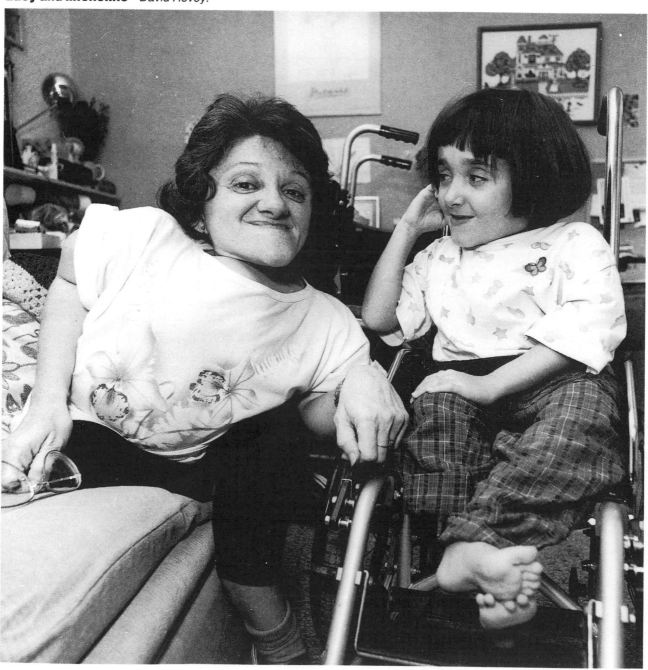

five months old. For almost six years, I brought Hazel up on my own. I always worked full-time and had very little assistance generally. My family lived quite a long way away in Milton Keynes and rarely visited. I had a home help once a week to clean the house and a very good child-minder. Hazel seemed to know right from the start that I had a disability. She was a very placid baby and slept a lot. I could feed, change and bath her by touch and the only real problems arose when she started on solids. I was not very good at feeding her with a spoon; her little head would waver from side to side as she looked at things and very often the food ended up in her ear rather than her mouth. She started feeding herself when she was thirteen months and never made a mess. She must have got tired of being hungry! She was a very easy child: she did not walk until she was seventeen months and never crawled, she never ran away, emptied cupboards, climbed furniture, in fact, she was not very active at all. This was a great relief to me although I was always careful about safety gates and would never allow her in the kitchen while I was cooking.

I'm not a good cook and I don't enjoy it. Hazel and I lived on convenience foods, things like beefburgers and tinned spaghetti. I rarely fry things but use the grill or the oven instead. We used to eat a lot of baked potatoes and salad. I always go for things which require least effort. We eat much better these days because Matthew likes cooking and is good at it!

I sometimes feel a bit sad about Hazel missing out on things when she was small, but we were very close and I gave her lots of love and played with her a great deal at weekends and in the holidays. I had some books for children in Braille which I read to her over and over again but I could never do painting with her or take her to the park on my own. Hazel never did learn to ride a bike and now that she is thirteen, she says it's too late. I had many friends, however, who would take us to the beach during the summer or take us to the pantomime or the zoo and so on. I will always be grateful to them for making Hazel's life very full and normal; in fact, I think she probably had more outings than many children.

Our first holiday was when Hazel was six and we went camping in France with some friends. There were six adults and two children and we really had a good time. It worked well because there were enough adults to share taking me from place to place so that I didn't feel I was being too dependent on one person. One of the worst things about being blind is the lack of choice and the lack of freedom. When I'm in a strange place, i can't even go to the toilet when I want to. I have to wait until I think someone is free to come with me. Sometimes when I'm out with Matthew, I dread going to the toilet and purposely drink as little as possible so that I won't have to go too often. Matthew and I lurk outside the Ladies at a cinema or theatre for instance, until a woman comes along and I have to ask a complete stranger to take me inside. I really hate it! Some people are very nice and don't mind at all, while others are thrown by it and are obviously very frightened and don't know how to react. I suppose it's because they have never met a disabled person before: I think able-bodied people are often frightened because they know it could be them one day. Disability can strike at any time after all.

Being a parent is a difficult job, and those of us with disabilities have found for the most part that there is no recognition of our role, and therefore no statutory support, housing, domiciliary assistance or anything else yet designed to assist us, with our task. This is especially critical if you are a single parent.

Education for parenthood would be a desirable thing for all young people in schools, and even more so for disabled people and people with learning difficulties.

At the same time, it needs to be recognised that some conditions will make it very difficult, or impossible to have children. Our experience has shown that it is not only difficult for 'lay' people to get accurate information about the implications for childbirth of particular conditions, but it is also very difficult for us. Doctors are often (not always!) fearful and prejudiced in this area, and there are many examples of people being given accurate information which is not based on clinical evidence, but on imaginings:

"So one time I went to the hospital and this doctor talked to me about having a child, and I was asking him some questions. And he said "You know that you will never be able to have a child, because you are small and the kid might not live through that, or you either".
Frances Delroach.

This young woman has the same condition and is about the same size as me (3ft tall). By contrast, my consultant studied my pregnant body and said

"There's not much of you is there! Still, nature is wonderful. Babies make the room for themselves. We'll have you in at seven months though, because there is a small risk that cramped conditions might make the baby decide to be born early, like twins often do".

My approach to the medical profession was to present them with a 'fait accompli', but I respect the fact that not many others would think this wise.

Information about hereditary conditions is also an incomplete science, and still leaves the potential parents with extremely difficult decisions to make.

These issues are slightly easier to think about if put into a broader context. A surprisingly high percentage of couples, able-bodied or not, have difficulty conceiving, or are unable to have children. There are also people who have life styles which make it very unlikely they will become parents, e.g., gay men or nuns and monks. So it cannot be assumed that *anyone* will want, or be able to become a parent. However, if the person concerned wants to be a parent and cannot be a parent, whether they are able bodied or not, the issue is the same - loss. It seems that in our culture parenthood is such an expectation

that the experience of not being able to have children is one of bereavement. You have to grieve for the children you have never had.

However, it cannot be stressed too much how much influence the wrong or right attitude of 'allies' can have on our perceptions of what is possible:

"I had understanding consultants looking after me who said, you know, come back when you want to be a mother and we will advise you, and almost, well the nice feeling that they assumed that you were going to lead a normal life, have children, which I always feel very grateful for, because I realise it sinks quite deep into my subconcious and it did. It oriented me towards leading a much more normal and full life then perhaps some other people might be able to do with the same disabilities" *Mother with Polio - wheelchair user.*

DISABLED MUM'S FIVE-YEAR WAIT TO BE RE-HOUSED

By Claire Hynes

Brave Angela appeals to council to honour its promise of a new flat

A paralysed mother is at her wits end after waiting to move into a council flat promised to her five years ago.

Wheelchair-bound Angela Whitelock is virtually a prisoner in her home, because the height of her doorstep prevents her from leaving the flat without assistance.

And now the 24 year old is unable to cope with looking after her six-month-old baby in the cramped east London flat. If a fire broke out, both mother and child would be trapped.

Angela, who was confined to a wheelchair after falling from a window nine years ago, battled with Hackney Council to secure suitable accommodation, way back in 1984.

Eventually, after over 200 people organised sit-ins in council meetings and petitioned councillors, the

council decided to renovate a property for Angela which would meet her special needs.

Hoped

Persistent Angela received a letter from the council, saying that they hoped she could move into the flat in 1985, and that her case was a shining example of housing need.

But Angela famed: "I'm supposed to be an example and I've been waiting five years. I sometimes get up in the morning crying, I can't get around the flat as it's so small".

Her husband Delroy Findley added: "It's really

difficult for Angela. The council have kept her waiting for too long and it's making her miserable."

The council's director of housing, Ian Booth, said: "Delays with repairs contributed to the five-year wait, because of the delapidated state of the property plus the Government closed down the council's repairs department."

Ready

But he estimated that the flat would be ready for Angela within six to nine months.

"I've asked the allocations department to look into providing her with temporary housing as a matter of urgency, because it's clear she is struggling to cope with the baby," he said.

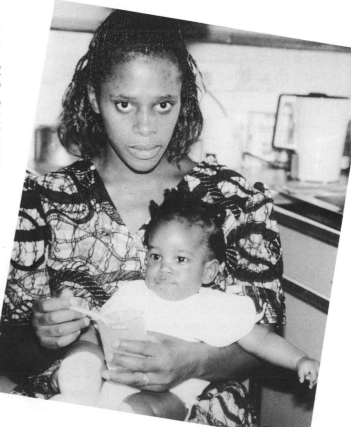

Disabled Parents and Schools

The same things which prevent disabled children and disabled teachers from being involved in schools, also prevent disabled parents from active participation in our children's school life.

This is unacceptable, especially now that parent governors are to have greater influence over the running of schools. Our participation as equals must be actively sought and made possible by the policy and practice of each school.

Reading:
'The Emotions and Experiences of Some Disabled Mothers'
National Childbirth Trust 1984

Video:
'Giving them the Best' 4 parents in conversation (see resource list)

On Being a Parent with a Disability
by Lois Keith

When I started looking for a local primary school for my first child I looked at the school's educational policy, the facilities and the attitudes of the teachers. By the time she was ready to start, I was also looking at wheelchair access.

The school nearest our home had been built in the '60's and although it looked from the outside if it was on one floor, there were short flights of stairs everywhere. A school just a little further away was in a typical Victorian three decker building but at least the ground floor was accessible to a wheelchair user. It also had the advantage for me of having another mother who had a similar disability and a child the same age as mine. I knew that her support would be very valuable.

The first couple of years were not too difficult since the nursery and infant classrooms were traditionally on the ground floor and it wasn't too much trouble to arrange talks with the Head or medicals in the Schoolkeeper's office on the ground floor. It took us two years, a lot of hassles and many 'phone calls and letters to Divisional Office to make the dustbin ramp which was steep and treacherous, safe for independent wheelchair users and to get the door widened. At this stage we still hoped that we would be able to get a lift installed which would give us access to the entire school. At this time I was also having a battle to get myself re-employed as a secondary school teacher with the ILEA and was running out of fighting energy.

As Rachel began to move through the Infants and her sister joined the Nursery, I began to worry about their future. I didn't know which would be worse; me not being able to get into their classrooms when they moved upstairs or them feeling different and isolated from other classes of similar age. The one class of big children among all the little infants. And what would other parents of children in their classes have to say about these arrangements?

On the day I deputised my husband to discuss this with the Head teacher, it became clear that the Authority was not going to provide a life and that the Head, in these difficult times, did not consider this issue anywhere near the top of her list of priorities. It was in this conversation that she mentioned that she had in fact had complaints from other parents about wheelchairs 'clogging up the corridors' at the beginning and end of school. I found this very upsetting, not so much at the comment - I could imagine a harassed mother with a double buggy and a couple more children saying this in irritation. But I doubted whether the Head would have repeated a racist remark to a black parent who had come to discuss an issue of equal opportunities with her. Perhaps she had assumed that since my husband was a walker he would share this point of view. It was yet another example of both the prejudices and the lack of awareness of the issues around disability.

It was in discussion with Rachel's class teacher who is both very good at her job and a sympathetic listener that it occurred to me for the first time that I should not have to think of it as MY problem but as an issue for the school to deal with. By this time there were three parents who use wheelchairs and we have four children between us. It was a great relief to me when this teacher took it to a staff meeting in much the same way as they might take on responsibility for involving parents who are not fluent English speakers into the life of the school.

The staff took on the issue of where our children were to be taught and incorporated these needs into a policy they were already thinking of developing. This was to mix up age groups in the various areas of the school and not to keep Infants and Juniors on entirely separate floors. This might encourage Juniors to be more aware of the needs of the little ones and the Infants would learn about the kinds of things they would do when they were older.

Parents of little ones (not the littlest but still pretty

small) soon accepted having to go up a flight of stairs and my own child doesn't feel isolated because her class of first year Juniors and the parallel classes are next to each other on the bottom corridor. I am sure there will be difficulties in the future and people's prejudices and nervousness around disability go so deep that it would be foolish to assume that all the battles have been won. Of course things won't be right until myself and other disabled parents have access to every bit of the school but in the meantime little things do help. Concerts are now arranged as a matter of course in the downstairs hall and there is also a ramp to the back entrance of the school. Following a nasty row with a temporary schoolkeeper, there is now a list in their office to remind them to open the door which leads to the ramp in good time for evening meetings.

I feel more confident that I have the right to be able to go into my children's classrooms regularly to see their work, meet their friends and talk to their teacher. The school is accepting their responsibility to think about the best ways to do this, so that my own children and those of other disabled parents are not set apart from their peers.

Lois Keith, January 1990

'Lois Keith with her daughters Rachel and Miriam'.

Credit Jane Dibblin.

Organizations Controlled by Disabled People

British Council of Organizations of Disabled People (BCODP)
St. Mary's Church, Greenlaw Street, London SE16 5AR
Southern Office: 01-316 4184
Northern Office: 0773 40246

Spinal Injuries Association (SIA)
01-444 2121
Yeoman House, 76 St. James Lane, Muswell Hill, London N10

Asian People with Disabilities Alliance
01-965 3860
105a Melville Road, Stonebridge, London NW10

British Deaf Association (BDA)
Vistel: Carlisle 28719
Voice: Carlisle 48844
38 Victoria Place, Carlisle CA1 1HU

National Federation of the Blind
0924 377012
Unity House, Smyth Street, Westgate, Wakefield,
W. Yorks WF1 1ER

Association of Blind and Partially Sighted Teachers and Students (ABAPSTAS)
0772 37027
BM Box 6727, London WC1N 3XX
and c/o Equal Opportunities Section,
Nottingham County Council, Guildhall, Notts

People First
Kings Fund Centre, 126 Albert Street, London NW1
(Self Advocacy organization of people with learning difficulties)

Association of Blind Asians
01-609 3590
14 Stranraer Way, Freeling Street, London N1 0DR

Sequel (Formerly Possum Users Association)
01-622 3738
27 Thames House, 140 Battersea Park Road, London SW11
Self run association offering advice and help in obtaining communication aids for people with major physical impairments

National League of the Blind and Disabled
01-808 6030
2 Tenterden Road, London N17
(Recognized Trade Union)

Disabled Drivers Association
01-692 7141
Drake House, 18 Creekside, London SE8 3DZ

Association of Disabled Professionals
0737 352366
The Stables, 73 Pound Road, Banstead, Surrey SM7 2HU

Union of the Physically Impaired Against Segregation (UPIAS)
Flat 2, St Giles Court, Dane Road, Ealing, London W13 9AQ

Greater Manchester Coalition of Disabled People
061 224 2722
11 Anson Road, Manchester M14 5BY

Nottinghamshire Coalition of Disabled People
0602 475531
32a Park Row, Nottingham NG1 6GR

Avon Coalition of Disabled People
c/o 81 Valentine Close, Whitchurch, Bristol, Co Avon

Derbyshire Coalition of Disabled People
0246 865305
117 High Street, Clay Cross, Chesterfield, Derbyshire

Milton Keynes Council of Disabled People
0908 677415
c/o Oliver Wells School, Farmborough, Netherfield,
Milton Keynes MK6 4AL

Glasgow Forum on Disability (The Voice of Disabled People)
041 2276125
Room 21, 1st Floor, McIver House, 51 Cadogan Street,
Glasgow G2 7BR

Hampshire Centre for Integrated Living
0730 68208
39 Queens Road, Petersfield, Hants GU32 3BB

Nottingham Centre for Integrated Living
0773 40246
Long Close, Cemetry Lane, Ripley, Derbyshire DE5 3HY

Greenwich Centre for Integrated Living
St Marys Church, Greenlaw Street, London SE16 5AR

London Disability Arts Forum (LDAF)
Tel and minicom: 01-935 5588/935 8999
The Diorama, Peto Place, London NW1

People First - London and Thames
01-267 6111
c/o The Kings Fund Centre, 126 Albert Street, London NW1

Greenwich Association of Disabled People
01-305 2221
Christchurch Forum, Trafalgar Road, London SE10

Waltham Forest Association of People with Disabilities
01-509 0812
Old School Building, 1a Warner Road, London E17

Kingston Association of Disabled People
53 Canbury Park Road, Kingston-on-Thames,
Surrey KT2 6LQ

Disabled in Camden (DISC)
01-387 0700
7 Crowndall Road, London NW1

Gay Mens Disabled Group
c/o Gays the Word, 66 Marchmant Street,
London WC1N 1AN
(Aims to lessen the isolation of gay disabled men)

Gemma
BM Box 5700, London WC1N 3XX
(lessens the isolation of disabled lesbians of all ages)

Regard
88 Maidstone Road, London N11
Compaigning organization of disabled lesbians and gay men

London Dial-a-Ride Users Association
01-482 2325
St Margarets, 25 Leighton Road, London NW5 2QD
Advice and information on transport needs of disabled people

Organizations not known to be controlled by disabled people

Centre for Studies on Integrated Education (CSIE)
415 Edgware Road, London NW2 6NB

Parents in Partnership (PIP)
01-767 3211
Top Portacabin, Clare House, St Georges Hospital,
London SW17
Support organization for parents of children with 'Special Educational Needs' in London

81 Network
S. England: 0279 503244 N. England: 05652 666
52 Magnaville Road, Bishops Stortford, Herts CM23 4DW
National support organization for parents of children with 'Special Educational Needs', especially implementing the 81 Education Act

The Integration Alliance – London
c/o 34a Dafforne Road, Tooting, London SW17 8TZ
New campaigning organization of parents of children with 'SEN's'; disabled adults; people with learning difficulties; young people; disabled teachers; disabled parents; professionals; schools; organizations and any other allies who wish to replace segregated education with supported integrated education. Offers consultancy and Disability Equality Training

The London Boroughs Disability Resource Team (LBDRT)
Rooms 92-95, The County Hall, London SE1
Provide registered 'Disability Equality Trainers' for courses for LA employees

Centre for Motor and Associated Communcation Handicaps (CENMACH)
Charlton Park School, Charlton Park Road, London SE7 8HX
(Assessment and provision of aids for use in schools)

Disabled Living Foundation (Aids Exhibition/Advice Centre)
01-289 6111
380 Harrow Road, London W9

Centre on Environment for the Handicapped
01-222 7980
35 Great Smith Street, London SW1P 3BJ
(Provides advice on designing environments to meet the needs of all disabled people)

Banstead Place Mobility Centre
07373 51674
Park Road, Banstead, Surrey SM7 3EE
(Provides information on all aspects of outdoor mobility, assessments and driving lessons for disabled people)

Mobility International
228 Borough High Street, London SE1 1JX
(Offers 'International Experiences' to young people with and without disabilities)

HALO (Housing Association Liaison Officer)
01-352 0909
11 Apollo Place, London SW10 0ET
(Maintains a register of people with physical disabilities who need wheelchair adapted housing. Linked with Housing Associations throughout London)

Disability Alliance Educational and Research Association
01-240 0806
25 Denmark Street, London WC2
(Advice on rights and benefits)

Royal Association for Disability and Rehabilitation (RADAR)
01-637 5400
25 Mortimer Street, London W1
(Information and advice on all aspects of disability)

Condition - specific organizations

Asthma Society
01-226 2260
300 Upper Street, Islington, London N1 2XX

Arthritis Care
01-253 0902
6 Grosvenor Crescent, London SW1

Association for all Speech Impaired Children
01-236 6487
347 Central Markets, London EC1

Association for Spina Bifida and Hydrocephalus
01-388 1382
22 Upper Woburn Place, London WC1

British Epilepsy Association
01-403 4111
92 Tooley Street, London SE1

British Diabetic Association
01-323 1531
10 Queen Anne Street, London W1

British Dyslexia Association
Reading 668271
98 London Road, Reading, Berks

Brittle Bone Society
0382 017771
Unit 4, Block 20, Carbendie Road, Dunsinane Industrial
Estate, Dundee, Scotland

London Dyslexia Association
01-995 5316
2/20 Wellesley Road, London W4 4BN

Cystic Fibrosis Research Trust
01-464 7211
5 Blyth Road, Bromley

Downs Syndrome Association
01-720 0008
1st Floor, 12-13 Clapham Common, Southside,
London SW4 7AA

Friederich's Ataxia Group
0483 272741
Burleigh Lodge, Knowle Lane, Cranleigh, Surrey

Haemophilia Society
01-407 1010
PO Box 9, 16 Trinity Street, London SE1 1DE

Mencap
01-253 9433
123 Golden Lane, London EC1
01-250 4105
115 Golden Lane, London EC1 (London Div)
01-250 4250

Muscular Dystrophe Group of Gt Britain
01-720 8056
Nattass House, Macauley Road, London SW4

Royal National Institute for the Blind (RNIB)
01-388 1266
224 Great Portland Street, London W1N 6AA

Royal National Institute for the Deaf (RNID)
01-387 8033
105 Gower Street, London WC1

The Spastics Society
01-636 5020
12 Park Crescent, London W1

Sickle Cell Society
01-961 7795
Green Lane, Barrets Green Road, London NW10

UK Thalassaemia Society
01-348 0437
107 Nightingale Lane, London N8 7QY

127

Pride Against Prejudice

Transforming Attitudes to Disability

Jenny Morris

'This book is a celebration of our strength and a pride part of our taking pride in ourselves, a pride which incorporates our disability and values it.'

£6.95 Women's's Press

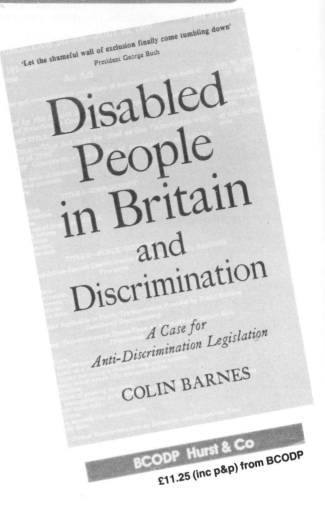

'Let the shameful wall of exclusion finally come tumbling down'
President George Bush

Disabled People in Britain and Discrimination

A Case for Anti-Discrimination Legislation

COLIN BARNES

BCODP Hurst & Co

£11.25 (inc p&p) from BCODP

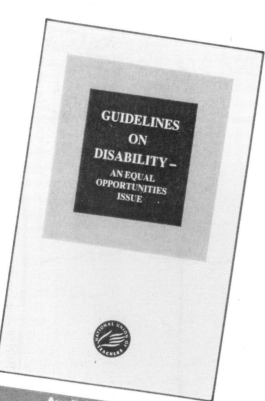

GUIDELINES ON DISABILITY – AN EQUAL OPPORTUNITIES ISSUE

Available NUT £1
1 Mabledon Place WC1H 9BD

THE POLITICS OF DISABLEMENT

Michael Oliver

POLLING STATION

Critical Texts in Social Work and the Welfare State

£8.99 Macmillan

Section 3
Good Practices

Disabled Women Protest Dec. 1991

'Field Trip'

Credit Sally and Richard Greenhill.

Summary:
A whole school policy should include a written committment to approaching disability as an equal opportunities issue in relation to:

Access to the environment.
Access to the curriculum.
Including disability issues within the curriculum.
Assessments and statements of special needs.
Disapplication and modification of the National Curriculum.
Support staff.
Co-ordination of peripatetic services e.g., speech and physiotherapy.
Communication.
BSL as a 'mother tongue'.
Language.
Images and literature.
Abuse - name calling and harassment.
Transport.
Trips.
Medication and nursing assistance.
Liaison.

Obtaining and maintaining 'special' equipment.
Consultation with parents.
Self-representation of disabled pupils.
Employment and support for disabled teachers and other staff.
Disabled parents.
Physical education and physical disability.
Sports and 'able-ism'.
Clubs and extra-curricular activities and services e.g., playcentres.
Medical emergencies.
Health and safety.
Involvement of Trade Unions and staff representatives.
Representation of disability and learning difficulties on Governing Bodies.
INSET for teachers, support staff and governors by Disabled Trainers.

Towards a Whole School Policy on Disability

by Richard Rieser

In 1985 the Fish Report: Educational Opportunities for All found (para 1.1.17) that while ILEA had a clear policy to promote equal opportunities and overcome disadvantage in respect of class, sex and race it had no such similar guidelines for children and young people with disabilities.

Fish puts forward a policy based on the view that disabilities and difficulties (learning) become more or less handicapping *depending on the expectations of others and on social contexts* para (1.1.25). Adopting the social model we use in the project Fish goes on to outline basic principles drawing on the Warnock Report (1978) and the 1981 Act.

The aims of education for children and young people with disabilities and significant difficulties are the same as those for all children and young people. They should have opportunities to achieve these aims, to associate with their contemporaries, whether similarly disabled, or not and have access to the whole range of opportunities in education, training, leisure and community activities available to all. Disabilities and (learning) difficulties do not diminish the right of equal access to and participation in society! 1.1.22.

Following the basic principle the report goes on to state that this principle requires respect and acknowledgement of all disabled children and young people as participants in society with equal access.

It then goes on that integration for all must be the only goal that fits these principles, but they acknowledge this to be a process and not a state, that merely placing disabled children in mainstream schools is not integration.

Special Educational Needs are relative terms. They are relative to the extent that schools and colleges can and do provide for a range of individual differences in organisation, regular programmes and curriculum, and in the attitudes of teachers to those differences. To illustrate this point there is clearly a great difference in the ability to cope with difference between a primary class taught from a well thought-out, child centred approach, and a more formal chalk and talk setting. In the first many more children will not have special needs being able to develop at their own pace. Similarly the old streamed grammar school class would have been far less able to deal with special educational need than a well run mixed ability comprehensive class.

However, one thing is clear. The child centred primary class and the mixed ability secondary class are far more vulnerable to failure if class sizes increase or are already too large. In Italy where they have integrated they did so with reduced class size and more support.

Unfortunately Fish expected to move to integration in ILEA without mentioning additional resources for support, INSET and smaller classes which are essential. Integration is expensive, but it is a right for disabled people.

Clearly any LEA or whole school policy that is seeking to give equal opportunities to all has to be based on mixed ability teaching groups of a reasonable size. The current 30 is too large and must be brought down significantly. This enables much greater teacher time to be given to each child including the many who will need to have the curriculum made accessible to them.

This last point Fish does recognise.

"Catering for individual difference within (primary school), comprehensive school and college system demands that *providing* equal opportunities and ensuring equal access to them are recognised as different issues as many children and young people with disabilities and learning difficulties need sustained help to make use of the opportunities available to them."

So far we have done no more than indicate the basis of a principle for a whole school policy.

Will Swann in his introduction to 'Including Pupils with Disabilities' (1987) makes the important point that in seeking to encourage the development of an education system which responds flexibility to children's abilities, interests and backgrounds and which does not devalue pupils on these grounds, we need to see children with disabilities participating in the curriculum on the same basis.

This does not only mean integrating pupils with disabilities into the existing curriculum as an access issue. Without widespread reform of the mainstream curriculum only a minority of disabled pupils can be successfully integrated. Indeed Swann points out the integration of the few on the terms of existing curriculum will reinforce barriers of attitude and complacency for the many.

The definition used here of the curriculum as the sum total of the pupils' experience at school is the right one to use when looking at equality for disabled children and students.

131

Language

Therefore any whole school policy must include making explicit what was often implicit and revaluating our assumptions against our policy goal of equality and access for disabled children and students (See Stereotypes/Language).

Language used must be examined. This will include taking up name calling or using impairments in a negative way. Ableist language with its evaluative connotations must be examined (see Lois Keith poem).

'Are you *deaf* boy. Didn't you *hear* what I said'.

'Its on the page in front of you can't you *see*? Are you *blind* girl?'

'Are you *stupid* an *idiot*, imbecile'.

'*Stand* on your own *Two Feet*'.

All the above I have heard teachers say. Neither are the following acceptable.

Thlid from Thalidomide
Spaso - Spastic - Cerebral Palsy
Cripple/Hop-a-long
Thicko or *Dummy*

These are more commonly heard in playground or staffroom.

'School-kids choir, Haringey'.

Images

The images in text books, wall displays, books in the library, reading books, videos and films used in the school must not reinforce the negative stereotypes of disabled people.

Last year I looked through the entire output of the ILEA Centre for Learning Resources. Apart from material expressly designed for 'Special Ed' there were very few examples of images of disability at all let alone positive ones.

ILEA Centre Learning Resources*

Nearly every ILEA infant classroom has the CLR ABC, brightly coloured, gender balanced, with lots of different ethnic groups, but only two boys with glasses as images of disability. Even the obvious stereotyped W is for Wheelchair isn't there. (Only 3% of disabled people are in wheelchairs).

Copy Art (1987) made an attempt to produce images that can be used in posters/worksheets. But nearly all the disabled are in wheelchairs or with great big hearing aids. No signing, using a stick.

'Everyone Counts' and Count Me In (1985) for primary maths materials did seek to include images of disability in maths work cards. Unfortunately this good practice has not been continued in more recent ILEA maths

*These are now published by Harcourt Brace and Jovanovich.

David Hevey.

productions. Out of about 5,000 SMILE cards one has a problem featuring someone in a wheelchair. 'Kevin and Lee Play Together' in the (PT6) photo-talk series for bilingual learners features in a positive way a disabled boy.

Many obvious opportunities to include disability and images of disability are missed. The environment series - 'Make Your Way' - only has two activities - a sensory walk and an access simulation using a wheelchair.

The ILEA Music Guidelines (1977) in Section B has six photos of disabled children but none are in an integrated setting and there is no discussion about music and sensory impairments.

Other Guidelines on the Curriculum like Health Education, Early Years, Food, RE approved syllabus, Extending Literacy have no images of disability.

Commonly used resources like 'Ourselves', 'Celebrations', 'Face Play', 'Just Like Us' and 'Look Out', also leave out images of disability. Perhaps the worst omissions are in the resources specifically designed for use with children with SEN. Looking at 'Myself', 'Makaton Pictures', 'Transport Photos' and 'Listening Skills' do not include any image of children or adults with disability. The underlying message to disabled children and indeed able-bodied is you/they are not in the picture and we would rather ignore you. There are a few other parts of the CLR output to comment on or recommend. There are some useful images of disability and information in the Teachers' Videos Series and Classroom Observation - Special Educational Needs.

All those shown in an integrated setting have mild learning difficulty except the last

CSEN
1 Wendy 8 Primary
4 Roger 12 Secondary
11 Jason S8 Primary
14 Jason V8 Primary
17 Jay 3 year Boy in Primary Nursery
18 Daniel 4 year old with Physical Disability in a Primary School

'Resources for the Visually Impaired' is an excellent book on strategies and resources for teaching the Visually Impaired.

'Talking with Signs' is based on Signed English rather than British Sign Language and gives 42 most commonly signed words. Mary Brennan (1987) in Booth and Swann, explains clearly that when signed English which reduces the gestural language of BSL into discrete signs that match individual words is taught to Deaf Children rather than BSL they are denied access to their own culture and language.

The Braille Numbers Pack (19.. .. resource both for partially sighted .. seeing children. As a different system.. is of general interest.

Children's literature is no more hopeful (see section on Children's Literature), with few publishers and illustrators just including people with disabilities as they do black people or girls in traditionally male roles, as a matter of course.

So clearly a disability monitoring group of images, books and resources would need to be set up in every school and college.

Access

This does not just mean physical access but also sensory and communication access.

Textured surfaces, ramping, handrails, lifts, widening of doors, positioning of switches, re-hanging of doors are basic, but can involve large capital expenditure. Every school as part of teacher INSET should undertake a full access survey and work out in consultation with local disabled adults what needs to be changed, then a list with rough costings for change can become part of the school development plan.

Facilities such as a disabled toilet, parking, rest room are also essential.

In specialist rooms an audit will need to be carried out and some practical work may have to be adapted to make it accessible. Benches need lowering, tools and apparatus will need adapting as will sports equipment. Much of this detailed work will tend to be done on a piece-meal basis to fit the needs of the actual disabled students.

Trips

All out of school activities and trips must also be made accessible, involving detailed pre-planning and booking necessary transport.

---

*Footnote on Access
1 Appendix 3 (p 239) Fish
2 Access for Disabled people to Education Buildings. DES Design Note 18 1984.
3 Lighting and Acoustic Criteria for Visually 'Handicapped' and Hearing Impaired in Schools. Design Note 25 DES 1981.
4 Design for Everyone. 1989 Manchester Planning Department, Manchester Disability Forum.
5 Code of Practice for Access for the Disabled to Building - British Standards Institute.

blind, partially sighted and deaf/partial hearing students, interpretation facilities for taping, brailling and signing will be needed. Modern computer technology is changing all the time and there is much new technology that can help in this process but it is still expensive. Speaking/reading computers and Keirsweiler brailling machines can make things much easier.

Deaf people are increasingly arguing for their first language, British Sign Language, to be treated in the same way as other 'mother' tongues. Much interest is now being shown in sign language and many hearing children, especially primary age children, are drawn to it.

This is one area where language development could be enhanced by the introduction of sign languages and finger spelling for all. (See Section Sign Language.)

The tasks in the curriculum being asked of children and students will need to be reassessed to make sure all can do them even if at different attainment levels. Ways must be developed with support teachers of getting the essential knowledge, skills and understanding across to a range of learning levels and speeds so the presentation is not acting as a barrier to cognition.

This type of exercise will have benefits to many children with various abilities. Many of these operations will have applications in existing 'special schools and units' where children will be following the National Curriculum unless they have been subject to disapplication.

Liaison

It is essential that an effective liaison system is developed where children may be educated in more than one class or institution.

The areas covered should be written down and cover

(a) Clear identification of responsible teacher for liaison. BUT ALL MUST SHARE RESPONSIBILITY.

(b) Provision of special equipment and negotiation with specialist teachers.

(c) Co-ordination of support staff, medication.

(d) Informing all who need to know of needs regarding playground, meal times.

(e) Alternative arrangements for PE and transport needs for trips.

(f) Liaison with other support services, Health, Social Services.

'Field Trip: Quintin Kynaston'.
Credit Sally and Richard Greenhill.

(g) Liaison with parents.

(h) Liaison about statementing and assessment procedures.

(i) Liaison on entry to primary, primary/secondary transfer and leaving secondary/post 16.

All of the above have considerable time implications requiring additional non-contact time and so more teaching resources.

Parents and Children

Part of any whole school policy on disability must be to get far greater involvement of parents and children. Especially asking for the children's opinion and valuing it. For too long other people have spoken for the disabled. Disabled children and young people must be encouraged to say what they think.

Parents have legal rights especially in the assessment and statementing process.

It is important that they can talk to a teacher who is in full possession of all information and tell them what point the process has reached.

Parents should be helped with legal advice over the statementing and don't forget parents, under Section 9 of 1981 Act can write to the LEA to initiate formal assessment. The teachers can't make the LEA assess.

'Michelle Smith: Castle Croft Primary Wolverhampton'. *Credit CSIE.*

It is important to establish the right type of rapport with parents, as a statement can mean equipment and additional teaching or non-teaching staff to help their child access the curriculum. This is vital if integration is to proceed effectively.

Under the 81 Act it is the duty of the LEA to secure, for a child it maintains a statement on, education in an ordinary school, (having taken the views of the parent into account) if it is compatible with her receiving the special educational provision that she requires, with the provision of efficient education for the children with whom he will be educated and with the efficient use of resources.

Special Needs

Many ILEA schools over the last couple of years, especially secondary have suffered a severe cut back in special needs/learning development support teachers. Much existing good practice remains but much has been lost and will need to be rebuilt. *This will include building up a resource base approach and working in the class with the class/subject teacher*.

Statement and Assessment

It is essential that all teachers of a child are familiar with her needs.

Children 'on loan' from a special school need to have their statements amended at the annual review to meet their needs for support in a mainstream school as do all statemented children.

The 1981 Act does not define how many children should have statements. The Government have said 2% but clearly more disabled children than this would benefit from a statement. As many children as possible should be statemented. Special Educational Provision in the Act is defined as something 'additional to, or otherwise different from' the educational provision made generally for children of the same age in the authority's schools'. So the statement can identify special staffing or resources and once agreed by the parents these are legally binding on the LEA.

The Government expect LEA'S to afford the protection of a statement to all children who have severe or complex learning difficulties which require the provision of extra resources in ordinary schools, and in *all* cases where the child is placed in a special unit attached to an ordinary school a special school, a non-maintained special school or an independent school approved for the purpose.

Under-Statementing

The recent OPCS Survey VOL6 (1989) On Disabled Children, Services, Transport and Education, has some very important data here about under-statementing.

They found that of 360,000 children under 16 with disabilities only 2% lived in residential establishments. This is a lower number of disabled than in other surveys.

Disability was classified in terms of severity from 1 - 10.

For all disabled children living at home, 63% had not been assessed. 30% had been assessed though only 14% had a formal statement (Table 6.2 p52). Perhaps we would expect only the more severely disabled to have statements. If we just look at the category of greatest severity 9/10, 62% only had been assessed and 35% had a written statement. (see Table 1)

The survey showed that the Government's intentions are not being carried out. While of the minority who had been assessed 83% were in special education 17% were in ordinary schools and 58% of these with no formal statement were in special education.

Lastly the survey also asked who requested the statement first.

	%
Teaching Staff	41
Parents	16
Doctor	8
Nurse	8
Educational Psychologist	5
Education Authority	2
Social Services/Police	
5% of parents	
not consulted at all	

Table 1

Where Disabled Children are Educated

(2 - 15 years)
(Children at Home)

Type of School	Severity Category					
	1-2 %	3-4 %	5-6 %	7-8 %	8-9 %	All %
Special Education	9	20	27	39	75	34
Special School	6	10	16	27	63	24
Unit in Secondary	1	5	7	6	3	5
Unit in Primary	2	3	4	2	8	4
Other Special Education	—	2	0	4	1	1
Ordinary Education	91	80	73	61	25	66
Secondary Class	25	29	24	19	7	22
Primary Class	45	38	34	33	15	33
Nursery/Play	11	8	8	6	1	7
Other Schools	10	5	7	3	2	4
	100	100	100	100	100	100

Based on Table 6.12 p57 OPCS Disability Vol 6

From these statistics it is clear that the benefits of assessment and statementing are being denied to many 1000s of disabled children.

Part of any policy in a school must be to rectify this position.

This is where the big problem lies. LEAs have inevitably been forced to slow down this process as education budgets have been systematically cut back every year since the 1981 Act was introduced.

This is in marked contrast to the PL94-142 legislation in the USA where all public bodies had to implement integration in schools. They had to mainstream disabled children and they could then claim back the additional expenditure from the Federal Government.

No such additional funding has been available here in the UK. This has led to many children who should have been statemented not being so. It has led to the wrong sort of staff support. The provision of cheaper welfare assistants when they should have teachers and it has led to lack of funds to adapt buildings and buy special equipment.

It has also led in many LEA's to piece-meal integration rather than planned with proper whole school change.

Some Authorities like Newham have decided on a strong policy but are then not able to fully implement it. For example, two secondary schools were to be made barrier free but these are caught up in capital cuts. (See Newham Policy.)

Employment of Disabled Teachers and Support Staff

An equal opportunities policy on disability must have an employment element if it is to be a whole school policy.

The Manpower Services Commission and now the Training Agency have produced various documents which form a useful basis for discussion*.

At the height of its employment ILEA employed 90,000 persons. Only 205 of these were registered disabled i.e. 0.03% a 100 times less than the legal quota required by both the 1944 and 1958 Disabled Persons Employment Acts. There are 1/2 million registered disabled people in the UK. The latest government figures show 2 million disabled of employable age. Only 31% of these were in paid employment compared with 69% of the general population.

Of the economically active - those seeking work: 27% of disabled men 20% of disabled men were unemployed compared with 11% of men generally and 9% of women.
(See section on OPCS Survey.)

When it come to teachers the medical restrictions on entry and continuing fitness to teach imposed by the DES 1/88 and implemented by LEA'S mean that the proportion of school teachers who are employed is even smaller than for ILEA generally. Certainly this leads to many with hidden disabilities not registering or mentioning it. (See Section on Teachers Employment.)

What schools and LEAs wishing to make disabilities an equal opportunities issue will have to do is break the mould.

They can operate (legally) positive discrimination to employ only disabled people until they meet the 3% quota. This could be done now in LEA'S and in every school employing more than 20 people once LMS is introduced.

However the problem is most schools are inaccessible and full of prejudicial attitudes.

Still it is interesting that Warnock (1978) recommended on Teacher Training that the number of disabled entrants to training and to LEA appointments should be greatly increased and that the medical fitness criteria should be much more flexible.

This the DES did not do and indeed in the 1989 Teacher Regulations the Secretary of State still retains to himself the power to classify teachers medically unfit.

LEA's do now have discretion and they must be forced to alter their categories, giving support in terms of variable work patters, ancillary support and resources for building adaption. A committee of disabled and able-bodied teachers would be best placed to recommend what support should be given once a disabled person is employed.

ILEA and many LEAS have included harassment and discrimination on grounds of Disability (1983) as basis for discipline and grievance. Yet all this is based on what is 'reasonable'. Who judges reasonable?

---

*Footnote

1 Code of Practice on the Employment of Disabled People 1984 MSC.

2 Employing Disabled People: Sources of Help 1985 MSC/Training Agency.

3 See also ILEA Disability Employment Pack which contains the above (1987).

4 TUC Guidelines on Employing Disabled People (1989).

Until quotas are filled it is unreasonable not to give positive discrimination to disabled applicants.

It is clear for things to change the structure and regulations must change. But it is clear steps to improve things can be taken now. This at the moment is a matter of isolated hard struggles by the disabled individuals concerned. However from their accounts it is possible to learn how practices and attitudes must change. (See Section on Disabled Teachers.)

The restrictions on entry to non-teaching jobs are not as restrictive and these jobs are determined on a school basis. These should be advertised asking disabled people to apply and positive discrimination and support should be shown to disabled applicants.

This policy will clearly need to be developed by school staffs and then taken to Governing Bodies for adoption.

But it is only if all employed in schools and colleges own such a policy, taking it to their union branches, staff meetings, parents meetings, assemblies, classes and tutor groups and Governors that it will succeed.

Health and Safety

Health and Safety is often given as a reason for not having disabled pupils/students or staff. This is discriminatory.

Ways have to be found to accommodate disabled users and employees on the premises.

The most commonly voiced concerns are about means of escape in the case of a fire for disabled people.

Firstly, concerns are expressed for the deaf and partial hearing. As an interim measure personal vibrating alarms can be worn. In the longer term flashing lights and sound alarms should be jointly fitted to accommodate the deaf, blind and non-sensory impaired.

Secondly, means of escape has led to some extraordinary schemes . ILEA sensibly in their new code of practice come down for supporting half hour fire resistant areas on every floor so disabled people can be taken out of the building by the trained emergency services. The alternative operating in some schools is that volunteers on the staff practice carrying disabled people out of the building in a dangerous, strenuous and demeaning activity.

ILEA previously recommended disabled people are equipped with EVAC lifts for fires and these can still be used when no fire resistant area can be found.

The overriding concern has to be that the vast majority of school and college buildings which could have been made accessible have not been.

These buildings are neither safe nor healthy for disabled people. It is a pity that more people do not see this as the main health and safety question and campaign for the necessary funds to bring it about.

Discrimination, Harassment, Name calling and Discipline

While we are all bound by law not to discriminate against people including pupils, students and other members of staff on grounds of sex or race no such legislation protects people with disabilities. As we have seen both entry criteria to teaching and other educational jobs and the whole process of assessing Special Education Needs are likely to exclude and separate people with disabilities.

We have to make Local Education Authorities and Governing Bodies adopt policies to deal with discrimination against disabled staff, pupils and parents.

Some LEA's have adopted such policies on paper such as ILEA in 1983. It took them until 1987 to issue a leaflet against harassment of people for their disability. It is worth reproducing part of it here.

'Harassment of people with a disability causes distress, interferes with their ability to work or to make full use of ILEA services, and can seriously restrict their opportunities.

Harassment of people with a disability can take many different forms, ranging from violent physical abuse to more subtle ways of making people feel uneasy, uncomfortable or angry because they have a disability. It includes:

- offensive jokes and comments that degrade people with a disability

- bullying, humiliating and patronising behaviour directed at a person because she or he has a disability

- physical assault

- circulation of leaflets, magazines, badges and other materials which degrade people who have a disability

- graffiti.

Proven harassment of women and girls, people from black and ethnic minority groups, people with a disability, lesbians and gay men is contrary to ILEA policy and is a disciplinary offence under the ILEA Staff Code.'

Table 2 Possible Discrimination/Harassment for Disability Incident Sheet

Date _____

Name of Pupil _____

Form _____

Teacher _____

Form Teacher _____

Head of Year _____

The course of action which must be taken is indicated by the empty boxes, which must be ticked as that action is taken. They indicate the minimum which must be done.

Description of incident – use separate sheet.

If staff do not follow the prescribed course of action, indicate why – use separate sheet.

Results of parental interview, letter to parents etc. – use separate sheet.

Column headings (left to right):
1. Discussion with Pupil.
2. Incident sheet to Form Teacher/Class.
3. Referral to H.O.D. (or H.O.Y. if outside lessons).
4. Formal discussion – Pupil, Teacher and Form Teacher.
5. Referral to H.O.Y. – Head in Primary.
6. Letter to Parents.
7. Parental interview to be arranged.
8. Pupil to Head with recommendation.
9. Pupil to be sent home.
10. Request to Governors for suspension.

(□ = empty box to be ticked; ■ = shaded/not applicable)

1 Verbal Abuse

(a) Incidental, no offence with Others on Grounds
(b) Persistent, intended to be offensive.
(c) Inciting others
(d) Vicious/threatening.
(e) Other

	1	2	3	4	5	6	7	8	9	10
a	□	□	■	■	■	■	■	■	■	■
b	□	□	□	□	□	■	■	□	■	■
c	□	□	□	□	□	■	■	■	■	■
d	□	□	□	□	■	■	■	■	■	■
e	□	□	□	□	□	□	□	□	□	□

2 Refusal to Co-Operate with Others on Grounds of Disability

(a) Sit next to/talk to/work with/help.
(b) Persistent
(c) Other

	1	2	3	4	5	6	7	8	9	10
a	□	□	■	■	■	■	■	■	■	■
b	□	□	□	□	□	■	■	□	■	■
c	□	□	□	□	□	□	□	□	□	□

3 Violence

(a) Jostling.
(b) Intimidation.
(c) Punching/kicking.
(d) Serious fighting.
(e) Using weapons.
(f) Other.

	1	2	3	4	5	6	7	8	9	10
a	□	□	■	■	■	■	■	■	■	■
b	□	□	□	□	■	■	■	■	■	■
c	□	□	□	■	■	■	■	■	■	■
d	□	□	□	□	□	□	□	■	■	■
e	□	□	□	□	□	□	□	□	□	□
f	□	□	□	□	□	□	□	□	□	□

4 Abuse of Personal Property

1	2	3	4	5	6	7	8	9	10
□	□	□	□	■	■	■	■	■	■

5 Graffiti

1	2	3	4	5	6	7	8	9	10
□	□	■	■	■	■	■	■	■	■

6 Propaganda against people with disability.

1	2	3	4	5	6	7	8	9	10
□	□	□	□	□	□	■	□	■	■

Disability and The National Curriculum

by Richard Rieser

Through the welter of circulars, orders and regulations following the introduction of aspects of the 1988 Education Reform Act two separate but equally important issues arise. Increases in the rights of disabled pupils to access the curriculum and the seeming decrease in the potential for raising "cross-curricula" issues like disability awareness.

It is the intention of the Government and the National Curriculum Council that all pupils share the same statutory entitlement and National Curriculum.

The Act requires all schools including *special schools:*

"to provide a balanced and broadly based curriculum which promotes the spiritual, moral, cultural, mental and physical development of pupils at the school and of society, and prepares pupils for the opportunities, responsibilities and experiences of adult life". The curriculum is to be relevant to the full range of pupils' needs. It requires every maintained school to provide for each pupil of statutory school age, as part of his or her curriculum, 10 foundation subjects (9 from age 5-11), each with nationally specified objectives - attainment targets -and programmes of study.

'Castle Croft Primary, Wolverhampton'.
Credit CSIE.

Pupils progress compared with the attainment targets will be monitored and formally assessed and recorded by prescribed methods throughout compulsory schooling and must be reported at the end of each of the four key stages - i.e. for most pupils at the ages 7, 11, 14 and 16." (para 8 DES Circular 22/89)

The Secretary of State believes all pupils, including those with SEN, should follow the National Curriculum to the maximum extent possible "it is expected that the flexibility offered.... will deal with *very nearly all* cases where pupils need to be taught outside the ranges specified for key stages, and that there should be no need, on this account for a significant increase in the extent to which statementing procedures are used (Circular 6/89).

However, Sections 17-19 of the Education Reform Act together with orders under Section 4 prescribing attainment targets, programmes of study and assessments, offer three ways of taking account of SEN.

The view of the National Curriculum Council in Circular 5 (Para. 10) is contradictory. It hopes planning for participation by pupils with SEN will minimise the need for detailed statutory modifications or exemptions to be written into statements. But in 'Curriculum for All' 2 they say 'However, details of statutory support, how much

142

and what kind need to be specified in order to ensure it is provided'. This can only be done through a statement.

But it is the Local Management of schools that is going to push many heads to recommend assessment.

The LEA remains responsible for assessment but they have a choice whether to delegate the additional funding to the school for statemented children or to retain control over the staff and funding. The school can decide how best to deploy its overall resources in order to offer the necessary provision but *it will be obliged to provide what is specified in the statement.*

Children without a statement will not have this protection.

Circular 22/89 has been issued and deals with many of the problems thrown up by I/83 on statementing. It follows on from the House of Commons Select Committee investigation of the workings of the I98I Act. Evidence was submitted by National Association of Headteachers of a survey of 400 special school heads. Some 80% felt that childrens statement of needs were being prepared directly in keeping with what was available rather than in terms of the specific needs of the child. The new procedures insist all needs should be identified in Section II even if the L.E.A. can't provide them under Section III. Parents and pupils also have more rights and the time limit is reduced to 6 months for the L.E.A. to produce a draft statement. (See Appendix)

Given all the above it seems extremely likely that there will be a large increase in statementing.

Many now believe as Michael Sterne (I987) that section I9 will increase the number of statements.

HMI Criticism

The recent report of the HMI on physically disabled pupils in mainstream and special schools I986-87 found a great variation in the quality of children's work.

In special schools relationships are generally good and there is some high quality work. While close co-operation by all involved with pupils is reported, much of the work underestimates pupils' abilities; the curriculum lacks breadth and there is a shortage of equipment for specialist work, largely as a result of the schools perceptions of what it needs.

For pupils with SEN working in mainstream classes with in-class support, standards are very uneven. Where they are good, a key factor is the effective joint planning of the children's work by all the teachers concerned.

Special schools will have to broaden their curriculum offer and work more closely with neighbouring schools in order to offer the full curriculum to their pupils. Much work here and in mainstream schools with pupils with special educational needs will have to be carried out by teachers to adapt programmes of study, attainment targets and assessments to the developmental needs and provisions to be made.

'Kirsty Arrondelle integrated in a Hertfordshire Primary'. *Credit BBC TV.*

'Finger Spelling at Laburnum'.
Tolu and Moshkura

To be effective this will require considerable teacher time and additional resources. The National Curriculum Council in 'A Curriculum for All' paint a somewhat rosy picture of how all this can be achieved from existing good practice. So at the very time when teachers are having to prepare to teach the national curriculum for the first time they are also being expected to modify it for disabled children and children with learning difficulties.

A National Curriculum for all?

If integration is going to proceed apart from the additional resources a major change of attitude is required in mainstream schools towards disability.

The DES leaflet from Policy to Practice makes the following point.

"The whole curriculum for all pupils will certainly need to include an appropriate (and in some cases) all stages ...... coverage of *gender* and *multi-cultural* issues" (Sec 3.8).

However no such concern is expressed for disability issues, despite recent Government evidence of 6.2 million disabled people in this country and at least 500 million worldwide.

It is essential that disability is raised throughout the curriculum. The fact that many teachers are currently re-examining what they teach and how

means that this is a good time to suggest they take on the perspective presented here and raise disability as an equal opportunities issue with their pupils. Disability and how it is perceived fits into the definition of the National Curriculum (page 125) put forward in the Education Reform Act.

It is my experience from raising disability issues with infant, junior, secondary and 6th Form students/pupils that this is an area of immediate relevance and interest and that a great variety of experiences are recounted. As a disabled teacher I start by talking about my own disability and how I have been treated now and when I was a child at school. Disabled people must be involved in teaching about disability.

I believe it is very important to develop the idea of a continuum of disabilities. Many of the more minor ones are present in the main-stream class even if no statemented children have been integrated.

(I) Orders under section 4 for different subjects. These may make different provision for different cases or subjects. The Order for English key stage I, for example, allows a headteacher to exempt pupils from AT5 - handwriting - if they need to use a non-sighted form of writing-braille- or have such a degree of physical disability that the attainment target is unattainable.

144

Great emphasis is laid on flexibility so pupils can be taught for part of the time (half or more) at levels below their key stage. If they are to be taught for most of the time they will need to be *exempted* through their statements. The option is also there for them to be taught with pupils below their chronological age. This is not acceptable to the NCC and would not be educationally acceptable to most teachers. Section 17 also allows for general variations in 'cases and circumstances' as may be later specified.

(2) Section 18 provides that for an individual pupil an LEA may, by a statement of special educational needs, modify or disapply any or all of the National Curriculum. So any departure from the National Curriculum can only take place after a full assessment of pupils' needs including parental views. Section III of the statement must contain details of modifications or exemptions.

(3) Section 19 allows a headteacher for 6 months to give a *general or special* direction to modify or disapply the National Curriculum on a temporary basis for an individual pupil. The general direction is for temporary problems while the special is used where the headteacher believes the child has special educational needs which require the L.E.A. to assess with a view to a statement.

It is possible and preferable that even very young children are involved in work on disability.

The National Curriculum Science/Disability module in the next section was developed out of teaching 5-7 year olds about disability. The advantage of such units are that they fit readily into the requirements of the core subjects of the National Curriculum. Firstly, it appears to me this is the best way of getting the question of disability into the school curriculum rather than in a ''cross curricular' area. Teachers over the next four years will be so busy especially in primary schools developing 9 core subjects that there will be no time for innovation outside these areas.

Secondly, a systematic approach to science is now required in the primary school and so developing such units will help develop this curriculum area.

Thirdly, project based work including English and Maths, design and technology, IT, geography and history can be built up around the curriculum units. This module for the science curriculum is aimed at 6 year old infants.

A similar type of unit could be constructed for 3rd and 4th year Juniors for Key Stage 2 with more emphasis on hidden disabilities, the biology of impairment, learning difficulties and the social

consequences and attitudes towards disabled people.

In the Secondary curriculum if schools still teach integrated humanities, social studies and Personal Health and Social Education every effort should be made to raise the topic of disability in a structured way.

However, again it seems that the most likely way of raising disability is within the core and foundation curriculum areas.

Judy Watson has developed a unit for GCSE English/English Literature which shows how a unit can be put together to fit work for key stage 4. Lois Keith has suggested ways of re-examining classic children's literature. Some of the works Judy has chosen portray negative stereotypes of disabled people and these need to be pointed out to students.

CDT - Craft Design and Technology is an area where a great deal of work can be done to raise awareness of disability. The Community Service Volunteers pack on this a good starting point also the project developed at Northumberland Park is a good example. The motivation for this later project come from the presence of disabled students at the school. The sheets on Design for Everyone are a good starting point.

The Unit on disabled people and the Nazis could be introduced into GCSE History work on the causes of Second World War or work on fascism. The unit on Pictures in the Mind raises points for History or Social Science.

Accessibility surveys and plans for change, drawn to scale can be used as a way in as a special maths or CDT project.

Clearly there are many areas where disability can be introduced throughout the curriculum. But it is necessary for teachers to feel confident about the issues and so it is important to familiarise yourself with the issues raised in this pack prior to raising with students/pupils. It is also important to try and arrange for disabled people to come into the school on a regular basis and create the time for fruitful discussion with the classes.

the things I like doing most are listening to music, watching T.V. and going out.

I like to be treated like any other person. All my friends treat me as if I am able-bodied.

People always talk above you and not to you. I think the word 'handicap' sounds like we are from outer space. I'd rather use the word disability.

I hate it when someone comes up to you and talks to you as if we are mentally disabled. They come right up to your face, and use simple language, for example 'Are you alright?' in a different voice from their normal one.

They would prefer us to be isolated from the world, from everybody else.

The thing that makes me angry with people is when they don't listen to what you say, as if it's not worth hearing.

Lydia Bent

Integration v Segregation
by Micheline Mason

'Integration is an education in itself - an education for life'
Headmaster - Northumberland Park School

The Segregated School - It's A Rap

I woke up in the morning
for my first day at school
I was off to the country
they told me it's the rule

my uniform was neat
and my calliper was clean
I took my wheelchair with me
to the school ... Oh what a dream

they told me it was special
I tend to disagree
I left my friends behind
'cos they're different from me

teaching based on therapy
never expected to achieve
like all the other children....?
No - don't be so naive

the problem was our bodies
was the idea that they sold
we must strive to be normal
or stay out in the cold

"You'll have to come to terms" they
say
"Accept the way you are"
but accepting our oppression
won't get us very far

it didn't take us long to see
they hadn't got it right
physical perfection
put a stop to their insight

to fit into their world
we must obey the rule
to be upright is normal
no legs, no arms - "How cruel!"

the cruelty was theirs
denying us our right
chip on our shoulder
just because we fight

we'll define the problems
just you wait and see
it's the construction of society
which most oppresses me

Steve Duckworth

The 1981 Education Act decreed that children with special educational needs should receive their education within a mainstream school wherever possible. However, a report prepared by Will Swann of the Open University shows that in 1987 the percentage of pupils being educated in a segregated setting has been reduced only minimally, and in some LEAs has actually risen.

Just as disturbing was the discovery of high percentage of children in segregated schools who did not have a statement of 'special needs' which is a legal right. (In seven LEAs the proportion of non-statemented pupils in special schools was more than 75%.) There has obviously been a lack of will to make the change. We will suggest some of the reasons for this.

INTEGRATION

Disabled people have worked out together an analysis of our situation, which we have already described. When we apply It to the education service, our point of view is that:

QUESTIONS

(a) Firstly, 'special' education has been seen as an issue for professionals, and more lately for parents to decide. The consumer of Special Education has been completely overlooked as having any valid reason for consultation. Children are traditionally not consulted as to their opinions about services which they are compelled to attend, disabled children and children with learning difficulties even less so. Because of the historically based attitudes able-bodied people inherit towards disabled people, the 'we know best' approach is extended from childhood into adulthood, so that even ex-consumers of special education are not asked whether it was what we wanted. Our experience of special education is often so different from the view-point of the providers, that you could be forgiven for thinking we were describing two completely different things.

Not only is it unacceptable that segregation is the only choice for many disabled children but even more unacceptable that provision for many means *boarding* school. Most parents of able-bodied children would never accept this imposition on their rights.

(b) The training of specialist teachers with consequent financial rewards confuses the issue for 'ordinary' teachers who feel they are possibly being exploited by the call to teach children they had previously been told they couldn't teach without extra training, especially when the children are currently being taught in small, unpressured groups by people who are being paid more to do it. Conversely, the teachers in special education who do have extra training and extra experience in being with disabled children, are worried that integration is going to mean a loss of status for them.

(c) The inaccessible nature of many school buildings and the apparent expense of adapting them to accommodate people with mobility disabilities, is an excuse often held forward as a major obstacle to integration.

RESPONSES

(a) Disabled people and people with learning difficulties are the consumers of 'Special Education'. We are beginning to do our own research into the effects of segregation, restricted curricula, special classes and units and we will publish our findings. However, the vast majority of disabled people already feel that the 'Special Education System' is based on the medical model of disability which we do not want perpetuated. The social model of disability would state that integration means the removal of disabling factors from the mainstream education system so that even the most severe disability can be accommodated.

(b) Experience of disabled children who have been educated in mainstream schools is that they do better educationally and socially, as long as the school responded in a positive way to their 'special needs'. Able-bodied children also report that it has been a positive experience for them as do their teachers.

(c) The training and payment of teachers needs restructuring, as regards the 'normalising' of disabled children. We feel much more emphasis should be placed at Teacher Training Colleges on learning about the whole range of needs present in the child population and that this should 'upgrade' the status of all teachers, not just a few specialists, who are a very undervalued profession anyway.

(d) Disabled Teachers should be assisted to teach, not barred from teaching as at present (see Disabled Teachers Section).

(e) A State Education System is paid for by the people. It is supposed to be for the people, not for the people who can walk. The fact that so many school buildings are inaccessible to people who cannot walk easily, or climb stairs is an injustice which should be remedied without delay. It should also be mandatory that schools have a changing room as well as properly adapted toilets for disabled pupils, teachers and parents, and a room

(e)   Continued

set aside for speech therapy and physiotherapy.

All this will involve major, but one-off capital costs. (All schools built after 1972 have to be accessible by law.) Until this happens there can be no such thing as equal opportunities for disabled people.

(f)   Both primary and secondary schools should have Special Needs Resource Bases - not units - which are run by people experienced in the practical, educational and emotional needs of disabled children. This could be a role for people currently employed within the segregated sector, as long as they also show some understanding and commitment to the issues of disability as outlined in this pack. This could also be a role for disabled teachers if they so wish.

(d)   Another reason is the fear expressed by parents of children who are currently settled into special schools, that the talk of 'integration' is a thinly disguised ruse to reduce expenditure on a group of children already maligned, mistreated, devalued, misunderstood and under-resourced as a matter of policy (i.e. oppression) by an increasingly competitive and uncaring society, a fear shared by many teachers and disabled people.

(g)   The issue of what happens to children currently placed in segregated schools, especially when that placement is supported by the parents, is on the surface quite tricky. However, if the mainstream 'host' school is properly resourced and prepared and the children are moved in groups with their friends, then it is usual that initial apprehension is replaced by great enthusiasm from everyone concerned, *once* it has taken place. Perhaps one thing that has not been addressed is the fact that the parents may also be getting a lot of support from other parents and the welcoming attitude of staff in 'Special Schools'. This support needs to be acknowledged and maintained within the mainstream provision.

(e)   Some disabled people, particularly those who are deaf have a history of non-disabled people attempting to wipe out their language and culture in favour of the dominant 'Oral' culture. This has proved to be educationally socially and psychologically damaging to deaf people who were denied the right to communication in their early years. For this reason deaf people fear the move to integration is a move back to a 'normalisation' process that denies who they are and what they want.

(i)   The issue of 'on whose terms' integration should happen is an important one for all disabled people. We support deaf peoples' right to represent their own issues and make their own demands. At the same time those of us who are part of the hearing world are demanding that the education service enables us to learn to communicate with deaf people by the recognition of British Sign Language as a modern language, included in the curriculum of all schools. This must be the first step if there is to be any equality of interaction between deaf and hearing people. 'Total Communication for All'.

(f)   Designers of the education system, education officers, local councillors, etc., who decide on funding priorities, and many other decision-makers are produces of a segregated system, and are usually grossly ill-informed of the issues around disabled children. A comparatively few people know about, or have seen examples of

(h)   Disability Awareness Training should be a requirement for all people who make decisions about young peoples' education and this training should be provided by disabled people familiar with the Disability Movement and with the Education Service.

149

(f) Continued

good practice in integration, or are even aware of what is happening on an individual basis in their own localities. 'Mainstreamed' families, or 'Mainstreaming' teachers have no organised voice to share their often positive experience, or to share their concerns, whilst the 2%, the segregated sector are well organised and seen as the 'experts'. Consultation therefore is less than one sided - no children, no mainstream teachers or parents, no mature ex-consumers are a serious part of the decision-making process.

(g) The last reason we will suggest is an overtly political reason. Disabled people, especially young disabled people occupy a powerless place in society and therefore are an openly admitted low priority in Government policy or expenditure. The responsibility for disabled people's needs and interests are largely given away to voluntary bodies and in so doing they GIVE AWAY OUR RIGHTS to be included in services and structures which are a right for other people. The consequent lack of resources available to mainstream society to mend their discriminatory ways is stated as if it were an unavoidable FACT, which people believe, rather than understanding that the unspoken sentence would say: AS WE, THE GOVERNMENT SEE YOU DISABLED PEOPLE AS UNABLE TO FORCE US TO MEET YOUR DEMANDS, WE SHALL CONTINUE TO CHOOSE TO MAKE YOU A LOW-PRIORITY, FUNDING INSTEAD THOSE THINGS WE DEEM TO BE MORE IMPORTANT, AND THOSE PEOPLE WHO ARE MORE POWERFUL. The argument that 'Special Education' is awash with money is not really true and even what there is, is heavily subsidised by private and charitable sources of funding. These dilemmas do have to be faced.

(j) Our response to the last reason is that our powerlessness is kept in place by our inequality of education, lack of social skills, the divisive nature of medical model provision, our lack of political awareness as disabled people and the gulf between disabled adults and non-disabled parents of disabled children. Disabled adults are, at last, uniting and becoming a much more powerful group than ever before. We are challenging in every way possible our fourth class position in society and are learning not to take 'no' for an answer. We are encouraging parents, teachers and many other professionals to do what my four year old daughter taught me to do in the face of injustice - GET MY OWN WAY!!

Recommended Reading:

'Nothing Special' A book for all ages describing a properly integrated primary school as experienced by an eight year old girl in the school. All good practices exist, but school and child are fictional. Many line drawings. Excellent for stimulating discussion in classroom, staff room and amongst governors. Published by working press, ISBN no. 1870736 028 Central Books Warehouse, 14 The Leathermarket, London (£2.50).

'Each Belongs. Integrated education in Canada': A report by Linda Shaw CSIE ISBN 1 872001 01 7 £2.50. A fascinating account of how the Catholic School Boards of Waterloo and Hamilton, Ontario have moved to a fully inclusive school system. "Full inclusion on the premise that each belongs because all are valued is routine for thousands of children". These two School Boards are at the cutting edge of the fight for fully inclusive schools. Explains some of the techniques

used – Circle of Friends, MAPS – Marketing Action Plans and Co-operative Education/Work Experience, which concentrate on friendship, increasing participation in the classroom and preparation for work.

Further Information – The Integration Alliance, C/o 34a Dafforne Road, Tooting, SW17 8TZ. A campaigning organization for Inclusive Education.

The Centre for Studies in Integrated Education, 415 Edgware Road, London NW2 6NB. Advice, support and information.

Mrs Ingar Hempstead, Head of Hounslow Integration Support Team at the Martindale Centre, Martindale Road, Hounslow W4 7HE.

London Boroughs Disability Resource Team, Bedford House, 127-133 Camden High Road, London NW1 7JR. For Disability Equality Training.

Park Barn Comprehensive School
Park Barn, Guildford, Surrey

A report by Micheline Mason

Surrey Education Authority has provided for 12 years units in mainstream primary and middle (junior) schools where children with disabilities are integrated, or at least partially integrated, into the school.

Parents and teachers requested that there should be provision at secondary level to continue this work, and about eight years ago Park Barn was chosen as the "host" school for a few practical reasons.

As there was no shortage of room, no extra buildings were necessary, and existing classrooms, superfluous cloakrooms and toilet areas were modified to provide:

1. a resource/class/common room
2. an adjoining physiotherapy room
3. a treatment room
4. a speech therapy room
5. two sets of toilets adapted for the use of disabled pupils
6. two new laboratories were built on the ground floor
7. all entrances/exits used by pupils at Park Barn were ramped; internal ramps were provided giving internal access to all rooms on the ground floor

Two teachers were appointed with experience of physically disabled pupils. Two part-time helpers were also appointed. The local HA granted six hours of physiotherapy and six hours of speech therapy a week. At the present time, October 1989, there are 22 disabled children in the school, and the numbers of helpers and teachers, physio hours, etc, have increased significantly.

Surrey Education Authority have installed a lift in the main building and negotiations are in progress about installing lifts in the two separate blocks, the stairs of which are negotiated by the use of a "caterpillar" stair climbing chair, which the pupils do not like. Parents and teachers have fund raised for a school bus with a tail lift which they now have.

The pupils are totally integrated. *The special needs base is not a unit.* The staff in the base see their duties as:
- making the school environment fully accessible
- acquiring special equipment or adaptations as they are needed
- timetabling physio and speech therapy so as not to interfere with exam lessons, etc
- providing physical care when needed

Making the curriculum fully accessible by:
- Assessing strengths and weaknesses, determining the "Special Eduational Needs"
- Ensuring correct set in English and Maths on entry, also in French (other subjects taught in mixed ability groups)
- Providing remedial help within the classroom and possibly for "booster" periods on a withdrawal basis
- Checking on classroom skills, study skills, ability to deal with homework
- Continuous support and encouragement
- Providing a welfare assistant in practical lessons
- Keeping teaching staff informed about educational implications of each pupil's disability
- Regular communication with parents of the pupils

Evaluation of the appropriateness of the support provided is structured into the whole school timetable, and the pupils themselves *are* consulted regularly.

In addition to the curriculum, the disabled children are enabled to participate in all extra-curricular activities including field trips, trips abroad, drama festivals and art and literary competitions. The presence of the disabled pupils and their support staff has broadened the scope of extra-curricular activities for the benefit of the whole school, e.g. a weekly PHAB club, and a very popular life skills class, designed initially for the disabled young people but open to, and enthusiastically used by, a large number of non-disabled pupils.

Special arrangements for school leavers include motorbike and wheelchair proficiency course and assessment, mobility assessment at Banstead Place for car driving, sexual and genetic counselling, and work experience placements. The pupils are "followed up" and are doing well following very "normal" paths into FE and work.

The "emotional" side of disability is being faced to some degree, particularly aorund the issue of dealth and dying. Staff were asked to go on a bereavement course, and the young people are not particularly protected from knowing about possibilities. Pupils who are very ill have been encouraged to attend school "Even if they just lie down in the common room all day. At least their friends can get to see them". The two deaths that have occurred have, in fact, both been able-bodied young people. Their classes attended the funerals and wrote letters to their parents. The staff said they would not refuse a child a place on the grounds of the severity of disability. They have had blind, deaf and severely physically disabled pupils. They also have children with learning difficulties, dyslexia, and some whose behaviour has been "bizarre". They also, now, include in the special needs department gifted children whose needs are also not "average".

Examples of pupil profiles written for the classroom teacher show some of the range of needs:

"P--- has Duchenne Muscular Dystrophe. This is a progressive disability and P--- must use his wheelchair at all times. He wears a spinal jacket to maintain his posture. This makes bending and leaning forward very difficult and tables must be at the right height and close enough for him to work in comfort. P--- cannot lift his arms or hands. He might need help to lift his hands off his lap onto the desk or table to start writing. If P--- wants to ask questions in class or answer, he will let you know by pressing his buzzer. Please ensure that books and pens are within his reach as he cannot reach out for them himself. So far his handwriting has not been affected and he is keeping up with his work.

P--- attended an ordinary middle school and is used to an integrated setting. He is rather quiet and slow to make friends. He is reluctant to ask for help but must learn to do so. He has good ability and is very conscientious. He enjoys directing activities where he himself cannot join in. He has a helper available in all practical situations."

"G--- joined Park Barn this year after attending a special school for seven years. He had not learnt to read at this time. At Park Barn he has followed a restricted timetable and an individual SN programme. This arrangement together with G---'s own positive attitude and hard work have resulted in his rapid progress in literacy and numeracy skills. From reading age 0.0 he has progressed to 8.6, sufficient for the moment to enable him to write simple accounts and to cope with most of the textbooks in the lessons. There is still much scope for improvement and G--- will need regular SN lessons and much encouragement to reach his potential. He shows good retention of taught material. This and his pleasure at having "broken the code" augur well for his future. He is friendly and polite and popular with his peers."

"R--- is using programmes which will help him to improve his recognition of suffixes such as -ture; -sion; -cial; -tial. His copying skills are also very poor. R--- is a lively and chatty pupil who has a tendency to rush his work. He has no problems in voicing his opinions but he does have a tendency to read too quickly, misreading words. He is currently working hard on a sports-based topic and responds well to tasks set. He does tend to have a low profile of himself which may manifest itself in him becoming a classroom "pest" so firm encouragement is necessary from all staff".

There has been no resistance to the integration of a large and visible number of disabled pupils from parents, teachers or pupils. They all speak of initial apprehension, quickly giving way to a sense of gain in friendship and experience and a sense of achievement for the school as a whole. After eight years they are pretty bored with publicity and interest in their "difference" which they feel is in fact very "ordinary".

There is a still scope, even within such a powerful example of good practice, for more awareness of the social aspects of disability. There was a strong emphasis on "We don't notice" pupils' disabilities, almost a wish for invisiblity, rather than any fostering of a positive identity as disabled people. I was not aware that thought had gone into the images of disabled people - there were charity posters stuck on the wall of the

'What we need'

Progressive Conditions like -
Friedreich's Ataxia
Cerebellar Ataxia
Muscular Dystrophy
Spinal Muscular Atrophy

Written by seven students
3rd, 5th, 6th years

There are different causes for these conditions, but they all involve progressive weakening of muscle power. None of them are apparent at birth and seldom before the child has reached school age. Around that time, the affected child becomes clumsy, falls a lot, loses normal co-ordination. It often takes a while before a correct diagnosis is made; it may take the parents and child forever to come to terms with it.

The speed and extent of deterioration differs from child to child. The progression cannot be halted but sometimes slowed down by regular physiotherapy and hydrotherapy. As muscles are affected. We slow down and become weaker. Walking, sitting down, getting up, lifting and carrying things, writing, speaking, becomes more and more of a problem. We are fighters though, and try to keep on our feet and on top of our work as long as we can. Unfortunately, most of us will be in wheelchairs before we are fourteen years old, if not before then. Most of us will need a typewriter or word processor eventually, to cope with our writing. Several of us will start speaking more slowly and less distinctly.

So you see, not only we but you, our teachers, have to learn to be patient. Typewriters and such like will not necessarily make us much faster at written work, but it conserves our energy of which we have very little. If practicable, handouts from you would be a great help. Homework also takes us a long time and we need encouragement to finish projects at home.

Academically, we have no specific learning difficulties. Pupils with Friedreich's Ataxia do however sometimes slow down mentally.

You will find all of us determined to do our best at school but we need your understanding and support to cope with our increasing loss of physical strength, of choice and independence. Don't hesitate to ask us how you can help. We can explain it better than anybody else.

common room displaying both positive and negative images of disabled people - and speaking to the pupils themselves made me aware that for some pupils their self-image as disabled people was not good ("I can't get a boyfriend because I'm handicapped") although this undoubtedly varied. I was not aware that any information about their place in the scheme of things (which to me as a school leaver would have been so useful) was forthcomimg. The depoliticalisation of disability was still evident.

'There's one small lift'. Northumberland Park. *Credit CSIE.*

their 'allocation' of welfare assistant time or teaching support time, or whether it was negatively affected by the fact that most of the pupils had come from a Special School where detailed statements are sometimes considered unnecessary, because 'everything is provided'.

The fact that there were no staff available who could assess and modify the curriculum for pupils with learning difficulties seems a discriminatory factor in the provision, and one which was divisive for the remaining pupils. How had the remaining pupils at the Vale been affected by the 'creaming off of its most able pupils?' The fact that only the pupils with statements were under the umbrella of the Special Needs Team was another divisive factor, drawing a line between pupils with visible disabilities and pupils with hidden disabilities.

Transport in the form of a bus from the Vale was still employed to bring pupils to school and to take them home, making the day very long (7.45am start). This seems a poor alternative to individual taxi schemes or owning its own school bus.

Our overall impression was of having visited people 'out on parole' not willing to complain, taking the attitude that 'You cope' because the alternative would be worse. The history of the integration scheme has greatly affected its form and structure and does not compare favourably with other schemes such as Park Barn where there have been no such umbilical cords to cut.

It seems very important therefore that for a scheme of integration to work well, *the mainstream school takes COMPLETE RESPONSIBILITY for all its pupils*, using the expertise, if appropriate of staff from Specialist Schools. It is also important that the Education Authority involved funds the school adequately, especially for the initial capital costs of adaptions *worthy* of their users. Disabled adults should be consulted as advisors on this matter. The DES Guidelines for 'Access to Educational Buildings' should be enforced.

Issues which need addressing in Northumberland Park were connected to each other. The gap between school life with a disability and adult life with a disability was entrenched with fear and lack of information on the part of the staff, who consequently felt ill equipped to support their pupils through the transition. Careers advice, sex education and information about 'Independent Living' were all mentioned as missing or inadequate by staff and pupils. The same issues have been identified in other schools, as has our own perception of a common lack of a 'political' perspective on disability, or any positive link between disabled school pupils and disabled adults.

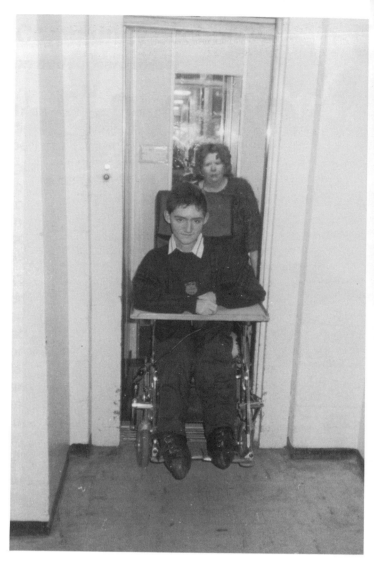

"There's only one small goods lift. Simon and Lift".

Possible solutions would include:

More relevant 'Special Needs' input at Teacher Training College.
More in-service training for staff by disabled Trainers.
More involvement with Arts and Disability Culture within the School.
The recruitment of more disabled teachers.
Visits and lectures to and by disabled staff of Integrated Living Centres.
Special 'Disability Equality Training' courses run by disabled adults for 4th, 5th and 6th form pupils.

The B6 Incident: Pupil Perceptions of Integration - David Cropp*

This Chapter tells a story of political development among a group of adolescents with disabilities and difficulties. These pupils challenged a number of features of school life which, in their view, forced on them a disabled identity which they rejected. Equally important, they did so in a co-ordinated and politically effective manner. But their demands did not attack any fundamental features of the structure of their schooling. The pupils wanted participation on equal terms: they wanted the same rules applied to them as to all others. They did not challenge the rules themselves: indeed, their demands served to reinforce them.

Introduction

Wo ofton bclicve that we can predict accurately the viewpoints of adolescents, particularly those with special needs. The particular incident which I describe in this article tells us about how pupils may define their own needs. It involved thirty-five adolescents aged between eleven and seventeen, all of whom had some form of special educational need, and were placed in the Special Educational Unit attached to Bartley Green School.

The school is a six-form entry, eleven to sixteen comprehensive, though at the time of this description it was completing its final sixth form. When I became Head of Unit, I had to adminster to the needs and welfare of forty-seven pupils. The Unit was staffed by five teachers and a nursing ancillary. All Unit pupils were referred through the Special Education Department of Birmingham LEA. The school has a formal catchment area as part of a consortium of local schools, but pupils being admitted to the Unit came from a wider area.

From the start Unit pupils had received part of their education integrated into mainstream classes, each pupil having their own individualy designed timetable. Pupils registered within the Unit, and each Unit year had a Unit teacher acting in the role of form teacher.

The Unit was a conversion of the school's original library and staff rooms during the last phase of building on the school site. It is geographically at the heart of the main school building and is therefore not separate nor cut off from the school's physical or social structure. The Unit is not named or labelled but merely links with classrooms at both ends. It consists of a double-sized classroom (the original library), a standard-sized classroom, a half-sized classroom, an office, medical room, staff, boys, boys' and girls' cloakrooms, and an acoustically lined room for speech therapy. Recently, an additional room has been added to accommodate the peripatetic Teacher of the Deaf now attached to the Unit. The number of pupils has risen, and the Unit now caters for up to fifty-five pupils.

One third of the intake have speech and/or language difficulties, one fifth are hearing impaired. In addition the Unit caters for pupils with a variety of physical impairments, including road-traffic accident victims; emotionally and/or physically delicate pupils including those with terminal illnesses; children who have specific learning difficulties, and children who are mildly autistic.

When I became Head of Unit the pupils participated with some degree of success in the school, with decisions on their activities, as traditionally you might expect, being taken by the teaching staff of the Unit.

This, then, is the background to what happened on one particular occasion in the Unit which had a long-lasting influence on the inter-relationships between not only pupils and teachers within the Unit, but also in the way in which the Unit functions as part of the whole-school community. It also raises the wider issue: the nature of any synthetically created or managed adolescent group, and what the group's actual potential for decision-making may be.

The B6 Incident

Shortly after my appointment to the Unit, an open letter signed by some thirty-five or so Unit pupils arrived on my desk requesting a meeting with me. Fortunately the headmaster of the school consented to the meeting taking place. Therefore, it was with some misgivings that, shortly after, in a lunch-hour, I faced these pupils in classroom B6.

Sheep and Goats

Surprisingly, before any points could be raised, the status of those present was challenged by the pupils and all who had not had the courage, as they put it, to sign the letter were ejected from the meeting on the grounds that they had abrogated their right to join in any discussions or decision-making. Those who were most vociferous in their demand to stay were pressured out by the fact that nobody was going to start any meeting of any kind with them present.

*Reproduced from 'Including People with Disabilities' (1987) Ed. Booth & Swann - Open University.

Ground Rules

Having cleansed the assembly of non-qualifiers, the first pupil-spokesman wanted some clarification of the future of whatever might be decided, recommended, or requested during the meeting.

Unable to predict what was going to appear in the agenda, I stated that all items would be considered seriously, would be dependent on the head's view, and would be implemented if I felt them reasonable and/or possible. The principle of sanctions against those present in the meeting was then raised. I gave an undertaking that none would be invoked, and the meeting proper started.

Agenda

Given most people's knowledge and expectations of comprehensive schools and their pupils, one might expect there to be demands for derestrictions, relaxations, and freedoms from the school-rule system. What actually came up on the agenda was somewhat different.

All forms in the school are styled according to the year number followed by form teacher initials. Historically, the separate years in the Unit had been allocated the suffic 'G'' (thus: 1G, 2G....5G). Agenda Item 1 was a request to change this method of identifying Unit forms, and to adopt the standard main school pattern. Quite reasonably they felt that this would establish anonymity in form group classification.

Not surprisingly, you might think, Agenda Item 2 was the subject of school sanctions and punishments. Their view was somewhat unexpected. It was that Unit pupils should be subject to the same system as that meted out to meted out to main school pupils. As the school had at that time a well-established report, detention, and corporal punishment system, I asked for an expansion of their reasoning behind this request. They said that if they were seen to be able to avoid the sanction system by reason of being puils with special needs, then either they were seen as less of a person, or if appropriate the pupil sub-culture of the school would apportion a suitable substitute at some other time orplace tomake things 'fair'.

This led to the third point they wished to raise. They felt that all the Unit pupils should be required to present themselves in a school uniform which conformed exactly to the standard as laid down. The fact that in many instances pupils throughout the school did not conform precisely to the standard was not accepted as a legitimate argument by them. Their view was the while recognising that uniform was in a sense an arbitrary aspect of school life, nevertheless the closer they conformed to it the more likely they were to be assimilated into the school environment as 'just another pupil'.

Agenda Item 4 was based on an established link between the main school and the Unit. During their fifth year a number of main school pupils were, by choice, attached to the Unit, particularly to help the less able or physically handicapped younger pupils, either in class with their work, or with mobiity around the school. There seemed to be advantages for both groups, particularly in fostering an awareness of special needs, or so I believed. Without malice, the Unit pupils wished to reject their presence in this arranged side-by-side relationship, firstly because it implied a lack of independence of all Unit pupils, and secondly, as a result, a difference of status within the school. My response that their placement in the Unit was as much to help main school pupils recognise the needs of others cut no ice withthe group: status was the key to the rejection of this 'help-link' scheme.

Status and independence were the themes of the fifth area of discussion. There were a number of traditional arrangements which I had inherited, and which seemed to me at first sight somewhat innocuous. But not to them. And as it turned out, they were right. One of the provisions commonly found in special school placements is taxi-transport for those pupils who by reason of distance and/or disability are unable to reach their school within a reasonable time. Some pupils lived close enough to reach school on foot or by public transport. I was now asked to extend the provision of bus passes to whoever thought themselves capable of travelling to school by public transport and could successfully convince their parents. Another arrangement which should change, they felt, concerned school reports. Main school pupls received their school reports unsealed for them to read before taking them home. Unit pupils received their's sealed, as often they had apparently less successful reports to see. Item 6 of the discussion was that this 'sealing' practice should cease, and they would decide if they were competent to see their own reports, whether good or bad.

Following this, the seventh area of discussion was more general and concerned their independence within the physical and social environment of the school, with the right to be able to mix freely in and out of school in the same way as every other pupil, including being able, where reasonable, to leave the school premises without escort. Previously, Unit pupils had been given a number of 'safety-privileges', such as having school lunch before the main school 'rush' started. There was now a 'restriction-for-independence' move on their part to have themselves attached to their school year groups. Thus the outward signs of separate identity, however, trivial, were to be erased in favour of their being able to create their own identity within the society of the whole school.

Item 8 was based on academic 'access'. They felt they had the right to claim access at all levels and to all subjects as available in the school, where they would have been placed by merit and attainment if they had been a main school pupil.

It was at this point that the discussion ended; the main grievances had been given a public hearing. Strangely, there was no demand for either a follow-up meeting, nor for a reporting back session. It was as if the expression of the wishes of the group had been a sufficient action, and the response to their requests would be considered at a different and inaccessible level.

Aftermath

While the demands of the pupils may at first seem to have ben fairly mundane, the method of expressing a consensus view was quite radical, particularly when you consider that this was all taking place in a fairly typical comprehensive. Since that meeting there have been a number of evolutionary and natural changes within the Unit, most in those areas which they discussed.

Once the meeting concluded, the head of the school and the staff of the Unit were told the nature of the proceedings. Almost immediately most of the demands were implemented. The forms' numbering system was changed to match main school; in any list of forms it is now impossible to distinguish which is a Unit form. As far as is possible and reasonable Unit pupils are subject to the same range of school sanctions as that experienced by all main school pupils. The pupils in the Unit, with little prompting, presented themselves in school uniform, often impeccably dressed. No scheme to introduce main school pupils into the Unit now exists, unless these pupils themselves have some temporary special need, for example, following an operation, and on these occasions they seem to be readily accepted. Taxi provision still exists, though on a reduced level. Public transport passes are a common status symbol, almost at times a symbol of freedom, flaunted before other less fortunate or stillover-protected pupils (I hasten to add, not less fortunate by reason of handicap). More often it is parental rather than pupil opposition which prevents some moving to independent travel. However, a significant number of Unit pupils travel long or double bus journeys in preference to taxi provision. Pupils read their own reports, good or bad, in the same was as main school, before taking them home. Over the past years Unit pupils have been able to take part in all the main school activities, including the more physically taxing such as skiing and potholing, and in a recent sponsored walk one notable member of the Unit completed eight kilometres on crutches in one and a half hours, in company with his main school friends.

There have been more global changes in the school as well as the particular changes they requested. Because the pupils of the Unit found that sensible and thoughtful discussion appeared to bring positive gains without any retribution, individual pupils began to use this to re-examine their own position.

Now, when pupils of the Unit feel they have a position to justify, then they exercise their individual right to negotiate with their teacher or with the Head of Unit. One irate pupil who thought her view had been wrongly rejected, took it further by negotiating direct with the headmaster, somewhat to his surprise. This attitude does appear to be transmitted to newcomers who never experienced that original meeting. A pupil recently moved from a situation where she was close to suspension and a possible psychiatric referral, and within the course of one school term began to recognise that a pattern of negotiation and decision-making seemed to benefit her.

Certainly the consensus politics of the Unit turns the very idea of 'special needs pupils' on its head, as Unit pupils often have an almost tangible feeling of elitism in the school. When Unit pupils express a point of view now, they do so predominantly about things which affect them as a pupil of the school, not as a pupil with special needs: their concerns relate to the general quality of academic life. It is expressed reasonably, and thoughtfully, and as a result I think it is accepted precisely because the attitude that goes with such an expression presents no threat.

Conclusion

What I have described here is a single event and its consequences in the on-going existence of a Special Education Unit. It was important because it was the result of the spontaneously generated actions of a group of adolescents with special needs who clearly felt the need to change their world, who found successful strategy for doing it, and who as a result managed to deflect the Unit onto its present course where pupils can have a much more open and honest relationship with each other and with staff, and a much greater potential for individual decision-making.

159

Mainstreaming in a Primary School – A Parents Account

by Micheline Mason

My daughter has brittle bones, a syndrome caused by a genetic fault in the structure of collagen, the fibrous tissue which gives bones their strength, muscles their 'tone', blood some of its clotting ability and skin some if its protective qualities. In Lucy's case, her bones and muscles are affected resulting in her inability to walk, and a great vulnerability to fractures of the long bones. She is very bright, lively and assertive. My own experience of 'special education' led me to an absolute determination that Lucy would not be excluded from 'ordinary' education, as I did not wish for her to be further disadvantaged by the low expectations and over protective atmosphere of a segregated school. Also, because her condition could mean a broken bone at any time which would need my presence as quickly as possible, I felt it was very important that her school should be very close to our house.

I found out about 'statementing' by accident, in a casual conversation with a nursery worker. I was told that it could take a year to complete so I began the process immediately. Lucy was then only three years old, but I was hoping for a part-time nursery place. I could not find anyone who could really advise me about which school to choose, so I rang up the head teachers of all the close schools and made appointments to visit, explaining briefly our situation. Some were markedly less enthusiastic than others.

I took Lucy to the first school visit with very little idea of what to expect. I had never before entered the door of a mainstream school either as a child or an adult. I took a friend as my disability prevents me from carrying Lucy who, at that time did not have a wheelchair. I was nervous during my interview, and my normally extremely articulate and, I liked to think 'advanced' daughter, hung her head and became completely incomprehensible for the first time in her life (so it seemed anyway). Despite this, the head suggested we looked at the nursery and met the nursery teacher who would be the one who would actually have responsibility for Lucy.

I loved the nursery, and the nursery teacher. She sat like a solid rock tending to arguments, tears, confusions and exuberance with easy warmth. Lucy, determined to not co-operate in my desperate need for her to make a good impression, decided she wasn't interested in all the nice, safe, activities spread to on the tables and floors, but instead wanted to play football with the boys in the playground, to which end she crawled out of the door after a huge ball which she began to tap with her grubby and miniscule socks, to the delight of the other children.

I could not see the expected fear and horror in the teacher's eyes, but delight as she watched Lucy tackle the climbing frame with my friend holding her. As she began to look at the classroom furniture with fresh eyes, thinking aloud about ways of adapting the sand tray and other things for Lucy's benefit, I knew that this was the school for her. If the school were willing to give her a place, I had no need to look further. In retrospect this does not sound like a careful decision. In truth I did not study the access to the school, or take into account that the primary school was on three floors with no lift. Nor did I visit any other schools (then) to make comparisons. However, I have never regretted the decision as I realise that I made it not on the basis of Lucy's disability, but on the basis of her personality and educational needs, and it was the right decision.

The school agreed to give Lucy a place on the condition that ILEA paid for a one-to-one assistant for the whole time she was in the nursery.

Given that the school had a place for her, it was fairly easy to arrive at a 'statement' which included small physical adaptions to the nursery and the provision of a helper for 15 hours a week. As it happened, the nursery teachers who I had hoped to be Lucy's first teacher chose that particular time to leave the teaching profession. However, her replacement was also very good and had been known to the Head Teacher in the past.

A parent of a young child currently starting at the primary school was chosen by the Head and asked if she would take on the job of Lucy's helper, which she agreed to do. I was introduced to her before the term began, and she came to our house to spend time with Lucy and to familiarise herself with Lucy's needs.

The arrangement worked extremely well even though Lucy was, at that time, crawling around the floor amid a sea of hard little shoes and falling bodies. The children adapted themselves and their games intuitively it appeared. Whilst I and my wheelchair were a source of great curiosity to the children, Lucy was accepted without question. There were no serious accidents despite some quite hair raising escapades.

Half way through the first year, Lucy acquired a lightweight manual wheelchair which made a lot of difference to her independence in the playground. Indoors she generally preferred to crawl and climb and sit with the other children as she had from the beginning. As exercise is very good for Lucy's muscles, it was desirable that she did not become dependent on the chair unnecessarily, even though she may have been 'safer' in it.

Her successful integration at the nursery has led to her successful integration in the primary school. The staff were familiar with her. Her friends from the nursery are her classmates now. Her helper went with her for a few months before having to withdraw due to ill health, but another parent has taken her place. The hours of helper-time have been extended to 20 hours a week, but Lucy manages independently for the afternoon sessions before begin bought home by yet another parent.

The access to the whole school is not good. The dining room, and television are upstairs, and eventually Lucy's classroom will be upstairs. Luckily Lucy is not heavy and we have two wheelchairs, one up and one down, between which she is carried by her helper when necessary. A wheelchair accessible toilet is being built on the ground floor and all entrances to the school are now ramped. A passenger lift is needed however to give both Lucy and myself independent access to the whole school, as well as any other disabled children, teachers or parents.

Lucy has had one fracture in her arm whilst at school. It happened, as her fractures usually happen, doing nothing much. It was an illustration of how unpreventable such injuries are, and how pointless it is looking for fault or blame. The school rang me and I went and retrieved her. Later that day we went to casualty where a small plaster and collar 'n' cuff sling was applied. Within four days Lucy was back at school During this time the children and classroom teacher willingly pushed her chair and gave her the assistance she needed when her helper had gone home.

I am aware that being able to get me in an emergency is not always possible unless I spend my days next to a 'phone. To overcome this I have applied to Social Services for a "bleep" so that I can be contacted at all times.

Everyone is delighted with Lucy's progress in the school. Her 'reports' are good as she is clearly one of the more able children academically. Lucy's favourite lessons however are PE and music and movement, both of which she does with her helper obeying her instructions, which is in fact probably why she enjoys them so much. Being 'boss' is her favourite role in life. She was disguised as an angel in the Christmas play, and is beginning to get invitations home from the parents of her friends, although it must be said that the parents have been the slowest group to accept and include Lucy in all aspects of school life. This is an example of how long it can take to make an integrated placement work, and why I am still determined to keep Lucy in the same school despite some of the physical problems. To start all over again with a new set of non-disabled children, staff and parents feels like just too much.

Today Lucy has gone to school especially excited - her friend Meesha, another little girl with more severe form of brittle bones is starting her first term there. Lucy is very proud in the knowledge that she has literally 'paved the way' for her friend to join the school.

Reading this account to myself I realise that it sounds smooth and unproblematic, but it wasn't. I feel weary at even the thought of describing the battles that Lucy's placement has involved. The long drawn out statementing process; the fight to get her a wheelchair from the DHSS; the instruction to 'MOVE HER' from the 'Panel' of experts who reviewed the statement at transfer to infants from nursery; the unresolved battle for 'permission' to carry her up the stairs; the loss of her helper; the Head's battle for the money for the toilet; the battle to come for the lift. Another parent recently described his experience of mainstreaming his disabled son, saying "I feel like a constant visitor in someone else's house". This accurately echoes my feelings, as we are still amongst the first, 'unexpected' pioneers of integration. I have to remind myself constantly that we have a legitimate claim to the education service, and a responsibility to define the details of that service for ourselves. It is our house too.

Kirsty: The Struggle for a Place in an Ordinary School*

'There isn't a week that goes by without Kirsty being invited to a party in the neighbourhood. She went to the local integrated pre-school playgroup at the age of three - we looked at several in the area and the closest turned out to be the one we like the best - and it has been this normal contact with other children and their families, whether in their homes, or here in ours, which has made us feel so sure that pressing for integrated schooling was the right thing to do'.

Kirsty's parents feared there would have been a great upheaval out of the community if they had responded to pressure from the local authority, and the special school in particular, that segregated schooling was the proper kind for their child and not normal schooling somewhere in the neighbourhood. It was not an easy decision to take as Kirsty approach the age of five: she had earlier attended this ESN(S) school once a week for physiotherapy to help get her walking. These 3/4 hour sessions stopped about two when she began walking. Nevertheless, following this first contact with the special school which is three and a half miles away, it was always inferred that Kirsty would go there for both her nursery education and then her full-time schooling from the age of five.

'Over Protected'

Her parents felt otherwise. 'The weekly sessions to help get her walking were wonderful, but we saw that the other children were very protected in the special school - it's just the way things are. We're not critical of the school, or that kind of school: the staff are extremely dedicated, there's no doubting that. What we are critical of is the concept of withdrawing a particular child from its natural environment, its local community, and educating it in a place where children with a variety of handicapping conditions are brought together in a concentration'.

Having the support of the peripatetic home-teacher (home tutor) while trying to secure a place in a local ordinary school where Kirsty's friends from the playgroup naturally progressed on to, was obviously of great help to the parents. But they said that even with this support they felt very much on their own in their pursuit of an integrated setting for Kirsty's schooling. The pressure for Kirsty to take the traditional educational route was 'enormous', and rested on the fact that no alternative was ever offered. 'From the word go, all the different people involved in caring for her let us know that they expected an ESN(S) education for Kirsty and nothing more'.

Kirsty Arrondelle   *Credit BBC TV*

It was an uphill struggle for the parents who soon came to realise they were going against the majority of attitudes and opinions held by individuals as well as those in authority, the most devastating of which was shown early on by a senior hospital doctor soon Kirsty was born, when the parents were told: 'Don't expect her to live very long: don't look too far into the future as far as your life with Kirsty is concerned' The local education authority (LEA) also certainly expected her parents to follow the traditional route for children categorised as ESN(S).

'We were acting from instinct, and still feel we need all the help we can get. For example, diet is extremely important for Downs children and we're trying out a special vitamin booster for Kirsty with the help of the Down's Children's Association and our local doctor, and it seems to be helping at the moment, but we don't know for sure. You often feel you are in the dark over lots of things because the professionals, the education authority and the individual schools all make you feel that they have so much more information and experience than you.'

From the moment she was born Kirsty's parents, who had had no previous experience of disability at all, exposed her to a lot of stimulation, particularly in the first six months and they now feel they have seen clear benefits at various stages of her life. She is a great mimic, according to her parents, and this has been put to good

Centre for Studies in Integrated Education: Factsheet

effect both in playing and learning at home, in the playgroup and in teaching social and behavioural skills in the infants school where she has been for a year and two terms (April 1983).

Her progress in the playgroup, where she mixed easily with all the other children and often helped the smaller ones with various tasks, allowed her to benefit considerably from a normal environment. At that time Kirsty was the only handicapped child in the playgroup but they were fully supportive of the parents' wishes for an ordinary education.

Pressure

Thinking back to the pressure they faced to place her in the ESN(S) school, parents commented: 'Without any malice to the children there, to their parents or to the staff, we could so easily see Kirsty regressing, or staying still in that kind of environment. Putting her in the special school's nursery unit at three years of age definitely wasn't the right thing to do for her at the moment. The playgroup was not a particularly unusual playgroup - which was fine - but it did prove to us what we had felt for a long time, that Kirsty could mix, take part and benefit from remaining in the 'normal' community'.

A major factor in this example of integrated education is the clear support for integration shown by the headmistress of the Church of England infants school: without it, Kirsty's parents said they would have probably given in to those pressures. For her part, the headmistress said that from the moment she was first approached by the parents and met Kirsty, she was convinced by their arguments as well as their enthusiasm, and she agreed to take Kirsty on a term-to-term basis. 'We have had tremendous support from the parents and we could not have come this far without it: with considerable enthusiasm they have always been involved with the school, they have talked with the staff and carried on with Kirsty's education at home in conjunction with her teacher'.

It was agreed that a case conference at the end of each term would decide whether or not it was working. The ESN(S) school was aware of the arrangements and ready and willing to take Kirsty at a moment's notice if the scheme 'failed': everyone involved knew this as they embarked on the scheme.

The parents said they felt they could not ask for anything more in terms of rights or a guaranteed future for Kirsty, and they described this arrangement for them as being 'on tenterhooks' at times: 'it does highlight the difference in parental rights and security of a school place which parents of ordinary children enjoy compared to that enjoyed by us'.

Credit Mark Vaughan

The headmistress felt that bringing Kirsty into her school was a challenge to everyone concerned: 'If we are not educating Kirsty, then we are failing. There is always a place in the special school, so it is up to us to prove it works here'.

Kirsty's parents have observed her in the ordinary infants school and commented: 'She isn't protected from the outside world in that school, and that is just what we wanted. The greater the chance she has in taking part in so-called 'normal' society when the groups up, the better.

Yes, we have made a direct connection between this ultimate goal of trying to achieve some kind of normality for her when she leaves school, and our seeking an integrated education setting. We think ordinary schooling makes the goal much more likely than a special school does. She isn't molly-coddled at this school; she has become much more self-reliant; she has to speed up - literally. Downs children tend to be slower and appear to be lazy, but she has adapted and she can keep up with a lot of things in the classroom and elsewhere in the school.

'We are delighted with her progress, which is greater than we had dared hope for, particularly with her reading ability which has also impressed the speech therapist'. The infants school has given her greater independence as well as self-reliance, and this comes out after school and at weekends: for example the regular Saturday morning visit to the adventure playground will see Kirsty moving from one activity to another under her own steam; when she comes home from school she will happily sit down and decide to read to her parents from her Kathy and Mark reader for 20 minutes to a half an hour before going upstairs to play on her own in her bedroom for a further half an hour to an hour.

The headmistress said that the strongest benefit to Kirsty in the first year had been a social one. She had not learned 'academic' skills as fast as other children of her own age, but she had gained more by being in the ordinary school, than if she had been in the special school. She added: 'The plus side has been for people already in the school as much as for Kirsty: if it is going to make the ordinary children realise that there are others with greater special needs than themselves, than that alone makes it all worthwhile.

'Kept Away'

I feel that for far too long some children have been kept away from the 'ordinary' environment. In Kirsty's case, I will still have doubts until she has learned more concentration and until her spoken language improves. The elder middle infants fussed her when she first came and she lapped it up: even though she could do things herself she let her peers do things for her, and it was something we had to look out for and stop, because it was obviously holding her back'.

Everyone felt the first term was a great success. Kirsty had learned from the other children who played and chatted to her as much as she did to them, and as they did to each other; she was included in the class group for all activities, in spite of the stumbling block of being behind in language development compared with the others. She was also included in all the joint school activities involving other classes.

Those taking part in the first case conference were the headmistress, the class teacher, the support teacher, the home tutor, the area speech therapist, the educational psychologist, and, when this group had finished the bulk of their discussion, Kirsty's parents were brought in. They felt the decision had been made before they went in to the meeting, but of course they were extremely pleased that it went in their favour: Kirsty was to stay another term, by a unanimous decision.

No Complaints

The school staff, as well as Kirsty's parents, noticed that other children made her say things properly, rather than letting her get away with less than clear words and actions: in her parents' words - 'Some of the best teachers Kirsty could ever have are other children in the ordinary school.' The end of the first term also proved that one anxiety of the head and the parents was quite unfounded - that of complaints from parents of other children in the school: nor have there been complaints or any opposition since then.

The second term - the spring term - was not as good: the headmistress said progress had not been as marked as before, and said she was worried about Kirsty staying in the same class, mainly because the older children wanted to do too much for her and not get on with their own work, or they vied with each other for her attention. It was clear to see how the other children were benefiting and learning after two term's schooling. The other professionals involved in the second case conference were in agreement with the head and it was decided to put Kirsty in the new reception class for the summer term, rather than stay with the group she had come to know and work with.

Kirsty's parents felt they had to go along with the decision, and although they felt that this change might be construed as 'failure', they agreed with the head's advice and the decision of the case conference.

It worked. Kirsty's behaviour according to her parents changed significantly: suddenly she was older than the others, and it was the same as when she was in the the playgroup - the new reception class of children were six months younger, and she found she could teach them things in the class and around the school, because she had experienced school for eight months more than them. This third term, the summer of 1982, was crucial so far as Kirsty's continued integrated education was concerned - it was the end of the first year and the parents approached the case conference in June with a considerable degree of anxiety.

Things had gone well in the term and included a new dimension of Kirsty joining a small group of six Asian children who were getting half-an-hour's tuition a day on their own from a teacher of English as a second language: in addition Kirsty's mother started taking her to the local welfare clinic for half-an-hour's speech therapy each week, something suggested by the second case conference. This same speech therapist holds frequent sessions in the ESN(S) school and also visit the infants school itself. The term ended with the case conference deciding that Kirsty should continue in September, a decision possibly influenced more than anything else by the head's sincere belief that the school was doing the right

thing for Kirsty, that it could cope with her special needs and that it wanted to educate Kirsty, rather than simply 'contain' her.

By the new year (January 1983) Kirsty's fifth term in school and at the age of six and a half, her achievements included knowing all her colours and most of her numbers; writing her name with a little help; reading five word sentences from her Kathy and Mark reader with ease; a marked improvement in language development; a real understanding of what the teacher was saying; an ability to get herself around the whole of the school competently; a healthy appetite without any problems at school dinner time, and, according to a teacher at the ESN(S) school, much more self-sufficiency than children of a similar age and handicap at the special school.

Her ability to concentrate on her own work was improving slowly, and it was decided that this and her language development, which clearly marked her out from the rest of her class, were the areas where most effort was going to be put in future. On a comparative basis with the rest of the children, Kirsty's parents were told she was 'not bottom of the class in everything': there were one or two others, who at that point in time, had greater problems in some areas.

The head stressed that while her commitment to integration had increased markedly since the

Credit Mark Vaughan

scheme had been in operation, she felt she would not let the theory dominate the practice. If she and the staff felt they could not cope or adapt to meet Kirsty's needs, she would recommend that the scheme be ended. At the same time, she agreed that Kirsty's presence in the school implied a lot more than Kirsty simply fitting in with existing structures and curriculum goals. All the staff and some parents of other children had gone through various educational processes and changes in attitude as well as a readjustment of expectations, as a result of Kirsty being in the school; the headmistress added 'While the future might not be certain, nobody - from the director of education downwards - has said we are doing the completely wrong thing. Nothing has happened so far to make me think it has been anything but good'.

In her first four terms Kirsty had three different teachers which might have had a slightly unsettling effect, although she has always adapted quickly, once familiar with the teacher. In an effort to understand the problems involved, the head, and all the teachers who had Kirsty, went over to the special school 'to see what a child like Kirsty would be doing in that setting, to see if she was actually missing out on anything, and to see how we could improve the provision we were already making'. Kirsty's approval at the infants school also lead to some in-service training on special needs for the head and two staff.

In looking to the future the head and other staff are firm about needing extra support, if only part-time, although no formal application had yet gone into the LEA: so far, the class teacher was able to cope with the needs of all the children in the class, but everyone agreed that some degree of regular withdrawal for special tuition would be necessary in the near future; some has already taken place with the headmistress teaching Kirsty on her own.

The ESN(S) school was recently asked if it felt that Kirsty was losing out by not being there: the firm reply to the parents was 'No'. It was true that the pupil-teacher ratios were much better in the special school, but the inter-action in the infants school, as well as the chance to find greater independence in a wider variety of activities, far outweighed the advantages of being in the special school. Other skills such as training and domestic skills could be caught up with in later life.

Kirsty's parents added: 'We're still in the dark about the future, about where Kirsty should go. We have approached one local junior school, but like Kirsty's present school, they too would be breaking new ground, and the head there is not 100 per cent certain that he would take her. He said: 'The door is open - there's no objection so long as we can cope with Kirsty's needs'. We feel that raises a lot of questions not only about Kirsty's education, but also about the attitude of ordinary schools, so we have to keep a number of options open; one possibility is Kirsty staying on an extra year at the infants school.

'Any parent in the same position as us is going to experience doubts as well as certainties: we both feel very strongly that we're doing the right thing for Kirsty at the moment. You see, we want to give her the greatest possible chance of looking after herself, of living an independent life when we're not around, and to us, the best starting point for that is integrated schooling. After the success of the playgroup and now the local infants school, our hopes and aspirations have grown and changed as we have seen Kirsty thrive and develop from being in those environments'.

February 1983

Postscript
Kirsty has continued in mainstream education and is now progressing well at secondary school with the assistance of extra teaching support. I met her at a Conference in Nov. 1989 where she spoke to a roomful of about 80 people, through a microphone, about her experiences of school.
Micheline Mason

Policy of London Borough of Newham

Special Education in Mainstream Schools

The statement adopted in 1987, is regarded as one of the most fully developed policies of its kind nationally.

Newham Makes Integration Work: How special education provision is being de-segregated in the London Borough of Newham. July 1990, London Boroughs Disability Resource Team. Compiled by Ann Hollinger. This provides a fascinating account of the progress and obstacles of the process of integration.

As Linda Jordan, Chair of Education, states in the Foreword

"On reading this publication, I realise how far we, in Newham, have travelled along the integration road. New structures are being built for organising the delivery of special educational provision in ordinary settings.

Positive attitudes towards young people with disabilities and learning difficulties are evolving in all our schools and colleges.

Mainstream and special educationalists are developing collaborative styles of working.

Disabled adults and parents of children with disabilities are being enabled to play a central part in the planning of strategies to meet pupils' and students special needs . . . Our progress has only been possible because we began by putting in place a clear policy which shows what we hoped to achieve and why we believed it important to make an immediate start."

The London Borough of Newham believes in the inherent equality of all individuals irrespective of physical or mental ability. It recognises, however that individuals are not always treated as equals and that young people with disabilities experience discrimination and disadvantage. The Council believes that segregated special education is a major factor causing discrimination. We therefore believe that desegregating special education is the first step in tackling prejudice against people with disabilities and other difficulties. They have been omitted from previous Equal Opportunities initiatives, and it is now obvious that our aim of achieving comprehensive education in Newham will remain hindered while we continue to select approximately 2% of school pupils for separate education.

It is also the right of pupils without disabilities or other difficulties to a experience a real environment in which they can learn that people are not all the same and that those who happen to have a disability should not be treated differently, and more than they would be if they were of a different ethnic background. It is their right to learn at first hand about experiences which they will possibly undergo in future, either themselves or as parents.

Desegregating special education and thus meeting the needs of statemented children in mainstream schools will also contribute, by the entry of expert qualified staff into mainstream schools, to improved provision for the considerable number of children who already experience difficulties.

The following first steps will be taken:

1. The appointment in January 1987 of an Advisory Teacher who will co-ordinate support teaching for statemented children in ordinary schools.

2. A teacher will be identified in every school (in secondary schools this may or may not be the Head of the Special Needs Department) who will act as a point of liaison between the school, the new Advisory teacher and any other school involved with the needs of a statemented pupil.

3. How to identify and assess special educational needs will be a priority for teacher in-service training.

4. A project team of officers from the Education Department will be set up to progress policy. This team will prepare feasibility reports on all aspects of the policy, including resource implications. The team will work in conjunction with a Steering Group of Members of the Education Committee which will, include one parent representative and one teacher representative.

Ex-Pupil's Account

Jane Campbell

My name is Jane Campbell. I work as a consultant trainer in Disability Awareness and I am a whole hearted supporter and campaigner for the total integration of disabled children into mainstream schools and have been since the grand age of seven.

You may think that seven is a very early age to be aware of one's educational and social deprivation, but you have to believe me when I say that by that small age I was displaying the usual symptoms of someone who is ashamed or frustrated with their situation regarding school. I hated the school bus because it took me away from my local friends, who were beginning to wonder why I didn't go to school with them. It also highlighted my differences at a time that I desperately wanted to do/be the same, however, difficult.

The School Uniform Story

I remember sending my mother all round the shopping centre - I must have driven her mad - to buy me a local school uniform even though I didn't go there. I didn't particularly like the way I was treated by school staff - special, frail, in need of very special care. My memories of junior school were not learning to read, add or multiply, nor even how to keep pets.... No, they are endless hours of physio, tons of art and craft (this was recognised as something I could do and would content me in my adulthood, since no employment was ever envisaged), and pushing myself in my wheelchair down what seemed to be endless corridors and consequently being tired.

I am grown up now (so they keep telling me), but I still feel anger about those days, and *I am not alone*. In my work as a disability awareness trainer and also in my social life where I do a lot of disability rights campaigning work, I have been in a position to meet many, many other disabled people who look back on that time of segregation with mixed feelings of deep resentment, anger and sadness. Not a good combination. It can, and often does, lead to psychological problems that are difficult to ever exorcise. This may sound quite alarming to many of you here today, especially if you have not met many of us veterans! But it is a side to segregated education that is rarely discussed, let alone tackled, by those professionals who advocate segregated special schools, perhaps because they are afraid of what they might find. Or perhaps it has never occurred

to them to look. But there again, how could they? It would mean that they would have to come to us, the people who have experienced their system of education! And we might just prove all their traditionally founded theories wrong. No, that would never do.

Segregation is Bad for Everyone

We have been excluded from the policy and decision-making process for too long. In fact we haven't even been consulted in any meaningful way, and when (on the rare occasion) we are, we get told that we do not represent the needs and wishes of most disabled people and parents. WE ARE 'TOO ARTICULATE'. How many times has that been said to you campaigning ones out there? I have lost count of the times it has been said to me, when I have dared to advocate what disabled people really feel about their early teenage years. How can they say that to someone who has experienced the system first hand and who has probably met more disabled people in a month then they have met in years of their professional careers representing us?

Sometimes I am involved in disabled people's workshops on personal development or assertion, or even the politics of the disability movement, and do you know what we always seem to end up talking about or remembering? Yes our special schools, or our separate further education colleges. It makes for endless debate, a debate that more often than not ends up in tears. There is so much in here that we want to say and want you who are not disabled to hear. We want you to know our stories, to strengthen our common fight to end segregation, not to make you feel guilty or sorry for us. It is about time we, as older disabled people who have had a life experience of segregated education, came together with parents who don't want the same for their children. I am talking of course about parents of disabled and non-disabled children, because let's face it: segregation is bad for everyone.

Blasting a Hole

When Parents in Partnership approached me about this conference, I was thrilled. It really is about time you parents joined forces with us disabled activists, and perhaps together after sharing our expertise and strengths, we shall be able to blast a hole through what has seemed to be an impenetrable barrier of attitudes and inaccessible schools and teaching methods, and show them what we really want and need, and also how to go about it. Because I firmly believe we have the expertise (and we shall demonstrate that today in the workshops) we have to come together and produce our demands in writing, at meetings and wherever else we can tap into these alleged 'integration plans' that are at this moment being shaped by local authority officers and education professionals largely without consultation.

We must and will be part of that process. If we are not, children with disabilities and other difficulties who grow to be adults without skills, will never gain equality of opportunity.

Simon Gardiner

I went to a school for people who are partially sighted. I was identified as having learning difficulties soon after I was born, because I had lack of oxygen to my brain - it gave me this disability. I had the same teacher from nursery age until I was about 11 or 12. Then I moved up a form, and I had about four to five years of different teachers each term, and I got further and further behind - it got worse, and I just didn't enjoy school. Then this new class was opened up in the school for people with learning difficulties who were a bit slow. I started to pick up again when I went into the class just before leaving age.

Up until that time I went to school by coach. The start of my independence was when I started going to school by tube. I always look back at that.

Then I left school and I went down to Ringwood, to a Rudolf Steiner school where they were going to do tests. But I didn't like it. I got depressed and miserable because I was away from London. Mum came down and picked us up. Then I was at home for a long time. I went to an ATC, then I went to a boarding school with an FE unit at Redhill. And it was okay for the first part of the term. Then the education cuts came in, and I lost out again. The teacher I had was transferred, and I had this other guy who was a right jerk. I went to the head and said, 'I'm not getting a good deal here, and it's costing the Education Authority a lot of money'. Then the Education Authority refused to pay for me any more, and I landed up back home with my Mum. Then my Mum threw me out, and that's when I started being independent.

How to Change Things

Being separated at school was uncomfortable. I was being picked on, bullied quite a lot, made fun of, in the special school, for about three years - which made me very aggressive towards people, even teachers. My education wasn't really that good. I didn't enjoy my education as much as I would have liked to have done.

In an ordinary school, I wouldn't have been able to see the blackboard, but if I had closed-circuit TV I would. And I would have mixed with ordinary people. I think for integration you've got to start at the early age of, say, four or five. Because then the kids will accept the other kids that had learning difficulties or limbs missing, and they would grow up *with* learning difficulties or wheelchairs, and discrimination wouldn't be as bad as it is today. Because, you look at kids who are seven to 11. They're okay about other kids. But when they reach the age of 12, 13, 14, they get rebellious and start making fun of people, because they're a bit insecure themselves. A good way of integration is at nursery school, where they can play together and learn together.

I think another thing is teacher training. They should be more aware of disabilities, and there should be more disabled teachers in schools. I heard about one teacher in a wheelchair who didn't have a disabled toilet in her school, and had to wait till she got home.

I think they should bring self-advocacy into the curriculum in school, but I'm not sure, because then teachers might think the kids are taking over, because they might get more skills in speaking up for themselves. But I think that with young people aged 15 to 18, there should be assertiveness training, and those sort of skills, in the last two years of their schooling, so they've got some confidence in themselves. One way that helped me was by role-play; that's a good way of getting people interested in coming out of themselves. This is for kids with learning difficulties. It's no fun if you leave school and haven't got the confidence to walk into a shop and spend a couple of pence.

The Alliance

The idea of parents and people with disabilities getting together is a good thing. With young parents, they're more open to change and new ideas. Parents who are older - I'm not being ageist here - are harder to persuade. Younger parents will take more part. The thing that really annoys me is, if you've got disabled people, blind or in a wheelchair, they are denied their right to go to teacher-parent meetings because there isn't access for them to get in - which is discrimination.

In school, there's no training to be a parent. You learn to be a parent by your experience. There's nothing on the education curriculum on how to be a good parent. If we were trained to be parents, we could be trained to be parents of kids with disabilities.

We can speak for ourselves
June Statham

Many people with learning difficulties have spent a large part of their youth living in residential special schools. The memories of this group were mostly negative; memories of boredom or fear, of endless regulations like having to go to bed at seven o'clock, of not seeing enough of their parents and family. Lorraine was the only one who had enjoyed her schooling. She went to a small residential school 'for mentally retarded children' from the age of four to sixteen, and liked the sense of family that was lacking in her holiday visits to foster parents or children's homes. She still goes back to the annual reunion, and remembers fondly the long walks and shopping expeditions on Saturdays, the swimming lessons and the coach trips.

> **We didn't do 'O' levels or 'A' levels. You couldn't in that sort of school. But we had a really good time. I wouldn't have liked to go to an ordinary school. I'd be far behind. I wouldn't be able to keep up.** *(Lorraine)*

Julie did go to an ordinary school and had found it hard to keep up, but hadn't wanted to go to a special school.

> **I went there because I couldn't do the lessons in the junior school. All I could do was cookery and art and craft. I couldn't do anything else because they were too hard for me. No one gave me any help. I would rather have stayed if they had helped me but I had to move on.** *(Julie)*

Gary is in favour of integrated education too. 'There should be extra helpers. It means the teachers will have to have different education. They will have to learn'. Tony went to half a dozen different boarding schools, the last one of which he described as being 'like Colditz'.

> **The worst thing is you're stuck there for months on end. You work there, you sleep there. I didn't like it. They just put me there. I'd like to have gone to an ordinary day school. Your parents can come and pick you up at the end of the day and take you home, and when you're older you can find you own way there and back. I only went to an ordinary school for a year, and then they said boarding school is more suitable for him, he's a handicapped person.** *(Tony)*

David received little education in the school attached to the hospital where he lived. 'I went to a school in the hospital grounds. From nine till half past ten in the mornings. But I can read now, I can tell the numbers on buses'. He felt that school should 'teach you education. George adds 'how

to get about and use real money'. David says they've recently stopped having further education classes at his and George's training centre. 'They're packing it up now because they've cut it back. The teacher left. We asked for another teacher at the meetings but they say they can't do it'. *(David)*

Eileen's centre has also cut back on education classes. 'I don't get anything now at the ATC. I've really got a good brain and I just can't use it'. Her experiences of schooling have left her frustrated, and with strong views on segregated education:

> **I went to an ordinary school till I was nine. The headmistress didn't have no time for me. They said I was damaged in my brain and sent me for tests. The tests didn't show anything wrong but I still got sent to an ESN school. My mother fought it, she went to the County Hall, but I still had to go. They said it was for a short time but once I got there they didn't bother any more. I couldn't go back. It was horrible. I could have learnt a lot but I didn't get any education, nothing at all. I felt I missed out on everything that was going on. They shouldn't have special schools. They shouldn't even have special classes in ordinary schools because that's just the same. Like in one school there was a class called the Lower Class and all the Down's syndrome children were in that class. There's hundreds of people with Down's syndrome, hundreds of people with a disability, and they're probably brighter than anybody else. You're saying, 'You're Down's so you should be shut away' and that's not right. There's a little girl in the nursery (a nursery class for Down's syndrome children where Eileen is a helper) and they say she has to go to a special school, but we've fought it and the court has just said she can go to an ordinary school.** *(Eileen)*

Eileen doesn't like the term 'children with special needs' either. It's all the same. It's still a label. It's still saying you're handicapped. We don't want any label, we're just ordinary people'. Her dislike of the term 'mentally handicapped' is shared by most of the people it is used to describe. 'It's cruel and hurtful and doesn't tell people what we're good at. We want them to take the 'H' of the bus passes and put a star or some kind of mark on it instead. We don't like it because we're not handicapped' (Marion). 'If you're called a handicapped person, if people see you in the street with a pass they say "don't go near him or her because look, they've got a pass"' (Tony). The term 'learning disabled' has been suggested as an alternative, but they are not sure that it is any better. 'It's still saying you're handicapped.'

Most self-advocates feel that labels like 'handicapped' affect the way that society treats them, and hope that if the labels are changed, then maybe people's attitudes will change too.

At an Open Day to celebrate the first anniversary of the setting up of the London and Thames People First, there are many of the same faces. Marion is behind the registration desk helping people to write their names and addresses on a piece of paper as they arrive. Alice is selling T-shirts, with messages like 'People First' and 'Label Jars not People'. Another stall offers publicity material and a newsletter, and there is a display of all the letters Gary has received over the past year inviting him to speak to various groups and conferences. Gary is President of People First, and stands at the microphone to give an introduction.

> **This is the first anniversary of People First in London. It's an organisation for people who are self-advocates and who want to speak up for their rights and put new ideas forward and have a better position. It's for people who've been labelled mentally handicapped, though we don't like that word. We call them 'friend' or 'people with learning disabilities' or we call them by their name, which is the proper way of introducing somebody.** *(Gary)*

He describes how People First of London was set up by the nine people who had been to the American conference, and has now grown to about fifty members, including a supporters group, 'for the people we call professionals. But instead of the professionals running the organization it's the advocates running the organization'. Gary is an accomplished speaker, getting his audience's attention, putting them at their ease, introducing humour into his speeches. He studies the news on television, 'to see how they do it, and to pick up ideas'. He tells his audience that they will be split up by area in order to have small group discussions after lunch. 'There's a South-East London group, a North London group and lots more, so you can meet with people from your area'. A West Indian women in the audience asks, 'have you got a Jamaica?' Gary says no, 'but you could set one up'. Someone else in the audience tells her that, 'we've not got a Jamaica, but we have got a Jamaica Road'. They go off into their small groups, and at the end of the day several new local branches of People First seem likely to be set up.

Gary Bourlet. *Creidt David Hevey*

The self-advocacy movement is spreading rapidly. Groups have been started in Holland and Australia as well as America and Britain, and an increasing number of local groups are springing up around the country. People First has just sent its information leaflet to all the schools and hospitals in the London area attended by adolescents with learning difficulties, hoping to bring over-sixteen year olds who are still in full-time education into People First. They plan to hold the next international conference in London, in 1988. They want to set up training courses to help more people speak out for themselves. The interest in self-advocacy amongst both professionals and consumers is such that the founder members of People First are inundated with requests for information and invitations to speak and are having to learn to say 'no', often to the professionals who have held that power over them in the past.

Self-advocacy has given them greater control over their lives, but sometimes they can feel like it has taken over their lives as well.

> **I can't sleep sometimes because I'm always thinking about it. Even when I play pop music to relax and forget, it's still in my brain. It's not a one-day thing. You can't say, 'I'll do it today', and then tomorrow you forget. It's all the time.** *(Gary)*

It is a commitment to improving the world, not just for themselves but for all those who have been labelled handicapped.

> **I'd like us to go forward towards a better independence and a better life for handicapped people. We'd like to think that if a child is born in the future that might be called handicapped, it will have a better life than we've had. We don't want pity, we want a future.** *(Gary)*

*Reprinted from 'Including Pupils with Disabilities' June 1987, Statham Chpt. 25.

My School Experience

by Sharon Sullivan

It was my first day at school (1965). I was five years old. Were we going to be late? 'We'll be late Mum, hurry up!' I had my coat on and wanted to go. I was so sure it would be fun; I had seen children playing in the playground when I had passed the school. I had been daydreaming about what it would be like; writing things down in nice new exercise books, playing with other children, painting pictures, singing songs.... I was so excited, I just couldn't wait to get there.

I will never forget the shock of that first day (I suppose a lot of people don't). The reality sent me home to my mother who was waiting for me at the gate, stunned and quiet, I was unable to talk about it and was trying not to let on how terrible it had been.

At that time I 'suffered' from eczema (I still do) and the condition was very poorly controlled. Every part of my body was covered in sores, which often bled, alternating with dry scabs. Walking was often painful. I found it difficult to move my fingers - wherever I had joints, my skin cracked and bled. My whole body itched, sometimes worse than others; literally wanted to tear myself to pieces. At night, in my sleep I used to scratch myself so badly that the sheets in the morning would be covered in blood. My mother used to put mittens on me to try to stop me doing such terrible damage to myself. I used to take them off; to scratch was painful, it didn't bring relief, but not to scratch was torture.

I suppose I was not a 'pretty' sight but that was me. I couldn't help it and had never been made to feel bad for the way I looked. My family all loved me and although my eczema caused me a great deal of distress, it was because of the pain and discomfort that it caused me, not my appearance.

This all changed for me after my first day at infants school. I was singled out as 'different' from that day and there was no escape from the endless taunts of other children. 'Scabby, ugly, monster' might as well have been my name for that was all I ever heard. I know that their parents told them not to play with me for fear that what I had might be 'catching'. It was discovered earlier on, in my infancy, that I was allergic to cows' milk, so, instead of the bottle of milk that everybody else had, I brought my own carton of orange juice with me. The animosity that this provoked is still painful to remember. My juice was frequently taken from me, thrown on the floor, hidden or had milk put in it. All of this by five and six year old children..

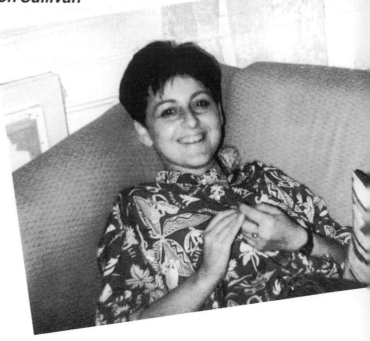

'Sharon Sullivan'.

My teacher seemed totally uninterested in taking control of the situation. I was plainly a nuisance and she refused to listen to my mother, who tried to explain the various allergies that caused my Eczema and Asthma.

For example, dust caused me to wheeze, but my teacher insisted that I took my turn to clean the blackboard inspite of the fact that I was always left coughing and wheezing after performing this duty.

I went through the infants' school, spending more time at home than there, learning practically nothing, becoming more and more unhappy and difficult to live with. My entry to junior school was a minor improvement. My teacher lacked the harsh attitude of the infant teacher, and was altogether more interested in me. I was still without friends, although the bullies had relented a little. They became tired of chasing the same person at playtime, but still nobody would sit next to me unless they really had to. I was desperate to be 'normal' and would look enviously at other little girls with their scab free knees who could run without pain, holding hands in the playground. My eczema stubbornly remained and showed no signs of improvement. The hospital that was treating me at the time tried a variety of creams and ointments to no effect.

It was suggested that I needed intensive treatment as an in-patient and I was offered a place at a hospital school some distance away from my Hackney home. My mother considered the situation very carefully and decided to accept the place. It offered accommodation with other

MY Eczema

when I'm in the susie class people play with me but people laugh at me in the playground. They say nasty I was sad. Some boy said dont sit next to me at diner. my eczema feels hot and I scratch cos I'm sweating It bleeds and it hurt and my cream hurt too. The big one1 the flat one not the little one. children play with me now. By Henry Doung

Henry swimming by Vid

"When the lift broke down, so did I."

'My Eczema by Henry Doung, aged 5, Laburnum School.

children with skin diseases, looked after by nurses, but during the day going to a school, on site, staffed by ILEA teachers.

Initially I was desperately unhappy. I missed my family so much. But gradually I settled down. I was now eight years old and for the first time I began to make friends with other children, to have fun. As I can remember my first day at infants' school I can equally remember vividly, the feeling of relief to be with other people 'like me'. It was a liberating experience. The child damaged by those lonely, isolated years at school in Hackney, began to change into a confident, slighting bossy (not bullying) child. Every weekend when my mother and sister and brother came to visit me, I had so much to tell them about school, about my friends, the teachers and the nurses that I lived with. The school was very small. There were about 10 children in class. My worst memory of the class is that for a lot of the time I was the only girl and any difficulties I experienced were because of this, not, because I had eczema. Boys, whether they knew I had skin diseases or not, tend to push girls around at school. This I remember being a real pain, but it was nothing compared to the victimisation that went before and was something that I found easy to cope with.

The experience in hospital on the whole was a positive one. I left nearly two years later, with a much improved skin condition, a lot of confidence, and a lot of optimism about the future.

Sharing the problems of coping with asthma with fellow sufferers can make a huge difference to life.

Sharon Sullivan joined the group four years ago: "I was twenty-two and completely incapacitated by my asthma. I'd been forced to give up work and spent long periods of time in hospital or at home in bed.

Then I got involved with the Asthma Support Group at Bart's. It helped me face up to the problems of my illness and learn to control the situation, instead of running away from it. It's no exaggeration to say that it transformed my life: I've lessened my drug intake by 80%, I have a demanding job — which I love — and do all the normal things a person of my age does.

I couldn't walk a few steps without suffering before. Joining the group was the best step I ever took."

Asthma Support Group for Adults.

I went home to live with my family again who had now moved to Islington, but it was back to school in Hackney again. This time, to a school for 'delicate children', something I shall never regret. All of the children, it was felt, needed someone on hand who could give them medical attention if the need arose. So along with the children with eczema and asthma there were also those that were epileptic, diabetic, with a whole range of disabilities. I remember it as a very happy place and it was here that I learnt to understand so much about my own disability and learnt about those affecting others. I have been able to grow up free from the ignorance that most people have about such disabilities and have been able to see how easily and readily people accept myths rather than facts.

I stayed at this school until I was 11, when I moved back into 'mainstream' education. By than my eczema was much improved, but my asthma and the allergies that caused it were becoming increasingly hard to control. Now I was dealing with a 'hidden disability'. I 'looked alright' now, but why was I always off school? Why did I run so slowly on the games field?

There were frequent question marks in my school reports and from teachers as to whether I was malingering or not, although I did achieve a certain degree of success in some subjects.

In short, I got through secondary school, just, but once again it was a lonely experience, drawing very much on inner resources learnt earlier on in my childhood.

In conclusion, I feel able to talk about my experiences at school now without too much pain. My initial experience of mainstream education was, to say the least traumatic and could have damaged me more severely than any illness or disability that I have suffered. Going to 'special' school was a very positive experience. It taught me how to like myself, to take pride in myself and most of all to be sensitive to the needs of others, to appreciate people for their 'differentness' as much as their 'sameness'.

Sharon Sullivan

'We Can Speak for Ourselves'.
Credit Sally and Richard Greenhill.

What disabled children have to say

Joys I'll never know

I would like people to know that 'What you've never had you don't miss' is not true. I do miss not being able to ride a bike or skateboard. I also miss not being able to do little things like splashing in rain puddles or being able to ride a double decker bus. I would like them to understand what it is like to have to spend a large part of your childhood in hospital, but I would not wish it upon them.

Heather Jones

'Understanding through suffering'

My hands are part of my body and they are guided by my heart ...

My hands are my best friends; I like them very much, because I have a disability in my lower limbs. If I didn't have hands, I couldn't walk with crutches so I wouldn't walk at all. There are hands that start wars and others that make peace. But my hands will never start wars but they will make peace, they will love the people, the poor, and sick and that's how all the hands of the world should be.

Cecilia, 14

I don't like it!

My worst experience of being in a wheelchair happened when I was eight years old. I was in hospital and two nurses were tidying my bed when one said to the other 'Isn't it a shame that she'll never be able to walk?' The other said , 'Yes it is.'' Then they went. Up to that moment I had always believed that one day I would be able to walk. I had no idea that I was going to have to spend the rest of my life in a wheelchair. People seem to think that if you have always been in a wheelchair that you don't have to learn to accept it, but they are wrong because I then had to learn to accept it.

Heather Jones

Hello! I am a disabled boy. I wish to be understood and may I tell you my feelings. We may be disabled but we have our abilities too. I always believe the value of life is not measured by the length of life but by what one can achieve during life.

A good friend of mine once said 'Life is like a "comet". It will light up and brighten the whole world, even though it may sparkle and disappear in a second.'

I wish people would give us the opportunity to reach our potential. I, too, sincerely hope all the disabled could understand the meaning of those words and try their best to contribute to their society.

Wong Chi Hang, 15

... the most important advantage of losing one's sight - you learn that people's appearances don't matter, and that it's far more important what they are as a person.

Anne Carter, 11

'The Rights and Needs of "Handicapped" People'

They need to be helped.
They need to be loved by others.
They need to be respected.
They need to be considered.
They need to be educated.
They need to be trusted.
They need to be appreciated as useful people.
They need to lead a good, happy life.
They need to be fed.

Mwaniki Makau, 10

I think my idea of a ful life is that I would like to do as many things as I could do and what I wanted to without people telling me what I can and can't do. I think that it is important, especially as you get older you must learn to be independent, to do things for yourself.

Sue Logan, 18

Towards independence

Usually when I want help nobody comes, but sometimes when I am trying to be independent, half a dozen people arrive to help.

Haider Tirmizey, 15

We have certain rights

What I need from you is only my rights and not a lot of sympathy.

Mutinda Kimilu, 9

All these quotes come from 'What It's Like to be Me' Edited and Published by Helen Exley 198
ISBN 185 015 0060.

Integration of Disabled Children: Lessons from Italy and the United States*

by Richard Rieser

In the last 15 years both the USA and Italy have embarked on major changes in the education of disabled children.

In the USA "The education of all 'Handicapped' Children Act" of 1975 (PL .94 - 142) guarantees all disabled children a free appropriate education in the least restrictive educational setting.

In Section 300.550-300.556 this is qualified:- that to the maximum extent appropriate, disabled children should be educated with non-disabled. That special classes, separate schooling or other removal from regular education occurs only when the nature of the disability is such that education in regular classes with the use of supplementary aids and services cannot be satisfactorily achieved.

In the USA Federal funding was made available to all public authorities to achieve the above.

Therefore it is perhaps surprising to find that of the 3,789,382 disabled children aged 6 to 17, 26.5% were in regular classrooms. (They spent less than 21 percent of the day out of class.) See Table 1.

Table 1 -USA Number and Percent of Disabled Children 6-17 years 1985-86 in Different Educational Settings

	Number	% of Disabled Children
Regular Class	1,002,809	26.5%
Resource Room	1,654,318	43.7%
Separate Class	907,500	23.9%
Separate Facility	158,660	4.2%
Residential Facility	40,342	1.1%
Homebound/Hospital	25,753	0.7%
Total	3,789,382	100%

(From Danielson LC Bellamy GT 1988)

So it is a professional judgement rather than a resource decision that is leading to 74% of disabled children not being education with their peers. However only 5.3% are being educated in the equivalent of separate special schools compared to England and Wales where 25% of all disabled children were educated in special schools. (63% of the most severely disabled.) This is far less segregated.

In Italy in the 1970's on the other hand anti-segregation sentiment led by the Italian Communist Party was developed into a rapid integration programme.

In 1971 the Italian Parliament passed National Law 118 which mandated the compulsory education of disabled children (pre-school to junior high) and their placement in regular classes.

The rapid application of integration for all proved to need educational refinement as mainstream teachers and schools were not equipped to teach sign language, braille or provide special equipment.

The passing of National Law 517 ended the 'integrazione selvaggia' (wild integration). It made the following impressive provisions:

1. A maximum of two disabled children can be integrated into one class.

2. Integrated classes are limited to 20 pupils including the two disabled pupils.

3. Support teachers (insegrati di sostegno) will be assigned by the State to assist regular teachers. For every four disabled students in the school one support teacher will be assigned.

4. The local health agency - Unita Sanitaria Local - USC will provide diagnosis and therapeutic services for disabled pupils and their families.

Since 1977 what has been achieved? 80-95% of disabled pupils in every school district are integrated. Children with Downs Syndrome, Cerebral Palsy, severe learning difficulty, autism, microcephaly and deaf and blind children are commonly found in regular classes. In 1987 101,388 disabled children were integrated in regular classes.

Children with mild to moderate learning difficulties and behavioural problems are not 'certified' but they do receive additional attention from regular and special teachers.

Some private special schools still exist but they are not publicly funded. There are 6,479 gravely disabled (graversim) pupils who the USC judge will not benefit from regular schooling.

Vitello observes positive attitudes among both teachers and non-disabled pupils to disabled pupils and a warm and friendly atmosphere on a visit to eight different integrated classes. This is in contrast to the current 'great controversy' over integrating mildly disabled pupils into regular classes in the USA under the Regular Education Initiative.

In Italy these pupils are not even classified as disabled.

There are communication problems between the USC and teachers.

Integration has necessitated educators moving to individualised instruction not just for disabled students but for all. This is now becoming part of the fabric of Italian schools. Integration is supported by the community and this has proved a very helpful support for teachers.

A multi-disciplinary support team visits schools from the USC and undertakes a comprehensive evaluation of the child and specifies the number of hours individualised tuition (limited to 18 hours maximum per week), and provides special therapies, e.g., speech or physical.

Italians have incorporated the Individualised Education Plan from the US.

The PEI 'Piano Education Individualizzato' is based on a functional diagnosis of students' abilities and disabilities. Italian educators have moved away from a medical model of assessment towards a curriculum-based model.

There is much we can learn from Italy and USA. Firstly State funding is essential. Secondly if integration is to be a rights issue to end segregation, it will require specialist support teams, teachers and reduced class sizes.

All teachers need an on-going INSET programme. This was advocated by Warnock 1978 and has stillnot been achieved. Individualised teaching and curriculum assessment lend themselves to the teaching of our National Curriculum to all.

Perhaps the most interesting point to arise from this comparison is the difference in what is meant by integration in Italy and the USA.

In Italy integration was part of a general political movement in 1970's to integrate the disenfranchised. In the US the Disability Rights Movement led the fight for legislation. The Italian movement had a wider and more generalised political base and has therefore been able to go much further than the movement in the USA. In Britain for those seeking equal rights for disabled students and faced with the lack of progress to

real integration it is important to see the need for such a generalised campaign to force sufficient funding from Central Government.

*Based on article by S. H. Vitello, 1989
'Integration of Handicapped Students in the United States and Italy' a comparison. In International Journal of Special Education Vol. 4, No. 1.

Disabled Awareness - Disabled People Lead in Haringey

> *Children of today are adults of tomorrow and we want adults of tomorrow to be better informed than adults today. We, therefore, go into schools to educate children for the future about how disabled people cope with everyday life and how they are treated.*

The History of the Schools Disability

Connexions, a Disability Arts Project based in Haringey has been running a committee skills workshop since November 1987. During these sessions there were discussions around personal experiences of growing up with a disability and the reactions of able-bodied people, particularly children. Everyone felt that the major reason for negative responses was ignorance, fear of the unknown and lack of contact. We felt that the experience of being disabled should be shared with children as soon as they were old enough to understand. At this point we decided we would go out and work in primary schools and also with teachers still in training. After further discussion we decided that talking to children about experiences would not be sufficiently gripping and we needed to evolve a way of reaching them in a participatory manner - a workshop format was developed and the whole thing became the Schools Disability Awareness Project.

As we got near to the time of going to our first school the people within the project grew very apprehensive - many of them had had very bad experiences with children.

The Workshop consisted of:

1   An introductory game.

2   Children in small groups with one or two people with disabilities and a travel agent, planning a holiday together.

3   Together again in a big group where the problems of planning the holiday were summed up.

4   Planning together a totally accessible holiday and leisure complex.

In Good Practices. 'Chicken Shed Disabled Theatre in Education Group'.

Credit CSIE: Brian Shuel

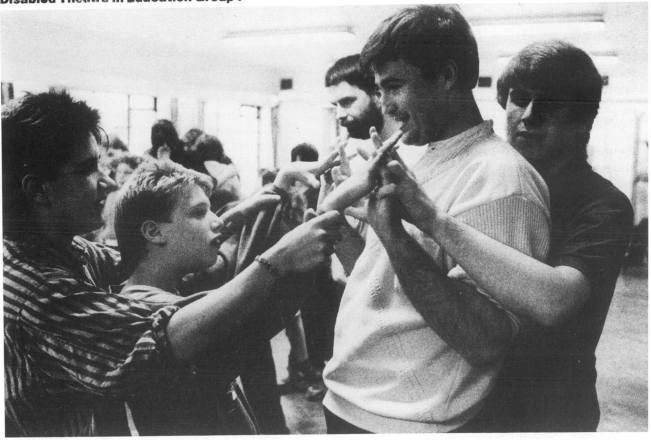

The children made everyone feel relaxed -they were very welcoming, attentive and caring. They were at ease and wanting to learn. (We were nervous!) They were direct and unembarrassed in their questions. It was felt that they really got the idea of the everyday problems of being disabled. It was, however, harder to convey the concept of hidden disabilities such as epilepsy to the children.

Aims of the Group

Children of today are adults of tomorrow and we want adults of tomorrow to be better informed than adults today. We, therefore, go into schools to educate children for the future about how disabled people cope with everyday life and how they are treated.

We felt that trying to plan a holiday to include disabled people would be a way to make clear the practical difficulties and problems in the environment and every day life for a disabled person that ordinary people don't have and take for granted. A shared activity would also open the doors to easy talking and discussion.

We also wanted, as far as was possible and appropriate for the age of the children, to give them some idea of the intimidation and humiliation that disabled people suffer. We felt that able-bodied people push others away because they are embarrassed and scared. We hoped that early contact between children and disabled people would avoid this and they would realise that disabled people are just ordinary people with disabilities.

Finally we wished to end the sessions on a positive note so we began, all together, to plan a totally accessible environment, using the knowledge gained of the problems and seeking some solutions. The children were practical, ingenious and fascinated.

Overall we feel that we have proved by these sessions that we can get the children not only thinking, but feeling about these problems and how to solve them. We felt the empathy of the children and there was a oneness of understanding.

Elia's Report

This was a new experience for myself and I presume all the others that attend the Day Centre. Many young children who attend the Nursery were coming to the Day Centre so that their school could be refurbished. We did not know what to expect and how it would turn out - how the children would actually react to people with disabilities. I felt it was necessary for these infants to actually experience being with people such as

Credit CSIE: Brian Shuel.

'Chicken Shed Disabled Theatre in Education Group'

us so I took it upon myself to go in and face them in my wheelchair. When I entered the room they were using I saw many of them step backwards. This is the reaction that most people make when they are faced with a person in a wheelchair. The question I had to face now was how to break down the barrier between us. The way I did this was to attend the Nursery and gradually get the children to come closer and find out what a wheelchair is, and to encourage them to push the wheelchair (my life in their hands). Once they had gained confidence they actually started clambering on to my lap. The question now is do they still remember?

After this all the members decided to give the children a Christmas party which was great fun for all. We invited their parents also and during this party one of the children started climbing up onto my lap. His mother leaped up in shock, saying 'Is he alright?'' and I told her not to worry as he had been doing this for several months and he knew what he was doing so she sat down in relief. Then in came Santa in a wheelchair and everybody became excited.

Written by Haringey Connexions

For further Information contact:
Jan Rubridge (Coordinator)
CONNEXIONS
340 The Broadway
Muswell Hill
London N10 1DJ
01 883 8598

Raising Disability in Primary Schools

by Richard Rieser

I worked at Laburnum Primary for half a day a week for two terms, starting with a full staff meeting on Disability. I then worked with five teachers and their classes for various lengths of time. The children were from four to eleven years old. The teachers were Christine Yorston (4 and 5 year olds), Susie Burrows (5 and 6 year olds), Paula Olurin (7 year olds), Carol-Anne Errington (8 and 9 year olds), Jean Banks (10 and 11 year olds).

With every age group I started by defining disability. Then I described my own disability as openly as I could, showing the children my different sized arms, hands, legs and feet. Because I talked personally even the youngest children could identify with this. (When I tell young children that boys I taught in secondary school used to mimic me they are shocked.) I talked generally with the children about all sorts of disabilities and attitudes in society. The idea of a continuum of disability was important. We discussed the disabilities of children in the class, adults and children in the school, other friends and relations, and their effects on people's lives. These ranged from the hidden to the very obvious. Children were able to talk about their own disabilities in an atmosphere of respect.

Dear Madam/sir   30 June 1989

Our Class been doing a topic on Disability and our friend Richard brought a wheel Chir into the school and our Class' went round our block. This is the obstacle we found 1. uneven and cracked pavements, rubbish, no ramps, cafe signs in the way, cars park in the Way. Can you make Disabled people's life easy?

Can you do something please

your faitfully

By Mayank Bhundia

To bring disability and differences into the open can be a great relief to any child who has tried to hide theirs, or 'cope', or who has suffered pain, teasing or worse in silence. By describing what they may feel is unique to them, and by initiating a positive attitude in the classroom they can lose their alienation and feel valued and good about themselves, maybe for the first time.

Most of the work we went on to do was practical or discussion. The drawings, writings and paintings were mainly done with their teachers afterwards.

The practical work included:

● Simulation work on being blind, using puzzles and special games designed for blind children.

● Simulation work on being physically disabled, e.g., catching with one arm, picking things up with feet.

● Surveys of barriers to access.

● Communication - braille, lip reading, finger spelling, sign language.

● Lesson on injuries to the central nervous system and safety. How these lead to disability and how to avoid them.

These ideas are in the National Curriculum Science and Disability Unit. This I developed with Christine Yorston from the work I did in the school.

It is crucial not to do such activities in isolation. As with work on anti-racism, anti-sexism and class bias, we have to help children look at the roots of discrimination against disabled people, and to counteract it in all its forms. It is not about being 'nice' to disabled people. This cannot be done without continuously challenging negative language, stereotypes and images, linked with positive discussion.

You do not have to be disabled to do this. You just need to have an understanding of what it is like to be disabled in this society. At Laburnum some good work had already been done in all areas of tackling oppression. I tried to build on this. As a disabled person I had my experience to draw on, as Black teachers have their experiences when tackling racism. But as every white teacher must take on the daily struggle against racism, so must every 'able-bodied' teacher take on discrimination against disabled people. Fortunately there are always children with much to teach us all.

R. Rieser

'Checking out the block'.

'Abraham shows what he found out about access.'

Teachers Comments

As a Black teacher who believes very strongly in equal opportunities, I was recently made aware that there was an area of equal opportunities that I had failed to take on board, both as an individual and as a teacher.

This awareness was prompted by Richard Rieser, who presented his paper on disability at one of my school meetings.

Richard changed my perceptions of disability and gave me the impetus to embark on a 'disability' topic with my first year junior class. We team taught and through his own positive image and open ability to share his experiences as a disabled person, the children began their understanding of disability and treated the subject with a great seriousness. A vast array of teaching and books and a variety of activities deepened their initial understanding.

Many of the activities the children undertook were of a practical nature and therefore recording took on a multi-media dimension not all accessible on a usual display.

These included many drama activities encouraging empathy; e.g., the crossing of the hall with apparatus representing a main road, with a blindfold and stick. A PE lesson that required work on the apparatus using three limbs and a great deal of thought and care. This lesson resulted in some of the most creative gymnastics work done all year and left the children with a positive attitude to Rachel (a younger child in the school who has one shorter arm). We also went on a visit to Globe Language Unit in Tower Hamlets, and on a tour of the local area In a wheelchair noting difficulties disabled people face in the environment.

Another of the activities the children enjoyed was learning sign language alphabet and signing for deaf people or hearing impaired; constructing their own sentences using signing; making up long stories and looking up signs in their sign dictionaries. I found this work invaluable as a teacher for it succeeded in appealing to and motivating a new ESL child in my class who had hitherto been extremely reserved. Every silent reading period she would chose one of the simple sign books and sit mouthing the words and signing. I was able to use this as a springboard for a great deal of language work with her.

The effect of this disability topic carried out in the school and others (also motivated by Richard's talk), have been extremely positive. The whole school attitude to disability and disabled people is now a positive one, as demonstrated by the reception of my classes' contributions to assembly concerning disability, which were received by serious interested faces.

I think that it is of vital importance that education and schools make a positive contribution in challenging and changing the discrimination that disabled people can counter in our society.

Paula Olurin
Laburnum JM

183

We went around the street with a wheel chair to see how it feels like and we saw dogs poos and tomato wichi is slippery for Richuds stick.

There was Lots of things in the way. There was a Big chair in the middle of the pavement. There was lots of rubbish and the pavement was Borokn. We nely fell Down. By the canal there was Lots of trees. In the middle of the path we kod only squeeze past with the wheel chair. There wer cars pact on the pavement. My mum is in a wheel chair and she haudiy ever goesout. Mowst people and the council dont seem to cer about disabled people and Bengali people. somepeople dont like Bengali paopk.

কেউ কেউ যা   আর আমি আর

২২ লে চোলা ঢালেরে না ২২ লে ৬৮ লাল

টিন আমিল আমনার না

by moshkura Rafique
7 years

Back row: Alvan, Bereni, Rachel, Femi, Henry.
Front row: Bradley, Kche, Bisi.

Burrows.

Richard come to susies
classand told me
about people disabled
He showed me his small
leg and his foot and his
big leg and his big
arm and his small arm
I saw them. He carries
Sahti. with his small
arm and one hand
and Sahti was heavy.
I like him. The two of us
played castles at the
seaside. I hugged him.
By ALVAN

'Richard'
by Alvan
Aged 5.

Left to right: Nicole, Moshkura, Indiana, Salma, Ashton, Mogfura.

Credit: Susie Burrows.

Richard
by Vid

'Richard' by Vid Aged 5½.

Rachel is in our school and she was born with one short arm and no hand. I like her. She used to cry a lot but now shes stopped because shes got friends. She can do most things - she can swim, tie her laces, carry her dinner.

by Louise

'Rachel', by Louise

Femi   and   Rachel   by   Louise

Rachel   was   born   with   one   shorter   arm.

R O A E L

A girl with no hands. I knock for her and she knocks for me. I help her to feed herself and I give her a drink. I hold the bottle and she puts it in her mouth. She's my best friend. She's 7.

"Rachel's Friend" by Rachel 5.

Rachel

I was born with one arm shorter. I can do laces with two hands. Shall I show you? I can do colouring with my short arm and I can carry my dinner plate on it. I can climb trees. I'm learning to swim. I can actually do most things, but maths is hard, not because of my arm, just because it's hard. Two boys used to make fun of me. They used to say "take that off"! because I used to have a two finger thing, you can pick stuff up with. I had to go to the hospital for it. I thought it would be better but when I got used to it I didn't like it. The strap keeps coming off. I don't use it any more. I think I can do things better with my arm. When I first went into the playground I used to cry, because people pointed at my arm and laughed. I had some friends called Mariam. I'm happy now because I know all the teachers and some of the children are nice to me. When I met Richard he had a different leg, and he was like me except for his hair, and his eyes which are not blue, are they?

Aged 5.

'Rachel – Writing about Herself.'

'Bereni has glasses'

Bereni
by Vid

'Paula'

'Leanne'

My teAcher paula has got ECZEMA. We didn't Know because it is under her clauthes. But Now she told us about it. She is Allergic to milk it makes her head hot.
By Moshkura

In Paulas class there is a girl called Leanne and she has

Asthma. When she came in this class I didn't know but

Paula told us. She's got a Asthma pump. it gives her more

air. by Nicole.

Nasty

When Richerd was a little boy at school the kids Made Fun oF him because he had Polyo. and said " ararrrr you are horrbie. look at your leg." when they said thak it made him Feel Sads. The Teacher didont let him yous the lift. People made Fun of uther people because they are in a Wheelchair. Sometimes they tip them out and beat them up and thay say they Won't get a girlFriend or a boyFriend because they think disabled people are horrible. sometimes disabled People think they are horrble them selFs. Disableld People seebeautiful People With No disability on the televishon or on advertisements. There arent hardy any disabled People in story Books. IF your black and you never see any pictures oF black People you might Feel invisible That's how disabled . People must Feel.

by Indianna   Age 7.

'Indiana Aged 7'

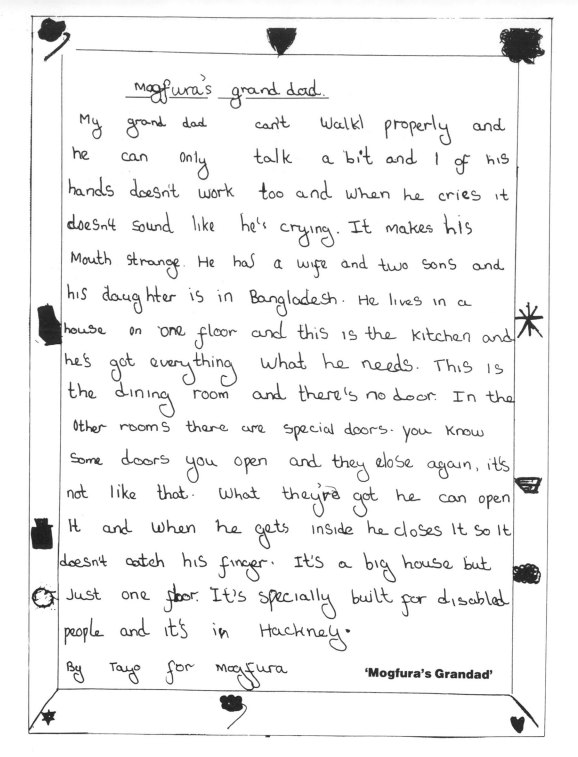

Mogfura's grand dad.

My grand dad can't walkl properly and he can only talk a bit and 1 of his hands doesn't work too and when he cries it doesn4 sound like he's crying. It makes his Mouth strange. He has a wife and two sons and his daughter is in Bangladesh. He lives in a house on one floor and this is the kitchen and he's got everything what he needs. This is the dining room and there's no door. In the other rooms there are special doors. you know some doors you open and they close again, it's not like that. What they're got he can open It and when he gets inside he closes It so It doesn't catch his finger. It's a big house but just one floor. It's specially built for disabled people and it's in Hackney.

By Tayo for Mogfura

'Mogfura's Grandad'

Richard's Work in my School: A Personal View

The invitation to consider our bodies - the functioning of our limbs, our senses, our minds - was radical and salutory in my school.

As we grow older (some of us) - a generation of teachers are noticing how our body works - especially as the National Curriculum takes its toll in stress.

The children we teach know that their bodies are growing. So they're interested in their bodies and, like the rest of us, they measure similarities and differences and are fascinated by what is different or new.

But in bringing disability as an issue to William Patten Infants' Richard Rieser brought to our school - in a staff meeting, assembly and subsequent work with classes and groups of children - a more radical message than the increased awareness of how we do or don't function.

When, in the presence of others, you look at yourself - and this applied to the children and the staff -you find yourself thinking of others.

Focussing on disability proved to be a radical catalyst enabling us to own up to our humanity, even to admit some frailties, difficulties and secrets, though the children were better at owning up than us.

Bullying.

All the children used to bully Richard when he was at school because his leg didn't work properly and they said he was ugly, and he'd never have a girl friend. When all the children are going swimming Richard didn't want to go because everybody stared at his body and thought he was ugly. He thought he was ugly because of the children going "her her her, you cripple" all the time. Richard felt horrid about himself inside his body. He doesn't any more. I think disabled people are <u>not</u> ugly.

by Roy Boateng 7

'Bullying' Roy Boateng 7

The staff meeting was, I thought, the best in living memory whilst the children were given an important moral context to the question as well as invaluable information and it was useful to have Richard there as a self-critical role model, prepared to use himself as an example.

The children studying - or suffering -the National Curriculum are going to have to look at how the body works and it would be criminal to present the body or body-mind as if it were in some way perfect in its functioning - or as if some mythic perfection were the norm - always a danger when presenting the biological and the human together.

It would be even more criminal to avoid teaching about the need to improve the situation - whether by children writing to the council, presenting careful and considered studies to the Education Authority or demonstrating.

The children who worked with Richard are involved in a vital investigation that really matters and the more reality we bring to school the better.

For teachers there is an urgent need to overcome Government policies of divide and rule. Our schools must not become little punitive well-run feudal systems competing in the world of public relations.

The collective must be re-asserted against the alienation of careerism and control and there is no better way of doing this than by honestly tackling the question of disability. Many thanks to Richard for reminding us of the dictum: 'From each according to their ability. . .'

Brian Simons
William Patten Infants'

Good Practices in the Classroom

by Micheline Mason

Teachers will have to modify this depending on which age group they are teaching.

Good practices within the classroom towards the issues of disability are the major teaching methods that should be used. Teaching by example.

1 The school should have a whole-school policy towards disability. All the school's practices should be examined with the assumption that some of the staff and pupils affected by the practices will have disabilities. This includes everything from fire drill to collecting the dinner money.

2 Structures should be developed whereby all incoming staff and students can define their own "special needs", e.g. all new pupils could introduce themselves to their class by answering the following questions:

(a) What's your name?
(b) How old are you?
(c) What do you like best about yourself?
(d) What do you like doing best?
(e) What do you find difficult to do?
(f) What things might you need some help with?
(g) What *don't* you like people doing to you?

3 In addition to this a short profile of each child's needs should be written for all the staff to refer to (see Park Barn example) if this is necessary. If the child is able, they should write their own profile (Park Barn example).

4 If a child defines a need which can be acted upon straightaway, then it should be done, e.g. a change of position so s/he can see/hear better.

5 If physical arrangements in the classroom have to be altered, or "rules" introduced to allow access to someone in a wheelchair for example, it would be better to do this with the presence and co-operation of the fellow classmates who will then understand the need behind the request, e.g. pushing chairs back under the tables instead of leaving them blocking up pathways through the classroom.

6 If a child cannot communicate on this level because of age or lack of speech/language, then invite an advocate to attend the first day(s) and ask them the same questions.

7 Make sure the teachers and other staff consult the parents of any child about their needs. All people are individuals and even the most extensive reading into disabilities will not give you the information you need about any particular child. Nor will "medical" information.

8 If a child's disability is affected by environmental factors, e.g. allergy to chalk dust, then make any attempt to lessen or eliminate these factors consciously and publically. You are "teaching" that people matter.

9 Make sure there are positive images of disabled people, especially children in the books, posters, photographs and other materials you might use. (See resource list.) Remember to include images of black and other minority groups amongst this.

10 Be aware of different cultures, attitudes and beliefs around disability. This is particularly important when in a school where many children speak a first language that may not be understood by the teachers. Disabled pupils *may* be being subjected to all kinds of teasing or abuse quite without the knowledge of the staff. Dealing wih this will have to be done with great sensitivity.

11 Bring up the issue of language and disability from nursery age upwards. Do not allow the names of disabilities to be used as insults, e.g. dummy, spastic, deafy, etc, and be very careful of your own language as an educator. Consider even the use of very common words - ugly, stupid, silly, daft, clumsy, naughty - what does it do to label anyone with these negative judgements?

12 Never confuse a person with their behaviour. "That boy is behaving in a destructive way" is very different to "That boy is destructive". It is important that children are reassured that a good person can behave in bad ways - including themselves - because once self-esteem is lost by the message "I am bad" then it will automatically follow that they will try to compensate by labelling others as "also bad" or "worse" - usually weaker and less able or more troubled persons than themselves. People with high self-esteem do not abuse others, nor are they usually victims of abuse. Having a disability is not a factor that alters this.

13 Encourage any child with a disabilty to organise some group activities around their own strengths, e.g. "crawling" games led by a child who cannot walk, "guess the object in the black bag by touch" game led by a blind child, "mime" games led by a deaf child. This may involve you in some careful observation of what a child's strengths may be. It is important that you point out though that if a child with a disability comes out as

superior at manoeuvring their wheelchair or differentiating objects by sound or touch, for example, that this is only because of practice, not because of some magical "compensation" that "normal" people don't possess.

14 Set up a structure, formal or informal, for disabled pupils to come together to give "feedback" on the school's policy and practice as regards their needs. This is one way of fostering a positive identity as a *group*, and it is important that children with mild or invisible disabilities are included (children with asthmas, diabetes, etc). Very young children can be included in this, and it should include such things as their relationship with any classroom aides, management of medication, fatigue, feeling "left out", etc. As they get older it would include self-image, etc.

15 Involve disabled people in the school at all levels, not as curios, invited to speak about disability, but as useful and interesting human beings. If a local disabled person has an interesting hobby, invite them in to talk about it. If they have a skill to share, ask them to come and share it. If they have time to spare, perhaps they could come and listen to children read, or do an art project, or cooking or photography. Perhaps a disabled person does puppet shows, or likes singing or is just great at playing with young children. The point is to allow contact so that questions can arise and be dealt with naturally, and at the same time the non-disabled pupils are experiencing disabled adults as having something to give.

16 Being aware that the able-bodied adult world moves at a pace that is faster than is good for anyone. Children, although often physically active are not 'driven' in the way adults are usually. That is why we are always telling them to 'Hurry up'. (How many times a day do you say 'Hurry up and ....' in your classroom.) People with physical disabilities and people with learning difficulties suffer from this one thing almost as much as everything else. People with learning difficulties are actually called 'Slow' as if there really is a correct speed to do things. 'Quick' is a compliment, 'Slow' is an insult. Do we ever stop and ask ourselves why?

17 At the same time as non-disabled people try to hurry us up, when *they* want *us* to do something, they use their power to make us WAIT in almost every situation when we need them to do something for us. Disabled people wait for transport, wait to go to the loo, wait for a bath, wait to go for a walk, wait in hospitals - you name it, we wait for it. But we mustn't get impatient because we might annoy our helpers. This is one of the dilemmas of dependence. It happens to young children and older people as well. Waiting is institutionalised in this country for disabled people. Our time, like our lives, is not considered to be important. As we move forward towards self-respect and equality, it can be expected that we will lose our endurance and false patience. However difficult it may feel to the non-disabled, this trend should be encouraged by our allies. Disabled people learn to use time in different, and often much more efficient ways than able-bodied people. We often do less and achieve more. This is also true of people with learning difficulties. People who are able-bodied are often most challenged by our different paces, feeling enormous impatience and frustration with having to listen for five minutes to something they could have said in ten seconds, for example. This difficulty needs to be acknowledged, but the problem needs to be firmly located in the 'speediness' of society, not in our challenging behaviour.

Teasing and bullying

There is no doubt that this goes on in all schools, 'special' or mainstream. Because young disabled people are likely to already feel 'different' in a mainstream setting, the teasing may feel worse if it comes from the non-disabled young people. It is not helpful to tell the person that it is 'normal', or that they are imagining it, if they feel that others are treating them unfairly.

Teasing and bullying should not be ignored or run-away from. The most helpful role an adult can take is to LISTEN to the person's feelings about the situation, help them to decide if it is something requiring some kind of action or not, and if it is, helping them to work out a strategy to deal with it. This may involve setting up a meeting between the 'victim' and the named perpetrator(s) where both sides can say what they think is happening.

'When you do such and such a thing it makes me feel so-and-so, or it makes me think so-and-so', is an effective, non-confrontational way of exchanging information where it is assumed there has been misunderstanding or mistreatment.

It should be made clear that the school has a policy which will not allow abusive language, or violence to be used against another pupil, including disabled pupils, nor will it allow disabled pupils to abuse others. What constitutes abusive language should be stated. (See Language and Harassment and Discipline in Whole School Policy.)

Dealing with questions

The essential issue is one of good practice. Don't ask someone what they have "got" or what's "wrong" with them. Give them a platform from which they can define their needs in relation to you (or the other pupils or staff or building, etc). With a very young child or a non-communicating child, then ask their parents. The parents can be a wonderful resource. When children ask "What's wrong with her" or some such question, they need a simple but accurate answer that explains the EFFECT of a condition, e.g. "She is a spastic" is not a good answer. The complexity of the answer should be related to the age/comprehension of the questioner e.g.,

Q. 'What's wrong with Jane?'

A. "Jane finds it difficult to make her muscles do what she wants them to do." or

A "Jane has a lot of difficulty co-ordinating her movements because of damage to certain parts of her brain." or

A. "Jane stopped breathing for a few minutes just after she was born. This meant that oxygen didn't get to every bit of her brain and some cells died. The part of her brain that was damaged was the part that sends messages to her muscles to tell them when to tighten and when to relax. If the messages get a bit mixed up it makes your muscles move in ways that you didn't intend. Sometimes it makes it very difficult to relax your muscles at all. This is called a spasticity in the muscles. Sometimes it is very difficult to stop your muscles moving all the time. This is called athetoid cerebral palsy. These involuntary movements are just as tiring as if you were doing them on purpose. Jane uses a lot of concentration and effort to do the things she wants."

Disability courtesy —
'good manners' towards Disabled People

One of the best things about having relationships with disabled people, is that it presents opportunities to learn lots of new skills, most of which are simply a wider understanding of 'Good Manners'.

Different kinds of conditions require specific responses, so we are dividing up the skills into groups that relate to particular needs.

Good Manners towards people who are blind or partially blind

1 Notice who they are. Totally blind people are usually easy to distinguish but partially blind people are often extremely clever at 'getting by' with limited eyesight, their other senses and guesswork. Therefore it is much easier to be unaware of their needs.

Good manners to blind or partially sighted people.

Credit CSIE.

2 Introduce yourself *by name* before starting a conversation 'Hi, it's Penny here. Is it raining outside?'.

3 Say a blind persons name when you are starting a conversation. Without visual clues they cannot know who you are talking to unless you say.

4 Speak before touching someone. It can be very frightening to be touched with no warning.

5 Be ready to describe things so as to give a person with little or no sight the basic information about the environment that a sighted person will take in automatically, e.g., Who is in the room, what they are doing, where they are sitting, anything unusual or interesting that is in the room, etc.

6 Don't move off without telling the person 'I'm going now'. Blind people are often left talking to thin air.

7 Do not avoid the words see, look, etc., also some totally blind people appreciate description using colours, because even though they have never seen them, they may have their own conception of them. Ask.

8 Ask a blind or partially blind person if they need help to get somewhere BEFORE giving it. If they do, offer your arm for them to hold. Do not push or propel someone in front of you. If the person is holding on to you and slightly behind you, they will feel in control as they can let go at any time, and they will be able to tell by your body movements whether you are squeezing past obstacles, going up or down slopes or steps, going through doors, etc. When having to go single-file, move your arm behind your back, still allowing the person to hold on. If you are a wheelchair user, you can easily guide a blind person by allowing them to hold a handle of your chair, following the same guidelines as above.

9 Tell a person where a chair or bed or whatever is, and put their hand on the chairback. Don't push them down into it.

10 Some blind people like to have food arranged on a plate like a clock. This helps them to know what they have to eat and how they can eat it the way they want. ''Your chips are at 12 o'clock, your fish at 6 o'clock and your peas at 9 o'clock. There is tomato sauce at 3 o'clock if you want it. There is a glass of water on the table in front of your plate on the right-hand side.''

11 Allow blind people, particularly young children, to touch things and get in a mess. This is the only way they can learn.

12 Allow blind people, particularly children, to touch you. This is how they find out what you 'look' like - how tall you are, how big, whether you have long hair or not, etc. When a blind child says 'Can I look at your toy', they usually mean, 'let me feel it so I know what it is like'.

13 In an environment that a person with little or no sight uses regularly, remember that order is vital, and that if anything has to be changed, tell the person and show the person what change has been made.

14 Warn a blind person about possible dangers in a new environment - e.g., very hot radiators.

15 Remembers that blind people and people with little sight are excluded from all information given in printed form. This is not just the obvious books, but birthday cards, notices on the notice boards, posters, letters, menus, instructions, photographs, maps, food labels, catalogues, insurance policies, bills and receipts, bus stop information, tickets, placenames, etc., etc. The inaccessibility of written or printed information can be one of the most 'disabling' factors of society for all people who cannot read for whatever reason. Braille and taped books redress only a fraction of the balance. Also white sticks and quide dogs cannot read either! Technology is being developed that can help, e.g., machines which 'read' print aloud, but nothing will take the place of aware friends and teachers who remember to 'translate' print into words, or an accessible form of literature.

16 Don't pat or distract a guide dog while she/he has her harness on.

17 Move out of the way of a person feeling their way along by the use of a long cane.

18 Don't make assumptions about what a blind or partially sighted person can do, e.g., blind children can play football, if the ball has a bell inside it. Similarly many activities are possible with small modifications or adaptions to equipment.

19 Explain to a blind child (or adult) any special needs of other children or adults with whom she/he may come into contact, e.g., Johnny walks with crutches and falls over if he tripped or knocked into. His crutches sound like this ... they feel like this ... they are used like this .... When you hear him near you, be extra careful not to walk into him.

'Good Manners towards Deaf or Partially Deaf People

1 Notice who they are. Totally deaf people will probably be obvious because of unusual or absent speech, and the use of a visual language. (They may or may not use hearing aids.) People who are partially deaf, however, may 'get by' by guess work and using visual clues to a great extent. They may use hearing aids and have a noticeable difference in speech patterns, or they may not. If a person has a hearing loss, get them to describe in detail how it affects them and what would be useful in terms of support.

2 Face the person before speaking or touching them.

3 Find out what form of communication the person prefers - signing, lip-reading, etc.

4 If the person uses British Sign Language as their first language then

   (a) learn how to do it and meanwhile,

   (b) make sure the person has an interpreter whenever she/he is expected to, or needs or wants to communicate with non-BSL users.

5 If the person lip-reads then make sure your face is in the light, face the person and speak normally, but clearly. Try not to change track mid-sentence. Don't shout. Don't exaggerate your mouth movements. Do use your facial expressions to emphasise your meanings. Do add mime. Fingerspell names or people or places as these cannot be guessed. Be patient. Be ready to repeat yourself if necessary. Don't put your hands in front of your face. Don't smoke and speak at the same time. Don't expect a lip-reader to understand you if your mouth is obscured by a hairy moustache.

6 In any classroom or other group situation where a deaf or partially deaf student or teacher is participating, arrange people in such a way that everyone can see each others faces - circles rather than rows. If rows are unavoidable, get any speaker to come up front and face the audience. Get each speaker to make a visible sign (e.g., raised hand) before speaking so that deaf people can locate which face to look at. This *includes* the teacher. Get people to speak one at a time.

7 Remember that deaf people cannot 'hear' or speak' in the dark, and this includes discos, parties, camping out at night, restaurants, night clubs, etc.

8 Do not assume being deaf is a tragedy.

9 Background noise can make it much harder for a partially deaf person to communicate orally. Leave your intimate conversations for quiet surroundings, not the playground, cafeteria, staff room or pub.

10 If the person uses a hearing-aid fitted with a T switch and can benefit from the use of induction loops, then have them fitted and use them in all halls and classrooms where the person is expected to function.

11 If an interpreter is being used, place the interpreter near the main speaker (if appropriate). The deaf person can then watch the speaker and the interpreter.

12 Do not use the words 'deaf' or 'dumb' or 'dummy' to denote lack of interest or stupidity. This is abusive to deaf people.

13 Remember that it requires a lot of energy and concentration for a deaf person to deal with a hearing community. They may get tired, frustrated and want to 'switch off', literally. This need should be acknowledged. A deaf member of any group should be asked to say when they need a break, or when they have had enough. Sometimes a 'writer' sitting next to a deaf person writing down the main points being said can take the pressure off.

Credit From Miller.

Good Manners to Deaf and Partial Hearing People.
East Park Junior Wolverhampton.

Sign Language

```
Joyous wealth of free expression
Pouring uninhibited
Body, hands communicating
Unlocked meanings fill my head.

This is where I find a freedom
Far beyond words framed by lips
Silently with understanding,
Ease and joy, there learning sits.

Signs of life and signs of reason
Signs that break through loneliness
Bringing feelings of belonging
I can find myself in this.


SARAH HEAD
```

Cartoon

Poem and Drawing IFTC.

Good manners towards people with hidden disabilities

1 Never assume that every person in a group is able-bodied. Many disabilities are not apparent.

2 Use the phrase 'hidden disability'. It paves the way for identifications.

3 If a person identifies themselves as having a hidden disability show an interest in the details of how they are affected.

4 Make realistic allowances, and acknowledge any extra efforts required to do ordinary things.

5 Do not use derogatory language about peoples' so called 'minor' disabilities or unseen chronic illnesses, or allow people to use such language towards each other. (You will not be able to stop every abusive word. What is more important is that you say that it is wrong.)

6 Bring things such as medicines, hospitals, doctors, special diets, etc., into ordinary conversations so that opportunities are presented for people with hidden disabilities to share their often very isolating experiences.

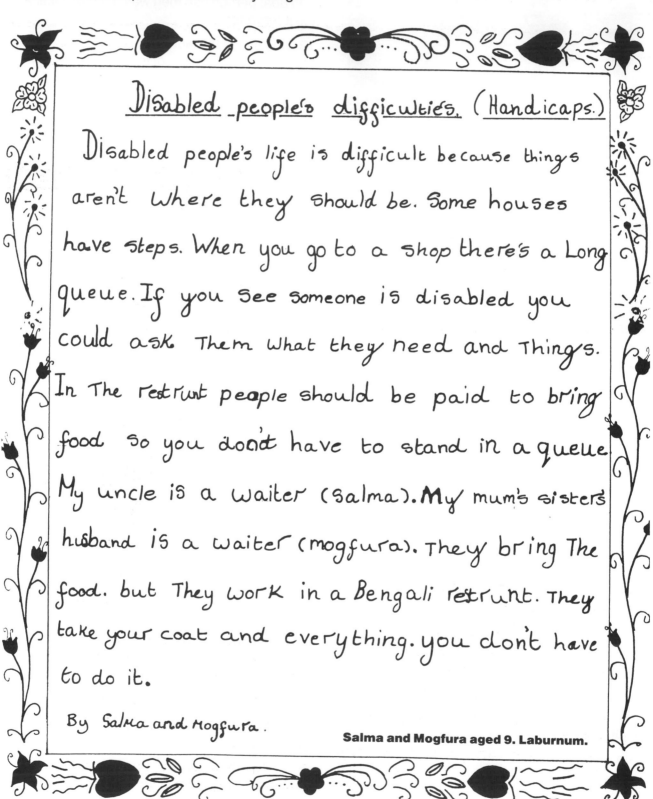

Disabled people's difficulties. (Handicaps.)

Disabled people's life is difficult because things aren't where they should be. Some houses have steps. When you go to a shop there's a Long queue. If you see someone is disabled you could ask Them what they need and Things. In The restrunt people should be paid to bring food so you don't have to stand in a queue. My uncle is a waiter (Salma). My mum's sisters husband is a waiter (mogfura). They bring The food. but They work in a Bengali restrunt. They take your coat and everything. you don't have to do it.

By Salma and Mogfura.

Salma and Mogfura aged 9. Laburnum.

7 Acknowledge and 'allow' the expression of frustration or disappointment. Intermittent conditions often bring a lot of sudden 'changes of plan', cancellations and 'missing out' on treats for young people. Never knowing if you are going to be well enough to go on some outing, sit an exam, meet the boyfriend, play in the match, etc., brings a particular distress which may lead to a generalised 'What's the point' attitude if these feelings are denied.

8 Ask 'how are you feeling' rather than 'Are you feeling better?' (This question is often experienced as having a silent 'YET' at the end of it.)

9 Believe a person when they say they are in need of medication or are feeling ill. Young people have died in both mainstream and special schools as a direct result of staff not taking a child's requests for attention seriously enough. It is always better to err on the side of caution. Most people MINIMISE rather than MAXIMISE their special needs.

10 Encourage staff with hidden disabilities to talk about them.

'Work in FE College: Coventry'.

Good Manners towards people with Physical Disabilities

1 Find out who has a physical disability, as not all are obvious, and ask them how exactly it affects them and what is useful assistance.

2 Learn to push a wheelchair safely.

3 Never push a person in a wheelchair without warning them or asking them first. Explain this 'role' to even the youngest of children. It is just the same as 'pushing' a person who is not in a wheelchair.

4 Do not fiddle with buttons or controls of powered chairs.

5 Come down to the head height of a person using a wheelchair if you are in conversation, especially children.

6 Learn how to lift without straining your back.

7 Learn to fold and store a collapsible wheelchair.

8 Make sure a person who uses sticks or crutches always has them within their reach.

9 Offer to carry books, etc., for anyone who has a walking difficulty and make sure they have somewhere to sit if needed.

10 Offer to carry trays and drinks when eating together and allow people to go to the top of the queue if standing is a problem.

11 Be aware of fatigue as a real issue for many people with physical conditions. Allow the person to define their own needs and limits in this area, even young children. Think of ways to lessen the effort involved in everyday activities. Don't force a disabled person to do everything they can do as a matter of false principle ('it is better to be independent' 'they must not be allowed to get lazy/manipulative/weak', etc.) It is an essential Life Skill for us that we make our own decisions as to how to spend our energy. It is one we have to learn and practice just like other skills.

12 Be patient. Some of us do like to do things for ourselves, but are slower than a non-disabled person might be.

13 Disabled people are the experts on our conditions and needs, and most of us like to be asked rather than have assumptions made about us by others. However, sensitivity is needed from adults in order to recognize that answering questions about ourselves requires different amounts of emotional effort on our part, depending on personality, self-confidence and the level of energy available on any particular day. It is preferable to ask very specific questions like 'Do you need me to open this door for you?' rather than general questions like 'How do you manage?' It is also preferable to set up pre-arranged information-sharing sessions with as many people as possible, rather than a disabled person having to repeat the same information to many individuals which, to us, can become tedious. It is also polite to consider whether your question is intrusive by first thinking whether you would ask a similar question of a non-disabled person e.g., 'How do you go to the toilet?'

14 If a person asks for help with a physical activity, it is courteous to do it, without sighing, complaining, saying 'I'm busy' or 'what, again!' or keeping the person waiting unnecessarily. People quite often have difficulty with this because it is sometimes a way of having power over someone else, to withhold assistance. This 'difficulty' may be unconscious and is usually a leftover behaviour pattern from our early childhood when we all needed help all the time and adults wielded all sorts of power over us especially when they didn't approve of our plans! A teacher of a class may need to set firm codes of conduct in this area, as well as being a role-model of a willing helper.

Sexuality and Disability

by Micheline Mason

There is nothing different about disabled people in regard to sexuality, except other people's expectations of us.

Disabled children are at least as vulnerable to sexual abuse as able-bodied children.

Disabled people have sexual feelings and will want to express them in exactly the same way as their able-bodied counterparts.

Disabled people have the same right to sex education, contraceptive advice and support around making relationships as any other young person of the same age.

Disabled people are no more vulnerable to the emotional roller-coaster of falling in and out of love than anyone else and are not less able to deal with it. Disabled people should be expected to follow the same life patterns as anyone else - finding a partner having children, getting married, getting divorced, etc., etc. Genetic counselling should be offered, but not in such a way that would insinuate that having a disabled baby has to be a bad thing. Parenting skills should be taught in secondary schools and it should be brought to people's attention that even severely disabled people have become successful parents.

AT THE SAME TIME, it should be recognised that the problems that society imposes on young people with regard to their sexuality are likely to attach themselves to disabled young people with a vengeance. In one's teenage years life becomes a market place for potential partners. It is fiercely competitive and largely based on superficial appearances. I have listened to many people talking about their adolescence and for nearly all of them it was a harrowing time, filled with confusion and insecurity. It is the time in their lives when they are most prone to feeling that something is wrong with them and that they don't fit in. Everyone talks about peer pressure, but can you remember the agonies felt at not having the right clothes or hairdo, or spots, or being flat-chested or skinny or short or fat, or not liking the right pop idol, or not having hairs where they ought to be? Well, disabled people are often left feeling that they have few, if any marketable attributes, especially if body image has been damaged by invalidating treatment in the past. It is a time when merging into your own age group is vital if you are to identify in the world as a young adult and not your parents' child. Yet it is the time when the social implications of being disabled may only just be being understood and the

Sexuality and Disability.

Credit Brittle Bone Society Newsletter.

differences between the disabled teenager and the non-disabled teenager may become acutely apparent. The choices open to young people may be far more restricted for a disabled teenager, especially as economic dependence may continue for years, with the added limitations that it brings. For example, it is not so easy to hang around the streets, stay out late, defy your parents and other such normal activities when you can't get out of the house without your parents' assistance.

Role models at this time are very important. Our jaded experience is that we cannot rely on non-disabled people to reassure a young doubt-filled, disabled person about anything to do with their futures. Most able-bodied people take the view that our fears are well-founded and that there are probably more problems ahead of us than we can anticipate! This does not draw us to open up our hearts and souls to most people, sometimes even to ourselves. What does make a difference is seeing people like oneself having made it - not the supercrip skiing on one leg whilst studying for a Ph.d - but making it in ordinary life as ordinary people, learning to drive or using transport systems, employing helpers, leaving home, getting work, having relationships, living together, having adventures, having children, having respect. It is probably true that achieving most of these things will be harder, require more effort and take longer than for their able-bodied counterparts, because of the way things are stacked against disabled people, but there is nothing about being disabled that inevitably closes doors to possibilities. Many disabled people *end up* with a greater sense of confidence, self esteem and inner security than many non-disabled adults because we are forced to question, think, challenge and develop our inner resources in order to survive. The relationships we do make are high quality. This is not bravery. We have no choice.

There are a few specific areas we would like to look at.

Sexual Abuse

It is with horror that the high incidence of sexual abuse of children is being uncovered. It is obvious that all children because of their size and relative powerlessness are vulnerable to exploitation by adults. This is no less so for disabled children or children with learning difficulties. One of the reasons disabled people have rejected all forms of institutionalisation, especially the common practice of institutionalising very young disabled children, is because we know that we are not always 'cared' for at all, but can be virtually helpless victims of all kinds of abuse from unscrupulous adults, including sexual abuse. As with all children it has often not been safe to complain or even acknowledge that the abuse was happening and memories have been suppressed and occluded.

An important book called 'Thinking the Unthinkable' is a collection of papers based on the proceedings of a conference on sexual abuse and people with learning difficulties held in London in May 1988. The conference was vastly oversubscribed by professionals who have been greatly concerned with the growing anecdotal evidence of abuse of children and adults with learning difficulties. Indeed it is being suggested that '... the experience of sexual abuse itself may be so confusing and damaging that developmental delay, cognitive dysfunction and intellectual handicap may actually result form the abuse experience'. Teachers in mainstream schools need to remember to include all their 'special needs' children in their awareness of possible signs of abuse. Teachers in Special Schools may need to include themselves in the general training on sexual abuse of children. The book also has a very useful chapter on sex education and on assertiveness skills which includes, Self Image and Self Assertiveness, A Sexual Vocabulary, Confidence to Confide and how to help young people with learning difficulties to 'Keep Safe'. Much of it is relevant to all young people.

KIDSCAPE 82 Brook Street, London S1Y 1YP Tel. 01-493 9845

The Kidscape Campaign provides practical guidelines for children, parents and teachers and their own separate workshops for all three groups. The overall theme is that everyone has the right to be safe and the right to own their own bodies.

Sexually transmitted diseases

Young people in mainstream or special schools need to be given clear information about 'Safe Sex', etc in ways that are accessible to them. The staff's possible assumptions that this kind of information is not relevant because their pupils are 'too disabled' should be over-ridden.

Further Information:
'Thinking the Unthinkable' edited by Hilary Brown and Ann Craft, published by the Family Planning Education Unit, 27-35 Mortimer Street, W1N 7RJ.

Homosexuality

Disabled people are as statistically likely to be homosexual or lesbian as non-disabled people. Everything that applies to assisting young non-disabled people to recognise their sexuality and the sensitivity needed from adults in their support of young people who may have feelings which society does not 'allow', needs to be applied to disabled young people and people with learning difficulties. The issue is not the feelings themselves, it is the awareness that you might belong to a group of people who are heavily disapproved of an discriminated against, using the sexual preference as an excuse for this mistreatment. An added issue for disabled people is the dimension of dependency on others who may not approve of how you want to spend your time, or who you want to spend it with. These issues call for careful exploration of the teachers and other 'enablers' own feelings around sexuality and homosexuality so that they can be objective assistants to young peoples own self-discovery.

A non-heterosexist curriculum? Can it ever be for children with disabilities?

Frances Blackwell

How it was in the Fifties

I was a baby girl born in January 1940, just a few months after the second world war had started; I was dying and the doctor decided to starve me, but for some incredible reason I did not die. My father was horrified and enlisted and was promptly sent to India so my mother had to cope alone with me; I had myopia, twisted legs and a cleft palate. After two operations on my mouth when I was two, I began to speak at three years old, but only my mother understood what I said. I had to have regular physiotherapy for my legs, and by five, they were strong enough to stand on; my eyes have deteriorated ever since. I had a brother who was older, and a middle brother had died.

My brother and I lived with my mother and grandmother near Bristol. I was sent to what was then called the Royal Asylum for the Blind; my memories at the age of four and a half is fish and standing in a row of other toddlers with our faces to a green and cream wall. It happened often and I have no idea why. The girls were allowed to mix with the boys but NOT in the toilets. One day, when I was five, a boy of four who I liked and who like me followed me into the actual lavatory: I was sitting on the loo with my knickers down and a teacher rushed in and whisked John away and we were not allowed to play together for that day; it must have made a great impression on me since I still remember it vividly.

At the age of eight I left the asylum and went to an ordinary school but I could not see blackboards or cope visually with the work, so I was sent away to school to Chorleywood College, the grammar school of the time, run by the RNIB for girls only. It was a good school in that it gave me a rounded academic education but quite hopeless in its emotional support of young women growing up in the fifties. Our sex education was page 62 of a biology book; thankfully, my mother had told me the truth about growing up, and having periods, and sex with men; a lot of parents had not, and some of my friends had no idea at all about what periods were, let along anything else. In the early fifties we had no contact with young men; there was always a special fuss when brothers came, and those of us who had not seen a young man since the holidays would rush down and peer or listen to this authoritative species of manhood. But by the sixth form there were links, usually debating, or some girls would go to actual lessons with boys at Watford Grammar. I just presumed I was never clever enough to be picked to go there.

So we were very insular. We would have dances, girls dancing with girls, to all kinds of music such as Guy Mitchell, Frankie Lane, and later it would be Bill Haley and the Comets, and by the time I was leaving, rock and roll had taken over the music. It always felt that MEN WERE NOT ALLOWED but the staff never appeared to consider lesbian activity or if they did, they certainly did not think it through. Most young girls have crushes, but if ever I was teased for liking one girl or teacher more than someone else I would hotly deny it was a crush: to me it was REAL love. But there was nothing sexual about our loving and caring; I was very innocent then, indeed I did not hear of the word 'lesbian' until my last year at school. But for the previous two years I had been getting in and out of beds of girls older than me for hugs and cuddles, but no sexual act ever occurred. But we certainly lay on top of each other. And one summer during a romantic phase I used to go and read poetry with a girl I was in love with and we would lie under the sun and blue sky in tall grass, just innocently loving each other.

In my last term I had a favourite aunt who died and I was very upset; I was comforted one evening by a teacher and got back into school through a door left open at about 10 pm; I found that the powers that be had been looking for me, and I hotly denied I had been with anyone since I knew instinctively that I could not get this teacher into trouble; and by the morning it just seemed that I could not have retracted my lie. In the event, nothing sexual happened, but I realise that it was implicit, and I learnt later that one member of staff could not make up their mind as to whether I had been with a man or a woman! It was then that I heard that a staff member had asked another Was I a lesbian? - she had to tell me what one was!

I grew up quickly then, for I realised that it was something you did not talk about - you just did it. This deceit coloured my life for the next 20 years, for I had lesbian relationships which I could never share with anyone except a psychiatrist who told me it was a passing phase; I then became promiscuous with men to prove I was 'normal' and 'het' and eventually married. It was not until my late thirties that I realised how foolish I had been, but I had loved my husband. Now, I am no longer married and I have been living a lesbian lifestyle for the past eight years.

All this would be fine if things had changed in special schools, but they haven't. Somehow, they are as claustrophobic as ever and as insular as ever. The argument is not that I would have been a heterosexual if I had been to a co-educational school; no, rather, I would not have gone through such hell at times if we had been free to talk about our sexuality and to have had information available for counselling or for discussion about it. Some schools have had this facility, but blind children cannot have full access to information unless it is read aloud to them, or taped or brailled. The institutions which control education for children with disabilities are still very prissy about sexual matters and the adults in such places still deny that children with disabilities have sexual feelings, let along sexual rights. It is pretty disastrous to talk about SEX with any seriousness; quite impossible to talk about being gay or lesbian. And Clause 29 is going to add to the problem: homophobia is rife.

In my case it was not primarily the curriculum which influenced my need to negate my lesbianism; but it must have played a part in the same way that it plays a part in any school. However, there was one subtle difference. All children in special schools are 'normalised' as far as possible: that is, they are told how they will leave school, meet Mr Right and all will be well - I was often told that I would get married and did not need to worry about my poor performance at school; the converse could also happen: you were too disabled and would never marry Mr Right. But it was made very clear that Mr Right did exist; there were never any possibility in our school for

girls that there might be a Miss or a Ms Right! Normalism also worked in that we were trained as far as possible for a further education and we had to be as near perfect as possible: this resulted in me having an inferiority complex for a very long time, since I could not see properly, there was no way I could ever be 'normal' or 'perfect' but the result is that I still overachieve to this day, but I am beginning to get better and not do quite so much to 'prove' I am as good as an able-bodied person.

Whilst it is right to write papers or articles such as this to highlight the problem, the institutions themselves need to be tackled: we can have lots of different go-ahead ideas, but they will not get further than the postbox unless those who run such schools are made to be aware of the needs for discussions and information about how to help young people who either define themselves as gay or lesbian or who are confused about their sexuality and need to know more. I write this just because I believe this is an important issue that cannot be continually denied a hearing.

Genetic Counselling: abortion v sterilisation

'Imagine if you will, what I would have missed if the doctors had not revived me.

Can freedom honestly be denied to the handicapped man? Can yessing be so difficult that rather than give a baby a chance at life man treads upon his brother and silences him before he can ever draw one breath of this world's fresh air?'

Christopher Nolan

Like every other issue concerning disability, our own view is almost the complete opposite of the 'accepted' i.e., able-bodied view.

If disabled people were valued by society, none of these issues would arise. The fact that they do arise with great emotion is a direct measure of the effects of the Medical Model of Disability on people's understanding of the 'Quality of Life'.

Much research into genetic conditions is aimed at identification of the 'rogue gene', with a view to early detection in Utero and the offering of 'Therapeutic Abortion'. A secondary purpose is to be able to advise people with inherited conditions as to the likelihood of any offspring being affected. This is a very complicated issue as there are so many different variations of medical conditions, each with its own pattern of genetics. Also individualised information can only be given when *both* partners' physical history is taken into account. Therefore genetic counselling in any accurate sense cannot be given to single people, but only to couples.

It is important to know, however, which conditions are hereditary and which are not. These are few, if any conditions where the chance of passing on the gene are 100% and some inherited conditions are only carried by females, although males may have the condition itself. Some conditions are likely to lead to infertility in males, e.g., Down's Syndrome. The real issue for young people is about the choice of having a baby with a disability or not. There is plenty of room for debate here, but remember that people with congenital disabilities who may be part of the debate are likely to experience the debate as a personal issue - 'should I be allowed to live?'

From child: care, health and development, 1981, 7, 183-186

Correspondence

Dear Doctors,

I do not have spina bifida, but I was born with a congenital disability which led doctors to say to my mother 'Don't worry, your baby will probably not live anyway'. I do not know whether I was subjected to the 'Only feed on demand' routine, but whatever happened I was Christened in hospital in the expectation that I would never go home. I did not die. I did go home and began my life as a proud and stubborn person with a disability.

I had to return to hospital many times as a child, and each visit did nothing to combat my conviction that doctors were not human beings at all. Nor did the doctors try to make me feel that I was part of the human race, but only a medical curiosity.

This therefore is who I am. One of the people who are discussed, considered and sentenced without trial, but luckily one who escaped the sentence.

There are many points I want to make about this. First, because it seems doubtful that you ever get told, I want to say how the attitude of the medical profession has affected me, personally. Secondly I would like to make some general points which I know I share with many other people with disabilities.

I was a few days old when the seriousness of my disability was discovered. I can remember the change in the attitude of the people around me from calm and loving to panicky and hostile. A message clearly and firmly slipped into my unconscious saying that people would prefer it if I died. It seems that since then I have spent nearly all my time desperately trying to prove that I should be alive, that I was not suffering (even when I was) and that I was not worthless, but indeed exceptionally worthwhile. This meant that everything I did had to be outstanding. I am now 30-years-old. Only now am I beginning to realize that I do not have to smile all the time, and that I can achieve mediocrity without feeling someone will come along and 'put me out of my misery'.

I wanted to tell you this so that you would know that babies are aware of what is going on around them from the moment of birth, if not earlier, and that one's welcome into the world profoundly affects one's feelings about oneself.

My parents were given a lot of information by the doctors at the hospital in which I was born. After the 'Your baby will probably die' piece, which, incidentally, did not cheer my mother up at all, the information all seemed to be of the 'she'll never be able to ...' variety. Even the good news was distorted - 'she'll probably be bright - poor thing', meaning, I presume, that I would be bright enough to realise what a terrible state I was in! Everything reinforced society's attitude that people like me are tragic.

This information has for the most part turned out to be inaccurate and misleading. I cannot blame the doctors for not knowing more than they did about my particular disability, but I can blame them for not admitting to their lack of knowledge and instead making statements based on the flimsiest of understanding to lay people who, like most lay people, believe what is told to them by so called experts. The effect of the misinformation was to make my family have much lower expectations of me than were helpful, and to create a much large fear for my future than was necessary. Luckily, after a few years of watching the gloomy prophesies not coming true, we all began to dismiss much of what we had been told.

It seems to me that there are two distinct issues facing doctors when a child is born with a disability. The first is what to do when a child is obviously going to die as a result of his disability. The question is whether or not one prolongs the life of medically 'interfering' in a natural death. This is not the issue about which I feel qualified to speak. The issue which seems quite different to me is whether babies who will not die as a result of their disabilities (as in the spina bifida cases) should be starved as a form of involuntary euthanasia because someone has decided that their 'quality of life' would be so severely damaged that their life wouldn't be worth living. As a person with a disability I know I have the complete right to determine whether or not I live. And I am the only person with the right to judge my quality of life. Most people fear unknown

situations and underestimate their adaptability. Consequently they imagine living with a disability to be far worse than it usually is. Doctors do not escape from this, and it must cloud their judgements. They, like everyone else, are affected by society's conditioning, stereotyping and general misinformation about people with disabilities - what we call ablebodiedism or handicapism. The root of the undervaluing of people with disabilities we would suggest, lies in capitalism - a political system which values people as workers, producers of wealth, and barely tolerates people who do not produce such as the elderly, the ill, people with disabilities, etc. Because we as a group are particularly discriminated against in employment, we are often stereotyped as 'burdens', 'dependents'. Because of this unavailability of work, we are often poor. Because we live in a society which warns us to 'Stay young and beautiful, if you want to be loved', and people with disabilities are often not conventionally beautiful (whatever that means) and we do grow old, the overall image that people have of us is ugly, dependent, poor and miserable. Those of us who, despite all this, have the audacity to enjoy our lives, get further stereotyped as exceptionally brave and courageous. What people do not seem to do is to question whether their original assumptions were false.

It was noticeable that, in the programme about spina bifida, not one person with spina bifida was interviewed. This is typical of the way in which such issues are presented to the public. It is as if our lives are not our own affairs and that we have nothing to say of relevance to the matter. Our lives 'belong' to others.

I think I speak on behalf of many other people when I say that our disabilities are tiresome, tedious and a downright nuisance, but the real distress, the tragedy, is that we are still not accepted for who we are, the way we are - disabled. This lack of acceptance shows itself in the way society architecturally, socially, economically and philosophically is designed to exclude us. It shows itself itself in huge amounts of resources being channelled into trying to 'cure' us or 'prevent' us. It shows itself in attempts to assimilate us, e.g., outlawing sign-language in favour of lip-reading, and in the lack of thought, funds or real interest in providing good support to families, friends and helpers of people with disabilities, or to those of us who choose to live independently. It shows itself finally in the vast amount of ignorance about disability in the general population. Only when all these additional factors have been removed from the argument, will any of us be able to make judgements about whether or not life with a disability is worth living.
Micheline Mason

Bereavement
by Micheline Mason

Death, Dying and Bereavement

One of the facts of life in 'special schools' is that young people die. During my three years at a Special Boarding school, seven children died. Their deaths were announced at Assembly in a very matter-of-fact way. We were not taken to their funerals or encouraged to contact their families. Most of them were not spoken about again. I never cried once over these deaths whilst I was at school. It was only ten years later that I could feel any grief or cry about them. I now realize that the distress of the staff was so great that they could not allow us any 'space' to feel what was happening.

In recent years loss and bereavement which have found no expression, have come to be seen as one of the major causes of depression and psychiatric illness. **Grieving appears to be a necessary healing process involving tears, rage, and shaking - all socially taboo activities.** Our culture in the west, and particularly in stiff-upper-lip Britain confuses the expression of pain with the pain itself - 'If you stop someone crying you are making them feel better' - whilst this is the opposite of the truth, as any young child knows quite instinctively. 'Mummy feels better when I stop crying'.

We recommend that a bereavement counselling course should be fitted in to the busy schedule of all teachers, as with the progress of integration, dealing with death and dying will become inevitable. Exploring these feelings and all the past losses in our lives which tend to get attached to death and dying in the present, is an extremely valuable process. Even the youngest children should not be 'shielded' from it, however uncomfortable their questions or reactions may make you.

Young children do not react in the same sentimental way to death as adults. Their worries and fears are often quite different, and their questions should be taken very seriously and answered as accurately as possible. Children, for example, quite often wish that people were dead, temporarily, when that person is annoying them or taking things away from them. They may harbour terrible feelings of guilt if that person actually does die and they do need to be reassured that it wasn't their fault.

For some children it may be the first time that they have realized that adults are not all-powerful, and cannot always stop bad things happening, and this may make them very scared, or angry.

They may want to know what colour the dead person went, or what he (she) felt like, or where the blood went. They may want to know what happens to the body when it is burnt or buried and other such interesting details.

They may also be scared of the ghost of the dead person, or of 'finding' the dead person in their cupboards or under their beds.

Another point about bereavement is that people don't want to be 'left alone to grieve'. If people want to express emotion that makes other people embarrassed then probably they will retreat to a safe place to do it. But what people really want to know is how valuable the 'lost' person was to others. If a classmate or teacher should die, **the most positive thing people can do is write (or dictate) the good things, the nice memories about that person, and send them to relatives who will treasure them, even if their initial reaction is to burst into tears when reading them.** It is important that we illustrate that whilst the person may be dead, their memory, their gifts to the world live on in other people. Keeping visible memoirs, photos etc., of classmates or teachers who have died, and bringing them into conversation for a long time afterwards, is very important. It is also important to point out, of course, that many disabilities and illnesses do *not* lead to early death, and that perfectly healthy people die in accidents etc.

For older children, it would be a very interesting thing to study how death is treated or viewed in other cultures, and also how funerals are a very visible sign of the social status of the person. How valuable people judge a person's life to be becomes painfully symbolic at the point of death e.g., compare the un-named wooden boxes of the Aids babies buried by prisoners in the USA, to a three day state funeral of some head-of-state or member of the Royal Family, or mass graves of Jews compared to The Tomb of an Egyptian Prince.

For the dying person themselves, like every other aspect of disability, it is coping with other people's reactions which are the main problem.

NETI-NETI THEATRE COMPANY have produced an excellent play GRIEF by Penny Casdagli. The play is a powerful examination of grief and bereavement. It is available on video with sign language and Bengali. It is suitable for age ranges from top juniors upwards. There is also a series of seminars on the play – Talking About Grief £2.50. The Video is £49.95. Both available from Neti-Neti Theatre Co., 44 Gladsmuir Road, London N19 3JU. Telephone: 071-272 7302.

'Facing death'

These comments were made by boys who know they're dying of a terminal disease:

"I would like to be considered as a normal person, but they do not consider normal for us that which is normal for a healthy person. That which is normal for a healthy adolescent, is no longer within our scope.

Death, sexuality, there is only that. We think of other things - of meeting girls just as we are. The problems which that poses are monstrous; you end up feeling abnormal and a little guilty as well. It's annoying that adults begin to gossip as soon as one meets a girl. They think immediately about sexual advancements, etc., whereas for me it is completely the opposite. I feel fine with a girl when I chat with her, when we smoke a cigarette together and that's all. Where in fact is the problem? I almost have something to laugh about!

There are some things which one just cannot talk about with adults. Death is one of these issues. People prefer to ignore it; they really do deceive themselves over the whole thing. If some of their friends are so ill that they land up in hospital, they end up saying that it really would be better if they died so that they shouldn't suffer too much."

"Adults talk about death; about our dying. They even anticipate it! We prefer to wait until it happens! We'll just wait and see, and in the meantime it's not worth worrying about. For the present, we are too busy living, being here and making the best of every moment and then we'll see!

One must dispel this fear of death. The only way to react, when you see the anguish which overtakes adults and the staff, is to laugh and react with a certain cynicism (turning to an adult and saying, for instance, 'Good morning, I'm going to spit.') That anguish and fear that they have, what one really wants is for it to just disappear because of what one has said.

Yes, it happens that adults dehumanise us. Grown-ups are afraid that reality is too hard for the young ones to accept and they have a tendency to class us all in the same category.

At the centre certain things are hidden from us. That way, it is easiest for adults and they also want to control our lives. Gradually, while we are here, we discover what's hidden from us, and it is that which upsets us. To speak of our death, of sexuality, the adults wear soft gloves or hold meetings and the young ones are excluded from these meetings.

There are discussions with us but they are useless because the adults do not say what they are thinking. They'll say it out of a meeting (they don't say the same things if the younger children don't go to it). They would do better to discuss things with us. They would not be off course any longer. One wonders if adults sometimes only have meetings simply to have a clear conscience, rather than to understand us better."

Exley 1981

Independent Living

Micheline Mason

In the course of researching for this pack, it became obvious that an area of great concern in both mainstream and special schools, is about life-after-school for the disabled students. This needs a good deal more time and research to present a properly developed unit in the pack, and one to which disabled adults will turn our attention. The following article is, however, one articulate example of the possibilities that life has to offer even severely impaired people.

A case of human rights
Simon Brisenden

When we are young we are supposed to be hopeful, but many young people with disabilities have given up hope of an independent life before they have reached their late teens.

Young people with disabilities need to know that they can lead independent lives, that they can control their own destinies, that they can avoid the internal exile from society that has been forced upon their predecessors. For internal exile has been the reality of much so-called 'care' in our society.

Let us look at what the word 'care' has come to mean to people with disabilities. Let us look at how it confronts with awesome finality the person growing up with a disability. For a start, the person who is cared for is a nonentity, someone who does nothing all day long except vegetate in front of the television. If you have to be cared for by somebody else you do not have a life of your own, you do not have opinions, ambitions, desires.

I can remember in my teens wondering how I was

Independent Living.
Credit Sally and Richard Greenhill.

going to manage. I thought that perhaps I would get a job and be rich enough to employ people to help. Or perhaps I would get married and have a devoted - and of course beautiful - wife to look after me. However, just like when I was at school, I must have been daydreaming when the riches and the devoted wives were being handed out, because so far I remain young, free, single and in debt to the bank.

Incidentally it is something to ponder on that if I were to get married to a non-disabled woman - or to cohabit for any length of time - the social services would remove financial help I receive to employ my own carers. This has happened in one recent case. The state, as always, remains eager to exploit the unpaid labour of women.

Anyway, even while still at school I knew that I wanted to avoid the fate of those who are 'cared for', for I realised almost instinctively that this was a sort of limbo existence, neither truly alive nor truly dead. It was almost ten years after I left school that I found what seemed to be realistic for the sort of independent life that I wanted.

It was then that I encountered people from the Hampshire Centre for Independent Living, a number of whom has moved out of residential care and into the community. They had done this by persuading the social services to give each person a grant to employ their own care support, proving it to be a more cost-effective option that institutional care.

Credit Sally and Richard Greenhill.

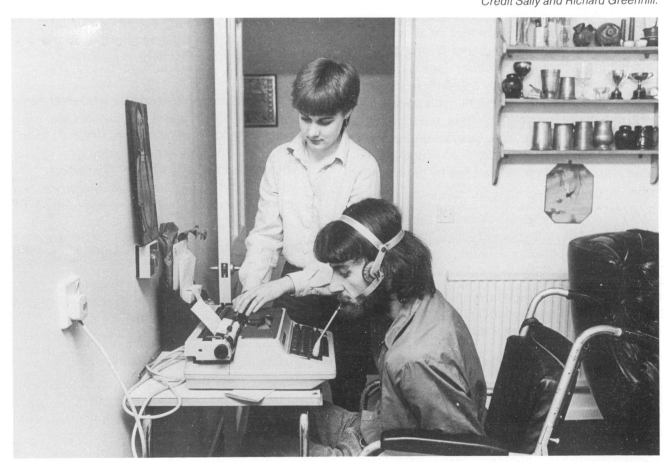

This was the model I was determined to follow. Indeed, it inspired me and turned my whole life around. I suddenly realised that I did not necessarily have to be submerged in the twilight world of those who are 'cared for'. I could actually have the personal care I required delivered under my control in such a way that it supported rather than submerged me. I could design my own package of care and get financial support for this from statutory agencies. This had to be the way for me.

And - to cut a long story short - it was the way for me. Since 1984 I have been living independently in the community of central Southampton, employing a team of three care-helpers who are finance by my disability benefits and a grant from Hampshire County Council. The dreams I had at school had finally connected with reality, and I have not really looked back since.

But after four years of independent living I realise that society still needs persuading and educating about notions of care and independence. For a start we seem to be confused about what care is, and this leads to a society in which care is delivered in ways that are inhibiting to individuals rather than enabling them.

The role of the carer should not be to control, but to facilitate. I define this as being the necessary intervention enabling the decisions of the individual to be carried out. Anything more than this is an infringement of a person's liberty.

We also need to be clear about what is meant when we talk about 'independence' in this context. We are not talking about being able to do everything for yourself. Neither does it imply cutting oneself off from the assistance of others. For what matters is not whether you do something with or without the help of others, but that it gets done under your direction. Being independent simply means that you have some control over your life, and that you do not live by the routine of others.

Most often professionals think that teaching people a lot of stuff about dressing themselves, making beds, cooking, washing clothes is putting them on the road to independence.

This is because those who work in the welfare professions have grave difficulties seeing things from the point of view of their clients.

But as consumers of welfare services we can no longer be satisfied with all this being portrayed as a welfare issue alone. It is not a matter that can be left to people who work in health related professions. We must see disability as a political issue and not just as a welfare issue.

Whenever we are talking about people's quality of life we must try hard and remember that they are people, that they are human and not just a inconvenient sub-species. I hey - I mean we - are human, and therefore we have human rights.

Living in the community is a right, not a privilege. To deny a disabled person the ability to live in the community is a abuse of human rights.

The right to a independent life is the most basic of all rights. The most fundamental right of all is that of living in the community alongside your fellow human beings. The only people who are not officially allowed to do this are criminals, and we have committed no crime that I am aware of. So why are we banished from society? Perhaps the reason is that we have no political muscle, we have not yet started to demand our rights with enough firmness and conviction. Once we have started to do this and we have given up putting all our faith in flag days and sponsored runs, then we can really start to change things.

This is not just a philosophical issue, a question of political theory which is of no relevance to real life, but is obviously also a practical issue. It is about giving individuals the opportunity to design their own package of care. And this means a real commitment to community care which is properly funded and which is not a smokescreen behind which government dismantles the services people rely on.

We have to try and make sure that the young disabled people of today still have a social services network to call on tomorrow. At the moment not even this can be guaranteed.

Written by Simon Brisenden, who died earlier this year. Simon was Secretary of the Southampton Centre of Independent Living. He was also a poet and a disability awareness/equality trainer. This article appeared in Community Care Magazine and is reproduced by kind permission of the Editor.

There is an Independent Living Centre in London:

The Greenwich Integrated Living Centre
St. Mary's Church, Greenlaw Street,
Woolwich, London SE18 5AR

ARDLEY, Neil and WEST, David (1989)
Giant Book of the Human Body

BASKIN, R and HARRIS, K (1977)
Notes From a Different Drummer; A Guide to Juvenile Fiction Portraying the Disabled
R R Bowker: New York. Reviews 311 books of juvenile fiction 1940-75

BASKIN, B and HARRIS, K (1984)
More Notes From a Different Drummer: A Guide to Juvenile Fiction Portraying the Disabled
R R Bowker: New York. Reviews 348 books of juvenile fiction 1976-81

BATTYE (1966)
The Chatterley Syndrome
In Stigma Edited Paul Hunt. Geoffrey Chapman: London

BIKLEN, Douglas and BOGDANA, Robert (1977)
Media Portrayals of Disabled People: A Study of Stereotypes
Inter-racial Children's Book Bulletin. Vol 8. Nos 6 & 7. p4-9

BOGDANA, Robert, BIKLEN, Douglas, SHAPIRO, Arthur and SPELKOMAN, David (1982)
The Disabled: Media's Monster
Social Policy, Fall 1982

BOOTH, Tony and SWANN, Will (1987)
Including Pupils with Disabilities: Curriculum For All
Open University Press: Milton Keynes. 335-159 77-X

BRADY, Mary (1983)
Farmers, Freaks and Fun: 142nd State Fair
Newsday 5th Sept 1983. p13

BRECHIN, LIDDIARD and SWANN (Ed) (1981)
Handicap in a Social World
Hodder and Stoughton: London

BRENNAN, Mary (1987)
British Sign Language: The Language of the Deaf Community
in BOOTH, T and SWANN, W - Including Pupils with Disabilities, Open University Milton Keynes. p274-305

BRISENDEN, Simon (1988)
What is Disability Culture
Disability Arts in London Magazine. December 88

BRISENDEN, Simon
A Case of Human Rights
in Community Care Magazine. Reprinted in Spinal Injuries Association Newsletter. Nos 53. Nov 89

BRISENDEN, Simon (1986)
Independent Living and the Medical Model of Disability
in Disability Handicapped Society. Vol 1. No 2. p173

BROWN, Hilary and CRAFT, Ann (1988)
Thinking the Unthinkable
Family Planning Education Unit, London

BROWNE, CONNORS and STERNE (1985)
With the Power of Each Breath
A Disabled Women's Anthology. Cleris Press: Pittsburgh

CAMPLING, Jo (1979)
Better Lives for Disabled Women
Virago: London

CAMPLING, Jo (Ed) (1981)
Images of Ourselves: Women with Disabilities Talking
Routledge, Paul and Kegan: London

COARD, Bernard (1971)
How the West Indian Child is Made Educationally Subnormal in the British School System
Pamphlet, New Beacon: London

Community Service Volunteers (1988)
In Our Own Right £9.50
Design with Disabled People £10

CONRAD, R (1979)
The Deaf Child: Language and Cognitive Function
Harper Row. London

CROPP, David (1987)
The B6 Incident
in Booth & Swann ibid

CROSS, Peter (1981)
In In From the Cold
Liberation Magazine for Disabled People. No 4

De JONG, Gerben (1989)
The Epidermiology of Disability
Into Rehabilitation Review. Autumn p3

DRIEDGER, Diane (1989)
The Last Civil Rights Movement
Hurst: London 850650594

DUFFY, Mary (1988)
Asking For It
in Fan Magazine. Vol 2. No 10

DES (1978)
Medical Fitness to Teach
Circular 11/78

DES (1983)
Assessments and Statements of Special Educational Needs
DES/HMSO

DES (1984)
Design Note 18 - Access For Disabled People to Educational Buildings
HMSO

DES (1988)
Medical Fitness to Teach
(Supersedes 11/78). Circular 1/88

DES (1989)
Educating Physically Disabled Pupils
Report of HM Inspectors. London: DES

DES (1989)
Assessment and Statements of Special Educational Needs
Procedures within the Education, Health and Social Services. Circular 22/89. (Supersedes 1/83)

DISABILITY ALLIANCE (ANNUAL)
Disability Rights Handbook
25 Denmark Street, WC2H 8NJ. Price £3.75

EXLEY, Helen (1981)
What It's Like To Be Me
EXLEY: WATFORD 1-85015 0060

FERGUSON MATHEWS, Gwyneth (1983)
Voices From the Shadows: Women with Disabilities Speak Out
Women's Press of Canada: Toronto

FINKLESTEIN, Victor (1980)
Attitudes to Disabled People: Issues for Discussion
World Rehabilitation Fund Monograph 5: New York

FISH, John (1985)
Educational Opportunities For All
ILEA

FRIEDBERG, MULLINS and SUKHENNICK
Accept Me As I Am: Best Books of Juvenile Non-Fiction on Impairments and Disabilities
Bowker: New York. See Ch 2 & 3 esp

GALLAGHER, H G (1990)
By Trust Betrayed: Patients and Physicians in the Third Reich
Henry Holt

GARTNER, A and JOE, T (Ed) (1987)
Images of the Disabled, Disabling Images
Praeger: New York

GROCE, N E (1985)
Everyone Here Spoke Sign Language
Harvard Univesity Press

GRUCHMAN, Lothar (1972)
Euthanasia and Justice in the Third Reich
Stuttgart

HALLWORTH, Grace (1982)
My Mind is not in a Wheelchair: Books and the Handicapped Child
Hertfordshire Library Service

HANK, J R and L M (1948)
The Physically Handicapped in Certain Non-Occidental Societies
The Journal of Social Issues. Vol 4. No 4

HARRIS, Merril (1985)
Making Our Students Aware of Ableism
Feminist Teacher. Vol 1. No 53. p8-10

HUNT, Paul (1966)
A Critical Condition in Stigma
Edited by Paul Hunt. Geoffrey Chapman: London

ILEA Learning Resources Branch (1981)
About Disability: A Guide to Material for Children and Young People
Materiography 2. (Reviews 55 books, kits and filmstrips)

ILEA (1981)
Race, Class and Gender

ILEA (1988)
Copyart Centre for Learning Resources
(A number of black and white drawings featuring disabled people)

Inter-Racial Books for Children Bulletin
1841 Broadway, New York, NY10023 especially Vol 8, Nos 6 & 7 on Handicappism 1977

KARPF, Ann (1988)
Crippling Images
Ch 5 in Doctoring the Media: The Reporting of Health and Medicine. Routledge: London

KETTLE, Melvyn (1987)
The Employment of Disabled Teachers
RADAR: London

KINRADE and DARNBROUGH
Directory for the Disabled
RADAR: London

LADD, Paddy (1978)
Communication or Dummification
in Montgomery (Ed)
Sound of Mind
Scottish Workshop publication: Edinburgh

LADD, Paddy (1988)
Hearing Impaired or British Sign Language User
in *Disability, Handicap and Society*
Vol 5. No 2. p195-99

LANE, H (1984)
When the Mind Hears
Random House: New York

LANGWORTHY, Jessica (1930)
Blindness in Fiction: A Study of the Attitudes of Authors Toward their Blind Characters
Jo of Applied Psychology 14. p269-286

LASS, Bonnie and BLOOMFIELD, Monica (1981)
Books about Children with Special Needs: An annotated bibliography
The Reading Teacher. February 81

LISICKI, Barbara (1988)
Nice Face Shame About the Legs: Confessions of a Female Stand Up Comic
Feminist Arts News, Vol 10. No 2

LITTLEWOOD, and LIPSEDGE (1982)
Aliens and Alienists: Ethnic Minorities and Psychiatry
Penguin: London

LONES, Jane (1985)
Integration at Teacher Level
Educare No 24. p21-24

MALE, Judith and THOMPSON, Claudia (1985)
The Educational Implications of Disability. A Teachers Guide
RADAR: London 0-900270-37-3

MARSHALL, Margaret (1985)
Ways into Understanding
Books for keeps. No 22. p8-9, July 85

McCONKEY, R and McCORMACK, B (1983)
Breaking Barriers: Educating People about Disability
Souvenir Press: London 2-85649949

MORRIS, Jenny (1987)
Progress with Humanity
in Booth, T and Swann, W ibid

MORRIS, Jenny (1989)
Able Lives: Women with Spinal Injuries Talking
Women's Press: London/Spinal Injuries Association

MOSLEY, Fran (1985)
Everyone Counts
ILEA: LMS

MOSLEY, Fran (1988)
Braille Numbers Pack
ILEA: LMS

NATIONAL CHILDBIRTH TRUST (1984)
The Emotions and Experiences of Some Disabled Mothers
NCT: London

NATIONAL CURRICULUM COUNCIL (1989)
Circular 5 Implementing the National Curriculum -Particularly Pupils with Special Educational Needs and *A Curriculum for All*
NCC: York

NATIONAL UNION OF TEACHERS (1984)
Meeting Special Needs in Ordinary Schools: A Union Guide

NATIONAL UNION OF TEACHERS (1989)
Anti-Racism in Education Guidelines: Towards a Whole School Policy

OLIVER, Mike and ZARB, Gerry (1989)
The Politics of Disability: A New Approach
Disability, Handicap and Society, Vol 4. No 3. p221-239

OPCS surveys of Disability in Great Britain
Report 1 - The Prevalence of disability among adults
HMSO, ISBN 0-11-691229-4, price £10.70

OPCS surveys of Disability in Great Britain
Report 2 - The financial circumstances of disabled adults living in private households
HMSO, ISBN 0-11-691235-0, ptivr price £11.50

OPCS surveys of Disability in Great Britain
Report 3 - The Prevalence of disability among children
HMSO, ISBN 0-11-691250-2, price £10.60

OPCS surveys of Disability in Great Britain
Report 4 - Disabled adults: services, transport and employment
HMSO, ISBN 0-11-691257-X, price £15.60

OPCS surveys of Disability in Great Britain
Report 5 - The financial circumstances of families with disabled children living in private households
HMSO, ISBN 0-11-691264-2, price £9.00

OPCS surveys of Disability in Great Britain
Report 6 - Disabled children: services, transport and education
HMSO, ISBN 0-11-691266-9, price £14.30

PAGEL, Martin (1988)
An Introduction to Self-organisation of disabled people
Greater Manchester Coalition of Disabled People

PARMAR, Pratilha
Fragmentations (L.B.D.R.T. Trainers Files)

POSTLEWAITHE, K and HACKNEY, Ann (1988)
Organising a School Response
McMillan: London

PRITCHARD, D G (1963)
Education and the Handicapped 1760-1960
Routledge, Kegan and Paul: Camden

QUICKE, John (1985)
Disability in Modern Children's Fiction
Croom Helm Ltd: London 0-7099-2102-0

RANA, Samena (1988)
Disability and Photography, Fan Vol 10. No 12. first appeared in Polareyes
A One Off publication of Black Women photographers

RALPH, Sue (1989)
Images of Disability as Portrayed through Print Media
Educare No 33 March 89

RIESER, Richard (1988)
Teacher Newspaper
21st March

RIESER, Richard (1989)
Disability and the School Curriculum
Unpublished paper

ROBERTS, Pamela (1988)
Videomaker Fan Vol 2 No 10

SAXTON, Marsha and HOME, Florence (1989)
With Wings: An Anthology of Women with Disabilities
Virago: London

SCHWARTZ, Albert (1977)
Disability in Children's Books: Is Visibility Enough?
Inter-racial Books Bulletin Vol 8. Nos 6 & 7. p10-15

SCHWARTZ, Albert (1980)
Books Mirror Society: A Study of Children's Materials
Inter-racial Book Bulletin Vol 11. Nos 1 & 2. p19-24

SERENEY, Gitta (1974)
Into the Darkness: the Mind of a Mass Murderer
Picador: London

SHEARER, Ann (1982)
Disability: Whose Handicap?
Basil Blackwell: Oxford

SLAPIN, LESSING and BELKIND (1987)
Books without Bias: A Guide to Evaluating Children's Literature for Handicappism
Kids Project Inc., 1720 Oregon Street, Berkely CA 94703

SMYTH, Margaret (1981)
Count Me In: Books for and about Disabled Children
The Library Association, Youth Libraries Group, Pamphlet 23

SOUTHGATE, Tim (1982)
Mainstreaming with Micros
CSIE Factsheet

STATHAM, June (1987)
Speaking for Ourselves: Self Advocacy by People called Mentally Handicapped
Ch 25 in Booth, T and Swann, W ibid

STEINKE, Gioya (1988)
A Venture into Art with a Magnifying Glass and White Cane
Fan Vol 2. No 10

STERNE, Michael (1989)
Exception Proves Rules Inadequate
TES 14/7/89

STONE, Deborah (1985)
The Disabled State
MacMillan: London 0-333-39312-0

STRAUSS WATSON, Emily (1982)
Handicapism in Children's Books: A Five Year Update
Inter-racial Book Bulletin Vol 13. Nos 4 & 5. p3-17

SUTHERLAND, Allan T (1981)
Disabled We Stand
Souvenir Press: London

TALWAR, Ramesly
Flashes of Joy
Anthology Women's Press

TOPLISS, Edna and GOULD, Bryan (1981)
The Charter for the Disabled
Basil Blackwell: Oxford 0631 127488

UPIAS (1976)
Fundamental Principles of Disability
London: Union of Physically Impaired Against Segregation

VESEY, Sion (1988)
Disability Culture it's a Way of Life
Fan Vol 2. No 10

VITELLO, S H (1989)
Integration of Handicapped Students in the US and Italy: A Comparison
Int Jo of Special Education Vol 4 No 1

VITTACHI, A (1989)
Stolen Childhood: In Search of the Rights of the Child
Blackwell: Polity Press: Oxford 0-7456-0720-9

WAHL, Otto and RATH, Rachel (1982)
Television's Image of Mental Illness: Results of Washington Media Watch
Jo of Broadcasting 26 p604

WARNOCK (1978)
Report of the Committee of Enquiry into Education of Handicapped Children and Young People
Cmnd 7212 HMSO

WERTHEIMER, Alison (1988)
Press Reporting of People with Learning Difficulties
Campaign for valued failures with people who have learning difficulties. 12A Maddox Street, W1R 9PL - looks at press coverage for 6 weeks in Spring 1987

WILLIAMS, Eugene (1989)
Surviving Without a Safety Net
Int. Rehab. Rev. Vol XL. No 2 & 3. Sept 89

WILLIAMS, P and SHULTZ, B (1982)
We Can Speak for Ourselves
Souvenir Press: London

WILSON, Christine (1989)
Educating on Disability - A UK Perspective
CMH Conference Paper

WOLFENSBERGER, Wolf (1972)
Normalization in Human Services
National Institute of Mental Retardation: Toronto

WRIGHT, John (1982)
Bilingualism in Education: Issues in Race and Education

ZAMES, Freida (1977)
Politics of Disability Movement
Inter-racial Book Bulletin Vol 8. Nos 6 & 7

We have not been able to cover pre-school education and further and adult education due to shortage of time. Here are some titles that might be useful.

CHAPMAN, Lynne (1986)
The Provision of In-house Disability Awareness Training for Staff in Colleges
Educare No 26 Nov 86. Details on curriculum in 32 colleges giving some form of training

HEWITSON-RATCLIFFE, Chris and MAUDSLEY, Liz (1987)
ILEA Special Educational Needs TRIST projects 1985-87
Looks at 9 London Projects. ILEA Webber Row

BRADLEY, Judy and HEGARTY, Seamus (1982)
Stretching the System
Further Educational Research

Further Education Unit (1986)
Special Needs Occasional Papers
Longmans/FEU

Adult Education Curriculum Development Unit (1986)
Special Needs Integration Project
ILEA

ILEA (June 1989)
Implementing the ILEA's Equal Opportunities Policies: Working with Young People with Disabilities: Guidelines for the Youth Service

Under 5's
CSIE Integrating Pre-School Children with Special Needs
Factsheet available 4th Floor 415 Edgware Road, NW2 6NB
01-452 8642

MENCAP
Ordinary Everyday Families
looks at under 5's with Learning Difficulties - forthcoming

Bibliography Update

BARNES, Colin (1991)
Disabled People in Britain and Discrimination: A case for Anti-Discrimination Legislation
Hurst & Co., London/BCODP £9.95

BCODP (1992)
Disability Stereotypes in the Media: A Code of Ethics

BRISENDEN, Simon
Poems For Perfect People
£4.00 from Hazel Peaseley, 19 Blighmont Road, Southampton SO1 3RH

FINGER, Ann (1991)
Past Due: A Story of Disability, Pregnancy and Birth
Womens Press £6.99

GREGORY, Susan and HARTLEY, Gillian (Ed) (1991)
Constructing Deafness
Pinter Press, London in association with Open University £12.50

HEVEY, David (1992)
The Creatures Time Forgot: Photography and Disability Imagery
Routledge, London

HOLLINGER, Ann (1990)
Newham Make it Work
LBDRT £2.50

MORRIS, Jenny (1991)
Pride Against Prejudice: Transforming Attitudes to Disability
Womens Press, London £6.95

NETI-NETI THEATRE (1991)
Talking About Grief
£2.50. 44 Gladsmuir Road, London N19 3JU

NUT (1991)
Guidelines on Disability: An Equal Opportunities Issue
Hamilton House, Mabledon Place, London WC1H 9BD. £1

OLIVER, Michael (1990)
The Politics of Disablement
MacMillan, London £8.99

OPEN UNIVERSITY (1990)
Disability – Changing Practice
Home Study Text K665XHST
Readings   K665XR
Dept. of Health & Social Welfare Open University, Milton Keynes

PROCTOR, Robert (1988)
Racial Hygiene: Medicine Under the Nazis
Harvard University Press £11.95

RIESER, Richard (1990)
Don't Disable Teachers with Disabilities
British Jo. of Special Education Vol. 17 No. 3

SACHS, Oliver (1990)
Seeing Voices
Picador, London £4.99

SHAW, Linda (1990)
Each Belongs: Integrated Education in Canada
CSIE, London £2.50

SIMPSON, Paul (1990)
Education's Equal Opportunities Policy No. Guarantee of Employment
Contact: RADAR Winter 1990

SPASTICS SOCIETY (1991)
What the Papers Say and Don't Say About Disability
Campaign Dept. £2.50

TAYLOR, George and BISHOP, Juliet (1991)
Being Deaf: The Experience of Deafness
Pinter Press in association with Open University £11.95

Four Books which help examine the experience of learning difficulties

ATKINSON, D and WILLIAMS, F (Eds) (1990)
Know Me As I am: An anthology of prose, poetry and art by people with learning difficulties
Hodder & Stoughton, London

BRECHIN, A and WALMSLEY, J (Eds) (1989)
Making Connections: Refleting on the Lives and Experiences of People with Learning Difficulties
Hodder & Stoughton, London

POTTS, Maggie and FIDO, Rebecca (1991)
A Fit Person to Be Removed: Personal Accounts of Life in a Mental Deficiency Institution
Northcote House, Plymouth £9.95

RYAN, Joanna and THOMAS, Frank (1987)
The Politics of Mental Handicap
Revised Edition. Free Ass. Books, London £7.95

A Struggle for Independence
by Leon & Yvonne Hippolyte

Leon Hippolyte, now 23, was diagnosed as having severe Cerebral Palsy at 5 months. This interview with Yvonne Hippolyte, his mother, is about her struggle against the "two crimes" of being black and having a disabled son.

Leon was not born disabled. He was 5 months old and he caught a cold and I took him to the hospital and he collapsed. That's the short of it all. He hates it when I talk about that.

In those days, there were very severe problems, the loneliness. I was out on my own. I thought I was the only one in the world who had a disabled child – the only Black person who had one. I used to get a lot of insults, when he was about six and was too big for a normal pram:

"I was totally mad".

"I was silly".

"I should get rid of him".

I met an old black man who had a stick. He told a friend of mine, "If Leon was his child, he wouldn't come through the door." She said, "If that's what you feel, why don't you tell her?"

I used to push Leon up to Hoxton Market. I saw this man often.

"You know me."

He said "No."

I said "Of course you do. I'm the one who had the wheelchair. Remember?"

"Oh yes" he said.

"Remember what you told my friend?"

He said "So what?"

I said "Do you want me to move your stick?"

"You can't do that, I'll fall."

I said "So. You'll fall if I move your stick, but I must put my son away. He's my son, you know. I had pain for him. I had nothing from people like you."

"You did mention that if he was your child, he would't come through the door. Well if you were my husband, you wouldn't pass that door either," and that was putting it nicely. I didn't put it nicely at all. That's some of the pressures you had to go through, especially from my own colour. A lot of them couldn't understand disability, especially the older ones who come from back home. You couldn't find disabled people back home. You don't know who they are. They were all hidden.

If you have a disabled child or something is wrong with you, then something wrong with the parent.

They have done something wrong and this is the wish of God.

The first thing I had to do was to get rid of the guilt of having a disabled child and I shed many a tear. But then in the early morning, I sat down and thought, "if I'm feeling like this and I'm not disabled, how about him who is?" So I started being positive and stopped crying and helped him out the best I could. And in every stage, it was not knowing how to get anything from anybody. Never being able to plan ahead. Just living from day to day.

I, myself, was involved with various organisations from the beginning, because I thought if you're disabled and you're black, you must be committing two crimes. I thought my son hadn't done anything to anybody. He's got to enjoy life. So my first aim was to break down as many barriers as I could. I did get some results.

When he was a little boy, he went to boarding school. It was certainly strange talking to all these white people. Hawksworth Hall, Guisley (near Leeds), out of 26 children the school can take, he was the only black child. I would go up there and you had to make an appointment and I said "where my child is, I don't have to make an appointment." When he got to Rutland House (Nottinghamshire), they said the same, and at Meldreth Manor (Royston, Cambridge). I didn't mind. Once the train could get there every Saturday or Sunday, weekdays or bank holidays. I had three other children after him and it was heavy, very heavy. But wherever I go, I take everybody. They were all mine and wherever I went, I took them all. I didn't make an appointment because then they expect you to turn up, especially a clever child like Leon. Then if something happens, it's terrible 'cause Leon would sit and cry for four days. If he didn't expect me and I just turned up, his face was so beautiful. So alive! God, it's worth it. You just hear a taxi at the door and his face was like a 1000 Watt bulb – you know.

In those days, my husband, he was never supporting me at all. He was out to have a ball. After a while, I thought well, I can't continue with him and I asked him to leave. I had to shout to get him to go, but he went. I set about getting the best I can, not just for Leon. I set about caring for my family and making sure they looked at life positively.

Leon was spoilt rotten at school. Because I didn't abandon him and the staff never knew when I was coming, they took more care. There was only one

Row over disabled man's homecoming hitch . . .

But council deny dragging their feet over special arrangements

THE long-awaited home-coming of a severely handicapped Hackney youth has sparked a row over the council's failure to make proper provision for his care.

Leon Hippolyte was forced to remain for a year longer than normal at a residential school for the disabled near Cambridge because Hackney's Social Services had not arranged help and support to enable his mother to look after him.

But a happy homecoming awaits him in two weeks time when his mum, Yvonne, and his three sisters have him back to stay at their home in Queensbridge Road, Haggerston.

Leon suffers from cerebral palsy and relies on a special electric wheelchair operated by head movements to get around, and a speech board and voice box to communicate.

The 20-year-old is totally dependent on others for his personal needs and hygiene, but is mentally alert, and a whizz-kid on the computer.

His case was used to highlight the plight of handicapped youngsters. The deputy head of Leon's school slammed Hackney's Social Services on a national raido programme for ignoring letters sent to them over a four year period asking for arrangements to be made for Leon when he leaves.

Peter Edmondson of Meldrath Manor School said: "What was required was someone to see to his educational needs at home and carers to help his mother look after him, because it would have been impossible for her to cope with him on her own.

"Leon has to be bathed and taken to the toilet as well as fed, and looking after him is a 24-hour-a-day job."

Hackney Council strongly deny they ignored letters, and say they kept in close consultation with both ILEA and Meldrath Manor School.

"We decided it was in Leon's best interest to keep him in an environment he knew for an extra year while we put together a package to enable him to live as independently as possible at home," said a council spokesperson.

"We have converted the flat next to his mother's into a self contained unit, installed computer equipment and made adaptions and modifications for his wheelchair, as well as providing home helpers to come in every day," said a spokesperson.

As Leon's mum made preparations for her son's home-coming, she said the help offered had been long overdue.

"All they offered at first was respite care, it took continous pressure, including letters from MP Brian Sedgemore, to get them to act."

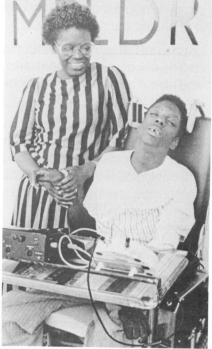

● Leon Hippolyte with his mum Yvonne.

occasion when someone put his calipers on wrong. The headmistress said "Well, I'm sorry." I said "Listen, if he was white, you would have done something to that man there. White or black, he's my child." I wrote to her to put this on record. When she found out who the person was, they were severely dealt with and they got the sack. They should know how to do it properly. They had 6 months training before coming to the school.

At the school, they met his needs. He had a severe disability and no communication, but they found ways of doing things. At the beginning he was rigid. There was nothing. The fact that he can shake his head and say "No" and smile and say "Yes" was the beginning. At Rutland House, his wheelchair was hand controlled. He had a terrible accident and Leon wouldn't go in a chair for 2 or 3 years. But they found a way of using a chair with a switch at the back of the headrest. It was only a matter of months and he was away and gone, zooming about.

Now Leon has a voice box (ORAC) hired from MARDIS, Lancaster University. It will cost £1100. It is activated by the head, everything is done by disc drive with different codes (Carnival or France) and it comes up on a visual screen. It can be linked to a computer, but that's for the future.

Leon's sisters used to have some discrimination at school, because he was disabled. On one occasion, a friend used to come to my house, play with Leon, play with the girls and have dinner with us. The friend told Joanne, at school, that Leon was 'a freak'. So Joanne whopped her. Then the girl wouldn't go to school for two weeks and I got a letter from the headmistress. So I went to see her and told her what had happened. And I told her, if I

was Joanne I would have done the same thing, and that if her father, mother and grandfather came, I would hit all of them, if that's how they are going to behave. She said "Mrs Hippolyte, I'm so sorry", so the teachers had a very different view of Joanne after that. I think she was victimised because after that, she was always getting into trouble with teachers. Eventually, I had to move her.

They are not ashamed of Leon either. Because I have met some who are ashamed of their disabled brothers and sisters. I have talked to many a young person, not just my own, to look at the person and do your best to help them. I've not only catered for my own, but I've learnt from my own how close they can be.

At 10-11 years old, I was having to carry him up the steps from the basement to the bedroom above.

I had to start a battle to get somewhere on the ground level, where I did not have to carry him. With help from the school and two social workers, both from South Africa, to cross with Hackney Council to get the present house. But it was adapted for a manual chair, and when Leon managed to use one independently, the adaption was way out. The doors were too small, he couldn't get into the bedroom at all. They had to knock walls down and widen doors for him to use it independently. He was over 19 and all that was offered by the school was a hostel. They didn't think I could cope at home. It was another year until he finally came home, I was so happy.

We forced them to convert this flat for him. Mine is upstairs with the three girls, although it is only 2 bedrooms. Someone has to be around most of the day and all night because if Leon is actually sick, then there's nothing he can do and he would choke. I'm trying to encourage him to be independent for the nights. I have heard of a Council scheme where you can get assistance for 24 hours a day, but then he would need a second bedroom. So I stay here with him every night.

When he came home, there was absolutely nothing for him. So we set about giving him a programme. For a start, he should have a social worker who would organise places for him to go and things for him to do. Finance is very difficult.

Hackney arranged for some money from the Independent Living Fund, and after two years, we received £16,000. I was asked if I had used any of the money for Leon's enjoyment! Then again, if you're disabled, you're only independent in your own home. He goes out in his chair, it breaks the rules, to me it's unfair. He can be independent in here, but when he goes out, he's not allowed to use a head controlled chair.

There are some new ones, but they cost £3,000 plus insurance. My idea of life is being active. Do your own shopping. He goes to the Cross (Dalston Shopping Centre) to Leo's and Sainsburys. I give him the money and he does the shopping. I don't need to do it. He goes to MacDonalds and has a Big Mac. You and I do that. I feel he shouldn't be stuck behind four walls.

If I had my own transport, that would make the world of difference. I'd learn to drive. I've got to find the money, £15,000 is what we need. I've written all over.

He loves drama. He got in on a course at Jackson Lane, in Highgate, but I couldn't get transport. His chair won't fit in a taxi and Dial-a-ride is useless. They have no priority system. He also does a cooking class and drama at Chats Palace as well as Perpetual Beauty Carnival Club.

I am now well involved with Equal Play, Huddleston Centre, and Perpetual Beauty. Leon takes an active part in the Carnival. There's nothing to say that just because you're disabled you shouldn't play a part in everything. My motto is "whatever's going, be there". I'm on the Carnival Committee because there was nobody there supporting the disabled people. It opened a few eyes. A few of the bars that we go to now provide access and toilets. 'Cause I say, if you want Perpetual Beauty, if you don't have disabled access, I'm not coming.

People seeing him on the chair have the idea he is totally stupid and that's what I used to get.

"Oh, hello Yvonne, is he alright?"

"Is who alright?"

"Leon"

"If you want to know how he is, ask him yourself", and that means you have got a problem, trying to understand what he is saying.

Eventually they don't ask me how he is, they mostly say "Hiya Leon", which to me is a big improvement – mostly black people.

So if I go anywhere where the club is having a show and I don't take Leon, they ask where he is. "Well Leon is doing his own thing." "So!", they say. So I arrange transport to take him.

There is no black Disabled Peoples Organisation in Hackney. They're mixed. To me, that's better. If you're disabled, it shouldn't matter if you're black or white.

When the Huddleston Centre first started, I felt strange. I was the only black person out of 15 or 20 parents. I sat in a corner. My experience was different, I didn't known who to turn to. I saw all these white faces and just did a reverse. After going there three weeks, I stopped. I felt so out of it. They kept asking me things I couldn't answer. I felt so completely out of it. I used to catch the bus, get to the door, turn around and come back home again. Three consecutive weeks this happened. On the fourth, I went as usual and there were two

Leon

people waiting outside who said "You're not getting away with it this time, you're coming in." Eventually, I could say what I had to say, Now I rum a parents support group at the Centre where parents can come and share their feelings. A lot of them who have disabled children over 18 find it difficult to let go.

At a conference the other day in Finsbury Park, of black disabled people, a chap was describing how he was treated by the police. They thought he was joking because they didn't understand that was his way of walking. So then he told them "if I'm joking now, I've been joking all my life." This was a young man of 25 who explained to them he had Cerebral Palsy. They didn't believe him and rang his parents to see if he was telling the truth. They gave no apology when they eventually release him.

I think myself, not only the police, but anyone who works with people in public service, should have at least 6 months training in disability awareness. Police, doctors, lawyers and teachers all need courses of 2-3 weeks.

Section 4

Work That Can Be Done In Class

National Curriculum
Science and Disability: Science Key Stage One and Disability: A Draft Unit for Second Year Infants

By Richard Rieser and Christine Yorston

This curriculum module for primary science arose from some successful work on disability and the primary school that was carried out at Laburnum JMI school Hackney from April to December 1989.

Arising from discussions between the staff and Richard Rieser it was decided that the school wanted to make the raising of awareness of disability a major priority. It was felt that many of the attainment targets at Level 11 of the primary science curriculum could be achieved while raising awareness of disability in a systematic way. Only parts of this unit have to date been trialed, but we hope to adapt and modify it in the light of experience. However it was our purpose to show how an awareness of disabilities could be developed within the framework of primary science for young children.

Certainly in our view this approach could be developed to deal with Level 2 and 3 Attainment Targets for Junior age children.

Wherever possible you should try and team teach this unit with a disabled adult who can come in and work alongside you throughout talking about her own experiences where this is appropriate.

National Curriculum Science & Disability: Key Stage 1

Introduction: Part 1

Attainment Targets	Objectives	Activities	Knowledge Skills and Understanding	Resources
ATT2 **Level 1** Know that there is a wide variety of living things which includes human beings. **ATT4** **Level 1** Know that human beings vary from one individual to the next.	(1) To introduce that there are a range of physical and mental attributes in class. (2) To develop simple measuring and recording skills.	**Are we all the same?** (1) Timing Activities - how long does it take to (a) complete a jigsaw puzzle (b) thread beads in a specific sequence (c) Put all the pegs in a pegboard. Memory Games: • matching pairs (pelmanism • *I packed my case....* each child has to remember what has already been packed then add a nother item. • *What's missing* - child has to identify missing object from a series of objects. Co-ordination activities • Catching a ball, measure the distance, how many correct catches at a certain distance, e.g. use left/right hand to see if there is any difference.	To understand that all children are different and develop at different rates and in different ways. Learning to measure simple differences between each other and recording them in a meaningful way.	Puzzles, beads, thread, sequence cards, pegs, pegboards, pairs game, set of everyday objects, balls.

Attainment	Activities	Objectives	Resources
(3) To discover whether there are children in class with visual impairment hearing impairment, asthma, eczema and or physical impairments.	Many of the results of the above games could be recorded simply and displayed to show some of the range of mental and physical attributes in class. Do all parts of our bodies work equally well? Discussion to find out if there are parts of their body that don't work very well and need help conduct a simple survey to find out if children have the following in class - glasses, grommets, braces, inhalers, skin complaints, are any children on a special diet, do they have food allergies, do they suffer from hayfever? etc.	To know that many children have a range of minor disability and need to make minor adjustments and or use aids. To understand that there is a range in their own class, by carrying out surveys and recording results.	*Books* 'Just awful' 'On my way home' 'Cromwell's glasses' Glasses, grommets, inhalers, etc. if available
(4) Use the knowledge and experience of the children in class to establish a continuum of minor impairments to more major disability.	**Are some people more disabled than others?** (3) Can they provide examples of friends and/or relatives who suffer from more major disability: blindness, deafness, use of wheelchair, etc., stories, pictures, photographs and whenever possible visits or visitors would supplement this objective in different ways. Learning to measure simple differences between each other and recording them in a meaningful way.	To know that some people have major disability which has a major effect on their lives often through society's attitude towards them.	*Books* 'The Franny Series' 'I have series' 'Garden in the City' McDonald's children Magazines T.V. (soaps?)
ATT3 **Level 1a** Be able to name or label the external parts of the human body. To be able to name the external parts of the human body, to identify how we use the various parts and to envisage what happens if a part doesn't work or we can't use it.	**What are the parts of our Body?** (1) Using the magnetic board with visuals reconstruct the human body naming all the parts and or use the Giant Book of the Human Body. (2) Draw pictures or write about people they know with a body part that doesn't work properly (permanent or temporary). What do they do?	To know the main parts of the body and what they do. Making hypothesis based on own experience and knowledge. Testing hypothesis.	Magnetic board. Visuals of all major external body parts. Giant Book of the Human Body (Neil Ardley and David West) Writing and drawing implements.

Attainment Targets	Objectives	Activities	Knowledge Skills and Understanding	Resources
		(3) Using the magnetic board and visuals ask children to hypothesise about body parts that don't work. How would it affect people if they didn't have ...... going through the major body parts. Use 1 or 2 examples to test hypothesis (a) P.E. lesson - moving without one leg, catching a ball with only one hand (b) writing without hands. Discuss adaptation of skills and use of appliances and aids to suit needs. **Definition of Impairment** - Impairment is when any part of the mind or body doesn't work as it should.		
ATT3 **Level 2b** Know that personal hygiene, food, rest, exercise, safety and the proper use of medicines are important.	To establish the difference between not being able to use your body or part of your body because of short term illness or injury and long term impairment leading to disability. To understand that without proper care, food, exercise, hygiene and safety they could become ill or disabled at any time.	**What is the difference between illness and impairment?** (1) Set up hospital corner or doctors surgery in class, children can relate their experiences of illness or injury and how they got better (role play). Have any of the children had injections? Talk about danger of hypodermic needles. Chart a common childhood illness (measles, mumps, chicken pox) from beginning to end emphasising that rest, proper food, hygiene and proper use of medicine helped to and their recovery. N.B. - Measles can be very dangerous. In some parts of the world it can be a killer.	To understand that cuts, breaks and most infections, can be healed up if given proper treatment. To understand that senses, nerves and large parts of skin cannot be repaired.	Bed, bandages, themometers, plasters, stethescope. Bottles for medicine, toy needles for injections etc. Pictures or photographs of potentially dangerous situations. C.S.V. pack. In the home road playground park

Show children a series of pictures or photographs showing potentially dangerous situations and ask them to describe what they think may happen.

ATT2
Level 2a and b

Know that plants and animals need certain conditions for life.

Understand how living things are looked after and be able to treat them with care and consideration.

To look at themselves over the pattern of a day and identify how they get things that are essential for their life.

To look at a day in the life of someone who is disabled.

How do we get what we need to live?

Using sequence books, pictures, circular charts, ask children to look at a sequence of a day in their life.

Discuss do they have the essential ingredients of a healthy life? (Food, rest, exercise, care, safe, environment, hygiene (water is very important, clean and dirty water systems must be kept separate - in some parts of the world they are not and typhoid is prevalent).

How is it the same and different for disabled people?

Introduce in them the three books on disabled children "I am blind", "I am deaf" and "I have spina bifida". Discuss fully how their lives are the same and if they are different and why.

To know first hand the handicaps imposed by society that disabled people have to try to overcome.

'I have series'

'I am blind'

'I am deaf'

'I have Spina Bifida'

This could be represented in a comparison chart.

ATT3
Level 2b and c

Know that personal hygiene food, rest, exercise and safety and the proper use of medicines are important.

Be able to give a simple account of the pattern of their day.

What things do people do that makes disabled peoples daily lives harder?

Perhaps they could also talk about a day in their own life and someone they know well who is disabled.

Skills of comparing, contrasting and recording similarities and differences.

Construct a chart of the disadvantages people make for disabled people.

e.g. Getting about
Entertainment
Shopping, School, Homes, Jobs.

Develop a knowledge that there are specific difficulties which disabled people have to deal with.

National Curriculum Science & Disability

Part 2 - Vision and Light

Attainment Targets	Objectives	Activities	Knowledge Skills and Understanding	Resources
ATT4 **Level 2** Be able to measure simple differences between each other.	To measure the variation of sight in class. To be aware of a continuation of visual abilities to blindness.	**Do all our eyes see as well as each other?** In groups test each other (a) standard children's eye test chart. (b) Field of vision looking straight ahead (someone carrying coloured sheet approaches in circular motion from behind) (c) Colour blindness. In class point out that certain eye problems can be corrected - glasses, operations, exercises. Colour blindness cannot be corrected. Read Cromwell's Glasses - story (discuss name calling). Give children a brief view of how the eye works.	(1) Administer tests, record results, draw conclusions. (2) Know that there are a range of visual abilities. Develop empathy with people who have visual impairment and an awareness that it is wrong to make fun of people with disability. Knowledge of how the eye works and what can happen if it is damaged.	Eye test chart (school medical room) seeing colour chart (McDonald Science) sheets of coloured card. 'Cromwell's Glasses' (Holly Keller)
ATT1 Observe familiar materials and events in their immediate environment at first hand using their senses.	(a) To become conscious of the use of touch taste, sound and smell to identify objects. (b) To establish that if one is blind you learn to rely on other senses.	**What do our senses tell us?** Some people can not see or see very well. They are either blind or partially sighted. (a) In hall set up an artificial road scene with certain obstacles in place. Blindfold children and in turn using a cane given them the opportunity to try and cross the road. Discuss the hazards they encountered.	Developing an awareness through practical enquiry of the information they get through different senses. Recording and interpreting result.	Bamboo cane or long-cane. Giant Book of how the body works. Blindfold. Wine gums, opal fruits. Scratch and smell stickers.

Attainment Target	Objectives	Activities	Learning Outcomes	Resources
ATT6 Level 1 Be able to describe familiar and unfamiliar objects in terms of simple properties.	(a) Be able to describe attributes of various materials. (b) Develop an appreciation of how much non-visual information there is available. (c) Appreciate that we learn to see by means of visual clues.	(b) In hall in pairs 1 blindfolded and 1 guide arrange for various sounds to be heard in different parts of the hall, blindfolded person has to identify activity by its sound. (c) Smell and taste in blindfolded children have to identify (only the flavour should vary in what they eat). Blindfolded, scratch and smell cards - identify the smell. (d) Touch trail, round school/classroom blindfolded with a guide identify by touch objects they encounter on their way round. (1) Measure the time it takes to do a familiar puzzle/construction e.g. lego wall, brick tower. (a) Without a blindfold (b) with a blindfold. (2) Feely box in class, each day replace objects inside. Children must be able to describe objects based on the characteristics they can feel e.g. rough/smooth, light/heavy, sharp/blunt, soft/hard. (3) Look at photographs of familiar objects from an unfamiliar angle. Close observation drawings of what they actually see not what they think they see. Visual tricks - shadows and shapes at night.	Record and measure by time list attributes and identify objects. Be able to identify object by non-visual attributes. Appreciate the difference between seeing and recognising.	Jigsaws, lego, bricks. Feely box, selection of objects. Photographs.
ATT2 Level 2b **ATT3 Level 2b** **ATT11 Level 1,2a&b** Know that many household appliances use electricity and that misuse could be dangerous.	To know that the kitchen is a potentially hazardous place particularly for a blind person. To examine ways that touch, smell, taste and sound could be used in	**What is dangerous in the kitchen?** Through discussion, photographs or simulation of a real kitchen what objects do the children feel are dangerous and why would they be particularly dangerous to a blind person. Can they visualise how a blind person might change things. How might a blind person make the kitchen safer?	Understand how useful other senses and devices can be used to provide a safe environment and therefore independence for a blind person.	*Liquid level indicator. Kettle. *Bread board, bread knife. Flour, salt, sugar in containers.

Attainment Targets	Objectives	Activities	Knowledge Skills and Understanding	Resources
	the kitchen to give a blind person safety and independence.	Examine devices and strategies that might help. (1) Whistle of kettle - sound (2) Cutting bread - touch (3) Pouring out tea - sound liquid level indicator (4) Keeping everything in a set place - memory (electric cables tucked away) (5) Distinguish - salt, soap powder, baking powder - taste. However, taste wouldn't always be safe. Children could develop a tactile code for identifying food. (6) How useful would magnets be for picking up utensils. Experiment with magnets to see what they do pick up. How useful would that be to a blind person.	Ability to develop a set of tactile symbols to enable them to tell the difference in food without looking. Know that magnets can attract certain materials and could be useful to a blind or partially sighted person.	Magnets of different strengths, set of utensils.
ATT15 **Level 1a** Light and colour. Know that light comes from different sources. **Level 1b** Be able to discriminate between colours. **ATT12** **Level 1 and 2**	To know the different sources of light. To know that without light there is no colour. To know that a blind person will want to identify colours and how they can do this of touch symbols, braille or scratch and smell. Learn how touch can be used to read and write. Moon/braille.	**Where does light come from?** List light sources - sun, electric light, car light, torch, mirror, moon, stars, phosphorescence, luminous, watch etc. **Is light needed for colour?** Experiment - a large box painted black inside apart from 1 wall - coloured -above cut a little hole and from a distance shine a torch with head inside box - how far/near do you have to shine torch before colour becomes recognisable. Blind people use colour/shape buttons to identify clothes. Can you match the colours using a blindfold?	Know where light comes from. Know that colour comes from light, and where there is no visible light there is no colour. Know that people can read and write by touching. Learn basic skills of Braille.	Black box, torch. *Identifying colour buttons. *German Film *Braille Cards Braille number resource sheet ILEA LMS *(All

from RNIB)

Using "German Film" draw familiar objects and have someone identify them by touch.

Can they recognise name, alphabet, numbers using Braille.

National Curriculum Science & Disability

Key Stage 1 - Sound and Hearing

Attainment Targets	Objectives	Activities	Knowledge Skills and Understanding	Resources
ATT4 **Level 2** Be able to measure simple differences between each other.	(1) To measure the variation of hearing in class including ability to identify objects according to sound. (2) To be aware of a continuum of hearing abilities to deafness.	**What can you hear?** (a) Can children hear a pin drop, how close do they have to be to hear bubbles bursting in a fizzy drink, or their breakfast cereal crackling? Children can do some simple measuring and recording and interpreting results. (b) Blindfold child (not covering ears) and slowly have someone bring a ticking watch towards their head from about 1 metre away stop when the child says it can hear. This distance can be measured in standard/non-standard measures. (c) Blindfold child, make a distinct noise, ask child to pin point direction of sound (the height of the sound should be at the same level as the persons ear). Try doing this	To understand that there is a variation in the hearing ability of children in class. To be able to measure and record distances that children can hear. To be able to measure variation in direction that children can hear. To be able identify objects according to the sound they make. To make generalisation about hearing loss from statistics.	Pins, fizzy drinks, rice crispies, metre stick, watch, blindfold. Various objects that make different sounds tin box. Tape recorder. Statistical information on hearing loss available from RNID.

Person sitting facing forward

227

Attainment Targets	Objectives	Activities	Knowledge Skills and Understanding	Resources
		experiment from different directions, could be recorded like this:	Portray information given as a statistic visually (bar graph) (no line).	
		(d) Try to recognise certain objects by rattling them inside a tin - try using different types of objects, chalk, rubber, matchstick.		
		(e) Drop various objects from behind a screen on to a table and have children identify them by their sound e.g. coins, rubber, knife, comb. Children can record answers on a tick sheet. How many did they identify correctly.		
		(f) Make a tape recording of various sounds e.g. sandpaper being rubbed on wood, pouring water into a container, blowing through a straw into a jar of water, unlocking a door etc. Children must guess what produced the sound.		
		(g) To look at statistics of hearing disability, ask children to make a visual representation of information.		
ATT14 **Level 1 and 2** Know that sound can be made in a variety of ways. Know that sounds are heard when the sound reaches the eardrum.	To gain a simple understanding of how the eardrum works and how, if it is damaged, it can lead to severe hearing loss. To establish that sound moves through the air and that you can foresee it but when it hits something solid it vibrates.	**How does your ear work?** Make a model of an eardrum. Cut off the bottom of a plastic or polystyrene cup leaving a smooth edge and cover the opening with clingfilm making sure it is taut. You may need to use glue to secure the clingfilm. Hold the cup horizontally as shown in the diagram and a small polystyrene ball (2cm) suspended from a length of thread fixed almost but not quite vertically.	To understand how the eardrum works by making a model and testing it with different sounds. To understand through the working model, ways in which deafness can occur. Understand that if damage is done to the	Polystyrene cup, clingfilm, glue, polystyrene balls. Suppliers: Phillip Harris Griffin and George Stand Thread Tape recorder Radio Musical instruments

To know that different sounds have different amounts of vibration.

A radio or cassette tape recorder is then played next to the open end of the cup.

The sound wave will make the clingfilm vibrate and the ball will move in sympathy Try using different types of sound or music. Try using different pitch and sound.

NB - What happens to the ball. (Record)

Compare this model to the inside workings of the ear.

What would happen if we burst the clingfilm Establish link with hearing loss.

outer or middle parts of the ear it can often be corrected medically or surgically, but the middle - inner ear if damaged can only be helped by artificial aids if a person is not profoundly deaf.

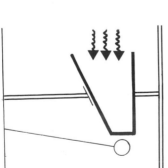

ATT11
Level 1

Know that many household appliances use electricity and that misuse can be dangerous

To establish that with electricity we are able to create devices that will amplify sound for partially deaf people.

NB - These aids are no good for people who are profoundly deaf.

To find out whether or not larger ears help us to hear more clearly.

How can electricity help?

Look again at the book used earlier called 'I am deaf'.

(1) Look at how Amina managers to hear What other electrical devices are used in the book to make hearing easier for Amina and her brothers.

(2) Ask the children if they know how hearing aids make hearing easier for Amina.

The children may like to try the following experiment.

Try making out of stiff paper large cones to fit over their ears. Do they make it easier to hear? Can they devise their own tests to find out.

NB - A mention of ear trumpets used in the past could be brought in here.

To understand that electricity in hearing aids helps the eardrum to do its work and that by amplifying sound we can help people hear more clearly.

Be able to create ways of testing artificial ears and devise fair tests to establish their effectiveness.

To understand that ear cones/trumpets can be an aid to hearing and that the electric hearing aid has now replaced it.

Books 'I am deaf'.
Stiff/cardboard Paper

Hearing aids if possible.

ATT12
Level 2

Know that there is a variety of means for

To establish that for people who are profoundly deaf there are other means of communication and

How do deaf people communicate?

(1) Learn how to lip read - using a mirror observe the shapes of the different words, try with a partner, how much can you understand. *

Understand that it is possible to be understood by someone who is lip-reading (although not

Mirror
Finger spelling and signing RNID

229

Attainment Targets	Objectives	Activities	Knowledge Skills and Understanding	Resources
communicating over long distances.	that deaf people learn to adapt the use of their other senses. To know that finger spelling and some signing is a useful skill for all to learn.	(2) Learn how to finger spell, can they spell their name and give simple responses. (3) Can they learn some sign language. Perhaps learning to sing a song. Consider the inclusion of sign language on TV as an important aid to deaf people. Some deaf people learn to talk using a computer and a microphone. (4) Simulate a situation in class where pupils might gain some understanding of being deaf. E.g. The whole class undertake to be silent for half a day whilst the teacher communicates to them by making word shapes and mime. Analyse the difficulties. *NB - Even the best lip readers, will only be able to understand 40%-50%. Profoundly deaf people prefer and use British sign language as their first language. Many teachers of the deaf do not agree. See section on Equality for Deaf People and Pictures in the Mind.	an effective means of communication). Understand that it is possible to communicate with someone using finger spelling and sign language. Understand the benefits of technology as a means to aid wider communication for the deaf. Understand a little of what it must be like to be deaf in a hearing world.	See also Signed Books in Childrens Books

National Curriculum Science & Disability

Key Stage 1 - Movement & Physical Disability

Attainment Targets	Objectives	Activities	Knowledge Skills and Understanding	Resources
ATT 10 **Level 1 & 2** Know that things move by pushing them. Understand that pushes and pulls can make things start moving, speed up, swerve and stop.	Appreciate that people in a wheelchair can lead an active life. Gain understanding of how we use muscles to walk. Learn how to use a walking aid if muscles don't work. Gain an understanding of different ways to propel a wheelchair and how gradients effect them. Learn the skills of pushing using a wheelchair. Have an appreciation of methods of using a wheelchair on pavements. Gain an understanding of barriers in school and local environment.	**How can you get about if it's difficult to walk?** Read stores of Franny. Look at picture or model of a limb, see how it works. If muscles or nerves carrying messages don't work, then we need to use an aid to help us walk. Stick-frame-wheelchair. **How does a wheelchair work?** Build a wheelchair in groups using: (a) lego - using ordinary bricks (b) from clockwork (this comes with lego) (c) Using electricity (with a battery) Test out different wheelchairs to see how far they go. Test them on a raised PE bench at different angles. Can they make conclusions about what they found out. How easy is it to get about in a wheelchair? Get a wheelchair. Demonstrate correct way and incorrect way of getting in and out. Learn Do's and don'ts of using/helping: (1) Always ask the person in the chair what they want.	Have the manual dexterity to design and build lego wheelchairs. Set up a test. Draw a conclusion. Know that it requires more work to get up slopes than to travel on a flat surface. Know the difference between pushing stored energy and an electric motor. Practical skills of pushing a wheelchair. Assessing barriers. Knowing what forms a barrier. Know these barriers don't have to be there. Make a graphic representation of barriers.	Franny series. Lego. Lego 810 Lego 895 motor. Great book of the Human Body The Body and how it works. Wheelchair (St Leonards hospital will lend. Ring Jackie Kennard 739 8484 ext. 4507). Other day centres will lend if arranged in advance. Design for everyone. Manchester disability Forum (DES booklet on Access). Worksheets on Access. See Section on access.

Attainment Targets	Objectives	Activities	Knowledge Skills and Understanding	Resources
		(2) Push at a steady slow pace.		
		(3) Go up kerbs on back wheel.		
		(4) Tip back going down.		
		(5) Don't get out without footrest up and brake on.		
	Gain an understanding of how those barriers could be changed/removed.	Assess school for access. Go round block assessing different obstacles. Write to council. Invite a regular wheelchair user to come in and talk about the barriers they have to deal with.		
	Draw an area plan without barriers.			
ATT 10	Gain an understanding that the built environment is not designed with disabled people in mind.	**What gets in the way?** Draw up a list of all barriers children found for disabled people, school, buses, shops, pavements. Draw up large scale plan/map of school/local area, to include list of barriers.	Gain an understanding of correspondence of birds eye view plan/local area.	Large piece of paper to draw up plan. Use large scale map if needing more detail.
		Conclusion	Be able to see barriers in various places from the point of view of a wheelchair user.	Available borough planning office.
ATT 10	Try to reach an understanding that while disabled people are impaired it is society that handicaps them.	Ask why the children feel life is made so difficult for disabled people. Can they think positively about how society can change it's attitude to disabled people.	Know that attitudes help make things more difficult for disabled people.	
Communication & Technology ATT 12 **Level 1, 2a & b** (1) Know about some everyday devices that receive text sound and image over a long distance using info. technology.	Gain an appreciation that disabled people can benefit a great deal from info. technology.	**How can Technology help disabled people?** (1) List all the ways of sending information over long distances. Make a poster using cuts from magazines. (2) Look at an ideal house for: (a) A blind person. (b) A severely disabled person. Devise aids that may not yet exist.	Know that technology is advancing all the time and that it does make life easier for everybody especially, disabled people.	Old colour magazines Set of brochures from aids/appliance companies.

232

(2) Know that there is a variety of means for communicating info. tech. over long distances.

(3) Know that info. can be stored in a range of everyday devices, including the computer.

(3) Know that there exists speaking computers, 2-way braille printers, electronic control of house. Fax, videophone, telephone, computer. Travelling to and from work may cease to be necessary.

Things ThaT Richard cant do easily.

1. he cant walk easily.

2. Wan It.s Sonw or fan his stik Slips.

By Nicole

USEFUL VIDEOS ON DISABILITY

(With thanks to Images of Physical Disability from Mental Health Council).

A. General

1 'Breaking Barriers' UN. 30 min

Looks at problems for 500,000,000 disabled people in the world. Available UN. 20 Buckingham Gate, SW1. (UN want £3.00 for it)

2 Rights Not Charity: Open Space 1989 BBC 13 October.

Outlines movement for rights for disabled people and problems we still face.

3 Dreams are the worst

Distributed by: Royal Society of Medicine (sale) 1 Wimpole Street, London, W1M 8AE.
Producer: Medicus Productions for the GLC
pd: video; 30 mins; 1985

Shows a disabled young man's efforts to reintergrate himself into society after a nearly fatal car crash. As the drama unfolds, we see through the young man's eyes a world that is frequently insensitive to the needs of people with disabilities and a society which makes a handicap a disability. Such issues as access and personal relationships are explored as well as the problem of employment and the possibilities that computers offer people with disabilities.

4 Disability: aspects of physical handicap,

80 Wood Lane, W12 0TT
Distributed by: BBC Enterprises (sale)
Producer: BBC
pd: 16 mm; video; 25 mins each; 1982

A series of five programmes which examines the problems faced by the physically disabled, their attitudes to their own disabilities, and the care they receive in their respective countries, including Holland, Ireland, Sierra Leone, and the UK.

1. One in Ten

2. Far Better Off in a Home?

3. A Question of Attitudes

4. A Feisty Group of People

5. Two Sides of the Coin

Watch out for use of 'handicap'

5 Hold Up

Distributed by: CFC (hire); EMI (sale) 25 Boileau Road, W5
Producer: Gibson Group
pd: 16mm, 30 mins, New Zealand; 1982

An entertaining film about disability, in two parts. In the first section, a blind man, a man with cerebral palsy and a deaf women have all witnessed a robbery. All have observed things which could help the police catch the robbers but all are ignored or misunderstood because they are disabled. The actors are disabled people playing themselves in this drama. In the second half, the actors discuss the points raised and give viewers an insight into what it really feels like to be disabled.

6 United in Fury

Distributed by: Central TV (sale) Broad Street, Birmingham, B1 2JP
Producer: Central TV
pd: video; 52 mins; 1987

Two thirds of Britain's disabled people are living on or below the poverty line. Changes and cutbacks in the benefits system have finally driven them to lodge a protest and suggest their own solution. This film considers the plight of 'sufferers' and examines the proposed solution.

7 Stolen Childhood

1 Gompamma - Polio in India in Stolen Childhood 23 min
2 Martina - Downs Syndrome in Sweden 30 mins £9.99. North/South Productions Woburn Buildings, Woburn Walk, WC2

B. Self image and self representation

8 Best Boy, 104 minutes, colour, 16 mm
Filmmaker: Ira Wohl. Distributor: Concord Film.

The life of Philly Wohl, a developmentally delayed fifty two year old man, is thoughtfully and livingly examined, as he learns to become more independent and his elderly parents learn to let go. This film won an Academy Award in 1980.
201 Felixstowe Road, Ipswich, Suffolk, 1P3 9BJ

9 People First

Distributed by: CFC (hire); EP (hire) Concord, 201 Felixstowe Road, Ipswich, Suffolk, IP3 9BJ
Producer:
pd: 16 mm; 29 mins; Canada; 1979

Self-advocacy groups are groups of disabled people, including in many cases people with learning difficulties, who have united to press for their own rights and services, a contrast to the usual situation whereby others campaign on their behalf. The American film shows some of the activities of the original group, People First In Oregon, which includes the organisation of a convention of disabled people. There is a growing development in the UK that a similar philosophy is needed.

10 Disability/Capability

Distributed by: Valley & Vale Community Arts (hire), Blaengorw Road, Blaengorw, Nr Bridgend CF 32 8AW
Producer: Valley & Vale Community Arts
pd: video; 26 mins; 1986

Produced with a group of peripatetic, physically-disabled and mentally ill adults at the Ty'r Ardd day centre in Bridgend, Mid Glamorgan.
Looks at attitudes to disability expressed by those attending the day centre as well as those of the general public. Available on free loan to schools.

11 I Can First Chance

Distributed by: Connections (sale/hire)
Pallingswick House, 241 King Street, London, W6 9LP
Producer: Connections
pd: video; 20 mins; 1987

I CAN is a training video produced by disabled people. It documents what activities disabled people can and like doing. These activities range from art to sport to film animation.

12 I am not what you see

Distributed by: CFC (hire) Concord (as above).
Producer: Pegasus Films
pd: 16 mm; 27 mins; Candada

Sondra Diamond, who has cerebral palsy, speaks about her struggle against ever-present barriers: the doctors who held little hope, the reluctant teachers, the wary employers and the norms of society as a whole. 'I am not what you see visually, I am a woman'.

13 57 Varieties

Distributed by: Commedia, 32 Rontallor Street, Edinburgh, EH8 9HZ or SCFL (hire)
Producer: Commedia for Calouste Gulbenkian Foundation
pd: video; 16 mins; 1984

Made by a mixed group of disabled (both developmental and physical) and able-bodied young people. Looks at education, deprivation and disability in a light comic style.

14 Moving in

Distributed by: Film Workshop Trust (hire); ICA Good Video Guide (sale) The Mall, London SW1Y 5AH
Producer: Film Workshop Trust for Channel 4TV
pd: video; 52 mins; 1984

Documents the progress of three severely disabled people as they move from institutional care to independence within the community. Intended for health education, disabled campaigners and housing action groups.

'Very realistic; gives hope about what can be done. Makes some very important points about the individualism of physically disabled people'. - Self Help Group Support Worker.

15 The impossible takes a little longer

Distributed by: EMI (sale/hire) 25 Boileau Road, London, W5 3AL
Producer: NFBC
pd: video; 45 mins; Canada; 1986

A documentary which gives an insight into the resourcefulness of five different disabled women who have overcome barriers in their personal and professional lives.

16 Walter (Channel 4 1982)

Concord: Story of intellectually disabled man and his family held at two points in his life, when he is in his twenties and then in his fifties.

17 Captives of care

Distributed by: CFC (hire) Concord as above
Producer:
pd: video; 28 mins; Australia; 1982

About the struggle by a small group of severely disabled people in a large and impersonal institution in Australia to be accepted as human beings with their own standards of dignity and autonomy. A dramatic reconstruction acted by the people themselves, alongside professional actors.

H. Aids, Appliances and Technology

35 With a Little Help from the Chip Nos. 1-6

Distributed by: BBC Enterprises (sale) 80 Wood Lane, W12 0TT
Producer: BBC Television
pd: video; 6 x 25 mins; 1986

A series of six programmes which reveals how recent developments in micro-technology can benefit disabled people.
No. 1 Christopher's magic cupboard
No. 2 Communicating
No. 3 Learning
No. 4. Getting about
No. 5. Working
No. 6. Inventing

36 Walk on Wheels

Equinox, Channel 4, October 89
Ch TV productions
All about wheelchairs.
Charlotte Street, WC1

37 Access
Let's Get Together

Distributed by: CFC (hire); Touch Point Productions (sale),
6 Ardencraig Street, Castlemilk, Glasgowe, 45
Producer: Touch Point Productions
pd: video; 15 mins; 1986

Made for 'Strathclyde Forum on Disability', highlights the difficulties of modern life for disabled people. The video concentrates of four central issues: housing, transport, access and information, and also encourages a united stance by disabled people on issues which affect them all. Also available with George McKay signing for the deaf.

I. Attitudes

38 So Clear in My Mind

Distributed by: Living Archive Project (Sale); Pillingswick House, 241 King Street, W6; Connections (sale/hire); The Go
Producer: Jerry Rothwell, Sharon Jones
pd: video; 29 mins; 1986

About attitudes towards the disabled and about changing the preconceptions of the able bodied. Documents the work of 'Theatre of Fact', a theatre-in-education group in Milton Keynes. Using the words and experiences of disabled people as their source material the company take a programme of exercises, role-play and theatre into local schools. Intended for those involved in training about disability -teachers, unions, social services, community groups - and also general audiences.

Feature Films all on Commercial Videos

39 Annie's Coming Out

Distributed by: Enterprise Pictures (hire); Blue Dolphin (hire)
Producer: Film Australia
pd: 16mm; 35mm; video; 93 mins; Australia; 1984 - commercial

This is based on a true story concerning a child born with cerebral palsy. Her innate intelligence is nurtured by a playworker. The film documents Annie's struggle to be allowed to leave the institution.

40 Rainman

1989. Feature film available on video. About Autism/sevants syndrome. About attitudes and institutionalisation. Dustin Hoffman and Tom Cruise a good film with good music makes many good points on disability cert 15.

41 My left Foot

1989. Feature film out also on video. About the life of Christy Brown. Gives many good insights into having a severe physical disability in a working class Dublin household in 1940's/50's.

42 One Flew Over the Cuckoos Nest

Starring Jack Nicholson. Has much to say about institutions and how people are treated especially when intellectually or severely emotionally disabled.

43 Coming Home

Jane Fonda and Jon Voigt. About disabled Vietnam war veteran and his relationship with Officers wife Jane Fonda.

44 The Elephant Man

John Hurt as 'the freak' and his tragic story in Victorian London. Would need careful discussion before showing a class.

45 Born on the Fourth of July

Story of Ron Kovaic and other disabled Vietnam War Veterans and the beginnings of the Disability Movement in USA.

46 We're Here Too

Video made for Youth Service with young people talking about disability. 1990.
£20 Individio, 80 Mildmay Grove, N1 4PJ.

Resource Cards to use in the Classroom. Teacher Notes.

We have not had a lot of time to develop these cards. We feel sure that having read this pack many teachers will be able to construct much better materials. In addition, see sections on childrens literature, raising disability in primary schools, whole school policy and National Curriculum for other ideas and resources. Many other parts of the text are adaptable for classroom use. We would be very interested in seeing copies of any work schemes you devise so we may carry on developing this project.

Cards

1A Here a simple presentation of the position of disabled adults in the UK is given, drawing on the OPCS statistics. For more detail see section on Disability in Britain.

1B (i) Here we give a regional breakdown of regional rates of disability (based on OPCS) which can be graphed and mapped.
(ii) Here are given two estimates of the prevalence and degree of deafness in the UK. (Note it is very difficult to get international data that is comparable although the World Health Organisation does provide some).

2A This cartoon by Micheline and Keith can be used as a talking point for a lesson on access and is suitable across the age range.

2B This account of Access USA from 'Same Difference' booklet is a useful way of discussing access by public transport by means of comparison. Suitable top forms junior.

3A & B/4A & B
These four cards are based on a booklet produced by Manchester Planning Department and Manchester Disability Forum (061-273 5033). While containing technical information we felt this could be used as the basis for an accessibility audit and for design work in CDT in secondary schools.

5A Hazards in the Home
5B Hazards in the Street from CSV. In Our Own Right. These can be used for a discussion on safety and possible disability arising from accidents as point of source curriculum or cross curriculum PHSE courses — different ages.

6A 'The Myth of Independence' raises questions for groups to discuss about Independence and inter-dependence in different settings (Secondary).

6B Disability/Race and Class possess in different situations what the likely effect of disability is going to be on a persons life chances and shows that both disability and handicap are relative terms and socially defined (see section on the language we use).

7A *Communication.* The Braille system devised by Louis Braille. Usually punched to raise dots on paper here shown – as a dot system. Copies of braille magazines can be obtained from RNIB as can Braille learning cards and cubes. The ILEA Braille Mathematics pack see Fran Mosley gives a lot of useful ways of using the braille system. Work can also be done on code messages and putting braille labels round the school.

7B Finger spelling alphabet. As good manners to deaf people everyone should learn to finger spell. All ages of children are very interested in it. For younger children and ESL children it certainly helps with language and literary development. Many silent games can be devised using finger spelling.

8A Signed numbers. The idea of non verbal communication can be reinforced using the number system in mental arithmetic and as another number system.

8B Language to Avoid, Exercise on positive and negative language useful generally and in Social Studies and English.

9 A & B British signed language is the first language of the Deaf Community. After many years of oppression (see 11A & B) much interest and recognition is now being given. This song 'Ten in the Bed' comes from a book of sayings in signed English from Beverley school. Infant children have shown great interest in sign language. [see Childrens Booklist].

10A & B Some basic signs for nursery and infant children. The books from Beverley school are well worth getting as are the 'Signed Spot' and 4 A-Z Books.

11 A & B This card summarises the history of the Deaf Community as shown in the Video 'Pictures in the Mind' available from Concorde Films for hire £11.35. More background is given in the section on Equality and the Deaf Community. This can be raised in History, Biology, PHSE and Social Studies lessons.

12 A & B   This account is for 4th year secondary and above in history, social studies and PHSE lessons, but could be simplified for younger children. It can also be used in RE lessons. A sad chapter of history with many lessons for debates on sterilisation, abortion and euthanasia (see 15A) and section on Genetic Counselling. This part of history should not be denied or covered up, all children should be made aware of it during their education as they should the Holocaust.

13 A & B   A Stitch Too Late: Polio in India. Taken from the book and Video Stolen Childhood. This story and information are relevant in Geography, Humanities, both in primary and secondary. The points on development are of general importance and can also be linked into Biology lessons on viruses and immunization.

14 A & B   Disability in Brazil. Another aspect of the growth in disability world wide is unsafe working conditions set up by multi-national companies and others in poor South countries like Brazil. This piece also talks of self-help and the disability movement in Brazil. Geography, Social Studies and Economics.

15 A & B   Martina a child born with Downs Syndrome, causing a moderate learning difficulty. Martina's story is in Stolen Childhood and the Video available from North South Productions. Kirsty's story can also be used. Raise many questions about how we judge people with learning difficulties.

16 A   Pre-Natal Diagnosis and Abortion can be used as a follow up to 15. In RE, Biology and PHSE and Social Studies. Would Martina be alive today if her mother had received Genetic Counselling. Also links to the current debate on embryo research.

17 A & B   Extracts from classic childrens literature were compiled by CSV 'In Our Own Right'
Heidi,
Treasure Island,
Christmas Carol,
Peter Pan.
[See section on childrens literature and stereotypes]

18 A & B   Three poems. Lois Keith on language. Helen Todd on deafness and Carmen Tunde on racism and mental illness. All raise much to talk about in GCSE literature and generally.

19   National Union of Journalists. NUJ Guidelines from the Campaign for Real People. List ways Disabled people are mis-represented and how they should be portrayed in the media.

20   Four examples of press presentation of Disabled People. Can be used with above guidelines. Any weeks national and local papers contain more examples.

21   Charity posters also draw on negative stereotypes. These are all taken from the 1989 Solicitor magazine supplement (Making Wills!) Get children to identify how disabled people are being portrayed.
a) multiple sclerosis
b) Metropolitan Society for the Blind
c) British Diabetic Association
d) Association of Spina Bifida and Hydrocephalus
e) Blesma
f) Break Through Trust

Footnote

Resource Card 12 Disabled People in Nazi Germany. Recently the Nazi extermination programme of disabled people has received some publicity. Observer 22nd September 1992 and a Channel 4 documentary 'Selling Murder: the killing films of the Third Reich' see also Robert Proctor's 'Racial Hygiene: Medicine Under the Nazi's' Harvard Press 1988 ISBN 0 674 74578 7.

Resource Cards

1A Statistics OPCS – Disability in Britain
1B (i) Regional Variation in Disability
   (ii) Prevalence of Hearing Loss in Great Britain

2A Access Cartoon
2B Access USA

3 A&B Design for everyone

4 A&B Design for everyone

5A Hazards in the Home
5B Hazards in the Streets

6A Myth of Independence
6B Disability/Race and Class

7A Communication: Braille
7B Communication: Finger Spelling

8A Signed Numbers
8B Language to use/avoid

9 A&B Signed Song – 10 in the Bed

10 A&B Some Basic Signs

11 A&B History: Pictures in the mind

12 A&B History: Disabled People in Nazi Germany

13 A&B Geography: A stitch too late: Polio in India

14 A&B Disability in Brazil

15 A&B Martina

16 A Pre-natal Diagnosis and Abortion
16 B Cartoon

17 A&B What we learn from books

18 A&B Poems

19 A&B NUJ Guidelines

20 A&B Press cuttings

21 A&B Charity Posters

Disabled People: The Facts and Figures

Incidence:

6,202,000 disabled adults in Great Britain

14.2% of the adult population

Where do they live?

93.2% (5,780,000) live in the community

6.8% (422,000) live in institutions

Age:

41.8% (2,595,000) are 16 - 65 years of age

5.8% (340,000) are 16 - 30 years of age

Sex:

58.5% (3,631,000) disabled women

41.5% (2,571,000) disabled men

Percentages of disabled people:.

Working		Not working
Men	36%	64%
Women	31%	69%

52% of disabled men under 30 years of age are not working

H.M.S.O. 1988 (Sept.), OPCS Surveys of Disability Among Adults: Report 1.

1A

(i) GEOGRAPHICAL VARIATION IN DISABILITY IN THE U.K.

Estimates of prevalence of disability among adults by region and severity category (cumulative rate per thousand population)

Severity category	North	Yorks and Humberside	North West	East Mid-lands	West Mid-lands	East Anglia	GLC	South East	South West	Wales	Scotland	Great Britain
In private households (cumulative rate per thousand)												
10	2	2	3	2	3	0	2	2	4	5	2	2
9–10	10	9	10	8	9	8	7	8	9	14	10	9
8–10	17	18	16	14	18	15	17	15	18	22	18	17
7–10	31	27	25	23	31	27	27	24	31	34	28	27
6–10	45	39	37	35	43	36	37	35	41	53	40	39
5–10	64	58	52	50	59	51	51	50	56	71	58	55
4–10	83	74	70	65	75	61	61	65	73	93	76	71
3–10	108	92	88	81	91	81	76	79	91	114	94	88
2–10	130	114	105	99	112	100	94	95	110	138	94	88
1–10	162	148	130	128	135	127	117	124	135	164	147	135
1–10 standardised for age	162	148	131	131	141	123	119	123	124	160	131	135
Total population (cumulative rate per thousand)												
10	4	4	6	6	4	1	4	5	7	8	4	5
9–10	13	13	15	14	12	10	11	13	15	19	12	13
8–10	21	23	23	21	22	18	22	21	25	27	21	22
7–10	35	33	32	31	35	30	33	31	39	41	31	33
6–10	50	46	45	44	48	39	44	43	50	60	44	46
5–10	69	65	60	60	64	55	58	58	65	77	61	62
4–10	87	82	79	76	80	65	69	73	83	100	80	78
3–10	112	100	96	91	96	85	84	87	101	121	98	95
2–10	134	122	113	109	116	104	102	104	121	145	120	114
1–10	166	156	139	138	139	130	125	132	145	170	151	142

HMSO 1988: Based on OPCS Table 3.9

(ii) THE PREVALENCE OF HEARING LOSS IN GREAT BRITAIN
2 sets of estimates
(based on data from the Institute of Hearing Research)

Degree of Hearing Loss (dBHL)	% of Adult Population * (numbers in millions for GB in brackets)
25+	17 (7.5m)
35+	8 (3.5m)
45+	4 (1.8m)
55+	2 (0.9m)
65+	1 (0.44m)
75+	0.5 (0.22m)
85+	0.25 (0.11m)
95+	0.13 (0.06m)
105+	0.05 (0.02m)

* Institute of Hearing Research Data

Description of Hearing Loss	Approx.no. of Adults affected in G.B.	(Percentage of adult pop.)
Mild (25-40dBHL)	5.7 million	(13%)
Moderate (41-70 dBHL)	1.58 million	(3.5%)
Severe (71-95 dBHL)	0.185 million	(0.42%)
Profound (96+ dBHL)	0.035 million	(0.08%)
Total	7.5 million	(17%)

RNID Research Group
March 1989

I thought ACCESS was a credit card
..... until I discovered STEPS

steps affect us all ....

ACCESS USA

Getting public transport on the right track for disabled people

Laurie Tranter goes to work each morning by public service bus and metro train, despite the fact she has multiple sclerosis and is in a wheelchair. A journey that in Britain, at the moment, would be inconceivable. Fortunately for Laurie, she works in Washington D.C., where the subway train system was built after legislation was passed requiring all public-service facilities to be accessible to disabled people.

The system is quite a revelation to disabled British visitors. Train doorways are level with the platform so that a wheelchair can be easily taken on and off. All stations have lifts and elevators to enable disabled passengers to get down to the right level. On the trains themselves, the first few seats inside the doors are reserved for disabled passengers. Ticket-vending and change-giving machines are set at a height so that they can be operated from a wheelchair.

They've also borne in mind blind and partially sighted travellers. A sound-warning of an incoming train is given as well as the visual one from winking lights set in the well of the platform. Voice announcements on the train itself give a clear indication of the stop you are about to reach and which side the doors will open.

The metro system has also been adapted for use by blind people. A small hole has been punched in tickets to enable them to be inserted the right way round.

STEPS ARE AN OBSTACLE TO PEOPLE WHO USE WHEELCHAIRS

RAMP THEM!

THIS IMAGE IS *OFFENSIVE* TO PEOPLE WITH DISABILITIES

2p each plus S.A.E.

WHY IS THIS BUILDING NOT ACCESSIBLE ???

On The Buses

The bus system works on the basis of making the whole system available to the disabled public, rather than making specific routes accessible. A percentage of Washington's stock of buses have been fitted with a ramp which can automatically be lowered to the road if someone in a wheelchair wants to board. You can always guarantee that an adapted bus will be available on your route, but you are asked to give about twenty-four hours' notice of your needs. The bus company hopes that as more buses are adapted, the need to give an advance warning will be diminished. Services aren't perfect; breakdowns on the subway system are often slow to be repaired, the bus ramps are also vulnerable to mechanical failure and one quite common scenario is for a bus-load of able-bodied passengers to be held up when a ramp gets stuck. Such bugs in the system sometimes cause a little friction; there is a school of thought which says spending so much more for such a very small minority of travellers is a waste of tax payers' cash. Our impression, though, was that most of the community supported the idea.

We looked at other alternatives too, such as taxi buses in Sweden. For a long time, Sweden was regarded as something of a trail-blazer, in Europe at least, in the field of accessible transport. Their answer in the sixties and seventies was to provide a service of special buses which picked you up at your door, although you had to give a couple of days' advance notice. However, in the eighties, the emphasis has been changing in response to the feeling that disabled people want to use the same kind of service as everyone else. Taxi buses are ordinary taxis for hire which have had a space cleared so that they can take wheelchairs; they are also equipped to take people who have to remain lying down.

In comparison to the US and Sweden, progress in Britain is slow and piecemeal. We filmed a service in Leicestershire which, while it doesn't yet have the Washington flexibility, does accept the principle that people with disabilities should use the same service as everyone else. They now have at least one bus in a week equipped with a ramp on all of their routes. The bus will either pick you up at a regular stop or, in some cases, collect you from your door. It means you have to do your shopping to fit in with the timetable, but the people we talked to thought it was worth it to be part of the mainstream bus service.

half actual size

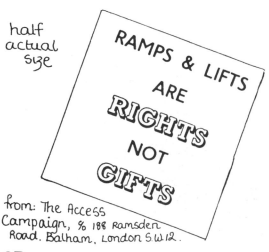

RAMPS & LIFTS ARE *RIGHTS* NOT *GIFTS*

from: The Access Campaign, % 188 Ramsden Road, Balham, London S.W.12.

DESIGNING FOR EVERYONE 1

ENTRANCES AND EXITS

Ideally all access points into and out of a building should be on the same level as the external pavement. This includes fire escape exits. Where this is not possible, a ramp or combined ramp and step facility should be provided. (see illustration)

Recommended Features for Ramps

Approach route to ramp should be a minimum of 1800mm wide.

Preferred gradient is 1:20 with a maximum of 10 metres between level resting places (1200 x 1200mm) on long ramps. A gradient of 1:12 is accepted in some circumstances.

All ramps should have a durable non-slip surface.

Recommended Features for Steps/Staircases

Step dimensions should be uniform and as follows:—

- treads not less than 280mm
- risers not higher than 150mm
- long flights should have platforms (1200 x 1200mm) at intervals: vertical rise without any landing should not exceed 1200mm.

Part M of the Building Regulations 1987 – applies to offices, shops, factories, school or educational establishments to which the public are admitted whether by payment or otherwise. The regulations lay down specific requirements regarding facilities for disabled people. These should be taken into account at the time that consent is obtained under the Town and Country Planning Acts.

New Buildings – ramped or level access should be made to all principal entrances for both the public and employees using a building. Sanitary conveniences should also be provided for use by disabled people wherever toilet provision is made for use by employees or the general public.

New buildings are deemed to include major refurbishment projects where a substantial refitting takes place behind a facade which remains largely unaltered.

Lifts – should be provided in all two-storey developments exceeding 280 square metres per storey and all three-storey buildings exceeding 200 square metres per storey. In similar buildings, where the floorspace does not exceed these thresholds, the design should seek to provide suitable access to principal entrances and toilet facilities on each floor and to enable movement between floors by means of a suitable stairway.

Plan of standard 900mm internal doorset

900mm doorset

300mm min on leading face of door

To give min clearance opening width of 760mm

NB Not to Scale

DOORS

Preferred doorsets – 1000mm external 900mm internal

Avoid heavy doors, or doors with strong spring closures.

Provide automatic (sliding) doors where possible.

Provision of lever-type handles is preferred. Position all handles 1040mm from floor level. Contrast their colour with door colour to indicate their position.

Use bold colours (e.g. orange) to indicate the edges of frameless glass doors. A bold coloured strip should also be placed across the centre of any glass door.

Avoid the use of revolving doors.

With double doors, at least one leaf should be 800mm min. width.

Alterations – when a building to which the new regulations apply is altered, the provisions for disabled people must not be made any worse. For example, steps cannot be constructed to replace ramps.

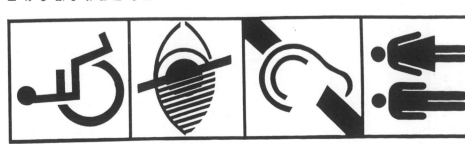

Handrails at 850mm above ramp to both sides

Platform min 1200mm x 1200mm at head of ramp

Ramp min 1200mm wide preferred width 1800mm

50mm high kerb to exposed side of ramp

Handrails with return ends to remove all sharp projections

Gradient not to exceed 1:12 preferred 1:20

NB Not to Scale

MANCHESTER DISABILITY FORUM

MANCHESTER PLANNING

Credit: Manchester Disability Forum/Housing Department

3 A

EXTERNAL FEATURES

Kerbs – where any pavements are laid, dropped kerbs between 10mm and 15mm above the road surface should be provided at crossing points, road junctions and parking areas. However, the dropped kerbs should be flush with the road surface where textured paving is provided in association with pelican, zebra and traffic signals which include a push button operated 'cross now' indication to pedestrians. Ideally, ramps associated with dropped kerbs should extend over the whole width of the footway. Where a ramp is being inserted in an existing footway the maximum gradient should not exceed 1 in 12.

Obstructions – locate all 'street furniture' such as signposts, bollards, litterbins, flower tubs, lamp-posts and seats to one edge of pedestrian through routes keeping the kerbside edge clear. Indicate their presence to blind and partially-sighted people by a change in surface texture and colour around the feature, thus giving a visual and tactile warning on approaching it. For safety reasons attempt to confine contact with street furniture to **waist** level (litterbins and bollards for example, should reach to that height).

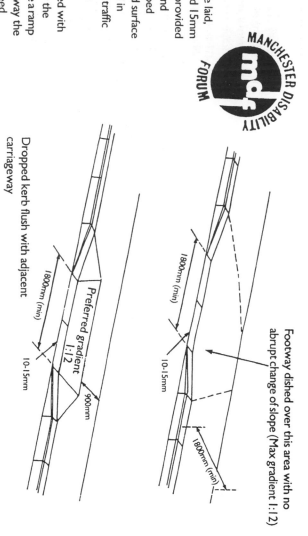

Dropped kerb flush with adjacent carriageway

Preferred gradient 1:12

1800mm (min)
1800mm (min)
10-15mm
900mm
1800mm (min)
10-15mm

Footway dished over this area with no abrupt change of slope (Max gradient 1:12)

Where possible a 1200mm clear passage should be allowed for unimpeded movement. Features should be coloured to contrast strongly with the background environment.

Gratings and gulley covers should have drainage holes with a max. size of 20mm square. Service covers should be non-slip and be flush with the surrounding surfaces. Avoid using open dished drainage channels.

Pedestrian routes – all routes should be level, without obstructions and with a preferred minimum width of 1800mm. Provide a firm, non-slip surface which does not deaden sounds, and which can therefore offer directional guidance to partially-sighted and blind people. Seating should be arranged at regular intervals along the route. Proper signing is also important – see section on 'Signs'

Parking – locate parking bays adjacent to the most accessible entrances. Off-street parking bays should be 4800mm x 3600mm wide to accommodate transfer from vehicle to wheelchair. Economy of space can be achieved by combining a pair of standard 2400mm width bays with a common 'transfer zone' 900mm wide. Indicate reserved nature of bays on tarmacadam and pole-mounted signs, and include dropped kerbs where necessary.

Marked out shared space between two standard parking bays for Orange Badge Holders

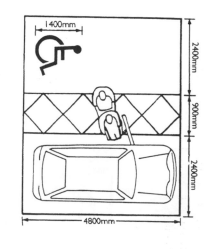

1400mm
2400mm
900mm
2400mm
4800mm

SIGNS

Directional – incorporating an arrow to a specific facility.

Locational – at the place where the facility is provided.

Informative – advising about the availability of a facility (e.g. an Induction Loop)

Ideally all information throughout a building should be communicated both audibly and visually.

Where audible delivery is not possible the recommended typeface for signs is 'Helvetica'. Use should also be made of:

● braille
● raised/embossed letters and numerals
● raised/embossed floor plans of buildings
● contrasting colours; for example large lettering on a dark background.

Where special facilities are provided for partially-sighted or hearing-impaired people, use the appropriate symbol:

Partially-sighted

Deaf

LIFT →

ramped entrance

Credit: Manchester Disability Forum/Housing Department

MANCHESTER DISABILITY FORUM
mdf

DESIGNING FOR EVERYONE

3 LIFTS

Recommended Features for Lifts

Lifts must stop flush with floor level.

Position control panel on the side wall. Control buttons should be placed horizontally at a recommended height of 800-1400mm.

Use control panel with raised braille and embossed numerals with illuminated and audible systems inside lift-car and at landings.

Link lift intercom with Induction Loop system.

Provide clear space in front of lift, not less than 1500mm x 1500mm. Seating close the lift will assist those who are not able t stand waiting for long periods.

Position mirror inside lift-car at a height which enables wheelchair users to view a floor indicator located above lift door.

See also earlier comments on provision of lifts under Part M of the Building Regulations 1987.

Places of Entertainment

The Building Regulations state that at least six spaces or 1/100th of the seated area (whichever is the greater) should be made accessible to disabled people. The spaces must be dispersed amongst the seating area in a suitable viewing position.

Wheelchair spaces in a theatre should be located in a manner shown in diagram 1. In a stadium or arena, wheelchair viewing positions should be designed as shown in diagram 2.

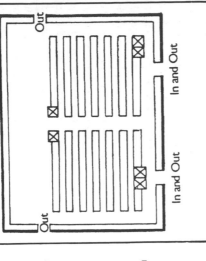

Diagram 1
Showing acceptable locations of 900mm x 1400mm wheelchair spaces in a theatre

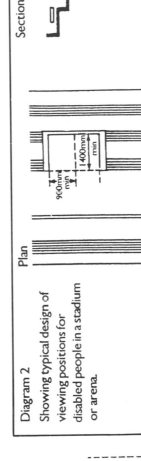

Section

Plan

Diagram 2
Showing typical design of viewing positions for disabled people in a stadium or arena.

REFERENCES

A selection of technical references should more information be required:

- Part M of the Building Regulations 1987
- Chronically Sick and Disabled Persons Act 1970
- Chronically Sick and Disabled Persons (Amendment) Act 1976
- Town and Country Planning Act 1971
- Disabled Persons Act 1981
- BS 5810 : 1979 Code of Practice for Access for the Disabled to Buildings
- BS 5619 : 1978 Code of Practice for Design of Housing for the Convenience of Disabled People
- BS 5588 : Part 3 1983 British Standard Fire Precautions in the Design and Construction of Buildings
- Designing for the Disabled, Selwyn Goldsmith, RIBA, third edition 1984
- Access in the High Street, CEH, 1981
- Access for Disabled People – Design Guidance notes for Developers, Access Committee for England/CEH 1985
- HDD Occasional Papers 2/74 Mobility Housing, DOE
- HDD Occasional Papers 2/75 Wheelchair Housing, DOE
- Providing for People with a Mobility Handicap, Institution of Highways and Transportation 1986

Controls

Handrail

Mirror

Collapsible Seat

Lift car min width 1100mm

Lift car min depth 1400mm

850mm min
1000mm max
800mm
1400mm max

800mm clear door opening

NB Not to Scale

Hotel Bedrooms

The diagram below shows one example of a suitably designed hotel bedroom with en suite bathroom.

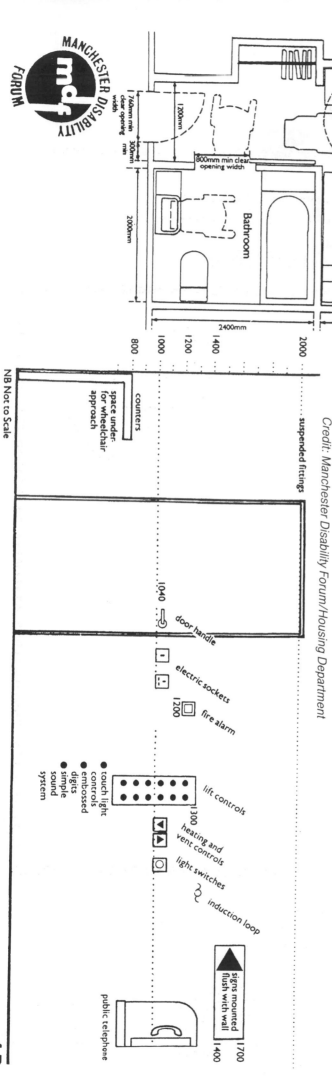

Bedroom

Bathroom

1500mm turning circle

Alternative 1500mm turning circle

800mm min clear opening width

760mm min clear opening

300mm min

1200mm

1200mm

2000mm

3600mm

2400mm

3500mm

LOBBIES/CORRIDORS

Lobbies

Where possible use sliding doors. If lobbies have outer and inner doors both doors should open in the same direction (i.e. not towards one another).

Where double doors are provided to an entrance lobby the minimum dimensions must be 2000 x 1800mm. Elsewhere, the minimum dimensions are:

● lobbies inside building entrances 1800mm x 1500mm

● lobbies off internal corridors 2000 x 1200mm or 1700mm x 1500mm

Corridors

The preferred width is 1800mm to allow adequate two-way flow.

Keep corridors/aisles clear of obstructions. Recess fire equipment into walls. Keep all projections from walls (signs, lights, etc) at least 2000mm above floor level.

Sign plates should be flush with the wall at a preferred height of 1400-1700mm above floor level.

Use a floor surface which is non-slip wet or dry.

Avoid deep pile carpets. Do not use floor pattern which simulates steps.

Use changes of colour and texture to warn of differences in floor level and to indicate doors, switches, handles.

Avoid glare from light sources and glossy surfaces.

Inclined lifts should be provided for access over small internal flights of steps.

Lobbies/Corridors diagram

NB Not to Scale

800
1000
1200
1400
2000

counters

space under for wheelchair approach

suspended fittings

1040 — door handle

electric sockets

1200 — fire alarm

lift controls
● touch light
● controls
● embossed
● digits
● simple sound system

1300 — heating and vent controls

light switches

induction loop

signs mounted flush with wall

1400
1700

public telephone

Credit: Manchester Disability Forum/Housing Department

ACCIDENTS

Many people become physically disabled as a result of serious injuries received in an accident.

Look at the illustrations 'Hazards in the Street' and 'Hazards in the Home'.

Make a list of all the hazards you can spot in both pictures.

HAZARDS IN THE HOME

NOW DRAW IN YOUR BEDROOM. HOW MANY HAZARDS?

Credit C.S.V.

Keir Wickenham

Now draw your bedroom. How many hazards can you spot?

KITCHEN
1 Stove — pans boiling over, handles sticking out
2 Baby on floor near stove playing with tin of bleach
3 Sharp knives within easy reach
4 Mother ironing from bulb
5 Overloaded socket
6 Rubbish bin with jagged tin on top

BATHROOM
1 Electric fire with cable coming from outside
2 Geyser
3 Ordinary light hanging over bath
4 Long flex with towels draped over
5 Boiling water coming out of tap
6 Shirts dripping onto fire
7 Medicine chest within reach of child
8 Empty first-aid kit
9 Faulty water-closet cistern about to fall

LIVING ROOM
1 Cigarette burning in ashtray
2 Open fire without guard
3 Mirror above fire
4 Papers on mantelshelf above fire
5 Chairs with only three legs
6 Curtains resting on radiator
7 Teddy bear laying in front of fire
8 Picture about to fall down
9 Cracked window pane
10 Television lead stretched across room, under carpet
11 Plant with poisonous berries

HALL OUTSIDE FRONT DOOR
1 Rug on slippery floor
2 Vacuum cleaner to trip over
3 Suicidal steps
4 Broken milk bottle
5 Marbles

5A

HAZARDS IN THE STREET

Draw your own people in all the vehicles.

Can you invent some more hazards?

Keir Wickenham

Credit C.S.V.

5B

The Myth of Independence

by Micheline Mason

Exercise:

Ask each person to list on a piece of paper everything they did in the first half-an-hour after waking up that morning.

Ask them to make a list of the amount of people whose labour made those activities possible.

Ask each person to make a list of the aids and appliances they used,

e.g.

I woke up in bed. An alarm clock woke me up. How many people were involved in the collection of the raw materials, design, manufacture, retail, delivery of the alarm clock? the bed, the bedclothes, the house you woke up in? Your nightclothes? I went to the toilet (Where did the water come from? Where does it go? The toilet paper, etc) Food for breakfast, etc. Did someone else prepare it for you? Did you prepare it for someone else?

I used a toothbrush, a flannel, a comb, I put on my glasses, the fridge, the cooker, the kettle, cutlery, tin opener, telephone, car, etc.

Lesson 1

Everyone is totally dependant on others for our so-called "independent" lives. Disabled people may or may not need direct human assistance with a few more of these activities than the majority of people. These seem quite consistent with normal human social behaviour. *Inter*-dependence is the reality for all of us. Disabled people have dependants too.

Lesson 2

Everybody uses aids and appliances all the time. Disabled people may need one or two uncommon aids to assist with particular activities, in addition to the hundreds we use daily in common with everybody else.

What then is the difference? The "Disability Factor"?

Lesson 3

Availability, cost, choice and control. These are the issues for us around the concept of independence.

Able-bodied people do not have to be assessed by an "expert" on their need for a toothbrush or a comb. You do not have to put in an application for a front door to get into your own home with a two year wait on the doorstep. You do not have to get a doctor's certificate before you can get yourself a bicycle. You do not have to pay your partner to make the tea.

You have organised your societies in such a way that those services and aids which you need to function within the society are freely available, have some measure of choice, are self-selected, and are within the economic means of nearly everyone. You call them "*normal*".

We want this range of normal provision to include all those things presently called "special" (by you) and for them to be as available to us as a toothbrush. Our only "special" provision should be in the financial resources available to us to "buy" these necessities. A comprehensive disability pension - not means tested, related to *need* only.

Disability - Race, Class and Nationality - A Worksheet

by Micheline Mason

A three year old child catches polio. After recovering from the crisis, she cannot walk unaided and has a weak left arm.

Describe her future life if she were born to:-

A White upper-middle class family in Surrey, UK.

An Asian (Hindu) working-class family in Wakefield, Yorkshire, UK.

A Black family in a village in Kenya, Africa.

A Chinese peasant family, working on the land.

A White middle-class family in Sweden.

A Black working-class family in California, USA.

The disabling factors in the world are not equally spread, because human needs are not equally met. This exercise will show that disability is linked to race, class and nationality as much as to any particular medical condition.

Video: ''Breaking Barriers'' produced by the UN shows many disabled people from all over the world describing the different barriers they are faced with.

THE BRAILLE SYSTEM ... for reading raised dots by touch

LETTERS:

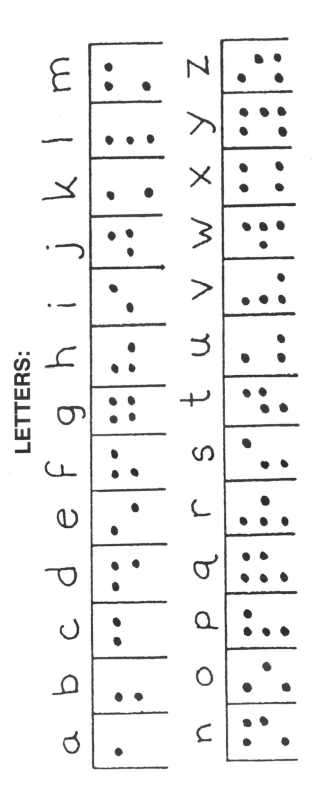

a b c d e f g h i j k l m

n o p q r s t u v w x y z

NUMBERS:

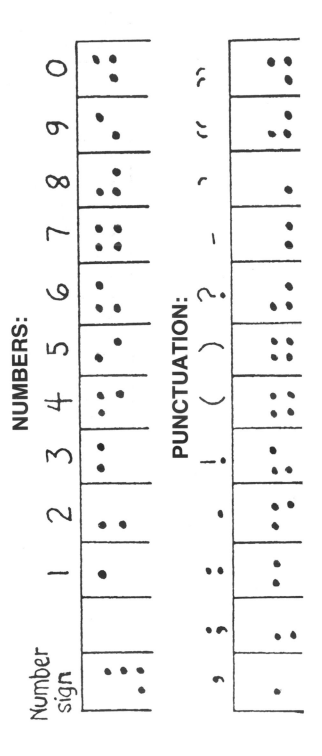

Number sign   1 2 3 4 5 6 7 8 9 0

PUNCTUATION:

, ; : . ! ( ) ? - ' " "

STANDARD MANUAL ALPHABET

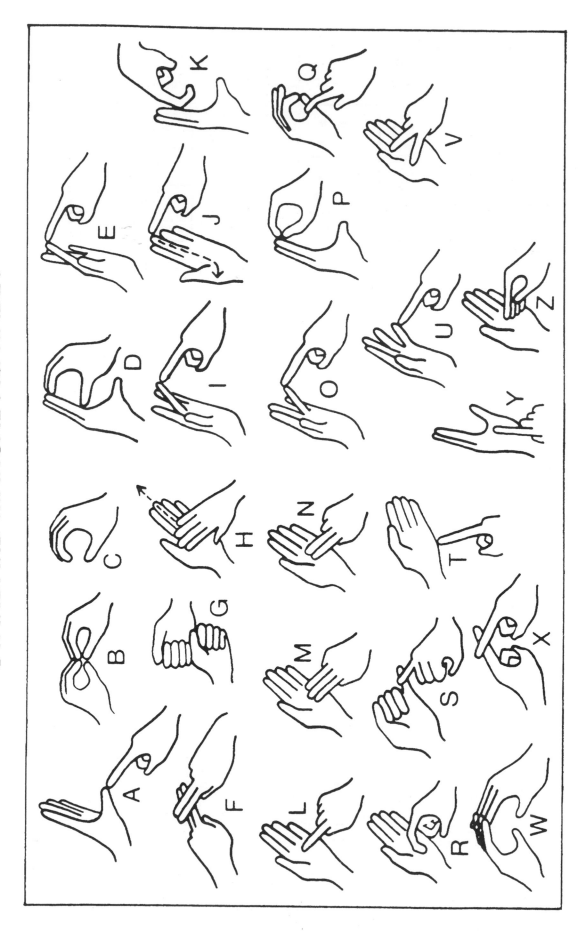

SIGNED NUMBER SYSTEM

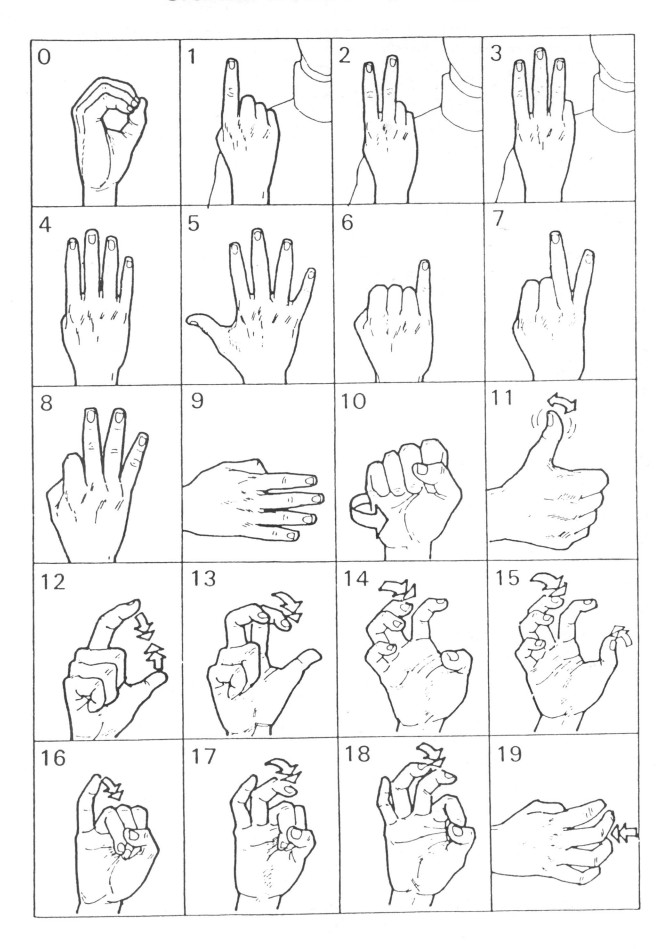

LANGUAGE WE USE

Word-Power

The issue of language with regard to disability is an important one.

Look at the following words and ask yourself whether they imply a positive or negative image.

wheelchair-bound .....positive/negative/neither

the disabled ....positive/negative/neither

people with
disabilities ....positive/negative/neither

disabled person ....positive/negative/neither

cripple ....positive/negative/neither

invalid......................positive/negative/neither

integrated ....positive/negative/neither

spastic.....................positive/negative/neither

handicapped.............positive/negative/neither

people with learning
difficulties ....positive/negative/neither

spina bifida ....positive/negative/neither

independent ....positive/negative/neither

sufferer....................positive/negative/neither

special....................positive/negative/neither

mental patient..........positive/negative/neither

Avoid	Use
Victim of	person who has/person with/person who experienced
Crippled by	person who has/person with
Suffering from	person who has/person with
Afflicted by	person who has/person with
Wheelchair bound	wheelchair user
Invalid (means *not* valid)	disabled person
Mental	disabled person

Offensive	Preferred
Handicap, Handicapped Person	Disability, Disabled Person
Spastic	Cerebal Palsey
Deaf and Dumb, Deaf/Mute	Deaf or Partial Hearing
Mongoloid	Downs Syndrome
Cripple/Crippled	Disabled Person or Mobility Impaired ambulatory disabled
The Blind	Blind Person, Partially sighted
The Deaf	Deaf People
Mentally Handicapped, Backward/Dull	Learning Difficulty,
Retarded, Idiot, Imbecile, Feeble Minded	Developmental Disability
Mute, Dummy	Speech Difficulty
Crazy, Maniac, Insane,	Emotional Disability,
Mentally ill	Mental Disturbance
Abnormal	Exceptional/ Different

8B

Sign a Song: Ten in the Bed

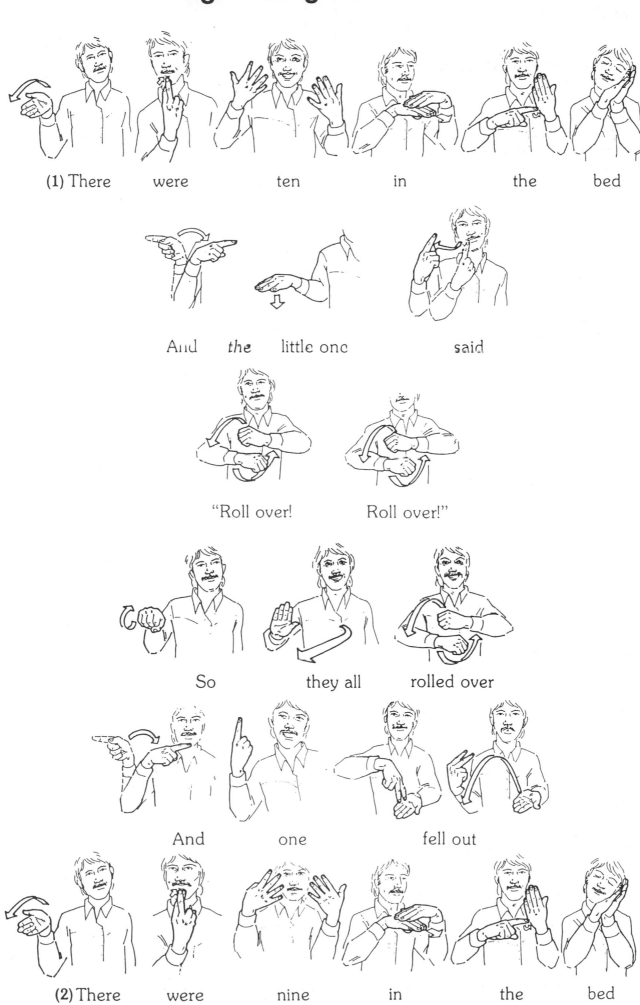

(1) There were ten in the bed

And *the* little one said

"Roll over! Roll over!"

So they all rolled over

And one fell out

(2) There were nine in the bed

"Songs in Sign" Beverley School, Cleveland

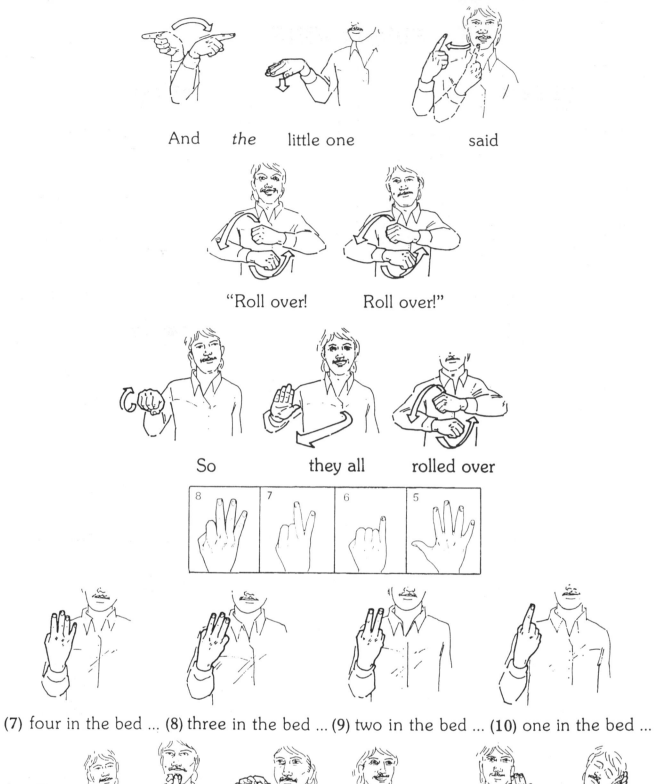

And   *the*   little one   said

"Roll over!   Roll over!"

So   they all   rolled over

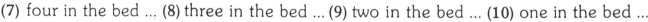

(7) four in the bed ... (8) three in the bed ... (9) two in the bed ... (10) one in the bed ...

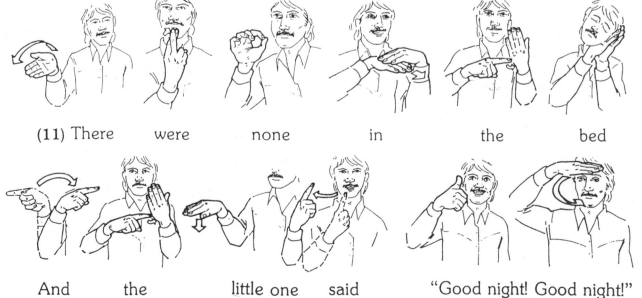

(11) There   were   none   in   the   bed

And   the   little one   said   "Good night! Good night!"

9 B

FIRST SIGNS

girl

Stroke Rt. side of mouth with side of extended Rt. index, palm forward.

boy

Brush Rt. index pointing left across chin.

cat

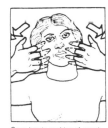 

Open hands at sides of mouth move out slightly twice whilst flexing to indicate whiskers.

fish

Rt. flat hand waggles forward like a fish swimming.

coat

Mime pulling a coat over shoulders.

book

Two flat hands pointing forward, palm to palm, open to palms up.

dog

Two "N" hands pointing down, move up and down slightly, like dog begging.

cup

 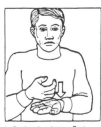

L. flat hand, palm up. Rest blade of Rt. wholehanded "C" on L. palm.

rabbit

 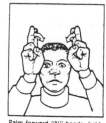

Palm forward "N" hands, held at either side of head, bend several times to indicate ears.

drink

Mime having a drink.

bird

Index finger and thumb open and close in front of mouth like a beak.

car

Mime holding and moving a steering wheel.

tree

Right elbow cradled in L. hand. Rt. clawed hand, palm up/ left twists from side to side.

bicycle

Two fists held a few inches apart make pedalling action.

baby

Mime cradling a baby in the arms and rock.

biscuit

 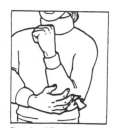

Fingertips of Rt. clawed hand tap near left elbow twice.

"First Signs" Beverley School, Cleveland

History of the Deaf Community: 'Pictures in the Mind*'

by Richard Reiser

For many hundreds of years deaf people had been treated as if they were 'mentally defective' or stupid by hearing people. By seventeenth century it was clear that born deaf could communicate with each other. However, there was no way of getting deaf people to learn to read and write.

This video film in two parts shows the history of the deaf community by means of a memory museum.

Our guide is Jean Massieu. He was a deaf shepherd who lived near Bordeaux in France.

His teacher, the Abbé Sichard, a hearing person had taught himself sign language so he could communicate with the deaf.

Together the Abbé and Jean worked out a sign language which could be translated into written language so it could be used to teach deaf people to read and write. It broke down the illiteracy barrier.

Their method revolutionised deaf education throughout Europe. Deaf people became teachers, writers, architects and politicians. Sign language made possible a full education and a career for deaf people.

Schools and clubs and a deaf culture and language was widespread.

Hearing people who could not understand sign language felt threatened and worried by sign language. Richer parents of deaf children wanted their children to be able to speak. They paid out for ways of getting their children to speak.

This was called oralism.

Hearing people in the 1870s - 1880s also thought quite *wrongly*, that if deaf people had their own language schools and clubs and married each other and had children, then there would be a big increase in deaf people: Social Darwinism.

So in 1880 an International Conference was held in Milan, Italy. Deaf Teachers of the deaf were not allowed to attend. The Conference resolved that only oral methods and *not* sign language should be allowed in the education of the deaf.

All deaf teachers of the deaf who had taught deaf children with sign language were dismissed or pensioned off.

The effect of these measures in Europe and America were fully in effect by 1910.

Vast amounts of time and effort and money were put into trying to teach deaf children to speak by copying hearing teachers -some called it parroting - lip reading, copying without understanding. For children who could hear a bit - partial hearing - when they used hearing aids the methods worked.

But for the completely deaf children these methods did not work. They had to sit on their hands and only 1 in 10 could be taught to speak so you could understand them. So the deaf children were again thought of as defective or stupid.

Sign language survived in the deaf clubs and was passed on from parents to children, but it was not part of deaf children's formal education. So by the 1980's deaf children were leaving school at age 16 only being able to read as well as an average 8 3/4 year old. They were after a century of oralism largely illiterate.

Young children who are born deaf can acquire language structure from the age of 6 months up to 4 years old if they are allowed to communicate with signs. They learn quickly and gain real understanding. They can then do better at lip reading and speech. As it is now 90% of lip reading is guessing. If you have already got a sign language structure you are going to have a better chance of understanding.

There is still much resistance to using these total communication methods. Still only a small number of schools use these techniques.

So, deaf campaigners still have a great deal to achieve to give all deaf children a proper chance of education. Perhaps they could be helped by hearing people learning about sign language.

Today quite a few television programmes are signed and more people are taking an interest in sign language.

*Pictures in the Mind: The History of a Community. Video film 55 mins. Directed by Nigel Evans.

Available from Concorde Video Film Council, 201 Felixstowe Road, Ipswich, Suffolk, IP3 9BJ, tel. 0473-726012 - £10 to hire - £50 to buy.

Also available from Video Arts 01-636 9421.

In this film the main language is sign but there are subtitles and voice over.

PICTURES IN THE MIND

THE HISTORY OF A COMMUNITY

EDWARD JONES ....THE ABBÉ SICHARD
PADDY LADD........................JEAN MASSIEU
DOUG ALKER......................THE MAGICIAN
DAVID PORTSMOUTH ....THE BOY

Written and Directed by NIGEL EVANS

Abbe Sichard and Jean Massieu.

Disabled People in Nazi German: the beginning of mass murder

by Richard Rieser

The National Socialists adopted a false theory of race science. There were superior races and inferior races.

Aryans — superior (Germans)

Jews
Gypsies — inferior
Poles/Slavs

Disabled and Black people - sub-human.

The Nazis also believed they should get rid of disabled people who were unworthy of life.

This was started first of all with compulsory sterilisation of men and women suffering from hereditary diseases - 25 July 1933.

Sterilisation means an operation to men and women to make them infertile. In men it is permanent. In women it can be reversed. Women don't produce an ovum or egg, as the Fallopian tubes are cut. Men don't produce sperm as the sperm ducts in the testes are cut.

This was expanded on 8 October 1935 into a law "to safeguard the hereditary health of the German people!" This introduced abortion where either partner had a hereditary disease.

Hitler when he expounded his crazy beliefs in 'Mein Kampf' in 1923, had talked of Euthanasia: The killing of people suffering from incurable and painful disease by 'gentle means'.

However, Germany was still a 'Christian' country and Hitler did not think he could introduce Euthanasia until war had begun.

Nazi medicine believed the health of all the people - 'Volk' - was more important than the individual.

But he prepared secretly. An opinion was got from a well known Catholic professor of theology - Professor Dr Josef Mayer - which argued that in Christian terms it could be accepted.

Representatives of the leaders of the Protestant church and a representative of the Pope (Pope Pius XII) were consulted on this view in private. Though they were not happy no public fuss was made.

In October 1939, after war had been declared Hitler issued a secret decree backdated to 1 September.

'Reichsleiter Bouhler and Dr Brandt are charged with responsibility for expanding the authority of physicians who are designated by name, to the end that patients who are considered incurable in the best available judgement after critical evaluation of their condition can be granted mercy killing.'

400 doctors, nurses and SS worked on the programme.

It was not mercy killing. It was a programme of mass murder of mentally and physically disabled people.

A Questionnaire was issued by the ministry of the Interior to all mental institutions asking them to list all patients who were:

Credit Ideas: Berkely CA.

Hartheim: more than 14,000 disabled people were killed here.

(a) Senile.
(b) Suffering a variety of mental debilities.
(c) Criminally insane.
(d) Under care for more than 5 years.
(e) Incapable of work.
(f) Only capable of routine work.

Copies of this form were returned, secretly to Department T4 and they were marked plus or minus - Life or Death. A red cross meant death. Doctors administered, chose the victim and carried out the killing.

The inmates, if they were chosen, were taken at night in blacked out buses to intermediate institutions, and then to one of 6 centres where they were within a few hours, either gassed or

Credit Ideas: Berkely CA.

Hadamar Institution: Over 10,000 disabled people were killed in the basement of this hospital over an 18 month period.

given an injection and killed. Their bodies were then burned. Their relatives were given their ashes and told they had had a heart attack.

Children were treated differently. Kinder Fachablechungen - Special Sections for Children.

Parents signed authorisation for severely

disabled children to be transferred to special wards where they were told there would be 'a unique chance for recovery'. The programme started with 'deformed infants', then expanded to include 2, then 5 and finally up to 17 year olds' by the end of the war.

There were 11 such sections each with 20-30 beds. After a period of observation the children were 'put to sleep' and all died. They never knew what was to happen to them. The programme continued in some hospitals until 1945.

Such a large programme in Germany could not be kept a secret for long.

Disabled people fought for their lives, ran away, seeking help from their families. 'Wild scenes' of public unrest occur. Towns folk support patients and fight police.

From March 1940 up to August 1941 more and more bishops and priests spoke out against euthanasia. Following riots in Bavaria in August 1941 Hitler ordered the killing to stop.

But 96 of the 400 staff went on to run the extermination camps of Chelmno, Treblinka, Sobibor and Belsen where more than 2 1/2 million Jews were exterminated along with Gypsies and Poles.

It is true to say that the killing of the disabled had made mass killing acceptable to the people who were to run the extermination camps.

Altogether 80-100,000 disabled children and adults were Nazi victims of mass murder. They were just the beginning of a mass murder programme of 12 million Jews, Communists, Gypsies, Poles, Russians, Gays and Lesbians and also more disabled people.

The above comes from Part 1 of 'Into the Darkness' by Gitta Sereney, 1974, Picador.

Simon Wisenthal (1967). The Murderers are Among Us: Heinemann, London also gives details of the Euthanasia programme and the Holocaust.

For details see:

Lothar Gruchmann -
'Euthanasia and Justice in the Third Reich'. Stuttgart 1972.

Hugh G. Gallagher, By Trust Betrayed: Patients and Physicians in the Third Reich Published Henry Molt 1990.

A Stitch too Late: Polio in India

by Richard Rieser

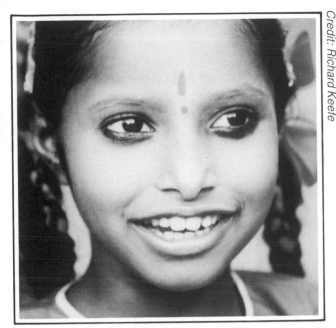

Gopamma

Gopomma is eight. She is disabled by Polio. She walks on all fours or with callipers and crutches. She caught Polio when she was two from a pool of dirty water in her village in Eastern India. This pool is still the village water supply.

For years she could only drag herself along the ground or slither on her belly like a snake.

'I couldn't go to school and I couldn't play.' The other children either ignored her or made fun of her.

Gopamma has had several expensive operations her family could not afford. Now she can get to school.

Her parents did not know about vaccinations. Now they do and have had their other children vaccinated .

Gopamma's brother carries her the 3/4 of a mile to the local school. She is trying hard to catch up all the schooling she has missed.

Like millions of other children in India and around the world Gopamma could have been vaccinated as a baby to prevent her being permanently disabled by Polio.

What is polio?

Polio is a virus that causes paralysis by killing the nerve cells leading to muscles. It stops muscles working in different parts of the body: legs, arms, back, chest. Children are the most vulnerable to the virus and it can result in severe lifelong disablement.

In 1956 a vaccine was discovered that is cheap and effective at immunising the body against the Polio virus. If 90% of the population are vaccinated Polio does not spread. Yet by 1974 in the Third World only 5% of children had been vaccinated. In 1980 5 million children died in the poor south from vaccine preventable diseases:

Diptheria	Polio
Whooping cough	Measles
Tetanus	and TB

This amounts to: 1 million in India alone.

The main problem is letting people know. This requires setting up a health network to reach everyone. Huge efforts have been made in India, China and other poor South countries. Through a massive campaign of communications using every possible means including cinemas, schools, sports personalities, religious leaders and youth groups a much larger number have been vaccinated. But many of the destitute and poor are not vaccinated. Still 200,000 children a year are disabled by Polio in India. There has

'I am going to be an immunisation teacher when I grow up.'

Gopamma

INDIA

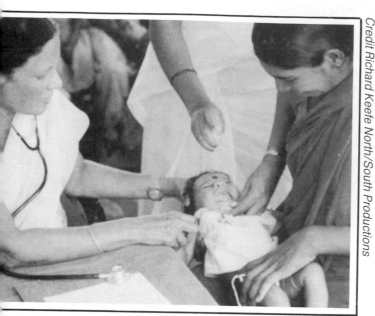

Vaccination in Gapamma's village

But those who are not will be the least well fed and the poorest. 5 million children are still dying needlessly every year.

As the price paid for commodities like cocoa, cotton and sugar has continued continued to fall Third World families have been getting poorer in the 1980's and their children are therefore more vulnerable to disease, death and disablement.

The poor South pays the rich North $20 billion more, in repaying debts on old loans than they received in Aid from the rich North. During the year when Live Aid and all the other fund raising efforts were made to send money to the famine in Ethiopia, the Ethiopean Government were forced to send four times as much money to banks in the rich North to repay interest on loans.

These two factors alone make it unlikely that the successful polio vaccination of the other 50% of children will occur, unless the rich North changes its policies and increases Aid, cancels debts and pays a reasonable price for Third World Commodities.

been a decrease of 25% in the numbers getting Polio in the last decade. In 1988 4,800 doctors, 72,000 paramedics and 30,000 community workers were all busy trying to get 100 percent vaccine coverage. But now the lack of political will and the widening gap between rich and poor countries throws the future progress in doubt. UNICEF say "Polio *could* be eradicated by the year 2000". But will it be?

Rush and Relay - China Success

China with one fifth of the worlds population is a success story.

In 1979 China began producing vaccines at seven regional institutes around the country. These were distributed to provincial health authorities on a set day. They rushed the vaccines to townships where 'bare foot doctors' bicycled them to their village. This had a dramatic effect on death and disease rates. By 1987 only 49% deaths were recorded from measles, diptheria, whooping cough and polio combined.

The 'bare foot' doctors are paramedics trained to give simple medical advice and administer remedies. They are not doctors but have saved millions of lives by their intervention in the villages.

50% of all children still vulnerable

Half of all the worlds children are now immunised.

Children with Polio in Morocco playing football

This information is taken from "Stolen Childhood: In Search of the Rights of the Child". *Pub* Channel 4 1989 by Anuradha Vittachi.

A video film of 23 minutes -available from North-South Productions, Woburn Buildings, Woburn Walk, WC1, £9.95. Channel 4 also produced a free booklet, send stamped addressed envelope 28p to Channel 4.

Disability in Brazil: the price of economic growth?

by Richard Rieser

"Mutilados", workers mangled by sisal grinding machines, demonstrate in Bahia. An inexpensive safety guard could cut accidents by 80% but it is not provided.

Throughout the 1960's and 1970's Brazil was hailed as an 'economic miracle'. From 1968-73 it had an average economic growth of 11% and from 1974-80 6% a year. Many large multi-national companies invested in factories in Brazil attracted by the 'stability' of the military dictatorship.

Although during this period there was an increase in the number of middle class and skilled workers the distribution of wealth did not change.

The richest 1% had as much wealth as the poorest 50%. Health was also unequal. The richest 8.5% of the population had a life expectancy of 70 years, where as the 46.7% of the people earning the minimum wage (US $40-60 per month) had a life expectancy of 54.6 years. There were some improvements up until 1982 with a steady drop in infant mortality (now 90 per 1000). Then the economy began to stagnate, with the burden of debt repayments to the rich countries the International Monetary Fund

insisted on a limit on social spending. Since then inflation has gone up by 14,000 times.

All this has led to poverty and 80% of children not completing 8 years of schooling, high illiteracy and a large number of unskilled poor workers. In this situation there is little control on employers to make their factories safe.

"In the last 10 years 50,000 Brazilian workers died in industrial 'accidents'. There are 3,000 accidents a day.

In 1988 500,000 Brazilian workers were mutilated in work related 'accidents"

O. Globo 28 May 1989

Research has shown low wages causing hunger and fatigue to add to the risk of 'accidents'.

Those disabled by accident join the 50% of the working population in the 'shadow economy' becoming street vendors, sellers of lottery tickets, roadside mechanics, car watchers/cleaners, drug dealers, prostitutes, thieves and beggars.

Social Security only exists for those long term registered employed workers who have paid into a scheme. Those who have never worked including disabled children, persons in the shadow economy and the large number of day and contract workers are not compensated for injury.

Through a strong Disability Rights movement disabled people have managed to fight for their welfare and rights despite there being no 'safety net' for most of them.

Apart from the 'middle class militant elite' of the Movement for the Rights of Disabled Persons with a theoretical and legislative approach ABRADEF from San Paulo represents a significant number of disabled street vendors. They fight collectively for day to day survival against the police, city government and mafia.

Many disabled activists have entered politics and the movement forced the inclusion of disability rights into the 1988 Constitutions.

With the lack of greater equality of wealth or access to hospital and social services, the implementation of these rights remains to be fought for. Self help activity fills some of the gaps **But disabled people have made political alliances with other disadvantaged groups and the Church to press for greater equality. They still have much to fight for.**

Based on an article by Eugene Williams in September 1989 Issue of International Rehabilitation Review.

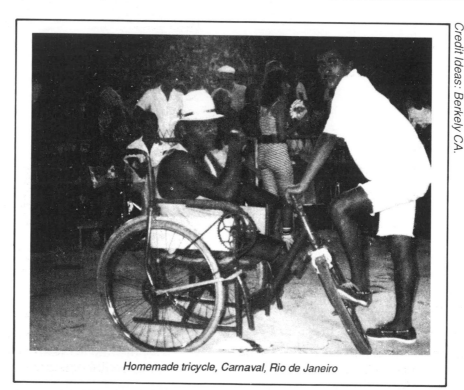

Homemade tricycle, Carnaval, Rio de Janeiro

Credit Ideas: Berkely CA.

*Martina: A Unique Human Being

Credit Richard Keefe N/S Productions

Martina is Swedish. She was born in a hospital to Berit her mother who sensed something was wrong, but the doctors did not tell her for more than three months.

Martina was born with one chromosome too many (47 instead of 46): a condition known as Downs Syndrome. About one in 750 babies are born with Downs. The possibility of it occurring increases the older the mother. Downs Syndrome effects the appearance and the functioning of parts of the brain. As Martina's story shows children with Downs will develop differently depending on how they are brought up.

When the doctors finally told Berit, they said Martina was 'mongoloid' (the old word for her condition no longer acceptable), that there was no hope for her and that she was an 'idiot'. They suggested Berit forget Martina and have another baby at once.

Martina, they suggested, should be given up permanently into residential state care, never to be seen again by her mother.

In the ancient societies of Greece and Rome and during the middle ages such children were left to perish - infanticide. This still is practised by some doctors withholding treatment.

More recently 'imperfect' infants were shut away in large residential institutions where they spent the rest of their meaningless lives, fed and clothed by the state and forgotten by their families.

Berit did not agree with the doctors. She wasn't interested in taking home a perfect baby. She wanted to mother and care for her baby as she was.

Gradually through singing, music and games, side by side with her younger brother Martina learned to speak. She was allowed to attend a

Martina when young

day centre with normal children, then on to a nursery school (up to the age of 7 in Sweden). And then on to a primary school and junior high school. If she was allowed to work at her own speed according to her own ability, Martina managed.

When Martina reached secondary school her mother persuaded the headteacher to let Martina be in a special class of visually impaired children, rather than in a segregated special school.

This proved a success to the head and many doubters, and helped change attitudes toward the integration of children like Martina.

Soon after in the early 1980's laws were passed in Sweden to allow children with learning difficulties and other disabilities to live at home and attend ordinary schools. Ninety percent of Sweden's nursery age children (under 7) with learning difficulties are now in ordinary schools. The government has provided money for teachers to receive special training and to provide technical aids.

Fifteen years ago Sweden had 500 children under 7 with severe learning difficulties living away from home in institutions. Now there are less than 30.

Martina is now aged 20. She loves music, lives away from home by choice and just wants people to accept her as she is. Now she can do many things, look after herself, read, write, play the piano while admitting to things she finds difficult like time.

One day when Martina was playing the piano, her brother shouted to her from the other room 'Martina' you shouldn't play that so well. You must remember you are 'mentally retarded'. She laughed and was pleased.

Society's perceptions and expectations of people with learning difficulties have in the past condemned them to institutions and their humanity has been denied. Martina and her mother's fight that she should be accepted have changed views in Sweden, but in the UK and USA and many other countries these attitudes still have to be changed.

In Sweden community care is not seen as a cheap option as it has been in the UK with the closure of many large institutions. The state provides help and resources for disabled children not just to those requesting it, but officials have a duty placed upon them to find out where help is needed, to offer it, and make sure it is given.

Martina has a lot to give - her openess, her sensitivity and patience, her .... and now timlessness, which are as much her strengths as her limitations.

> **'I can see a black bird**
> **that flies through life's door.**
> **A bird that shows its golden wings for me.**
>
> **It comes from a freedom that is open,**
> **with unlocked doors**
> **The bird is released from my hand**
> **like a freedom without wounds.'**
>
> *Martina*

*Based on Chapter 8 of 'Stolen Childhood' by Anuradha Vittachi. Martina's story is on a 30mm video from North-South Production £9.99. Woburn Buildings, 1 Woburn Walk, London, WC1H 0JJ.

Martina loves music – here at 20

Pre-Natal Diagnosis and Abortion - A Worksheet

by Micheline Mason

A mother has just been told that her unborn baby has spina-bifida. Her pregnancy is five months old and she has started to feel its movements inside her.

The doctor has said that he cannot say how severely disabled the baby will be, but he/she could be completely paralized in the lower limbs, be doubly incontinent, and may have an associated condition called hydracephalus which could cause learning disabilities. In any case, surgery after birth will be necessary to close the spinal opening.

The doctor says he would perform an immediate termination if the parents wish.

How will the mother decide what to do?

Take the part of:

(a)   The doctor
(b)   The mother
(c)   The father
(d)   An older sister
(e)   The unborn baby
(f)   A Catholic priest

What are the factors that will influence their decision?

What factors could have made them come to a different decision?

What will be the consequences of the decisions either way?

What support will the family need?

Did the family have enough time to weigh up all the pros and cons?

Notes

Some factors that should come up are the doctor's attitude towards disability, his/her own experience of treating spina-bifida children.

The family's class and financial circumstances

The family's race and cultural background

The family's religion

The family's support system

The extended family and their attitude towards abortion and or disability

The family's previous experience of disability

Do either of the parents have a Spina Bifida? Another disability?

Their knowledge of Spina Bifida in particular. Good/bad/non-existent

Their self-confidence at dealing with challenge

Their hopes for their new child

What does the older sister feel? What would she imagine having a disabled brother/sister to be like? Would she be jealous or would she look forward to 'mothering' the new baby? or both?

How do brothers and sisters feel about abortions

If the baby could talk, what would he/she say?

Catholic Priests are believers in the sanctity of life regardless of disability. What would be his argument?

'A Disabled Child is Born'

Micheline

Why do they all look so sad?

Why is the baby smiling?

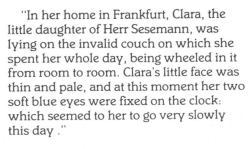

Extracts from 'Heidi', by Johanna Spyri

"In her home in Frankfurt, Clara, the little daughter of Herr Sesemann, was lying on the invalid couch on which she spent her whole day, being wheeled in it from room to room. Clara's little face was thin and pale, and at this moment her two soft blue eyes were fixed on the clock: which seemed to her to go very slowly this day ."

Clara is waiting for the arrival of a new companion, Heidi, who has always lived an open-air life on the mountains. We are not told why Clara cannot walk. Later in the book, however, when Heidi has become her friend, we learn that the two girls can only go out, "on rare occasions when Clara was well enough to drive out, and then they only went a very little way, as Clara could not bear the movement for long." *Eventually Heidi returns from the city to her mountain life. Clara, after much worry and persuasion, is allowed to visit her there in the spring.*

"Clara could not feast her eyes enough on all the beauty around her. 'O Heidi, if only I could walk with you,' she said, longingly, 'If I could but go and look at the fir trees and at everything I know so well from your description, although I have never been here before!'"

Clara's wheelchair is destroyed by Peter, a young boy who is jealous of her friendship with Heidi. She is carried about by Heidi's grandfather and spends much time sitting in the Alpine meadows.

"Clara found a strange new pleasure in sitting all alone like this on the mountainside, her only companion a little goat, that looked to her for protection. She suddenly felt a great desire to be her own mistress and to be able to help others, instead of herself being always dependent, as she was now."

Soon, with help from Peter as well as Heidi, she learns to walk unaided. Everyone is delighted, including Clara.

"For she could think of no greater joy in the world than to be strong and able to go about like other people, and no longer to have to lie from day to day in her invalid chair."

Macdonald Publishers

THINGS TO DO

1. Re-write the first paragraph, about Clara, so that, although in her wheelchair she does not seem pathetic and sad.

2. Make up a happy ending for the story if Clara did not learn to walk.

3. Long John Silver is more impressive because he has only one leg, not less. Amputation is often seen as the mark of a hero — why? Should other forms of disability also confer 'hero' status? Think of a favourite story and imagine the main character as disabled — in a wheelchair, perhaps. Could the same story be told, or would you have to change parts of it to accomodate the wheelchair?

Extracts from 'Treasure Island' by Robert Louis Stevenson

This story has two characters with physical disabilities: the 'seafaring man with one leg' — Long John Silver — and Blind Pew. Both are seen through the eyes of a young person, Jim Hawkins.

Long John Silver

"As I was waiting, a man came out of a side-room, and at a glance, I was sure he must be Long John. His left leg was cut off close to the hip, and under the left shoulder he carried a crutch, which he managed with wonderful dexterity, hopping about on it like a bird. He was very tall and strong, with a face as big as a ham — plain and pale, but intelligent and smiling.

"Aboard ship he carried his crutch by a lanyard round his neck, to have both hands as free as possible. It was something to see him wedge the foot of the crutch against a bul-head and propped up against it, yielding to every movement of the ship get on with his cooking like someone safe ashore. Still more strange was it to see him in the heaviest of weather cross the deck. He had a line or two rigged up to help him across the widest spaces — Long John's earrings, they were called; and he would hand himself from one place to another, now using the crutch, now trailing it alongside by the lanyard, as quickly as another man could walk. Yet some of the men who had sailed with him before expressed their pity to see him so reduced."

Later, on the island, Long John, representing the mutineers, comes, under a flag of truce, to talk to the ship's captain. He manages to get over the high fence around the compound where the captain and loyal crew members are, but:

"Silver had terrible hard work getting up the knoll. What with the steepness of the incline, the thick tree stumps, and the soft sand, he and his crutch were as helpless as a ship in stays. But he stuck to it like a man in silence, and at last arrived before the captain, whom he saluted in the handsomest style."

Silver agrees to sit on the sand for the talk, ". . . you'll have to give me a hand up again, that's all." *But no agreement is reached and when Silver asks for help to rise,* "Not a man among us moved. Growling the foulest imprecations, he crawled along the sand till he got hold of the porch and could hoist himself again upon his crutch. Then he spat into the spring."

Credit CSV

Blind Pew

"He was plainly blind, for he tapped before him with a stick, and wore a great green shade over his eyes and nose: and he was hunched, as if with age or weakness, and wore a huge old tattered sea-cloak with a hood, that made him appear positively deformed. I never saw in my life a more dreadful-looking figure.

"I held out my hand, and the horrible, soft-spoken, eyeless creature gripped it like a vice. I was so much startled that I struggled to withdraw; but the blind man pulled me close up to him with a single action of his arm."

Later Blind Pew comes again to Jim's home, with a gang of friends. They are surprised there by revenue officers, searching for smugglers. The blind man's companions escape.

"In half a minute not a sign of them remained but Pew. Him they had deserted, whether in sheer panic or out of revenge for his ill words or blows, I know not; but there he remained behind, tapping up and down the road in a frenzy, and groping and calling for his comrades." *Because he cannot see, Pew falls under the hooves of the approaching horsemen and is trampled to death.*

4. Take the second paragraph, about Blind Pew, beginning "I held out my hand ." and complete it with the blind man's words to him. Make these words change Jim's opinion of the man.

5. Instead of being 'as good as gold' in church, imagine Tiny Tim being very naughty. What do you think he would do?

6. In Captain Hook, J M Barrie has created a comic character who is funny because of his handicap. Do you think this is unkind to disabled people?

Extracts from 'A Christmas Carol' by Charles Dickens

In the family of Bob Cratchit, clerk to Scrooge, there are several children, one of whom is physically disabled. When we first meet Tiny Tim, he is being carried on his father's shoulder.

"Alas for Tiny Tim, he bore a little crutch, and had his limbs supported by an iron frame!"

Mrs Cratchit asks her husband how Tiny Tim behaved when they were out together:

"'As good as gold,' said Bob, 'and better. Somehow, he gets thoughtful, sitting by himself so much; and thinks the strangest things you ever heard. He told me, coming home, that he hoped the people saw him in the church, because he was a cripple, and it might be pleasant for them to remember upon Christmas Day who made lame beggars walk and blind men see.' Bob's voice was tremulous when he told them this, and trembled more when he said that Tiny Tim was growing strong and hearty."

In a vision of what will happen in the future, Scrooge is shown the Cratchit household after the death of Tiny Tim. Bob remembers the child,

"I know, my dears, that when we recollect how patient and mild he was, although he was a little, little child, we shall not quarrel easily among ourselves, and forget poor Tiny Tim in doing it."

But Scrooge's vision of the future does not come true,

"and to Tiny Tim, who did NOT die, he was a second father."

Extracts from 'Peter Pan and Wendy' adapted from JM Barrie's play, 'Peter Pan'.

In the magical Neverland, Peter Pan's enemies are the pirates, 'extremely hideous to behold.'

"Anybody would have run a mile to escape from this horrible crew. But they were treated like mere dogs by their captain, Jas Hook, who was the biggest and most dreadful of them all. He lay in a rough chariot which was pushed and pulled by his men: smoking two cigars at once by means of a clever contraption he had invented, and waving his terrific iron claw. The most unpleasant thing about Hook (next to the iron claw) was his politeness: the more dangerous he was, the politer he grew. And there was only one thing on earth of which he was afraid — that was, the sight of his own blood."

Captain Hook hates Peter, and with some reason —

"It was he who cut off my arm' said Hook, with dark looks. 'Oh I'll tear him for that!' and he brandished the iron claw. 'He flung my arm to a crocodile that happened to be passing by."

Credit CSV

17B

POEMS

I'M GOING TO HEAR WITH MY EYES

Above me is a blue sky
filled with clouds so white
I see the trees move slowly
from side to side
but all is silence
and I feel uneasy
sometimes
I just want to run away and hide

Feeling unaware of sounds around me
sounds high, low, fast and slow
I feel these sounds with my hands
the rest I hear with my eyes

I'm not going to let my emotions take control
I'm going to pull through strong
whenever I feel ready to let go
I shall force myself to go on

I shall succeed
through anger, fear
happiness and love
I can and I know it
be something and someone
I thought I could never be

I'm going to come out
and stay right out
of my shell I've lived in for so long
I'm going to take control of my emotions
not let them take control of me

Above me is a blue sky
filled with clouds so white
I see the trees move slowly
from side to side

but now - I feel strong

I can't change the silence
but my hearing is back where it belongs
- back in my eyes

I'm going to hear with my eyes
and move side to side with the trees
and I will continue to succeed
until I reach a point as high
as that clear blue sky.

Helen Todd

Racism and Disability

Shut Down

There was a madman on the train today,
He walked right up and shouted in my face.

I could smell the drink so strong and stale,
His dress was ragged and his skin was black
His skin was black Two shades darker than mine.

I knew why he was mad
Inside he was so terribly sad though he smiled, a terrible smile.

I had to shout back –
Move!
He was invading my space,
who knew what he might do next?

But I knew why he was mad
He was a Black man in this land,
He was a Black man in this land,
Black like me

The tube was packed
and only this could shift
their locked gazes.. yet still
they disguised their interest.

After he'd gone,
My eyes followed,
And watched his every pain.
How could this man have suffered so?
To the point where his mind had to say —
NO
And shut down
And shut down
This Black man had shut down.

I was feeling strong today
Had it been another
I would have just cried broke down and cried
Broke down
Shut down
Shut down.

From 'Charting the Journey: Writings by Black Women and Third World Women' 1988 SHEBA

Tomorrow I am going to re-write the English language

Tomorrow I am going to re-write the English language
I will discard all those striving ambulist metaphors
Of power and success
And construct new images to describe my strength
My new, different strength.

Then I won't have to feel dependent
Because I can't Stand On My Own Two Feet
And I will refuse to feel a failure
Because I didn't Stay One Step Ahead.
I won't feel inadequate
When I don't Stand Up For Myself
Or illogical because I cannot
Just Take It One Step at a Time

I will make them understand that it is a very male way
To describe the world
All this Walking Tall
And Making Great Strides.

Yes, tomorrow I am going to re-write the English Language,
Creating the world in my own image.
Mine will be a gentler, more womanly way
To describe my progress.
I will wheel, cover and encircle

Somehow I will learn to say it all.

Lois Keith
from Able Lives
©Spinal Injuries Association

It's About Disability...

Access

- Blind, partially-sighted and deaf people's right to information is hampered by the lack of materials on tape, in large print and braille, and sub-titles and signing on television.

- Complete access details should be given when publicising events.

- People with disabilities rarely get the opportunity to work in the media. Yet no-one can represent people with disabilities better than they themselves.

The media has both created and perpetuated the negative representation of people with disabilities which has led to discrimination against them. It must now work towards showing the real picture and redressing the balance.

- Include more positive and varied images of people with disabilities, even when disability is not the focus.

- Responsible journalism demands accurate representation – contact representative groups.

- Avoid sensationalism which exploits individuals.

- Any audience will include people with disabilities – reflect their concerns too.

All members of the NUJ are bound by the Code of Conduct which is part of the Union's rule book. Clause 10 says: 'A journalist shall only mention a person's race, colour, creed, illegitimacy, marital status (or lack of it), gender, sexual orientation or disability if this information is strictly relevant. A journalist shall neither originate nor process material which encourages discrimination on any of the above-mentioned grounds.'

For further details about the Campaign for Real People write to the Equality Council, the NUJ, Acorn House, 314 Grays Inn Road, London WC1X 8DP.
This leaflet is also available on request for the partially sighted, in braille and on tape.
The Campaign for Real People is supported by: the Campaign for Press and Broadcasting Freedom, 9 Poland Street, London WC1; Equal Opportunities Commission; Women's Media Action Group; Commission for Racial Equality; Campaign for Homosexual Equality; NUJ Lesbian and Gay Group; NUJ Race Relations Working Party; members of the London Liberation Network; National Union of Students: Arts Media Group; Women's Film, Television and Video Network; MIND (National Association for Mental Health); Age Concern; Association of Cinematograph, Television and Allied Technicians; Down's Children's Association; Campaign for People with Mental Handicaps.

CAMPAIGN FOR REAL PEOPLE

PEOPLE FIRST

This leaflet outlines general points about people with disabilities are represented by the media. It has been put together by a joint working party of the NUJ and the CPBF, made up mostly of people with disabilities. It is hoped that NUJ members will want to take up the issue of disability and report it in a more sensitive and informed way.

The Campaign for Real People, which is an NUJ initiative, is backed by a wide range of organisations with a common aim: to change the way people are portrayed through the media. We hope to get journalists thinking more about the way they work. And we're encouraging other people to expect more from the media. We want to see real people coming through the media. We want all journalists to break the mould.

The Campaign for Press and Broadcasting Freedom is a broad-based non-party campaign working for greater diversity, access and accountability, and against all forms of bias and discrimination in the media. It has a semi-autonomous group working on the issue of disability.

At least one in ten of the population has a severe disability. Most of us will have a disabilities at some temporary or permanent diablity at some time in our lives.

- People with disabilities include those with physical, mental, sensory, learning and speech difficulties. Sometimes the disability is not recognisable. People with disabilities should not therefore be seen as a homogenous group.

- People with disabilities are not "the problem" — it is society that handicaps people by its environments and attitudes. So how do the media contribute to the misreprentation?

Invisible and marginalised

- The media tend to assume that their audience are able-bodied. If people with disabilities are seen at all, the focus is on the disability, even when the disability is irrelevant.

- Issues important to people with disabilities are often not seen as newsworthy, and are marginalised into specialist publications or programmes.

- News about disability is most often represented by able-bodied "experts". People with disabilities are the real experts on their own lives. The organised collective voice of people with disabilities is rarely consulted.

Stereotyped

Stereotypes are; insulting and can be damaging. The most common of those

which purport to describe people with disabilities are:

courageous – pathetic – helpless – tragic victim – recipient of charity – eternally cheerful – grateful – "abnormal" – constantly searching for a cure or miracle aids – asexual. It is rarely acknowledge that they may also be black, lesbian or gay.

Stereotypes distort reality. They perpetuate false notions of "normality", emphasising the difference between "them" and "us". They lead people to fear that disability inevitably means a tragic end to a life of fulfilment. They focus on the personal aspects of disability that can be relieved by charity rather than the political and economic changes required to end discrimination.

Language

Language used to refer to disability is often inaccurate and offensive.

- People with disabilities are people first – "the disabled" focuses only on the disability. Do not use words like "cripple", "deaf and dumb", "abnormal".

- Use the correct term for the disability, e.g. Down's Syndrome, not Mongol; cerebal palsy, not spastic. Misuse of language is unprofessional.

- Words associated with disability are frequently used perjoratively, e.g. lame duck, blind stupidity, deaf to reason. Avoid such usage.

PRESS CUTTINGS

THE Sun

ursday, July 30, 1987   20p   TODAY'S TV IS ON PAGE 14

YOU SPASTICS

Master blaster . . . Peter Phillips yells at newsmen during yesterday's clashes   *Just like mum? . . Zara appears to stick out her tongue at photographers*

Shock taunt as Anne's children face newsmen

By SUN REPORTER

PRINCESS Anne's son Peter Phillips was at the centre of a storm last night after two photographers were told: "Get lost, you spastics."

Master Phillips, nine, was out riding with his six-year-old sister Zara and six young pals when the taunt rang out from the group.

Agency photographer Paul Walters, who was taking pictures of Zara, turned to see Peter with a wide grin on his face.

He said: "I heard one of the riders shout, 'Get lost, you spastics.' It sounded like young Peter.

"I can't be sure if it was him

but one of the group was certainly out of order.

"I was flabbergasted. It is not the sort of behaviour one expects from the class of person in that group, even if they are children."

NOTORIOUS

The youngsters, who were unaccompanied by an adult, were trotting along a road outside a pony club summer camp at Minchinhampton, Gloucs.

It is near the Gatcombe Park home of Princess Anne, the Princess Royal—notorious for her "Naff Off" outbursts at pressmen. Walters, who works for the

Bristol-based South West News Service agency, said Peter was "discourteous" throughout yesterday.

He added: "I spent the day watching him in the club grounds.

"Master Peter appeared to shout abuse at me and other photographers.

"I was keeping a respectable distance and did not hear what he was saying. But going by the expression on his face, it wasn't particularly polite."

Peter's mother Anne—patron of the Riding for the Disabled Association—has had many similar run-ins with photographers.

In January she shocked first-class train passengers by scream— *Continued on Page Two*

A

THE Sun

onday, April 6, 1987   18p   TODAY'S TV IS ON PAGE 14

QUEEN'S COUSIN LOCKED IN MADHOUSE

By IAN HEPBURN

A COUSIN of the Queen has spent the past 40 years locked away in a mental hospital, The Sun can reveal today.

And the locked-up woman's sister—another Royal cousin who was also mentally handicapped—is buried in an untended pauper's grave after dying last year.

The shocking truth about Katherine and Nerissa Bowes-Lyon came to light after The Sun discovered an extraordinary cover-up.

The women are first cousins of the Queen, nieces of the Queen Mother and aunts of top photographer Lord Lichfield.

They have been listed as DEAD since the 1963 edition of Burke's Peerage, the Who's Who of British

The Queen . . . close relative

The Queen Mother . . . aunt

40-year nightmare of abandoned Kate

aristocracy. Yet Katherine, 60, is very much alive.

She is a long-term patient in the state-run Royal Earlswood mental hospital in Redhill, Surrey—once blasted as a hell-hole by a watchdog committee.

Nerissa also spent most of her life there before dying, aged 67.

"Members of the hospital's League of Friends would drop in simply because they were abandoned."

Last night, leading ancestry researcher Hugh Peskett said: "This is definitely a cover-up."

WRITTEN OFF AS DEAD—See Pages 2 and 3

B

20 A

Haringey Weekly Herald

AND NORTH LONDON ADVERTISER

WOOD GREEN, EDMONTON, TOTTENHAM and HARRINGAY   JANUARY 10, 1990

The best of British

MOVE over Gary Kasparov. It's time to check out Phillip Gardner who's on the way to becoming king of the chessboards against stiff East European competition.

For Phillip, of College Road, Tottenham, is a member of an extraordinary chess team which will be taking part in an international tournament this year.

The 32-year-old computer analyst and his four team-mates are fighting their way to the top with the odds stacked against them. They are all deaf.

Phil fights deafness to lead chess challenge

C   D

STAR SUNDAY SPORT, September 27, 1987

27 YEARS OF HELL—

● THE only remedy for people suffering from APERTS Syndrome, like Andrew, is plastic surgery. Bones in the skull, fused from birth, need to be separated early in life to prevent mental handicap.

If you want to help sufferers, donations can be sent to the APERTS Syndrome Supporters' group run by Mrs Pam Walker, Sandhill House, Middle Laydon, Bucks.

and he's still SMILING

EXCLUSIVE by CHRISTINE RODERICK

HEARTLESS idiots laughed at his knobbly face... and webbed hands and feet.

Children drove him to tears with cruel taunts. And pretty girls broke his heart. But ugly duckling Andrew Dickson refused to hide away.

And now, after a staggering £2 million worth of hospital treatment, his smile says it all.

Andrew has suffered 27 years of torment — and 70 operations. His story is one of immense courage.

" I looked like Frankenstein when I was born ... drooping forehead, webbed hands and feet, and a nose as flat as a snout.

My parents, Vera and Eric, were shattered. But they refused to hide me away like the legendary Victorian freak John Merrick.

I had my first operation when I was just five weeks old.

Great Ormond Street surgeons defied nature, slicing my hands, building a nose, and transplanting a rib to my forehead.

The National Health Service must have spent £2 million on me.

It was sheer hell. But I'll never regret it, even though I still have webbed feet.

When I was ten I was offered a life-or-death operation. It had only been tried once before and it was very risky. But it worked wonders. I began to hope that one day I might look normal.

I shake with pain at the memories of my teenage years.

I never used to go out in the evenings as I only had a couple of friends. Most kids made fun of me.

And I nearly cried when I saw the Elephant Man film, because that was what it was like for me. Children at school were so, so cruel.

I'm 27 now, but I still feel nervous if I go swimming at strange baths because I'm afraid people will stare.

But that's the only time I worry – except when it comes to girlfriends.

I've only asked two girls out and they turned me down flat.

But there is still time. I'm not a bad guy. I'm normal in that way.

I used to get crushes on the nurses in hospital.

Nowadays I'm more outgoing. I'm

CHEERS... Andrew toasts the future

popular at the shirt factory where I work and I'm a friend of all handicapped and old people.

I spend every spare second raising cash for the League of Friends of Musgrove Park Hospital in Taunton.

It's my way of paying back the medical profession for all they've done for me. "

ANDREW'S birth should have been the happiest day of her life.

But Mum Vera recalled from the family home in Taunton, Somerset: "I knew the minute the nurses took him away something was wrong.

"I saw him and felt sheer bewilderment. It took 10 days to find out what was wrong. It was an enormous hill to climb."

ANDREW suffers from APERTS Syndrome – Accro-Cephalo-Syndactily. And before he helped pioneer the miracle Tessiers operation, victims were unlikely to reach adolescence.

Harley Street paediatrician Dr David Morris said: "If Andrew had been born a decade earlier, he would probably have died in his teens."

20 B

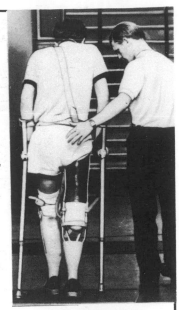